Hollywood in the Holy Land

*Essays on Film Depictions
of the Crusades and
Christian–Muslim Clashes*

Edited by
NICKOLAS HAYDOCK *and*
E. L. RISDEN

McFarland & Company, Inc., Publishers
Jefferson, North Carolina, and London

Nickolas Haydock is the author of *Movie Medievalism: The Imaginary Middle Ages* (McFarland, 2008)

LIBRARY OF CONGRESS CATALOGUING-IN-PUBLICATION DATA

Hollywood in the Holy Land : essays on film depictions of the Crusades and Christian-Muslim clashes / Edited by Nickolas Haydock and E.L. Risden.
    p.   cm.
Includes bibliographical references and index.

ISBN 978-0-7864-4156-3
softcover : 50# alkaline paper

1. Middle Ages in motion picures.   2. Crusades in motion pictures.   3. East and West in motion pictures.   I. Title.
PN1995.9.M52 H65   2009
791.43'643580907 — dc22   2008055208

British Library cataloguing data are available

©2009 Nickolas Haydock and E.L. Risden. All rights reserved

No part of this book may be reproduced or transmitted in any form or by any means, electronic or mechanical, including photocopying or recording, or by any information storage and retrieval system, without permission in writing from the publisher.

On the cover: Thousands of Saracens lay siege to Jerusalem in *Kingdom of Heaven*, 2005 (20th Century Fox/Photofest); background and border ©2009 Shutterstock

Manufactured in the United States of America

McFarland & Company, Inc., Publishers
Box 611, Jefferson, North Carolina 28640
www.mcfarlandpub.com

*For our dear wives,
Socorro and Kristy,
in loving appreciation*

Acknowledgments

We both owe a deep debt of gratitude to José Irizarry, who deftly and patiently saw to all the technical aspects of preparing the manuscript. His expertise, good sense, and fine eye for detail have made this a much better book. Though listed neither as editor nor author for this volume, José proved an invaluable co-conspirator.

Nick Haydock's work on the volume was supported by a sabbatical leave during the 2007–2008 academic year granted by the Faculty of Arts and Sciences and Dean Moises Orengo at the University of Puerto Rico, Mayagüez. Part of this sabbatical was passed happily as a guest at the University of St. Louis researching alongside Thomas Shippey. Tom and his dear wife Catherine worked hard to make the sojourn in St. Louis a happy and productive one. Nick's profoundest thanks as well to co-editor Ed Risden, whose energy, persistence, and unflappable friendship have made working with him a real joy. Final words of thanks go to Nick's beloved wife Socorro, who makes all things possible.

Ed Risden includes his thanks: to his friend Nick Haydock for asking him along on the journey that became this volume; to all the contributors, without whom there would be no book; to those scholars, medievalists and medievalism-ists, upon whose work this book is built; and to his wife, Kristy, who once again encouraged him through "just one more project."

Table of Contents

Introduction:
"The Unseen Cross Upon the Breast:"
Medievalism, Orientalism, and Discontent
NICKOLAS HAYDOCK — 1

1. Framing the West, Staging the East:
Set Design, Location, and Landscape in Cinematic Medievalism
JOHN M. GANIM — 31

2. Homeland Security:
Northern Crusades through the East-European Eyes of *Alexander Nevsky* and the *Nevsky* Tradition
NICKOLAS HAYDOCK — 47

3. Now Starring in the Third Crusade:
Depictions of Richard I and Saladin in Films and Television Series
LORRAINE KOCHANSKE STOCK — 93

4. SaladiNasser:
Nasser's Political Crusade in *El Naser Salah Ad-Din*
PAUL B. STURTEVANT — 123

5. "La geste que Turoldus declinet":
History and Authorship in Frank Cassenti's *Chanson de Roland*
LYNN RAMEY — 147

6. Agenda Layered Upon Agenda:
Anthony Mann's 1961 Film *El Cid*
KEVIN J. HARTY — 161

7. *El Cid*:
Defeat of the Cresentade
TOM SHIPPEY — 169

8. Nobody but the Other Buddy:
Hollywood, the Crusades, and Buddy Pictures
E. L. RISDEN — 186

9. Medieval Times:
   Bodily Temporalities in *The Thief of Bagdad* (1924), *The Thief of Bagdad* (1940), and *Aladdin* (1992)
   KATHLEEN COYNE KELLY 200

10. Chivalric Conspiracies:
    Templar Romance and the Redemption of History in *National Treasure* and *The Da Vinci Code*
    SUSAN ARONSTEIN and ROBERT TORRY 225

11. On the Border:
    Merging East and West in Cadfael's Twelfth-Century Shropshire
    WILLIAM F. HODAPP 246

12. Movie Millenarianism:
    Left Behind, Script/ure and the Sleeping Dragon
    CHRISTOPHER POWERS 269

Epilogue
   Resisting Manichean Delirium
   E. L. RISDEN 290

About the Contributors 299

Index 303

Introduction: "The Unseen Cross Upon the Breast"

Medievalism, Orientalism and Discontent

NICKOLAS HAYDOCK

*You may forget about Eros and Thanatos,
but you can be sure they will not forget about you.*[1]

The Crusades have become an embattled theater of operations for a mass-society intent on waging its wars of demagoguery over analogies between medieval and the contemporary "clash of civilizations."[2] The essays that comprise this volume testify abundantly to the long history and plasticity of these analogies in movie medievalism. The films discussed herein trade upon and at times attempt to realign projections into the medieval past, which serves both as the source and reflection of modern nation states, international conflicts, as well as ethnic and religious antipathies. With the attacks of 9/11 and what for many in the Bush and Blair administrations appeared the inevitable invasions of Afghanistan and Iraq, analogies between medieval and modern inter-hemispheric (and inter-faith) wars have been thrust to the center of mass-mediated political discourse. This perceived new relevance of the Crusades caused analogies to be drawn and withdrawn, often within the same news cycle. Some scholars of the Crusades have found themselves not only addressing the analogies between the present and the past, but also, like the dean of Crusade historians Jonathan Riley-Smith, being asked to review popular films and to lecture foreign policy makers on the relevance of the Crusades for contemporary interventions in the Middle East. Riley-Smith has sharply dismissed any such relevance, with an abiding contempt for the tendency of medievalism to blur important historical differences.[3]

However, beginning from the premise that what Erich Auerbach dubbed a *figura*[4] is by definition an imagined typology linking disparate times and places based on a faith in the relevance and meaningfulness of history, recent denials of the Crusades as *figura* are as politically compromised as the arguments of those on all sides who stress the parallels between millennia. Pope Urban II called the First Crusade in 1095, yet the contemporary occupant of the papal throne Pope Benedict XVI reverts to a potent orientalist medievalism when he quotes a medieval text in which Islam is characterized as a religion of the sword. Official responses from the Muslim world predictably compared his "medieval mentality" to that of the earlier Popes who in calling their Crusades made similar charges against Muslims.[5] Osama bin Laden has repeatedly cast the invasions of Afghanistan and Iraq as a *Crusade* called by George Bush. Bruce Holsinger (2007), in a study that provocatively spans both academic and political discourse, has devastatingly critiqued the linkage between neo-medievalism and neo-conservatism in what Bush in an unguarded moment called "this crusade, this war on terror." Yet leftists like Terry Jones and Tariq Ali also run roughshod over historical alterities to spark horrified delight at the ease with which they collapse medieval faith and modern fundamentalism.[6] Those on the right eager to support "Operation Iraqi Freedom" quote liberally from Riley-Smith and Thomas F. Madden in their denials of the Crusades as *figurae*. Yet best-selling, rabble-rousing books like Robert Spencer's *The Politically Incorrect Guide to Islam* (2005) are seldom content merely to shun historical analogies altogether; rather they engage in a recognizably orientalist discourse whereby historical continuities are denied for the enlightened West but underlined for the Middle East, conceived as an ideologically stable and technologically backward empire of faith.

Perhaps not surprisingly even before the release of Ridley Scott's *Kingdom of Heaven* (2005) experts and pundits could be heard weighing in from all sides, the very ferocity of their condemnations clearly motivated less by any dispassionate interest in popular film than by the analogies with the present the film was perceived to evoke. Riley-Smith accused Ridley Scott of sharing "Osama bin Laden's version of history," and UCLA's Abou el Fadl rather petulantly forecasted that Arabs would riot. In short, these academic experts from their entrenched perspectives saw the film in almost mutually exclusive terms, as a condemnation of western Crusades, past and present, or as a condemnation of Islam — it is neither, though of course both experts' opinions were compromised by the fact that neither had seen the film![7] Yet it is worthwhile to look closely at this film and at others like it that screen popular projections of present conflicts onto the medieval Crusades precisely because these *figurae* are as ineluctable as they are toxic. Riley-Smith tips his neo-con hand when he suggests that the Crusades are more analogous to the Liberation Theology movements in Spanish America than to contemporary interventions in the Persian Gulf. Yet in many of these films an ideology of "freedom" is made to calque the religious convictions of the Crusaders, an appeal perhaps similarly composed of belief and cynical manipulation. This is as true of Ridley Scott's film as it is of his major cinematic source, Cecil B. DeMille's *The Crusades* (1935), which likewise preached non-involvement to Americans in the face of an international menace. Ridley Scott also imagines late twelfth century Jerusalem as a *convivencia* of Muslim and Christian, not unlike that valorized in Anthony Mann's *El Cid* and appealed to by both academics and in popular culture as a model of multi-cultural tolerance. In the imagined friendship between the Arab Imad and the Frankish Balian, Scott's film valorizes a recurrent trope of interfaith and intercultural tolerance that finds its ultimate source in Sir Walter Scott's *The Talisman*, but the trope is evident too in films as varied as *El Cid* and *The Thirteenth Warrior*.[8] In short, Ridley Scott's *Kingdom of Heaven* demonstrates that the politics of these films are likely to be as ambivalent as the culture that produces and consumes them.

Our collection is designed to allow readers to take stock of the many films that depict medieval East/West encounters. The cinema archive yields an index not only of the variety and portability of these analogies, but it can also allow us to identify common, repeated strains in movie medievalism that give evidence of an underlying cultural imaginary: a construct that influences not only the making of these films, but also the making of public policy. Hence we attempt in this collection to survey the many incarnations and elaborations of the medieval East/West dichotomy in film from pre–Crusade encounters of Saracens and Vikings and proto-Crusade wars in Andalusian Spain, through Crusades launched against the Holy Land and North-Eastern Europe, down to what might be called the enduring inheritance of the Crusades in orientalist fantasies and secret conspiracies. The essays that follow speak eloquently for themselves, and they will be allowed to do so without any prior restraints or characterizations imposed here. Edward Risden's epilogue at the end of the volume takes stock of what these essays accomplish and attempts to plot some future coordinates for what we trust will become a growing concern. Here, though, we attempt to frame what follows by offering a series of vignettes: anecdotes chiefly from popular media that will help to stake out the area covered in this book while also demonstrating its thorough implication in the wider concerns to which we hope it makes some small contribution. Subsequent sections in the introduction return to the question of the Crusades as historical analogy and vet the notion of the film Crusades as historically uncanny. The introduction ends with the notion of repetition in the history of films about the Crusades through a discussion of the ubiquitous but mutable cinematic theme of "taking the cross."

At Play in the Fields of the Lord: The Crusades as Pastime

1. Muslim and Christian forces outside the walls of Acre in autumn of 1190 reach a stalemate and decide to pass the time by staging a mock battle between children, in what is arguably the earliest recorded dramatic representation of the Crusades. Baha al-Din describes the "strange incident" thus:

> One day the two camps, tired of fighting, decided to arrange a battle between children. Two boys came out of the city to match themselves against two young infidels. In the heat of the struggle, one of the Muslim boys leapt upon his rival, threw him to the ground, and seized him by the throat. When they saw that he was threatening to kill him, the Franj approached and said: "Stop! He has become your prisoner, forsooth, and we will buy him back from you." The boy took two dinars and let the other go [Trans. Maalouf 207].[9]

In this early theater of war we begin to see what is at stake in such representations: the pastime quickly spins out of control, as the boys' mimesis of their elders becomes too faithful and bleeds into the conflict it is designed to represent. Perhaps the scene also represents the attenuation of chivalry, especially its most vaunted facet, the duel. The two sides play with, even send up their wish to end the standoff by something so definitive as a duel, but end up reproducing instead the aporetic nature of the stalemate. The Frankish response to this dangerous slippage of pastime into mortal combat is not simply to separate the children; rather they adhere rigidly to the rules of the game by calling a truce (within the general truce already in effect) and by offering ransom. There is something uncanny about the episode that troubles hard and fast distinctions between actual and virtual war, like the Borges' story that imagines the true genesis of the *Iliad* in Homer's childhood memory of the shame he felt when teased by a bully and the bloody revenge he took with his father's dagger.[10] Baha al-Din's anecdote, like that of Borges, seems to expose the bloody kernel of an elemental shame which lurks beneath attempts by the combatants and by al-Din himself to paint warfare as a chivalric contest. Economic considerations also rear their ugly heads: the mock-battle concludes anticlimactically with a ransom. In the Middle Ages war (even "Holy War") like feudalism itself was based upon the redistribution of wealth. And whatever the stated *causae bellorum*, from Helen to a divine beauty pageant, from heresy to the recovery of stolen property, from WMDs and fighting terror to dethroning a dictator, the internal logic of warfare as profit by other means tends eventually to become manifest. Such admittedly base explanations have been recently denied by apologists for the Crusades as well as by those eager to defend contemporary interventions in the Middle East. Yet such motivations for both twelfth and twenty-first century "Crusades," despite virulent assertions to the contrary, continue to undermine both medieval and modern idealizations of warfare.

2. A more recent example of child's play, set in the same period (1191), is Ubisoft's videogame *Assassin's Creed* (2006) for Xbox and Playstation 3, which has sold more than five million copies worldwide — not counting the widely pirated PC version of the game that appeared in February 2008. Though in many ways a mishmash typical of futuristic medievalism (including not only the requisite Templars and an elaborate "scientific" pretext, but also the Syrian branch of the Ismailis whom their Arab victims contemptuously dubbed *hashishi*), the game represents perhaps the most fascinating in the plethora of mass-mediated responses to the "war on terror." The framing fiction for *Assassin's Creed* is set in 2012, where a bartender (*cum* Connecticut Yankee) is kidnapped by a corporation capable of reading genetic memories encoded in his DNA. The memories of the bartender Desmond and his twelfth-century ancestor, Altaïr ibn La-Ahad ("the flying son of no one") are "synchronized," allowing Desmond to experience his alter ego's perceptions. The deeply significant setting for the game, then, is the virtual world of memory, twenty-first century recovered memories of a twelfth-century terrorist/assassin, which are not simply screened passively by the "Animus" machine, but rather turn Altaïr into a kind of automaton whose moves are controlled by his distant ancestor and ultimately by the player of the game.

A radical branch of Shi'a Muslims, the Ismaili Assassins made preferred victims Sunni Muslim caliphs and power brokers. In fact Arab sources record some degree of cooperation during the Third Crusade by Assassins and Franks, perhaps ultimately based on the rationale that "my enemy's enemy is my friend." The Ismailis are also listed as tributaries of both the Templars and the Hospitallers. Assassins claimed their first Frankish victim, Raymond II of Tripoli, as early as 1151. Under the leadership of their Imam Rashid al-Din Sinan, assassins twice attempted to kill Saladin himself (in 1176 and again in 1185). Their most famous successful mission occurred at Acre in April of 1192 when disguised as Christian monks two Ismailis murdered the King of Jerusalem, Conrad de Montferrat. When captured afterwards the assassins claimed that the murder was bought and paid for by Richard I (see Lewis 97–124). Conrad is one of nine "targets" marked for assassination in the videogame, which begins in a kind of terrorist boot camp at the Ismaili stronghold of Masyaf and then searches out targets — including the Grand Masters of the Templar, Teutonic, and Hospitaller Orders in Acre, Jerusalem, and Damascus. Two tenets central to the beliefs of the Ismailis are markedly reflected in the game: *Taqiyya*, or the necessity of hiding in plain sight by disguising one's real allegiances, and the fundamentally apocalyptic doctrine of time as split between periods of occultation and revelation, characterized by the hidden and revealed Imams who led the sect. The game's hero Altaïr is disguised in the robes of the Teutonic Knights. He relies upon stealth and the forging of alliances with those on both sides in order to identify and kill his victims. At Masyaf Altaïr is shown a courtyard paradise filled with beautiful women, whom postulates are promised upon their martyrdoms — a promise reportedly still made by recruiters for al-Qaida. The famous stories of recruits to the Assassins being drugged and then awakened in "paradise" as a foretaste of what awaits them after their service to the Imam were most probably an invention of medieval western and eastern opponents. Yet the use of similar harem-in-the-sky promises by al-Qaida as well as contemporary western exaggerations of the practice offer ample evidence of the power of imagined continuities between twelfth and twenty-first century terrorism.

More crucial evidence appears when, for the Ismailis and their Imam, assassination and the terror it wrought were war by other means, waged against superior powers they could not hope to defeat by conventional tactics. For many and perhaps for himself as well Osama bin Laden has reprised the role of the Old Man in the Mountain, the leader of a sect of martyrdom-seeking assassins whose effect on political realities is obscenely out of proportion to their numbers. Just as in the twelfth century, the revelation of this "hidden Imam" — complete with cryptic and stultifying threats — has brought about a strain of antinomian eschatology, a fierce loyalty to a leader and a cause, that suspends the outward law of the prophets and heralds the apocalypse of a hidden truth that supposedly will transform the world. More profoundly than most video games, *Assassin's Creed* taps into contemporary western xenophobia about the enemy among us, hiding in plain sight: the nightmare that Arabs are not buying into the American Dream or the European Union, but rather, like the 9/11 hijackers, practicing the Assassins' *Taqiyya* and taking flying lessons. But the game allows its players to work through these anxieties by returning to the medieval source of Arab terrorism, assuming the role of a professional, well-nigh supernatural assassin. In an irony leaders of al-Qaida would no doubt relish, western children are encouraged to identify with a Muslim Assassin, receive weapons and stealth training, and ultimately direct their hidden daggers into Frankish necks. The result does for popular genetics what *The Manchurian Candidate* did for mind-control psychology. In an increasingly common form of "sublimity" the game also offers its players a titillating glimpse at the hidden truths of global and millennial conspiracies. The makers of the Animus machine, Abstergo Industries, are in fact a modern Order of the Templars, searching for the "Pieces of Eden" that can be used to alter human perception and induce mass-hypnosis. The twenty-first century Desmond's hidden Imam is al-Mualim, who we discover near the end of the game is actually a Templar himself, bent on world domination through the creation of Matrix-like, simulated realities. While the charges brought against the Templars in the early fourteenth century posited an unholy union of Templars and Muslims, this is the first contemporary conspiracy narrative of which we're aware that hypothesizes a modern link between secret orders of Templars and Muslim Assassins. Still, absent the medieval masquerade, conspiracy theories about the secret complicity of the Bush Administration with al-Qaida attacks are stubbornly persistent. The makers of *Assassin's Creed* are themselves complicit, however, in the production of an increasingly seductive and perhaps ultimately even dangerous hyperrealization of politics and history against which they encourage their many postulates virtually to contend. *Assassin's Creed* is the *Da Vinci Code* on steroids.

3. *Saladin: The Animated Series* is an *enfances* look at the early life of the eponymous hero targeted at 10–12 year old children and consisting of 52 half-hour episodes to be broadcast beginning in late 2009. The prologue/trailer for this animated series presents an adult Saladin facing off against Richard's forces across the Nile in what is a densely packed and culturally volatile exercise in cultural re-appropriation.[11] Richard the Lionheart, hugely obese, red-bearded, and red-robed, launches an impressive fleet of Viking-like warships across the Nile from his command post atop a hill. From the opposing hill across the river a young and handsome Saladin prepares to counter the invasion. The Muslim fleet is a kind of terrorist *bricolage*, freighted with coded references to the ancient world, medieval films, as well as recent al-Qaida highlights. Saladin's ships are equipped with metal battering rams like those the Athenians used to demolish Xerxes' Persian fleet in the fifth century BCE. The ships are piled high with timber stacked in the shape of pyramids. The Arabs soon launch these floating funeral monuments across the river, and just before they crash into the Frankish fleet a contingent of archers looses a barrage of fire arrows into the night sky, setting the pyramidal pyres alight and transforming them into resplendent Christmas trees. The scene is a rather extended parody of the cinematic "Viking" funeral, ubiquitous in popular American films (e.g., *First Knight* and *Thirteenth Warrior*), but as the floating bombs crash into their targets, "the rockets' red glare, the bombs bursting in air" give proof through the night that the Franks are no longer there. Just as in the flotilla that carries Balian to the Holy Land in *Kingdom of Heaven*, we watch as the whole Frankish invasion force sinks beneath the waves, like Eisenstein's Teutonic Knights in the Battle on the Ice (*Alexander Nevsky*), borne down by the weight of their armor. The Muslims, though, dive gracefully off their navigable torpedoes just before they explode, and in a nod per-

haps toward Issa, the famous swimmer/spy, they glide gracefully back ashore. The episode is cinematic pastiche and bears no relation to anything that actually happened in the Third Crusade, but it does represent an uncanny projection of the October 12, 2000 attack on the USS Cole in the Port of Aden, as well as the flying bombs that took down the Twin Towers less than a year later. The target audience of 10–12 year-old children is thus instructed on the Saladin/Osama bin Laden, Crusades/Gulf Wars analogies that are a crucial component of al-Qaida propaganda. And in being projected back onto the twelfth-century screen, acts of terror are cast as brilliant strategy employed against an invading force.

4. *Monkey Dust: The Crusades* is an episode from the second year of the popular BBC animated series that originally aired in 2004.[12] Fully and somewhat pretentiously in the tradition of Monty Python and Blackadder medievalism, this parody of action and epic films was made "In honor of all the Americans who died fighting in the early Middle Ages." Its send-up of American neo-imperialism around the globe leverages the widespread American ignorance of history and geography. Deep among the potato fields of Idaho a motley crew of teenagers engages in a neo-medieval joust, shot and scored to evoke the wildly anachronistic *A Knight's Tale*. Yet when the barking "coach" of this team turns up, it becomes clear that the rowdy teens are in fact recruits in a military training camp, preparing to ship out to the Persian Gulf. The class of '59 (1159!) is delighted finally to get the chance to "open a can of wup-ass on Saladin" and recover the stolen Holy Grail. The blurring of Saladin and Saddam Hussein represents an identification the latter repeatedly encouraged, but the series' Saladin is notably English and rather a bit too refined, sipping his afternoon tea from the grail. His prisoners are a group of Irish Ceilidh singers who await their rescue by the USA in a cheeky reference to American interference in *both* situations. That Saladin should be English was not unknown in earlier medievalist fantasies. In early films about the Crusades he was often played by English actors, but the real butt of the joke here seems to be the politically correct Middle Ages of more recent American films where the English are invariably the sadistic, imperialistic oppressors of freedom fighters like Joan of Arc, William Wallace, and, however improbably, King Arthur himself.[13] Our first sight of the desert comes via a quotation from the opening of *Three Kings* as a tracking shot from a low-flying helicopter brings us rapidly across the sands to the door of Saladin's tent. Now garbed like Templars, the American shock team stands in V-formation at the door of the tent, a formation that has a long history in film westerns as well as "easterns," from *Alexander Nevsky* and *The Magnificent Seven* down to the recent *King Arthur*.[14] The crowning parody though has the

trapped soldiers retrieve the Grail from the clutches of Saladin, whom the invaders quickly identify as an "English bastard." The ninja-Templars hold their own against Saladin's republican guard, but as a last resort liberate the Grail by means of a last second Hail Mary. The lone African-American is told to "go long," and he catches the bomb over his shoulder. One is left unsure as to what most vexes the makers of this engaging farce: American imperialism or American-style football. Still the imbrication of American medievalism and American invasions in the Gulf poses questions that will be repeatedly addressed throughout this book.

5. In Raymond Khoury's best-selling novel *The Last Templar* (2006), conspiracy medievalism is rightly shown to be based on forged documents, but it is no less influential for all that. Khoury wants the best of both worlds: his tale ultimately offers audiences an ironic perspective on grail legends and conspiracy—like that in Umberto Eco's satirical *Foucault's Pendulum*—but this distance is not achieved until the very end of the novel when the hoax is revealed to be the work of a Templar forger waiting to die within the walls of Acre in 1291. The novel chiefly works to enlist Dan Brown's *Da Vinci Code* audience in a knock off of the international quest through codes and grand Manichean conspiracies for an eschatological truth. The first scene is worth pausing over: the Metropolitan Museum of Art holds a gala opening for an exhibition of "Vatican Treasures" in the tense atmosphere of an orange alert in the aftermath of 9/11. At a time when many New Yorkers were anxiously fearing the drop of the other shoe, four mounted Templars ride up to the entrance of the Met provoking first shock and then excited glee in the thronging crowd, which assumes the Templar Knights are part of the elaborately orchestrated opening. Their excitement slowly changes to horror when one of the knights beheads a security guard who had tried to prevent their entrance into the museum. These four apocalyptic horsemen then charge into the building, which houses treasures on loan from the Vatican and one of the largest collections of art in the western world, destroying the priceless art in their path. The episode rather opportunistically evokes the damaged psyche of a city that had seen American films destroy New York hundreds of times over the years with an ever increasing believability, until one autumn morning they could watch it happening for real over and over again on their televisions. The crash of the imaginary into the real was met less than a month later by Bush's call for "this crusade, this war on terror" against enemies whose religious fundamentalism and low-tech weapons made them readily identifiable as "medieval." There at least popular culture and Neo-conservatism were reading from the same page: the clash of civilizations was really a clash of epochs, and America found itself under attack by the Middle Ages.

6. But now also seared into cultural memory, alongside the sublime and terrible images of 9/11, are the nauseating digital photos of torture at Abu Ghraib and Guantánamo Bay.[15] Torture and terrorism are the nearly identical faces of a two-headed monster, two sides of a cursed coin. And like terrorism, torture is routinely conjoined to that most abject of adjectives, "medieval."[16] Perhaps only America's diplomatic clout in international bodies will prevent its president, his cabinet, Vice President Dick Cheney, former Secretary of Defense Donald Rumsfeld, and high-ranking members of the armed forces from being tried for war crimes and crimes against humanity. In the hundreds of photos now widely available across the net, the most remarkable are not those which detail the workaday world of torturing detainees, but rather those which depict guards posing (and posing with) detainees. These staged shots also give a picture of abuse, but do not represent tortures such as waterboarding that were ostensibly designed to force confessions. As in the tournament for children in Acre discussed above stalemate and boredom give free rein to a ludic sadism, a photo album of what Mommy and/or Daddy did in the war, that has now become a primer for the world on American phobias: Islamic, homosexual, racist.[17] In one shot a detainee is tormented by being forced to stand on a box dressed in a black hood and make-shift cloak — the epitome of a bogeyman — and told that the wires attached to his body will electrocute him if he falls from his perch. The pose creates a warlock-puppet, but this puppet has been forced to assume the position of the crucified Christ. In another picture of hooded Iraqis, the thigh of one detainee has been inscribed with the message: "I am a rapist." In another the ubiquitous Lynndie England points at a naked Iraqi forced to masturbate in front of her. In still another, England and Charles Dean Graner embrace before a collapsing pyramid of naked detainees, Arab posteriors facing (and open to) the camera. The exposure of Iraqi anuses and penises, the pyramidal and crucifixion poses, bodies painted with graffiti and feces are chiefly designed to humiliate rather than cause severe physical damage to Iraqis. There was plenty of that on offer in the Baghdad prison as well, from sodomy with batons to burning with acid, from stress positions to brutal beatings of bound and wounded prisoners. But the more ludic, posed forms of torture bespeak a clear pedagogy: a presumed cultural superiority bent on converting Muslims from their backward ways. Since they insist their women wear veils, put soiled panties over their faces and force them to masturbate in front of women. If they are dirty and the consensus is that they smell, paint them with their own shit, making real their supposed descent from the muck. If they deny Christ's immortality, force them to hold his position on the cross in the belief that failure to do so will bring immediate death. If Arabs are proud of the pyramids and indeed of ancient and medieval societies more technologically advanced than

those in the pre–Enlightenment West, make them recreate the pyramids with their own bodies and enjoy the spectacle of that human pyramid collapsing at your feet in a tangled orgy of naked Muslim men. But these atrocities have had a short shelf life in American news media, pushed to the margins by the rise in gas prices. In a widely circulated political cartoon, an upside down Uncle Sam is "oil boarded" by an Arab Sheik. The image derives from a scene in *Three Kings* (1999) where a CIA-trained member of the Iraqi Republican Guard does likewise to an American POW. Arabs are now seen as "torturing" Americans with high gas prices.

Getting Mid-Evil: Medievalism/Film/Politics

The cavalry of Richard the Lionheart attempted to assassinate Cecil B. DeMille in 1935 during the shooting of his film *The Crusades*. DeMille managed to dodge the charging horses only at the last minute. The conspiracy to trample the director was the brainchild of the Gower Gulch Gang, a close-knit group of cowboy stuntmen seething over DeMille's imperious ways and the very real dangers to which he routinely exposed them (Cary 219–32). Of course the incident absurdly doubles a major plot point in the film, drawn from Sir Walter Scott's *The Talisman*, where Richard's own supposed allies attempt his assassination. More recently in November 2001, the American Anti-Slavery Group filed a billion-dollar class action suit on behalf of the Presbyterian Church in a New York district court against the Canadian "upstream" oil company Talisman Energy. Talisman was accused of funding and encouraging a policy of ethnic cleansing and forced depopulation in southern Sudan against Christian and other non–Muslim minorities in order to clear the way for oil exploration.[18] The charges against Talisman Energy and the Sudanese Government also included the destruction of Christian churches, enslavement, and rape — exactly the crimes we see being depicted in the opening scene of DeMille's loose adaptation of Scott's novel. Though a life-long Episcopalian Dissenter, Scott would probably not have approved that way of fighting Presbyterianism under his novel's banner.

The notion that Western interventions awake the ghosts of medieval barbarism is a surprisingly common one. In Vladimir Pudovkin's classic film *Storm Over Asia: The Heir of Genghis Khan* (1928), the colonial British regime in Mongolia invests absurdly in the reign of a peasant erroneously identified as the heir of Genghis Khan. The officers and their wives attempt to "civilize" the peasant Khan into polite society and seat him upon the throne of what they envision will be an ideal puppet monarchy, friendly to British interests. Predictably the puppet regime degenerates: the "king" is dethroned and imprisoned by the British, but he escapes to lead a rebellion against the occupying forces. As he rides recklessly and alone into the teeth of a modern British artillery campaign, the Golden Horde appears at his back and blowing with them is a powerful wind from the East that flattens all before it.[19] While Pudovkin's critique of Western imperialism in the Eastern hemisphere is certainly the product of a particular (perhaps even dated) Marxist valorization of revolutionary history, it has a parable-like relevance to more recent history in America's initial support of Saddam Hussein and subsequent attempts to overthrow and assassinate him, as well as to our disastrous backing of the Shah of Iran. Another *unheimlich* parable from the annals of cinema Genghis Khans is the infamous Howard Hughes production of *The Conqueror* (dir. Dick Powell 1958), which searched for desert steppes *vraisemblance* in the American West and found it on a nuclear test site in Nevada.[20] Some forty percent of the cast and crew, as well as many of the principals such as John Wayne, later died of cancer. Hughes reportedly screened the film obsessively in the last days of his life. In the recent, low-budget film *Afghan Knights* (2007), a black ops unit of American soldiers returns to Afghanistan after the first Gulf War to extract a collaborating Afghani politician. The group is trapped in a cave and possessed by the demonic souls of the Great Khan's Mongol warriors. The Mongols' souls reside in their "sewels," rods whose pointed tips carry blood-borne schizophrenia. In the *Alien*-like plot, members of the group are changed into automatons of Mongol battle lust, slowly killing off their comrades in an orgy of "delayed stress" and "friendly fire." Thus the mysterious Gulf War Syndrome ultimately becomes a supernatural malady resulting from the Western invasion of the Persian Gulf cast not as a new crusade, but rather as the reincarnation of Mongol barbarism in American bodies.[21]

States of emergency and of emergence voraciously digest the past to feed the hunger of identity for continuity and difference. The first point to be made here is a simple one: the ubiquity of the analogies between the medieval world and present-day conflicts irrespective of ideology or nationality. From all corners of the globe and throughout the political spectrum, these parallels are drawn and redrawn in what has become an elaborate and well-nigh inescapable web of analogies. Hollywood films can even play on the controversial nature of these analogies. In the recent *Lions for Lambs* a typecast Tom Cruise calls Afghani resistance "medieval." The Machiavellian senator insists: "We're fighting a brand of evil that thinks the last 1300 years of human progress is heresy punishable by violent death."[22] The mindset revealed in these words relies upon a general audience's recognition of the term *medieval* as the keystone of a Bush administration rhetoric in which the "clash of civilizations" becomes a war of historical epochs. Just as obvious is the way the tendentious use of *medieval* and perhaps the equally resonant phrase *brand of evil* entail the filmmakers' critique of an orientalist medievalism that has now twice successfully marketed wars in the Gulf as a long-delayed Enlightenment for a stubbornly "Middle" East. This collapsing of Middle Ages and the Middle East — the former a concept coined by the Renaissance and the latter a political construct[23] realized by the colonial powers France, Britain, and the United States after World War I — is the means by which wartime propaganda has skirted charges of racism and religious bias by changing race into region and religion into time. Western demagoguery has also combined medievalism and orientalism to construct a medieval Eastern enemy and to wage its wars against the evils of an unregenerate past — note the widespread American pronunciation of the word [mid-evil]. Fighting a war against mid-evil elements in Middle Eastern states allows the pursuit of American interests in security and oil to be sublated in a march of progress, a romance of enlightenment that figures invasion in the time-honored trope of a civilizing mission, the winding of a clock long stopped.

While Redford's film clearly sets out to critique what Homi Bhabha has called "Manichean delirium"[24] in the Bush administration's War on Terror, it lapses precipitously into the same binary thinking it attempts to critique. The film's soldier heroes are a pair of unlikely buddies, a black and Hispanic, shown in flashback to be both morally and physically superior to their rich, white classmates in a west coast university, where fashionable, attenuated liberalism suffices a disaffected, materialist generation. That these minorities have chosen to "get involved" when the American Dream is within their grasp exposes the fatuousness of campus radicalism in a post–Vietnam age. Despite the supposed majority of "tenured radicals" on college campuses, the wars in the Middle East (*sans* draft) have scarcely disturbed the peaceful pursuit of well-paying careers. Yet, oddly, the moral superiority of these minority students endures even on a mountain plateau in Afghanistan where their Taliban enemies lack not only air support and socio-economic back-stories, but also faces. In rejecting the white hero/minority sidekick prototype of action films, the casting would seem to flout racist conventions, but the film ends up simply re-inscribing them. The "Talis" (i.e., Taliban) exist in the film only as blips on a satellite infrared or as ghost-like shadows in the dark, cowering behind rocks.[25] As Slajov Zizek has recently remarked of a similar situation in a Serb film about the war in Bosnia: "The narrative device thus mobilized is, of course, taken from many horror films, and even Westerns, in which a group of sympathetic characters is encircled by an invisible Enemy who is mainly heard and seen only in the guise of fleeting shadows and blurred appearances" (38–9). Likewise even in the almost desperately didactic *Lions for Lambs*— a third of the film depicts a student/teacher conference — the Muslim enemy is a shadowy, even ghostlike presence and its heroes latter-day Rolands trapped in the dolorous pass by latter-day Saracens, awaiting the always too late rescue. The film ends up confirming the Middle East as precisely the historical uncanny it tried to satirize through Tom Cruise's self-righteous conservative.

This strange self-deconstruction is common to many American films about the Middle East, even those bent on a critique of the orientalist medievalism in American neo-conservatism. One reason for this is the conservative nature of the film industry itself, determined to put new wine into the same old Hollywood bottles. Redford's film — snatched from today's headlines and motivated by strongly held political beliefs — finds itself reproducing almost exactly the last scene from *Butch Cassidy and the Sundance Kid* (see note 25). The historical uncanny is perhaps even more ambivalent in *Three Kings*, a 1999 Gulf War I action-adventure film starring George Cloony, Ice Cube, and Mark Wahlberg. The film's ironies rely on the slippage between mythic subtexts: the three Eastern kings who brought gifts to the new-born Christ and the three thugs of Chaucer's "The Pardoner's Tale" who vow to kill Death but run afoul of their own greed. Like the bored, disaffected revelers of Chaucer's dark parable, most of the American army camped in the desert have never seen any action and spend the morning guzzling booze, until a treasure map is discovered in the anus of an Iraqi captive in yet another example of the western fascination with the Arab male anus: *radix malorum est cupiditas*. Like Chaucer's revelers this discovery quickly changes their goals from the peace-keeping role of warring against Death to the logistical problems of recovering, hiding, and transporting "Saddam's gold." Taking the gold out of Egypt was a medieval Christian trope for allegorical readings of the Old Testament that mined from literal stories the precious, hidden meaning of charity. So too do the heroes of the film slowly convert to the message of Christian charity, distributing alms in the form of gold bars to destitute Iraqis and bartering the remainder of their hoard to buy passage for Shi'a refugees out of Iraq. In turning from "The Pardoner's Tale" to its supreme cinematic expression, John Huston's *The Treasure of the Sierra Madre* (1948), the film's heroes return the gold whence it came: the poor and abused Iraqi people. What begins as an anti-war film — their leader Archie Gates early on bellows in frustration "just tell me what we did here" — turns from its satire of American greed to the ubiquitous post–Vietnam rescue narrative, evident in dozens of films from the *Rambo* franchise to *Tears of the Sun*. In granting American oil wars a pardon, *Three Kings* assigns the usual American penance of reinvestment in the spiritual as well as economic resources of the Middle East. The film's movement from cupidity to charity is a modern day calque of Chaucer's Pardoner: the paradox of an American Satan that in spite of himself ends up doing God's work in the Middle East.

Canning the Historical Uncanny: Crusade Analogies

Mahmoud Darwish's powerful work on the 1982 invasion of Beirut, *A Memory for Forgetfulness*, belongs to the ancient genre of the *satura*, anatomized by one of Darwish's intellectual heroes M.M. Bakhtin. The tableaux of the prose poem slide seamlessly between the raw nerves of the siege, the vagaries of personal memory, and the immediacy of medieval history. Desperately wanting his morning cup of coffee, but kept from his water tap by the shelling and snipers, Darwish recalls the now infamous anecdote from Ibn Fadlan's history:[26]

> I remember Ibn Fadlan's *Epistle* and feel nauseated by that one vessel of water used to wash a whole army. Our water has been cut by those acting on behalf of leftover Crusaders, yet Saladin used to send ice and fruits to the enemy in the hope that "their hearts would melt," as he used to say. (Darwish, no pagination)

However ridiculous the notion of "Zionist Crusaders" may sound to many Western ears, it is nearly impossible to read Darwish's *Memory for Forgetfulness* without gaining some sympathy for those who find the collocation meaningful. Later Darwish recalls the rise of Gamel Abdel Nasser and hears another historical echo when Nasser names "the banks of the river in such a way as to disguise the mud there — sects and dregs of the Crusaders coming back to life in the darkness under the ringing speeches. But when the nationalist thesis collapsed, these sects put forth their almost shared language." Even attempts at making peace in the twentieth century are for Darwish indistinguishable from the designs of the Crusader kingdoms in *Outremer*:

> Because the aim of partitioning the land into coast and mountain between Arab and Frank was not, under prevailing conditions, to guarantee for the Arabs whatever forts and terrain had remained in their hands but to grant the enemy a respite that enabled him to establish a pattern that sanctioned his transition from exception to rule. (no pagination)

The final sentence reads like an uncanny anticipation of Giorgio Agamben's thesis about "states of exception" being the foundational step in the establishment of legal governments (1–32). Darwish goes on to quote long passages from medieval Arab chronicles that depict the shamelessness of the Franks, such as Usamah's infamous tale of a Muslim asked to shave the pubic hair from the wife of a Frank or Ibn Kathir's apocalyptic description of the unnatural miracles wrought by Frankish occupation, as if they were news reports of conditions within the contemporary siege of Beirut.

For Darwish the historical uncanny is not simply a tool for satire; it is a way of accurately representing the Palestinian experience of western barbarism as only the latest manifestation of an enduring Crusade: their "memory for forgetfulness." Western historians have for the most part been contemptuous of such "memories," led by the Cambridge historian Jonathan Riley-Smith. He has written both popular and definitive studies of the Crusades and the Military Orders, as well as several denials of their relevance to 9/11 and its aftermath. Responding to the propaganda coming from al-Qaida in a talk delivered at Old Dominion University in 2002 (later widely reprinted), Riley-Smith suggested that the Islamist connection of the medieval Crusades to contemporary invasions was a "version of neo-imperialist crusade history which suddenly and spectacularly forced itself on the world outside, since it provided historical and moral justification for acts of extreme violence" (2005, 307). Both imperial and romantic versions of Crusade history are for Riley-Smith products of nineteenth-century medievalism in Europe, which found its definitive expression in the Crusade novels of Sir Walter Scott and in the history of Joseph François Michaud. The popularity of this view of the crusades, which descended from the Enlightenment rejection of religious warfare, persisted into the mid-twentieth century in Steven Runciman's powerfully told *A History of the Crusades*—like Walter Scott he was "another lowland Calvinist." In later pieces for newspapers Riley-Smith would tendentiously attack Sir Ridley Scott's *Kingdom of Heaven*, said to derive its vision of the Latin Kingdom from Walter Scott's *The Talisman*. The Cambridge historian further warned that the film "would help to fuel the terrorists" and, as mentioned above, charged that its director shared "Osama bin Laden's view of history." Central to Riley-Smith's denial of historical analogy and continuity is his insistence, initially supported by many Crusade historians, that after the fall of Acre in 1291 Arabs completely forgot about the Crusades until late in the nineteenth century when Abdulhamid II marshaled the analogy in the service of a pan-Islamic call for resistance to Western imperialism, based on "rhetoric that had washed around Europe for more than half a century" (2005, 304). Thomas F. Madden also laments this "recovered memory" in the contemporary Arab world that celebrates Saladin and sees the terrorist attacks as revenge for a continuing crusade against the East: "It is not the crusades, then, that lead to the attacks of September 11, but the artificial memory of the crusades constructed by modern colonial powers and passed down by Arab nationalists and Islamists. They stripped the medieval expeditions of every aspect of their age and dressed them up instead in the tattered rags of nineteenth century imperialism" (222).

The contention that medievalism is at fault for the 9/11 attacks is a provocative one and deserves to be investigated at further length than can be attempted here. The surprising claim that nineteenth-century Western writers and imperialists had to remind Arabs of the Crusades — now apparently taken as a given in both popular and scholarly discourse — is too critical to stand as an *ipse dixit* assertion without documentation. The claim is counterintuitive, has an orientalist flavor that remains to be proven, and should not be taken on faith. Less surprising is that the Crusades again became relevant for Arabs with the breaking up of the Ottoman Empire, the return of western military forces to the heart of the Middle East, and the division of Arab territories among the colonizing powers of France, Great Britain, and ultimately the United States. But the weakest part of Riley-Smith's argument doesn't concern Arab memories at all, but rather Western ones. The notion that what we might call crusading ideology was an isolated phenomenon invented by late nineteenth-century intellectuals in the West and then in a typical example of liberal recklessness taught to the Arabs simply doesn't hold water. Crusading ideology survived with little change into the early modern period, evident in the epic poems of Ariosto and Tasso, as well as in holy wars waged against Reformed Churches like the Spanish Armada of 1588. Crucially, as Mayer points out, the last of the crusading bulls issued to Spanish monarchs didn't expire until 1940, when there was "no longer a Spanish king to receive them."[27]

Humanism, the Reformation, and the Enlightenment profoundly changed European society, but there was little change in attitudes about "the Turk." As Tomaz Mastnak demonstrates, humanists such as Erasmus and Sir Thomas More were disheartened by internecine wars between European peoples (just as Pope Urban II had been) and also like the eleventh century Pope encouraged Western kingdoms to unite in a war against Saracen infidels. Even Martin Luther, who unsurprisingly condemned papal leadership of medieval Crusades, advocated a league of Christian princes, a *"gotselig Krieg"* or Holy War. As Mastnak concludes, "Protestants helped to secularize, yet not to desacralize, war against the Turks. Holy war ... survived the reformation" (218). Enlightenment thinkers did condemn the Crusades, most notably in Hume's oft-quoted characterization of them as "the most signal and durable monument of human folly that has yet appeared," yet crusading scenarios continued to be vetted throughout the Age of Reason and again caught fire with the Romantic fascination for chivalry and the Gothic. Indeed most striking in Mastnak's survey of crusading plans throughout the seventeenth and eighteenth centuries in Spain, Italy, and France is the consistency of the rhetoric urging European unity as a prelude to launching a renewed Crusade against the Ottoman Empire. Looked at from this perspective the triumphal evocations of the Crusades by the West in the First World War seem less whimsical and more like recognition of a widely shared goal finally achieved after the better part of a millennium. Whether or not Riley-Smith is correct in assuming that Arabs had to be reminded of the Crusades, the West on the other hand never forgot them — and that finally is the point. An unbroken if at times muted strain of crusading ideology in the West has never stopped dreaming of the day when Europe would unite in a final, decisive Crusade. If many in the Arab world since the nineteenth century have felt Western imperialism and military interventions were part of a continuing or returning Crusade, they are only incorrect in that assumption if we insist on defining a Crusade according to certain fashions in contemporary scholarship, rather than according to the mentalities of those Westerners who put boots on the ground in the Middle East throughout the twentieth century. Here medievalism trumps conventional historical scholarship because it is not the medieval wars themselves that are really at issue in the charge that the wars in the Gulf are a renewed Crusade, but rather an Arab response to an enduring and widespread imaginative investment by the West in this imperial, quasi-religious form of medievalism. A recent and influential survey of future conflicts by Samuel P. Huntington argues for the inevitability of wars along religious lines and urges the West to unite in preparation for these wars, an argument that stirs uncanny echoes. Despite belated attempts by many in the Bush administration to control the casting of the current conflict in religious terms, the formulation always oozes through the cracks: from the Muslim prayer posture transformed into a stress position with an American soldier on the back of an Arab detainee to the gun barrels of American tanks painted with the slogan "New Testament."

John Masefield, poet laureate of Britain and during the First World War a paid propagandist, re-imagines the disastrous British invasion of Gallipoli in 1916 as yet another instance of the historical uncanny. Unlike Darwish's, Masefield's references to crusading ideology are not simply elements in a wider net of historical and personal associations but rather a dominant figural grid that structures his romantic eulogy for the catastrophic invasion. Each chapter of the book begins with an epigraph from the *Song of Roland*, and its narrative — repeated victories against incredible odds, final heroic defeat, and the too-late arrival of reinforcements — also serves to structure Masefield's account of Gallipoli:

> Only, when all was done, their situation remained that of the Frank rearguard in the *Song of Roland*. In that poem the Franks could and did beat the Saracens, but the Saracens brought up another army before the Franks were reinforced. The Franks could and did beat that army, too, but the Saracens brought up another army before the Franks were reinforced. The Franks could and did beat that army, too, but then they were spent and Roland had to sound his horn and Charlemagne would not come to the summons of the horn, and the heroes were abandoned in the dolorous pass [90].

As Paul Fussell points out, "for Masefield a *crusade* constituted a useful metaphor, because one of his government's objects was to persuade the Americans to join a Christian war against barbarism" (193). And Masefield's way of furthering that agenda goes beyond the simple evocation of a holy war against the Turks/Saracens, but also imagines above the rut of mechanized slaughter a heavenly host calling upon the Charlemagne who lingers overseas:

> Surely all through the eighth of August our unseen dead were on that field, blowing the horn of Roland, the unheard, unheeded horn, the horn of heroes in the dolorous pass, asking for the little that heroes ask, but asking in vain. If ever the great of England cried from beyond death to the living they cried then. "De ço qui Galt. Demuret i unt trop" [113].

Masefield saw the wounded coming in from the front and surveyed the carnage on the battlefield after that appallingly bungled invasion, but unlike other war poets of the time, such as Wilfred Owen or Siegfried Sassoon, he didn't believe his eyes. For him the reality of what occurred at Gallipoli is invisible, and its significance derives from an historical uncanny pushed to the point of supernatural coincidence: martyrdom in a holy crusade against the infidel and the assurance of salvation "were but the end they asked, the reward they had come for, the unseen cross upon the breast" (63).

Yet however one chooses to judge the persistence of Crusading ideology, it is essential to consider as well a discourse that is inextricably bound up with it, one remarkably uniform throughout the centuries, an ideology we might dub the *Saracen doxology* to emphasize its descent from medieval ways of constructing the Saracen other as well as its perdurable, almost catechistic character. As Norman Daniel in his survey of Western attitudes toward Islam insists, "the cohesion of this integrated group of opinions, what we may call this established canon, proved to be so strong as to survive the break-up of European ideological unity, both the division into Catholic and Protestant, and the growth of atheism and agnosticism" (302).[28] The medieval portrait of the Saracen in general and of Mohammed in particular survives humanism, continues largely unabated through the Enlightenment, gains renewed if altered vigor during the nineteenth-century revival of chivalry and medievalism, and continues to surface unabashedly across Western culture today. As Europeans in the thirteenth and fourteenth centuries gained more direct knowledge of Muslims, they inculcated a vision of Islam that has had an almost miraculous persistence. Chief components of what I am calling the Saracen doxology include the notion that Islam is a political religion that grew out of worldly, temporal concerns. A central text in this synthesis is Nicholas of Cusa's fourteenth-century dialogue where he queries his opponent John of Segovia (a translator of the Qur'an) about what Islam has added to Jewish and Christian revelations, other than the use of the sword as a means to achieve political ends. Even Voltaire's more "Enlightened" approach did not disturb the basic Saracen doxology established in the Middle Ages: "Mohammed was seen as the inventor of a religion made up of bits and pieces...a deliberate deceiver...who established his religion by force" (Daniel 312). It is precisely this charge and its catechistic repetition through much of Western history that Pope Benedict quoted for discussion in 2006: "Show me just what Mohammed brought that was new, and there you will find things only evil and inhuman, such as his command to spread by the sword the faith that he preached."[29] Unlike George Bush's call for a crusade, Pope Benedict XVI, a more than competent scholar of medieval Latinity and someone who has read the Qur'an — cannot plead ignorance in the use of this old chestnut as a means to engage the Islamic world in dialogue. The implication that one must draw from reading the whole speech is, or so it seems to me, that Pope Benedict charges elements in the Muslim world with adhering to Manuel II Paleologus' medieval characterization of Islam and adopting a doctrine of forced conversion in direct contradiction of Qur'anic teachings. Hence Pope Benedict has the best of both worlds: evoking the Saracen doxa of the Middle Ages also permits him to encourage the equally stubborn inference that Muslim cultures are "stuck" in the Middle Ages, living within a faith uninformed by reason. Writing long before Pope Benedict's provocative invitation to dialogue on reason and faith, Daniel summed up the western "scientific" tradition of writing about Islam and warned: "even when we read the most detached of scholars, we need to keep in mind how medieval Christendom argued, because it has always been and still is part of the make-up of every Western mind brought to bear upon the subject" (326). Angry reactions to the Pope's words from Muslim intellectuals and religious leaders repeatedly characterized the speech as evidence of a "medieval mind" and a "crusading mentality." Though perhaps a case of the pot calling the kettle medieval, these characterizations of Benedict's speech as we have seen point to a real if polemically stated continuity in Western views of Islam. Similar controversies continue to brew over the survival of other medieval elements of the Saracen doxology, such as the supposed brainwashing of Muslim suicide bombers with the promised paradise of male sexual fantasies. Western medievalist critiques of contemporary Islam have also targeted the veil as a sign of the oppression of women. The veil has become the locus of many legal and extra-legal forms of interference with Muslim women and girls living in the West. Abu Ghraib became a study in many of these "medieval" prejudices: from the specter of forced conversions to Islam as a sham or parodic religion; from the supposedly oversexed nature of Muslim men to the enforced passivity of Muslim women.

But we are most concerned not about carefully orchestrated propaganda withdrawn in the next news cycle nor even with torture recklessly improvised to abuse a faith as well as its bodies. What interests and what frightens us most is the sheer, blinding force of recurrence itself, everywhere intimated: from satire that mocks repetition to tragedy which finds it ennobling, from analogies that teach the medieval past by rendering it relevant to travesties that stir echoes of which their creators are only dimly aware. Are analogies drawn to the medieval Crusades more than simply partisan politics, rather part of a compulsive return to the era of the Crusades? In attempting to think *Beyond the Pleasure Principle* (1961a, first published 1920) Freud hypothesized a "death instinct," initially defined as a surplus of instinctual energies that overwhelm the pleasure principle. In repetition compulsions the patient "is obliged to *repeat* the repressed material as a contemporary experience instead of, as the physician would prefer to see, *remembering* it as something belonging to the past" (1961a, 19). Yet for Freud the most disturbing kind of repetitions are those that take on the form of a curse "where the subject seems to have a *passive* experience over which he has no influence" (1961a, 24). Strangely Freud's chief example for this "fate neurosis" comes from Torquato Tasso's *Gerusalemme Liberata*:

> Its hero, Tancred, unwittingly kills his Clorinda while she is disguised in the armour of an enemy knight. After her burial he makes his way into a strange magic forest which strikes the Crusaders' army with terror. He slashes with his sword at a tall tree but blood streams from the cut and the voice of Clorinda, whose soul is imprisoned in the tree, is heard complaining that he has wounded his beloved once again [1961a, 24].

There are a number of complexities nesting within this ostensibly straightforward example. It's difficult to characterize the irascible Tancred as *passive* in any sense of the word. The episode in Tasso's poem has him first killing an enemy, albeit one whose identity he misrecognizes and then volunteering to cut down the trees in a haunted forest all the other Crusaders have fled in fear. The tree itself contains an inscription that concludes, "With us, the living have no cause to fight," yet Tancred begins hacking at the tree with his sword anyway. As Freud's own phrasing suggests Tancred only *seems* passive. He remains in despair over having killed Clorinda, and his impetuous slashing of the tree connotes the rampant passions to which he is still subject. Freud's example is also evidence of an intertextual compulsion to repeat; the scene reprises episodes in Virgil, Dante and Ariosto. These intertexts exemplify respectively the mortal sins of greed, suicide, and lust: the latter two most in force here are Christian counterparts to the death instinct and the sexual instinct that Freud will go on to explore in the remainder of the book. But perhaps the most evocative repetition of all is Freud's own quotation that sets as a kind of culturally primal scene the First Crusade, where Thanatos is first seen as an excess that overwhelms Eros, and the compulsion to repeat is driven by what has been repressed.[30]

Freud would go on in *Civilization and Its Discontents* (1961b, first published in 1930) to offer proof of the primal aggressivity in human beings — of the principle *homo (est) hominis lupus*— through a revealing series of examples: from "racial migrations," the Huns, the Mongol warlords Genghis Khan and Tamerlane, to "the capture of Jerusalem by the pious Crusaders, or even indeed the horrors of the recent World War" (1961 p. 69). The parallel between medieval atrocities and "indeed" World War I suggests a crucial strain of medievalism in Freud's evolving theory of the death drive. Medieval barbarity in his metapsychological, cultural criticism has itself become a kind of "fate neurosis," a compulsion to repeat wherein the modern world lapses into the primal aggressiveness of medieval conquests. During this period Freud was increasingly thinking in terms his biographer Peter Gay calls "phylogenetic fantasy," the Lamarckian idea that the development of the drives and mechanisms of defense in the individual were duplicated in the psychic development of civilization. We might postulate that the centrality of medievalism within Freud's developing theory of the death instinct (*Beyond the Pleasure Principle* and *Civilization and Its Discontents* include no extended clinical examples) suggests that perhaps in his dualistic reformulation of the drives the Middle Ages marked the point in cultural evolution when the compulsion to repeat was formed: a kind of primal trauma to which civilization is doomed to return. Indeed, Nazi medievalism's subsequent valorization of the crusades and the military religious orders suggests just such a benighted repetition.[31] Freud's survey of medieval barbarism begins with the "racial migrations" of the Goths who sacked Rome (a traditional starting point for the Middle Ages), continues through the itinerant Mongol tribes for whom war was — in the common understanding — a way of life, and concludes with the sack of Jerusalem, where we are told that blood ran knee-deep through the streets. Mongols and Crusaders are certainly the Eastern and Western epitomes for Freud of civilization's discontents. There could perhaps for him be no better example of a historical compulsion to repeat than the eight major Crusades to the Holy Land spanning two centuries and the roughly eighty lesser crusades across a dizzying array of fronts spanning half a millennium. In *Beyond the Pleasure Principle* the "war neuroses" of soldiers returning from World War I, the childhood aggression inherent in the famous game of *fort/da*, and the "fate neurosis" of Tancred the Crusader all significantly manifest the compulsion to repeat. The child is father to the man, just as the Crusading Era is father to the contemporary world, where Freud feared that we had not seen "the last of the barbarian invasions," as Sir Steven Runciman famously dubbed the Crusades. In all these repetitions there is something "demonic," an anarchic, primary sado-masochism.

This new theoretical turn in Freud's thinking can be traced from the essay published a year before *Beyond the Pleasure Principle*, "The Uncanny" (first published in 1919), which introduces the concept of a compulsion to repeat and connects our awareness of this instinctual compulsion to the *unheimliche*:

> It is possible to recognize the dominance in the unconscious mind of "a compulsion to repeat" preceding from the instinctual impulses and probably inherent in the very nature of the instincts — a compulsion powerful enough to overrule the pleasure principle, lending to certain aspects of the mind their daemonic character...whatever reminds us of this inner "compulsion to repeat" is perceived as uncanny [2001, 942–3].

The evolving concatenation — the uncanny, the compulsion to repeat, the death instinct — was widely criticized by subsequent psychoanalysis but has made something of a comeback more recently. Julia Kristeva usefully defines the uncanny as "the immanence of the strange within the familiar" (183), and Slavoj Zizek opines that: "we, the 'actual' present historical agents, have to conceive of ourselves as the materialization of the ghosts of past generations, as the stage in which these past generations retroactively resolve their deadlocks" (90–1). Both thinkers in their returns to Freud counter the growing pessimism that underwrote his development of the theory with something like optimism. For Kristeva our recognition of the abject within ourselves can lead us to respect without needing to comprehend the radical alterity that lurks within the other; for Zizek demonic instincts allow the present to serve as the stage whereon, rather than blindly replaying its bloody aporias, the past resolves them. As subtexts for our exploration of the historical uncanny in Crusade and orientalist films, these reformulations of Freud pay large dividends. Such films often focus on the formation of cross-cultural bonds — be they heterosexual or homosocial — and screen for their audiences myriad projections of the "strange within the familiar" and the familiar within the strange. Part of the attractions of any medieval/oriental film for modern audiences is the play of continuity and difference in their identifications with people and cultures of an epoch deemed both the origin and radical obverse of modern Western subjectivities and cultural formations. Crusade films often suggest a nascent personal or even cultural tolerance meant to serve as an example for the contemporary world. And many films set in a modern age haunted by the demonic return of the Crusades through time travel or in the miraculous survival of secret orders and sacred artifacts also — just as Zizek would suggest — pose the contemporary world as the *stage* of cultural development in which medieval conflicts are resolved and millennial secrets unveiled.[32] Yet there is an abundance of reasons in today's world to be skeptical of such attempts to disentangle Freud's compulsion to repeat from the death instinct.

Taking the Cross

A strikingly repetitive motif in Crusade films is the taking of the cross — a theme ubiquitous though mutable whose repetitions and variations point directly to the heart of the matter: a religion that launched a series of interhemispheric wars. Jonathan Riley-Smith directly confronts the vexed question of the Crusaders' motivations by insisting that the Crusades were chiefly penitential and that Crusading constituted an "act of love" (2002, 31–50). Pope John Paul II's apology on March 12, 2000, though deliberately couched in general terms, was widely deemed an apology chiefly for the Crusades, as indeed it was in part. Riley-Smith emphasizes the clerical organization of the Crusades and John Paul II the many regrettable outcomes of armed pilgrimages, but between these opposing characterizations of the Crusades as an "act of love" and "sins in the service of truth" nests the obscurity of particular pilgrims' motivations for taking the cross. If the tendency in earlier histories was to portray the Crusaders as adventurous and opportunistic victims of primogeniture, more recently the danger is a rather credulous acceptance of official or idealized accounts. The motivations behind the actions of any particular individual embarking upon a Crusade were likely as complex and mitigated by circumstances and personality as they are opaque to us today. Yet films (especially popular films) in their traditional focus on particular individuals must make motivations apparent for their audiences. Historical films typically employ back stories to explain their characters' motivations, which through the trajectory of the diegesis are supplemented, modified, and/or called into question by subsequent developments. In popular historical films motivation and its evolutions determine character and to a great degree plot as well. These films begin from what we know least about — the complex interiority of particular medieval subjectivities — and this imaginary prosthesis, not the historical details about which we can and do know a great deal, circumscribes the shape of the resulting film.

The importance of motivations in determining character and plot is perhaps nowhere more apparent than in the filmic theme of taking the cross. In this and many other ways Cecil B. DeMille's *The Crusades* (1935) provides the paradigm from which similar scenes in a number of later films descend. DeMille's film is based upon the dichotomy of violence and the sacred (albeit in a resolutely non–Giradian fashion). This dichotomy is symbolized by the film's frequent juxtaposition of the sword and the cross. *The Crusades* opens with the fall of Jerusalem to the Arabs, signified by Muslims toppling a cross from the Dome of the Rock. The Christian resolve is embodied in the "Hermit" who holds a wooden crucifix in front of the triumphant Saladin and promises to return with the Crusade. When next we see him he is back in

Europe preaching the Crusade and presiding over an elaborate ceremony in which King Philip of France takes the cross. King Richard (Henry Wilcoxon) is a no-show, more concerned with the forging of his sword and trading jests and blows with all comers. When pressed to fulfill his father's pledge for Richard to marry Princess Alice of France (played by DeMille's daughter, Katherine), Richard seizes upon the opportunity to escape wedlock by taking the cross. The Hermit warns Richard that his tomfoolery is evident to God and that the cross will burn its way into his heart — as indeed it ultimately does. For the present though Richard is proud of his newly forged sword and raises it high above the Hermit's cross as he calls on all his vassals to join him. Soon though Richard falls victim to a more expertly sprung marriage trap and is forced to marry Berengaria of Navarre in order to purchase her father's beef to feed his starving army. Richard sends his sword to the marriage ceremony as a surrogate, and Berengaria duly marries the sword, determining that it and not he will share her bed. As the Crusade falls victim to dissention and Berengaria is wounded and taken prisoner, Richard's priorities begin to change. He makes peace with Saladin and breaks the sword over his knee, swearing that it and his pride will stand between him and Berengaria no more. Richard's sword has not been beaten into a plowshare but rather broken into the shape of a cross, which Berengaria dutifully places as an offering on Christ's tomb. Jerusalem is made open to all faiths and Christ's message of peace reigns once again in the Holy Land. This pacifism was in stark contrast to the message sent by DeMille's earlier film, *Joan the Woman* (1917), which envisioned American entrance into the First World War as a sacred act. In 1935 he turned to preaching non-involvement and peaceful coexistence; in curbing Richard's pride DeMille also counsels American isolation from an increasingly unstable Europe. But that was not to be: General Dwight D. Eisenhower would famously dub the allied war against Germany the "Crusade in Europe" (see Eisenhower 1997 and Parnet 1972).

In a vastly superior film released three years later, Sergei Eisenstein's *Alexander Nevsky* (1938), the Teutonic warrior monks comically and impotently turn their crosses into swords but are overrun by Russian peasants. David Lean's influential *El Cid* (1961) begins with a scene in which the titular hero (Charlton Heston) shoulders a wooden cross to carry it from a burning church. The shot deftly negotiates the difficulties of the proto-Crusades in Spain by casting the Cid as a Christ-like savior, and it also looks forward to his sacrifice at the end of the film. At the end, his corpse lashed to his horse and his erect posture secured by prop, the Cid gallops "through the gates of history and into legend," putting the Saracen armies to flight. His freely made choice is to sacrifice his own life, becoming a potent symbol even in death for Christian resistance to Muslim fundamentalists like the war-mongering

Ben Jussuf. Youssef Chahine's *Saladin* (1963) undermines the cinematic trope of taking the cross by having Richard's palm imprinted with a bloody cross from the wound of a pilgrim thought to have been attacked by Saracens. That the real culprits are Frankish provocateurs who want war, not peace, calls into question the very injuries that motivated the Crusade in the first place.

In more recent films, even those attempting to portray particular Crusaders — though not the Crusades — in a positive light, the union of violence and the sacred in the taking of the cross is rendered much more ambivalently. Frantisek Vlacil's *Valley of the Bees* (1968) calls the agency of the Crusader himself into question. As a mischievous boy the young hero of the film plays a nasty trick upon his new stepmother on her wedding day. The boy's father angrily hurls him into a wall and quickly prays to the Virgin Mary to save his life, offering to give the boy to her if he survives. The boy Ondrej is duly dedicated to the Knights of the Virgin (the Teutonic Knights), yet the ceremony in which he takes the cross is full of shadows and haunted by claustrophia and pederastic undertones, which suggest that the Order is really a place of cruel incarceration. Indeed later as a young man Ondrej discovers that taking the cross has doomed him to a sado-masochistic and violently misogynistic world that he can never escape.

More recent still, though very much in the tradition of DeMille and Lean, is Ridley Scott's 2005 film *Kingdom of Heaven*. The hero of the film, Balian, every bit as agnostic as DeMille's Richard and every bit as dedicated to waging war as a means to peace as Lean's Cid, takes the cross from a priest (who also happens to be his stepbrother) as he murders him. In the dark of his blacksmith's forge Balian discovers his wife's tiny silver cross around the neck of the priest, who taunts him with the hell that awaits his wife because of her suicide. Balian is forging a sword and cooly plunges the red-hot blade into his stepbrother's belly, and the priest bursts into flames. Balian, though, is only interested in the cross, which he snatches from the flames, branding his palm with the sign of the cross in a shot that recalls the bloody cross on the palm in Chahine's *Saladin*. Balian leaves on Crusade in the hopes of remitting both his sins and those of his spouse. Once in Jerusalem he climbs Golgotha to bury the cross at the top of the hill. Though like DeMille's Richard Balian will ultimately become a peacemaker, also like DeMille's Richard he is meant to stand for the blessings America can incur by leaving the Middle East and returning home to peaceful isolation in the West.

Less bound by the big-budget requirement for happy endings is my last example, *Soldier of God* (2005), an independent film in which taking the cross is explicitly conjoined with a fatal compulsion to repeat. This engaging and little-known film begins with a dazed and blood-soaked Templar wandering through a forbidding desert landscape. Suffering from his wounds and sunstroke, the Templar Rene lies down on the desert floor to die, but he is rescued by a mysterious Saracen who gives him water to drink and takes him to the tent of a Frankish widow whose husband was an Arab. The widow Soheila tends his wounds and mends and washes the blood out of his Templar tunic. Rene begins to envision a life beyond the catastrophic Crusade. But re-donning the Templar tunic with its red cross also seems to doom him to a vicious cycle of crazed bloodlust. Rene's Arab friend, Hasan, turns out to be an assassin sent on a suicidal mission to kill Saladin. When the hunt for the assassin finally uncovers his hideaway and Saladin's raiding party attacks Soheila's camp, Hasan and Rene fight side by side to repel the invaders. The battle though stirs flashbacks and a rabid bloodlust in Rene. When Soheila runs up from behind him, he takes her for another attacker in the dark and Tancred-like kills his love in a fatal *meconaissance*. The film ends as it began with Rene, his white Templar robe spattered with blood, wandering through the desert and at last (and again) lying down to die in the sand.

Notes

1. Terry Eagleton, *Holy Terror*, page 25.
2. The term and its popularity in contemporary American politics descends from an article Samuel P. Huntington published in the journal *Foreign Affairs* in 1993. The more complete version of his thesis appears in *The Clash of Civilizations and the Remaking of World Order* (1996). A series of engaging and thoughtful responses from a Muslim perspective is offered in Qureshi and Sells, eds., *The New Crusades*.
3. See for instance the "Afterword" to his revised edition of *The Crusades* (2005, 299–309) and the essays "Jihad Crusaders: What Osama bin Laden Means by a Crusade" and "Religious Warriors: Reinterpreting the Crusades."
4. See the chapter *"Figura"* in *Scenes from the Drama of European Literature* (11–78).
5. See below in this introduction for a fuller discussion of Pope Benedict's remarks.
6. For Jones see *Terry Jones' War on Terror* (2005) and his four-part documentary, *Crusades* for the BBC, released as a "History Channel" DVD in 1995. For Tariq Ali see *The Clash of Fundamentalisms* (2002) and *Bush in Babylon* (2003).
7. See my *Movie Medievalism*, pages 134–50, for a fuller discussion of the controversies surrounding this film and a bibliography on the debate as well as Arthur Lindley, "Once, Present and Future Kings: *Kingdom of Heaven* and the Multitemporality of Medieval Film" in Ramey and Pugh, eds. *Race, Class and Gender*, pages 15–30.
8. See Edward Risden's chapter below for a discussion of what he calls the "other buddy" in *Thirteenth Warrior* and *Kingdom of Heaven*. On *El Cid* see the chapters of Thomas Shippey and Kevin J. Harty below.
9. Maalouf's translation of this incident differs in some relevant details from that offered more recently by Richards (2002, page 101), where it is the Muslim boy's idea to take the young Frank prisoner.
10. The story by Jorge Luis Borges is entitled "The Maker" (Borges 155–7).
11. *Saladin: The Animated Series* is a co-production between MDec (msc.com.) and JCC (jcctv.net). http://tv.muxlim.com/video/NROCGQPiDGX/Saladin-The-Animated-Series/ (retrieved 7/19/08)
12. Only Series One (2003) of *Monkey Dust* has been released on DVD. *Monkey Dust: The Crusades* was retrieved 7/19/08 from http://www.youtube.com/watch?v=vEVJ_48YgTg.
13. For Joan of Arc see Luc Besson's *The Messenger: The Story of Joan of Arc* (1999). For

William Wallace see Mel Gibson's *Braveheart* (1995) — as well as its similarities to Gibson's take on the American War of Independence in *The Patriot*. And for King Arthur warring on the side of the native Picts against Saxon imperialism see Antoine Fuqua's *King Arthur* (2005).

14. See Haydock (169).

15. My discussion is based chiefly upon the full archive of all the available photos on Salon.com (*http://www.salon.com/news/abu_ghraib/2006/03/14/*) retrieved on 8/30/08.

16. A restricted search on Google for "medieval torture" produces a list of 224,000 hits, most of which chronicle modern atrocities.

17. See the conclusion added to Melanie McAlister's powerful study *Epic Encounters*: "The photographs from Abu Ghraib were a new kind of racial politics, one that brought the symbolics of domestic racism — itself the product of the history of colonialism and imperialism — into the service of a new, overtly American imperial power" (302).

18. Talisman Energy divested its Sudan holdings in 2003, and the suit was dismissed without prejudice.

19. The scene was imitated via CGI in Peter Jackson's *The Return of the King*, where Aragorn, Gimli, and Legolas charge against the Orcs; the army of the dead magically appears at their backs, sweeping through the enemy like a bitter wind.

20. See John Ganim's discussion of this film in his chapter below.

21. The screenwriter of *Afghan Knights*, Christine Stringer, replied on 18 February, 2008, to a query of ours with the following description of the genesis of the film's mythology: "As the writer of *Afghan Knights* I was hired to construct a story about mercenaries in Afghanistan who get caught in a cave haunted by the ghosts of Genghis Kahn. That idea stemmed from the Executive Producer of the film, Brandon Hogan. I believe (and he could probably tell you more on the subject) that when he was in Afghanistan some years ago with the American military he came across folklore that Genghis and his warriors haunted a certain mountain range in Afghanistan. Upon researching the topic, I found that Genghis did indeed lead his troops through that mountain range and suffered the greatest losses ever suffered by his army. Further research into the topic gave me insight to the real event of Genghis Kahn's soul being loosed. The first scene in the movie of the Russian invasion of China is true history put to fiction. Monks were killed in the thousands and many mongul relics lost and destroyed."

22. One finds the same conservative Washington insiders spouting the same platitudes about Muslims who "want to roll back the clock to the eighth century" in the vastly superior *Syriana*.

23. American naval theorist Alfred Mahan first used the term in 1903. For a fascinating and thoroughly engaging history of American financial and spiritual investments in the Middle East see Michael B. Oren, *Power, Faith, and Fantasy*.

24. Bhabha, page 62, but see also Bhabha's chapter on "Articulating the Archaic" (175–198).

25. The whole belabored last stand of the wounded American soldiers plays like a homage to the final (suicidal) scene of Redford's *Butch Cassidy and the Sundance Kid*. Redford's Afghanistan and the Afghanis themselves are simply calques for the earlier film's Mexican mountain and the cowardly but patient Mexican army.

26. Darwish (1982, no pagination): famous because of the scene in *Thirteenth Warrior*.

27. Qtd. in Mastnak, "Europe and the Muslims" in Qureshi and Sells, eds., *The New Crusades*, page 230.

28. We might add that this portrait, as Jack S. Shaheen exhaustively demonstrated in *Reel Bad Arabs*, has continued to be employed in hundreds upon hundreds of films from the early days of cinema right down to the present. See also Stock's essay below.

29. Pope Benedict's quotation of the Byzantine emperor Manuel II Paleologus occurs in a speech given at the University of Regensberg on September 12, 2006. The complete speech in English translation is available at: *http://www.vatican.va/holy_father/benedict_xvi/speeches/2006/september/documents/hf_ben-xvi_spe_20060912*, retrieved 8/31/08.

30. Kathleen Biddick (206–209) suggests that both Tasso and Freud "encrypt" the textual, archival remnants of martyrs. This seems — in so far as I understand it — a misreading of both. The "speech" in the enchanted forest Tasso presents is so powerful that it expels and terrifies the invading force — they never do manage to desecrate the forest but have to get their wood elsewhere. In Freud's reading the point seems to be not that the deaths of Jews, Muslims, or Christians are forgotten or hushed up in a way that demonstrates some sort of bias, but rather

a fatal compulsion to repeat that overwhelms all distinctions between peoples — even between those one loves and those one hates.
  31. See my chapter below.
  32. See the chapters by Aronstein and Torry and by Powers below.

Bibliography

Ali, Tariq. *Bush in Babylon: The Recolonisation of Iraq.* New York: Verso, 2003.
_____. *The Clash of Fundamentalisms: Crusades, Jihads and Modernity.* New York: Verso, 2002.
Agamben, Giorgio. *States of Exception.* Trans. Kevin Attell. Chicago: University of Chicago Press, 2005.
Auerbach, Erich. *Scenes from the Drama of European Literature.* Minneapolis: University of Minnesota Press, 1984.
Bakhtin, M. M. *Rabelais and His World.* Trans. Helene Iswolsky. Indianapolis: Indiana University Press, 1984.
Bhabha, Homi. *The Location of Culture.* New York: Routledge, 2004.
Biddick, Kathleen. "Unbinding the Flesh in the Time That Remains." *GLQ: A Journal of Lesbian and Gay Studies* 13.2–3 (2007), 198–225.
Borges, Jorge Luis. *Jorge Luis Borges: The Aleph and Other Stories, 1933–1969.* Trans. Norman Thomas di Giovanni. New York: E. P. Dutton, 1970.
Brown, Dan. *The Da Vinci Code.* New York: Anchor Books, 2006.
Cary, Diana Sierra. *Hollywood Posse: The Story of a Gallant Band of Horsemen Who Made Movie History.* Norman, OK: University of Oklahoma Press, 1996.
Daniel, Norman. 1960. *Islam and the West: The Making of an Image.* Oxford: One World, 2000.
Darwish, Mahmoud. *Memory for Forgetfulness: August, Beirut, 1982.* Berkeley, Calif: University of California Press, 1995: http://www.escholarship.org/editions/view?docId=ftlz09n7g7&brand=ucpress retrieved 8/5/08.
Eagleton, Terry. *Holy Terror.* Oxford: Oxford University Press, 2005.
Eco, Umberto. *Foucault's Pendulum.* Trans. William Weaver. New York: Harcourt, 1989.
Eisenhower, Dwight D. *Crusade in Europe.* 1948. Baltimore: Johns Hopkins University Press, 1997.
Fussell, Paul. *Thank God for the Atom Bomb and Other Essays.* New York: Ballantine Books, 1988.
Freud, Sigmund. *Beyond the Pleasure Principle.* Trans. James Strachey. New York: Norton, 1961a.
_____. *Civilization and Its Discontents.* Trans. James Strachey. New York: Norton, 1961b.
_____. "The Uncanny" in *The Norton Anthology of Theory and Criticism.* Gen. Ed. Vincent B. Leitch. New York: Norton, 2001: 929–952.
Haydock, Nickolas. *Movie Medievalism: The Imaginary Middle Ages.* Jefferson, NC: McFarland, 2008.
Holsinger, Bruce. *Neomedievalism, Neoconservatism, and the War on Terror.* Chicago: Prickly Paradigm Press, 2007.
Huntington, Samuel P. *The Clash of Civilizations and the Remaking of World Order.* New York: Simon and Schuster, 2003.
Jones, Terry. *Terry Jones' War on Terror.* New York: Nation Books, 2005.
Khoury, Raymond. *The Last Templar.* New York: Dutton, 2006.
Kristeva, Julia. *Strangers to Ourselves.* Trans. Leon S. Roudiez. New York: Columbia University Press, 1991.
Lewis, Bernard. *The Assassins: A Radical Sect in Islam.* New York: Basic Books, 1967, 2002.
Maalouf, Amin. *The Crusades through Arab Eyes.* Trans. John Rothschild. New York: Schocken Books, 1984.

Masefield, John. *John Masefield's Great War: Collected Works*. Ed. Philip W. Errington. Barnsley, UK: Pen and Sword Books, 2007.
Mastnak, Tomaz. "Europe and the Muslims" in Emran Qureshi and Michael A. Sells, eds. *The New Crusades: Constructing the Muslim Enemy*. New York: Columbia University Press, 2003.
McAlister, Melanie. *Epic Encounters: Culture, Media and U.S. Interests in the Middle East since 1945, Updated Edition with a Post-9/11 Chapter*. Berkeley, CA; University of California Press, 2005.
Oren, Michael B. *Power, Faith, and Fantasy: America in the Middle East, 1776 to the Present*. New York: Norton, 2007.
Parnet, Herbert. *Eisenhower and the American Crusades*. New York: Macmillan, 1972.
Qureshi, Emran and Michael A. Sells, eds. *The New Crusades: Constructing the Muslim Enemy*. New York: Columbia University Press, 2003.
Ramey, Lynn, and Tison Pugh, eds. *Race, Class, and Gender in "Medieval" Cinema*. New York; Palgrave, 2007.
Richards, D. S. *The Rare and Excellent History of Saladin by Baha al-Din ibn Shaddad*. Burlington, VT: Ashgate Publishing, 2002.
Riley-Smith, Jonathan. *The Crusades*, 2nd ed. New Haven: Yale University Press, 2005.
_____. "The Crusades as an Act of Love." in Thomas F. Madden, ed. *The Crusades: Blackwell Essential Readings in History*. Malden, MA: Blackwell, 2002: 31–50.
Shaheen, Jack G. *Reel Bad Arabs: How Hollywood Vilifies a People*. Gloucestershire, UK: Arris Books, 2003.
Spencer, Robert. *The Politically Incorrect Guide to Islam (and the Crusades)*. Washington, DC: Regnery, 2005.
Zizek, Slavoj. *The Fragile Absolute—or, Why Is the Christian Legacy Worth Fighting for?* London: Verso, 2000.

Filmography

Afghan Knights, dir. Allan Harmon, 2007.
Alexander Nevsky, dir. Sergei Eisenstein, 1938.
Braveheart, dir. Mel Gibson, 1995.
Butch Cassidy and the Sundance Kid, dir. George Roy Hill, 1969.
Conqueror, The, dir. Dick Powell, 1958.
Crusades, The, dir. Cecil B. DeMille, 1935.
Crusades, documentary, dir. Alan Ereira and David Wallace, 1995.
El Cid, dir. Anthony Mann, 1961.
First Knight, dir. Jerry Zucker, 1995.
King Arthur, dir. Antoine Fuqua, 2004.
Kingdom of Heaven, dir. Ridley Scott, 2005.
Knight's Tale, A, dir. Brian Helgeland, 2001.
Lions for Lambs, dir. Robert Redford, 2008.
Messenger: The Story of Joan of Arc, The, dir. Luc Besson, 1999.
Patriot, The, dir. Roland Emmerich, 2000.
Rambo: First Blood, dir. Ted Kotcheff, 1982.
Syriana, dir. Stephen Gaghan, 2005.
Storm Over Asia: The Heir of Genghis Kahn, dir. V. I. Pudovkin, 1928.
Tears of the Sun, dir. Antoine Fuqua, 2003.
Thirteenth Warrior, dir. John McTiernan, 1999.
Treasure of the Sierra Madre, The, dir. John Huston, 1948.

1. Framing the West, Staging the East

Set Design, Location and Landscape in Movie Medievalism

JOHN M. GANIM

Since David Lean's *Lawrence of Arabia* (1962), we have had a certain set of expectations about what we should see when we look at a typical Western film set in the East: an uncannily stable visual projection of history, a message that the world it portrays is empty, silent and timeless, punctuated by brief images of crowds in the bazaar or armies on the battlefield. This limited visual topography supports the classic description of the West's vision of the natural and built environments of the Middle East is found in Edward Said's *Orientalism* (Said 1978). Said argues that the West regards the Middle East as an empty landscape, ranging from waste lands to underexploited resources, punctuated by crowded and decayed cities, faint echoes of an earlier glory. By and large, this orientalizing perspective is an accurate description of the preconceptions that the viewer brings to films set in the Middle East, even those supposedly taking place during the Middle Ages. What we expect, that is, is a variant on the Hollywood Eastern (a term usually used to describe films set in the Far East), resembling in its generic contours (and some of its specifics) its more famous parallel, the Western. Figures on horseback (or camel) ride alone or in small groups across a vast landscape that the camera only needs to suggest in a partial pan; hostile natives threaten outposts of authority, fragile settlements that seem both timeless and temporary in the face of natural and social upheaval.

The association of the Crusades film with the Western is not frivolous. Central to both genres is the land, which becomes as important as any narrative device or character. The Western film is a filtered account, variously tragic, heroic or ironic, of expansion into the American West and its associated ideology of manifest destiny. At its best the Western film often reveals the underside and forgotten costs, including the human costs of linear history, and it both reflects and is surprisingly frank about, often critically so, its associated racism. Nevertheless, it presents the national ownership of the landscape as either inevitable or natural. Such a perspective is revealed most dramatically in Robert Frost's poem, "The Gift Outright" (Frost 1942), written in 1942, but read at President John F. Kennedy's inauguration when the poet's eyesight left him unable to read the commissioned poem he had written for the occasion: "The land was ours before we were the land's," the poem opens, and it ends with "To the land vaguely realizing westward,/ But still unstoried, artless, unenhanced,/ Such as she was, such as she would become." Frost's poem could easily have been written about a John Ford western film as a about a documentary American history.

The Crusades film, however, is somewhat less assured in its view of the land. The Holy Land was always there, but it was not and is not always or wholly "ours." As a result, no matter how imperial and triumphalist the plot line of the Crusades film, its sets and locations tell a somewhat different story. A preexisting iconography of the landscape of the Levant in fact operated beneath and in conflict with the imperial gaze.

Early photography is the first model for the sets of the medieval Eastern film. Photographic technology was immediately seized upon as a way to record the treasures of Ancient Egypt, as a new technological parallel to the Napoleonic project. This project, the *Description de l'Egypte* (Neret and Gillespie), resulted in a massive inventory of ancient Egyptian architecture and culture. As Said points out in his important discussion of the *Description*, its ideological strategy was to place Revolutionary France in the lineage of the great empires of antiquity, relating to Egypt's past glories rather than its barbaric present. The plates and prints in the *Description* consisted largely of isolated images from tombs and architectural structures. Photography allowed a more contextualized record, and French officials such as François Arago defended the medium as early as 1839 as if it were akin to modern digital technologies, allowing investigators "to copy the millions and millions of hieroglyphics which entirely cover the great monuments at Thebes, Memphis and Carnac" (Arago: 1). Within a short time the Middle East became one of the most frequent subjects of early photographic anthropological travel, and the scenes they record also trace the development of photography from metal to glass plates, and to new chemical developers (Perez). As the technology developed, local people and everyday scenes begin to appear in photographic collections that at first consisted of buildings and objects, with only a few human figures in the foreground or middle ground to suggest scale.

A more dramatic tradition had existed in earlier prints, especially of the Biblical Holy Land, where artists such as Luigi Mayer in the early nineteenth century illustrated the present locations of events from the Old and New Testament. Mayer and others had exaggerated the form and color of geographic and geologic features to create an imaginary stage set for these events. A proto-cinematic experience was available in cycloramas — 360-degree paintings that recreated famous historical events or places — that were popular in international exhibitions. One such existing cyclorama was assembled for the Buffalo Cyclorama Company in 1895; it is now on display in Quebec City. It pictures Jerusalem and its surroundings around the time of the crucifixion. Early photographic images of these same scenes were much less dramatic and often required text accompaniments to emphasize their symbolic importance.

The medieval settings of the Biblical Holy Land and Egypt were not entirely ignored in early prints. Egyptologists, including the influential Edward Lane, were as drawn to the Islamic architecture of Cairo as they were to its ancient monuments. Islamic architecture was considered "medieval" because it corresponded to that historical nomenclature in Northern and Western civilization. Lane, in his *Manners and Customs of the Modern Egyptians* (1837), acknowledged the processes of modernity, but thought of contemporary Egyptian life as not very different from "medieval" Cairo. Lane's illustrations of bazaars and narrow Cairo streets became a model for a highly influential prefiguration of the staged settings of early films about the Middle East set in the Middle Ages, the so-called "Streets of Cairo" exhibition that was created and recreated for World's Fairs from the 1867 International Exhibition onward. The crowded street with its camel rides and other features and the stage-like pavilion in which Arab and other natives acted out their daily tasks, among the most popular attractions in World's Fairs and International Exhibitions through the early twentieth centuries, created expectations about what the Middle East should look like and how it should be displayed (Ganim 2005).

One aspect of such display is how interiors should look. After helping to organize the Great Exhibition of 1851, Henry Cole and Owen Jones were involved with the establishment of the Department of Practical Art (1852) and the South Kensington Museum, one of the forerunners of the Victoria and Albert Museum. They celebrated the artisanal productions of Eastern and Middle Eastern countries, which they judged both beautiful and functional, especially given the two-dimensional nature of Islamic ornament. In his influential *The Grammar of Ornament* (Jones 1856), Jones printed page after page of beautiful textiles (and collected many now available in the Victoria and Albert museum). Thus, rich hangings, carpets and wall coverings became the sign of the Eastern interior, especially in the Middle Ages.

The popularity of Grand Tours in the middle to late nineteenth century, as well as the rise of new photographic technologies, also helped shape the pre-cinematic stage set of the Medieval Eastern film. Stereographic projection offered the new experience of three-dimensional viewing, and since the slides were elaborately packaged (by such firms as the Keystone View Company and Underwood and Underwood) in boxes of stereographic cards with accompanying text on the reverse, they made an effort to be both informative and entertaining. As with conventional photography, if the scenes being captured were insufficiently exotic, the photographers staged the scenes purposely, especially those involving live subjects. Increasingly, however, as both conventional and stereographic views of the Middle East became more widely available, contemporary, everyday human subjects appeared in timeless Pharaohnic and Biblical settings. While often staged to reinforce preexisting stereotypes, the human present jostled uneasily with its natural or ancient scene. As with prints of Holy Land scenes, the point of view is of a Christian observer, mixing the eschatology of Protestant theology with the upper middle class perspective of a traveler. The pilgrim, the missionary, and the tourist become one from the view through the lens. This perspective remains a constant through Western films about the Holy Land, especially, but not only, films about the Crusades.

One of the most striking records the sets of early silent cinema is an Edison production entitled *Christian and Moor* (1911). The film was shot in Cuba. The scene is an interior, though shot in glaring daylight. A blackout screen comprises the rear of the set. Wooden scenery to the left and right of the set are painted to create the illusion of columns and hence a defined interior space. A tapestry or throne defines the rear of the set. In the center a blond Christian, presumably a king, looks towards his right. A Muslim captive or guide sits on the floor, his arms outstretched, also towards the right. On the left side of these two are a group of crusader knights. On the right side of the kings are two Christian ladies with anachronistic conical headgear. On either side of them are figures who may be Moorish ladies, and one, to the immediate left of the king, is gesticulating, presumably entreating the kneeling Muslim to speak or clarify what he sees. The photograph is almost as compelling because of the position and posture of the cameraman and director (and the relatively tiny production crew) as of the actors, for these naturally standing figures are arraying the actors and actresses into what we would consider stilted and artificial poses. The array of the figures is not what we would now consider cinematic.

Part of the reason for this artificial crowding is technological, since the tripod set camera is filming the scene from a fixed position. Such interior groupings are not uncommon in early silent cinema, especially at moments of a plot crisis. But another reason is that early filmmakers, working at an extremely rapid schedule with little reshooting, rely on stereotypical settings to complement the action or narrative. While it is to be expected as a usual cinematic pattern, the loose framing of exterior shots and the tight framing of interior shots result in a characteristic mood of crusades films. The conceptual framework of medieval films set in the Middle East is codified early in the development of the genre, and despite the growth in technological capabilities, the deep structure of this framework remains relatively stable throughout cinematic history. The sets and locations of motion pictures set in the Middle East comprise a remarkably consistent, but varied, visual array. As a result, the cartographic complexity of the region is reduced to a small number of stereotypical images. This is not an unusual pattern in film history, especially in other film genres and genre films, such as the western or the noir mystery. And within any genre it is possible to manipulate this expected setting in unexpected ways. Even when the plot and characterization of medieval Middle Easterns deploy the most appalling stereotypes about the behavior and motivations of the other, the visual background of the films sometimes tells a slightly different, and very occasionally very different, story.

Early films set in an imaginary medieval East show an interest in interiors. Early film pioneers such as Edison and Melies produced films with Middle Eastern themes as they did with other themes that they thought would attract viewers and lend themselves to the technology at their disposal. They inherited or exploited images from vaudeville and pantomime, but also, as we have seen, from World's Fairs. In addition to such virtual recreations as "The Streets of Cairo," international exhibitions also featured ethnographic displays, such as the "Damascus Arabs" at the 1904 St Louis Exhibition, which housed artisans in a tent going about their work. Such anthropological motives, however, gave way to scandalous sideshow activities, such as the belly dancing of a whole series of "Little Egypt" shows. Virtually all of the early film studios produced Arabian Knights or Aladdin-themed films. Melies' "Ali Barbajou et Ali Bouf à l'Huile" (1905) employs a Middle Eastern theme to show off cinema's magical capacity, as well as Melies' own training as a magician. The 1905 re-release of an earlier 1902 version offered hand-tinted colors, adding to the exoticism of the scenery. Some of Melies' early films were shown as intermezzos between magic acts at his own theater.

Indeed, pantomime and vaudeville are a strong influence on early films set in the Middle East, as was the "Little Egypt" belly dancing side show common at World's Fairs from the turn of the century onward. As an executioner flirts with some dancing girls, four men appear. The executioner beheads them, but the heads fly out of their container back onto the bodies of the condemned men, who proceed to cut the executioner himself in two, followed by his equally magical reassembly. The film is especially interesting in its use of stage flats to create a jungle-like setting, reflecting the one-dimensional decoration celebrated in nineteenth-century accounts of Islamic design. To suggest depth characters disappear behind layers and layers of curtains. While as typical of Melies' film as of orientalist visual vocabularies, the film does introduce a stagey excess of designs to indicate the Middle Eastern interior space. Even the outdoor scenes look like indoor scenes. The particular subgenre of oriental fantasies, in themselves outside my scope here, appear in such imaginatively conceived films as the two *Thief of Bagdad* productions (1924, silent and 1940, technicolor), which equate special effects with oriental magic.

Films set in the Middle East begin location shooting fairly early, though, as with later Hollywood films, and most of the films discussed below, North Africa and Spain substitute for the Levant. Though some scenes may be shot in Jerusalem or Crusade locations, the action scenes and most of the interior scenes are usually shot on sets constructed in countries with a larger cinema infrastructure and fewer logistical problems. Some early silent films were shot in Tunisia and Morocco. That is, the cinematic visual image of the Middle Eastern landscape, whether set within, before or after the Middle Ages, is a generalized semi-arid Mediterranean geography. Nevertheless, even in relatively low-production-value films, some sense of vista and open space becomes essential to communicating the idea of a Middle Eastern landscape. This new introduction of geography and vista in the cinema is inseparable from the enormous success of Lowell Thomas's account of the British war in the East against the Ottomans. Commissioned by Woodrow Wilson to report on actions that might distract American audiences from the carnage on the Western Front, Thomas reported on Allenby's success in the east against Germany's Ottoman ally. Upon meeting the charismatic Lawrence, Thomas produced a series of famous newsreels that became the visual basis for David Lean's iconic *Lawrence of Arabia*. But Thomas's often staged or restaged newsreels were dwarfed in impact by his film and lantern show *With Allenby in Palestine* (1919), which was enormously popular around the world and which, in sepia-colored slides and with music and dancing and Thomas's own narration, had as much to do with shaping the Western visual image of the Middle East as early cinema or Lawrence's own newsreels. Thomas's show restaged the modernity of cinema as something more traditional, even medieval, in its pageantry and ritual. As Lawrence's own reputation rose, Thomas changed his title to *With Allenby in Palestine and Lawrence in Arabia*. Clips from Thomas's archive show some sweeping desert combat scenes that will immediately strike the viewer as the model for Lean's *Lawrence of Arabia*. But many other scenes owe much to previous imagery, manipulated to emphasize a secular salvation. A sentry marches on a hilltop below which a postcard perfect view of Jerusalem spreads. Orderly lines of local residents enter and leave the newly liberated regions. Disciplined and triumphant Arab legion troops march in review. These scenes conflate a military utopia very different from the trenches of Northwest Europe with sacred geography.

As we have seen, the sources of film sets that predetermine the visual vocabulary of these films are surprisingly various, though these rich visual resources are called upon selectively. The visual representation of the Middle East in medieval cinema as expressed in set designs and location, from early silent cinema through the early twenty-first century, is influenced by late nineteenth-century and early twentieth-century forms: panoramas of Jerusalem and the Holy Lands in European buildings; colonial exhibitions in World's Fairs; melodrama and other popular theatrical entertainments; the collections of textiles designs at the Victoria and Albert Museum. These influences diverge in the early days of cinema with two film types: the fantastic Middle East of various silent films concerned with the Arabian Nights and other similar motifs on the one hand, and the documentary newsreels of Lowell Thomas tracing the operations of T. E. Lawrence on the other. In the former, even exteriors are portrayed as if interiors, and in the latter, the Western subject defines the desert landscape. The perspective of the European West extends beyond the frame of the image, but the perspective of the Middle East is limited as if a stage set by the borders of the frame.

This dialectic can be found operating in different permutations in films, especially Crusade costume dramas, through the 1940s. By the end of World War II, however, new film technologies change the terms of this dialectic. Aerial and reconnaissance photography and film, and both classified and unclassified films of the Battle for North Africa, introduce a dimension of time into the representation of desert space, no longer rendering it as mythically timeless. Entertainment technologies and new camera types in the early 1950s also change the visual relation between subject and landscape. This changing semiotics is most striking in *Lawrence of Arabia*, which captures the Western imagination as the default landscape of the Middle East no matter what period the film is set in, but it is also possible to trace in medieval-themed films from *El Cid* (1961) to *Kingdom of Heaven* (2005). Even when scripts and acting styles reassert Orientalist polarities, the *mise en scene* obscures and reverses these polarities. Such ironization of the Middle Eastern set is, however, relatively rare, and counter-discourses are usually expressed in the working out of plot, character and dialogue. Moreover, Hollywood and industrial scale cinema are not the only producers of the medieval Eastern. The film industries of the Eastern Mediterranean and North Africa have produced notable examples, though they are more sporadic. Typically these films are more careful to include local landmarks, including geographic features other than sand dunes, and also to include aspects of the built environment such as vernacular housing types.

In fact Crusades films are often surprisingly sympathetic in intention, if not in actual practice, to the Islamic defenders, even when, as in Cecil B. DeMille's *The Crusades* (1935), the plot and dialogue verge on parody. The Crusades not only take medieval Europeans to the Middle East, but they also bring Saracens and Crusaders back to Europe. Sir Walter Scott's novels, popular in Hollywood, offered one avenue of this cultural loop, and *Ivanhoe* remains an interesting example of cultural hierarchy, stacking Christian, Jew and Muslim infidel in that order, even while explaining everyone's stake. *The Talisman* even more interestingly codifies the idealization of Saladin for Romanticism. In other films the returned Crusader or alien observer provides a cultural critique of the West. In *The 13th Warrior* (1999) the cultured and rational representative of the East is able to see through the superstition of the barbarian tribes. In *The Seventh Seal* (1957) the crusading knight finds his real nemesis at home and discovers that his homeland has as much need of rescue as the Holy Land.

Another conceptual frame that photography provided, besides vast distance, is the mobility of concepts such as the "East" or the "Medieval." A predominantly Christian and usually Protestant perspective focused on the visual reconstruction of a Jerusalem and a Holy Land as it "really was" in Biblical times. Moreover, the mapping of the Christian world and its Judaic antecedent was always around and opposite to the Muslim world. The Middle East of photographic geography in the nineteenth century spanned from North Africa to Northern India. Its historical dimension could be Al-Andalus, or it could be anachronistic events and episodes in the present day that demonstrate how "medieval" the East remained. These historical and geographic vectors inform early films about the place and the period, not only in the early days of cinema, but even in the Hollywood and Cinecittá potboilers of the 1950s and 1960s.

Because of this mobility and this overlay of the temporal and the spatial, a number of films that might not be categorized as medieval Easterns by most standards, such as *El Cid*, *Lawrence of Arabia* or even *The Sheik* or *The Arab* (1924), are important for setting expectations. Yet, in a sense, though they satisfy the conditions of a postcolonial analysis, they distract us from the spatial imagery of Hollywood films set in the Holy Land. Most Crusades films are genetically related to Biblical epics more than to Westerns, for the reasons I have outlined above. A classic Hollywood Eastern, *The Conqueror* (1956), starring John Wayne as a young Genghis Khan, demonstrates the difference. One of the most controversial films set in the East during the Middle Ages, *The Conqueror* is notorious for something other than its miscasting and geographic substitutions. *The Conqueror* was produced by Howard Hughes and starred John Wayne as the Mongol Temujin, who will become known as

The western landscape of Medieval Easterns in *The Conqueror* (dir. Dick Powell, 1956).

Genghis Khan as he amasses his victories. In an attempt to communicate the exotic otherness of Central Asia, the filmakers shot the initial scenes near St. George, Utah, with its dramatic canyons, quite different than the starker landscape of the Gobi desert where it is supposedly set. The substantial publicity surrounding the film is full of authenticating details. It was based on the *Secret History of the Mongols*, though typical Hollywood liberties are taken with the facts. The film is notable for its reliance on makeup to render the largely Anglo cast somehow Oriental, though interestingly many of the extras were local American Indians. It is entirely possible that the Western China scenes in *Crouching Tiger, Hidden Dragon* (2000) were deliberate allusions to *The Conqueror*, especially the opening scenes when Temujin (Wayne) raids a caravan and meets his future beloved, Bortai, the Tartar noblewoman.

The Utah setting was presumably chosen to suggest the idea of what a Central Asian landscape consisted of, rather than a Central Asian landscape itself. The Mongols are filmed riding down the steeply raked hillsides, allowing dramatic camera angles and a sense of their invincible force. The battles often meld into one another, as if there were no setbacks in the progress of the hordes. Yet the geographic inaccuracy is not the reason the setting was so controversial. In the early 1950s Yucca Flats, not far from the area where the film was shot, was used for above-ground nuclear testing. The area around St. George had detectable amounts of dangerous radiation. The producer, Howard Hughes, even had dirt from the site transported back to Los Angeles to ensure authenticity in the studio shooting. The possibility has been hotly debated that the high death rate from cancer of so many of the cast and crew, including Wayne himself, was related to radiation exposure. For our purposes, however, the crucial aspects of the location were its immediate visual associations with Westerns, not least of all because of Wayne's casting, and the cowboy swagger he brought to the role. Even without Occidental characters, *The Conqueror* regards the world from an imperial vista, indulging in vast landscape pans.

In contrast with the wide expanses of the imperial film such as *The Conqueror*, Crusades films, from *Christian and Moor* to de Mille's *The Crusades* through *Kingdom of Heaven*, carry on an interior typology, even when it is no longer necessary for technical reasons. The history of the visual imagery of the Holy Land helps explain why a film such as Ridley Scott's *Kingdom of Heaven* should devote nearly half its scenes to interiors or enclosed street or framed street scenes. *Kingdom of Heaven* seeks in many ways to avoid or counter the stereotypes surrounding traditional Crusades films. Nevertheless, fresh and original moves, many of them related to setting, coexist with recent heroic film conventions. While seeking to be faithful to the military tactics of both Crusaders and Islamic armies, the new film technology results in a battlefield that feels like *Troy* (2004) or like Scott's own *Gladiator* (2000). No matter the shooting location, Scott's editing results in a faithfulness to the place of the action (as opposed to the location of the filming) down to a scrupulousness about geography and historical architecture that harks back to nineteenth century photography. Of course those nineteenth-century prints and early photographs of biblical landscapes combined an imperial Crusade with their ostenible pilgrimage dimension. Scott is careful to locate his battle scenes and his siege scenes against a recognizable landmark. This is not, his film says visually, an empty landscape to be conquered and cultivated, but an existing, living culture that is being invaded. Ironies attend such a visual lesson, however, among them the wave after wave of invasion that swept through the Holy Land from the Islamic conquest through the Turkish expansion. Scott's film also offers a neat contrast of medieval Western Europe and a resplendent Jerusalem and Acre that teaches a lesson in economic and architectural history as well as makes a thematic point. What is notable, however, is how many of his shots are interiors, and, when not interiors, courtyards or piazzas. Again such a visual emphasis communicates Scott's vision: the seriousness of subjective and interiorized faith being contextualized in terms of larger social forces.

The long shot of Jerusalem will become a visual trope in Crusades movies. De Mille's *The Crusades* opens with a postcard-like view as the titles end. Chahine's *Saladin* (1963) ends with a similar shot, perhaps answering de Mille, and attempting to communicate in image and sound (a call to prayers and a Christmas hymn) what history and film genre have disallowed. The interior scenes in *Kingdom of Heaven*, reflecting the inner turmoil and state of Balian himself (the film has about it the quality of a dream framed

The siege of Jerusalem by Saladin's forces in Ridley Scott's *The Kingdom of Heaven*.

by the beginning and ending scenes of Balian working his trade as a blacksmith), allow the drama of the battle scenes to achieve part of their effect by contrast. As Saladin's forces attack Krak, Balian engages in a holding action to allow civilians to take shelter in the citadel. Aerial shots show Balian's detachment riding into Saladin's cavalry. Then Baldwin's armies arrive, and a huge battle seems to loom, but is forestalled by negotiation. The tension is rebuilt towards the end of the film at the battle for Jerusalem, though there nothing is held back, and Scott engages in his trademark presentation of a wasteful but existential violence almost reluctantly unleashed by Balian and Saladin.

Here again the complex message of the set and wide shots is somewhat muddied by reliance on a fairly simple-minded film convention: closeups of "good" characters alternating with closeups of "evil" characters. It is an attempt at Shakespearian character drama that was one of the weaker (but essential) techniques in the Crusade films that *Kingdom of Heaven* pays homage to: Chahine's *Saladin* and Eisenstein's *Alexander Nevsky* (1938) (which like *Saladin* is as much anti–Crusade film as Crusade film). If, as I have argued elsewhere (Ganim 2007), Chahine's *Saladin* attempts to use the cinematic language of Hollywood historical films to write a counterhistory that is also a more universal history, Scott's film, for all of its intelligence, sometimes reinscribes the sources that Chahine, with only partial success, was seeking to subordinate.

Without the context of the many interior scenes, the spectacular defense of Jerusalem at the end of the film would not differ substantially from, say, similar siege scenes in *The Lord of the Rings: The Two Towers* (2002) or battle scenes from *Star Wars, Episode V: The Empire Strikes Back*, the latter of which innovated the digital techniques on which Scott's battle scenes depend. With previous allusions to *Alexander Nevsky* in the battle sequence of Reynaud's defeat, the allusions now run closer to that of *Ran*, with its tragic and ironic rather than heroic conception of warfare. The furious attack on the walls of Jerusalem by Saladin's artillery and siege engines is portrayed as an attack on sacred stones, since we imagine the many interior rooms and courtyards of the city now under threat. Shot from above, the breaching of the walls by the infantry, their round helmets moving like corpuscles, makes the city akin to the bodies that we have viewed strewn about. The ritual of truce between Saladin and Balian outside the gates of the city reasserts an almost unreal order as the city is apparently peacefully occupied by Saladin's troops, despite the harangue of the mullah who signifies instransigence in the Muslim ranks as Guy and the Templars did in the Christian ranks. Unlike *El Cid*, where the city is defended but the hero is lost (the body of Charlton Heston is tied to his horse to appear undefeated), heroism here is defined as an interior and spiritual triumph. By offering terms to Balian in the tent outside the city walls, Saladin is acknowledging a certain victory on Balian's part, which is to say the acceptance of Balian's actual belief in the vows of knighthood. Interestingly it is Saladin who acts like the true European knight, teaching the Crusaders how they really should behave. Saladin walks through the city thoughtfully at the end, and he straightens a falling cross, an unwriting of the opening of de Mille's *The Crusades*, with its burning icons, toppled crosses, and auction of Christian slaves girls. At the end of the film, the fairy tale opening — a common blacksmith learning that he is of illegitimate noble blood — is restated. Balian is surveying what is left of his previous life. Richard I comes looking for him as "defender of Jerusalem," but Balian identifies himself only as a blacksmith. But his dual-class status, necessary to his heroism, is now doubled in a positive way. He rides away from the humble buildings on a pair of noble horses with his princess, presumably to her ancestral lands.

In his earlier films, such as *Thelma and Louise,* Scott displayed his mastery of wide landscapes and also demonstrated his innovation in filming interiors freighted with meaning, such as in *Alien* or *Blade Runner*. In *Kingdom of Heaven* digital technology allows virtual techniques to substitute for the huge number of extras and props in de Mille's *The Crusades* or Mann's *El Cid*. Yet the obvious traces of digital imagery, such as the slight pixallation in scenes of rapid movement and the metallic color palate result in the film foregrounding its technological origin, even announcing it, in contrast to the almost obsessive accounting of physical reality in the great Cinemascope epics of the 1950s and 1960s. Tellingly, however, Scott's interiors in *Kingdom of Heaven* surpass the one-dimensional interior sets of earlier Crusades films (or even Eastern-themed silent films), with their emphasis on screens and tapestries and play of light and shadow. In interior shots Scott is able to give rooms and buildings and furniture an aura either sinister or sanctified, as befitting the tone of a scene, and he often evokes both moods at once, a skill honed on the Gothic sets of *Alien* (1979) and *Blade Runner* (1982). Were the Crusades predominantly about material ambition or spiritual quest? A largely idealistic interpretation dominated nineteenth-century scholarship, and a largely materialist interpretation dominated twentieth-century scholarship. Early twenty-first-century scholarship has moved towards a hybrid interpretation, which Scott's camera communicates in subtle ways, even against the sometimes blatant moves of the plot.

Youssef Chahine's *Saladin* (Egypt, 1963) served as an homage to Nasser's nationalist and pan-Arab politics (Aberth), but it now is viewed as one of the few presentations of the medieval East and the Crusades through non–Western eyes. I have argued elsewhere that the *Saladin* is constructed as a cinematic response to previous Hollywood films about the Crusades, including DeMille's *The Crusades*, often quoting and correcting them and that this quotation accounts for its superficially conventional appearance, surprising from the Middle East's most well-known *auteur* director (Ganim 2007). In fact, one of the two most experimental scenes in the film is the concluding shot, a scene of Jerusalem under a light snowfall with something like a Christmas carol as soundtrack. The shot recalls the importance of the image of the city in nineteenth-century photography, though it has a disjointed relation to the rest of the film.

Saladin alternates between exterior location shots, often chosen to reflect the actual historical terrain, and interior shots that seek to demystify the mysterious interiors of conventional Hollywood Middle Easterns. This patterning allows *Saladin* to be viewed almost as a silent film, akin to Eisenstein's *Alexander Nevsky*, on which several anti–Crusade films are modeled, including Aleksander Ford's *Krzyzacy* (1960). The opening scenes of *Saladin* show Crusaders attacking Arabs on pilgrimage, and these exterior scenes give way to the interior of the court of Saladin, where he is implored to defend the populace and to take Jerusalem back, associating Jerusalem with a built environment. The next sequence shows a long line of exiles, obviously alluding to the dislocation of Palestinian refugees. An Arab village falls silent, and a breeze crosses a pool of water. As the camera moves into the distance, Saladin's armies appear on the horizon. Saladin's face takes up the entire scene as the titles roll. The action again shifts to the interior, where Saladin gathers his officers to decide on a response. In contrast the hot-headed crusader Reynaud, against the advice of other Christian allies, is shown deviously planning an attack on Muslim pilgrimage caravans. This attack is shown in surrealistic style, including a spinning disk splattered with red to indicate the slaughter of the innocent civilians. Wisely rejecting a frontal attack on a hill, Saladin cuts off the Christian forces from their water supply, emphasizing again the imagistic use of water in the film. As if rewriting *The Song of Roland*, Chahine has the hotheaded Reynaud lead the Christian forces into the valley, where they face hidden spikes and flaming arrows, resulting in a rout. Emphasis is placed, both visually and dramatically, on Saladin's intimate knowledge of the landscape and his ability to deploy this knowledge against the crusaders. When Richard arrives in the Holy Land, the film continues this alternation of interior court and exterior battle scene, cutting back and forth to suggest the see-saw fortunes of the two armies, as well as the various intrigues and betrayals on both sides. Striking court scenes take place on the same set. Richard absolves the nurse Louise at the last moment after she has aided the escape of her beloved, a Christian Arab who is an ally of Saladin. Saladin, however, condemns a traitor to his side. The scenes are changed only by lighting. The alternation emphasizes one of the interesting themes of *Saladin*, which is the identification of Saladin and King Richard as doubles. While Hollywood Crusade films come close to making this connection, Chahine renders it explicit. At the end, as we have seen, the film concludes with pageantry that seems to take the events out of history. Refraining from attacking the Christian armies on Christmas Eve, Saladin invites Richard into Jerusalem: Chahine reshoots, almost, DeMille's opening scenes in *The Crusades*, which show Saladin and his comically evil cohorts entering the city. The inhabitants of Jerusalem wave olive branches at the departing Crusaders, and snow falls over the city accompanied by choir music, played simultaneously with the Muslim call to prayer. Chahine's critical manipulation of the visual language of the Crusade film represents heroism as a willingness to negotiate and victory as partial, contingent, and qualified. While critical of Western triumphalism, this visual message may have been understood by Nasser, who made continued employment in Egypt difficult for Chahine, though the nationalization of the film industry may have limited his preferred options in any case. However that may be, *Saladin*'s originality lay partly in its exposure of the anxiety underlying the typical Crusade film. The Holy Land escapes ownership by one side or the other, and the film shames any such attempt by exposing a common history.

What are the larger implications of this evidence? Our preconceptions of what motion pictures set in the medieval East should look like derive from the controlling images of the colonial film: *Lawrence of Arabia*, with its breathtaking vistas of empty deserts, or the many Foreign Legion films, with French soldiers and other expatriates peering from their fortications at an emptiness that might at any moment erupt. In actuality, however, a surprising preponderance of shots in medieval Easterns are interiors or architectural settings. As we have seen, this emphasis on the built or human environment as opposed to the pristine desert landscape has a number of sources, one of them the constraints of early cinematic technology and another of them the enormous freight of the memorial geography of the Holy Land. Both of these settings invoke polarities now familiar to us. The empty land awaits the Western subject to achieve its destiny. The crowded, sensuous and chaotic interior, often a harem or bazaar, with its riot of excess contrasts with the purifying sky of the desert that waits outside its screens and windows. Considered in this way, as movie still or movie poster, the alternation of symbolic exterior and interior conjoin to inscribe a colonialist message across the many films portraying the East in its (always) medieval phase.

At the same time this semiotic opposition between an interior setting of excess and an exterior setting of emptiness is not always as clear-cut as we might expect. The traditional freight of the image of Jerusalem and its environs invests each building and object with a historical, usually biblical, significance. The landscape of Crusades films, like that of biblical epic films, is a landscape of collective memory. Moreover, above and beyond the stereotypes of the other, such as the cruel and cunning local ruler (Turk or Arab) often portrayed in these films, is also an embodiment of the arbitrariness of patriarchal power, even in their exercise of sexual indulgence, so they are not simple, natural, or childlike as natives often are in colonial films. Saladin, purified of excess sensuality, as he was in contemporary accounts from many different perspectives (not, though, in de Mille's *The Crusades*), complicates the division of Christians and Infidels, allies and enemies. Both historically and thematically the message of the Crusade film is not total conquest or defeat, but negotiation, ambiguity, uncertainty. In Crusades films a dimension of time is introduced into space, which is, after all, how motion pictures first began.

Bibliography

Aberth, John. *A Knight at the Movies: Medieval History on Film.* New York: Routledge, 2003.

Arago, Francois. *Le daguerreotype: rapport fait a l'acadamie des Sciences de Paris le 19 aout 1839.* Paris: L'Achoppe, 1987.

Frost, Robert. *A Witness Tree.* New York: H. Holt, 1942.

Ganim, John. *Medievalism and Orientalism: Three Essays on Literature, Architecture and Cultural Identity.* New York: Palgrave, 2005.

_____. "Reversing the Crusades: Hegemony, Orientalism and Film Language in Youssef Chahine's *Saladin*," *Filming the Other Middle Ages: Race, Class, and Gender in Medievalist Cinema.* Eds. Tison Pugh and Lynne Ramey. New York: Palgrave, 2007. 45–58.

Gillispie, Charles Coulston. *Monuments of Egypt the Napoleonic Edition : The Complete Archaeological Plates from la Description de l'Egypte*. Princeton, NJ: Princeton Architectural Press in association with the Architectural League of New York and the J. Paul Getty Trust, 1987.
Jones, Owen. *The Grammar of Ornament*. London: Day and Sons, 1856.
Lane, Edward William. *An Account of the Manners and Customs of the Modern Egyptians*. London: C. Knight and Co., 1837.
Lindley, Arthur. "Once, Present, and Future Kings: *Kingdom of Heaven* and the Multitemporality of Medieval Film." *Filming the Other Middle Ages: Race, Class, and Gender in Medievalist Cinema*. Eds. Tison Pugh and Lynne Ramey. New York: Palgrave, 2007. 15–30.
Néret, Gilles. *Description de l'Egypte*. Köln: Benedikt Taschen, 1994.
Perez, Nissan N. *Focus East: Early Photography in the Near East (1839–1885)*. New York: Abrams, 1988.
Said, Edward W. *Orientalism*. New York: Pantheon Books, 1978.

Filmography

Alexander Nevsky, dir. Sergei M. Eisenstein. 1938.
Alien, dir. Ridley Scott.
Ali Barbajou et Ali Bouf à l'Huile, dir. Georges Melies. 1905.
The Arab, dir. Rex Ingram. 1924.
Blade Runner, dir. Ridley Scott. 1982.
Christian and Moor. 1911.
The Conqueror, dir. Dick Powell. 1956.
Crouching Tiger, Hidden Dragon, dir. Ang Lee. 2000.
The Crusades, dir. Cecil B. de Mille. 1935.
El Cid, dir. Anthony Mann. 1961.
Gladiator, dir. Ridley Scott. 2000.
Kingdom of Heaven, dir. Ridley Scott. 2005.
Krzyzacy, dir. Aleksander Ford. 1960.
Lawrence of Arabia, dir. David Lean. 1962.
The Lord of the Rings: The Two Towers, dir. Peter Jackson. 2002.
Ran, dir. Akira Kurosawa. 1985.
Saladin, dir. Youssef Chahine. 1963.
The Seventh Seal, dir. Ingmar Bergman. 1957.
The Sheik, dir. George Melford. 1921.
Star Wars, Episode V: The Empire Strikes Back, dir. Irvin Kershner. 1980.
Thelma and Louise, dir. Ridley Scott. 1991.
The Thief of Baghdad, dir. Raoul Walsh. 1924.
The Thief of Baghdad, dir. Ludwig Berger. 1940.
The 13th Warrior, dir. John McTiernan. 1999.
Troy, dir. Wolfgang Peterson. 2004.
With Allenby in Palestine and Lawrence in Arabia, dir. Lowell Thomas. 1919.

2. Homeland Security

Northern Crusades through the East-European Eyes of *Alexander Nevsky* and the Nevsky Tradition

NICKOLAS HAYDOCK

> *On borders, war is declared on borders.*
> Mahmoud Darwish, Memory for Forgetfulness

This essay explores historical analogy in Sergei Eisenstein's *Alexander Nevsky* (1938), Aleksander Ford's *Krzyzacy/ The Order of the Teutonic Knights* (1960), and Frantisek Vlacil's *The Valley of the Bees* (1968) as a function of film style, in particular the film frame itself as the stage for border transgressions and containments. Then I trace the ways in which Eisenstein's auteur medievalism has been domesticated as an essential part of popular American cinema's globalizing capitalization of Manichean nationalism. This development is readily apparent in the contemporary redeployment of Eisenstein's paradigmatic binaries to the battlefields of Dark Age Britain, pre–Columbian North America, and Tolkien's Middle Earth.

What is commonly called "art house cinema" in the United States seldom enters the discussion when medievalists excoriate popular films about the Middle Ages, and for good reason. The faults commonly found with the popcorn past in popular reviews as well as in much contemporary scholarship are if anything more integral to those works commonly included on lists of the finest films ever made. One would search in vain for a superior historical veracity in, for instance, Carl Theodore Dreyer's *The Passion of Joan of Arc* (1928), Eisenstein's *Alexander Nevsky* (1938), Roberto Rossellini's *The Flowers of St. Francis* (1950), Kenji Mizoguchi's *Sansho the Bailiff* (1954), Ingmar Bergman's *Seventh Seal* (1957), Aleksander Ford's *Krzyzacy* (1960), Frantisek Vlacil's *Valley of the Bees* (1968), Andrei Tarkovsky's *Andrei Rublev* (1969), Akira Kurosawa's *Kagemusha* (1980), Bertrand Tavernier's *The Passion of Beatrice* (1987) or Youseff Chahine's *Destiny* (1997). Common to the films in this admittedly partial list is a willingness to shape the past according to specific analogues or continuities and to mark such affinities with the stylistic signature of the auteur. Contrary to what is widely supposed, mainstream movie medievalism's failures typically stem not from its infidelity to history, literature, or legend, but rather from the lack of any thorough-going commitment by directors, screenwriters, and cinematographers to provocative anachronism and compelling idiosyncrasy.

In the long tradition of films that allude profoundly and persistently to *Alexander Nevsky*, one can trace a distinct pattern of dispersal and diffusion. For the Polish director Aleksander Ford (*Krzyzacy*) historical analogies between the medieval and modern *Drang nach Osten* (Drive to the East) remain a crucial part of living memory and contemporary experience, integral to the historical consciousness of the film's intended audience. While the Czech director Frantisek Vlacil (*Valley of the Bees*) remains an avid student of Eisenstein's compositional style in the service of historical allegory, his satire is if anything more deeply critical because his Teutonic Knights are not simply stick figures: they possess a complex interiority. Latent homosexuality and misogyny are not for Vlacil, as they are in Eisenstein and Ford, broadly comic reinforcements of gender boundaries, but rather elements in a profoundly fractured and ultimately tragic psyche. In more recent Western films such as the *Star Wars* and *Lord of the Rings* franchises, *King Arthur* (dir. Antoine Fuqua 2004), or *Pathfinder* (dir. Marcus Nispel 2007), historical analogy is colonized according to the new world order of an empire among whose chief exports are Hollywood spectacle and "freedom." Historical parallels are deracinated and disseminated across a fantasy space, as after the fall of the Berlin Wall, markets repackaged world war Manichaeism across a globalizing economy. Auteurism and imagined historical continuities are sublated by a commodity fetishism that — as Marx taught — tends to obscure actual conditions of origin and manufacture.

Alexander Nevsky

Was the Eisenstein of *Alexander Nevsky*, as Stalin reportedly exclaimed after seeing the film, "really a good Bolshevik after all"? Certainly the wedding of personal style and official ideology in this film — such an elusive union through the decade that separates *October* (1928) from *Nevsky* (1938) — would seem to suggest that Eisenstein had earned his way back into the good graces of the Soviet cultural bureaucracy (as well as to the Order of Lenin and the Stalin Prize) at some cost. Still the place of *Nevsky* within Eisenstein's career is more central than the all-too-common reading of the film as a concession to political exigencies suggests. If we look for the moment just at the seven major, finished films—*Strike* (1925), *Battleship Potemkin* (1925), *October* (1928), *The General Line* (1929), *Nevsky* (1938) and *Ivan the Terrible*, parts I (1944) and II (1958)—a considerably more revealing pattern emerges than the conventional division between "silent" and "talking" films. One quickly perceives a tripartite division of ideologically inflected historical cinema focused initially on the immediate past and present, followed by the medieval *Alexander Nevsky* set in the thirteenth century, and concluding with the early modern *Ivan the Terrible*. Modern, Medieval, Early Modern: the structure of this *gran recit* is epic and cyclical, turning on the crucial synthesis in *Nevsky* of a collectivity united behind strong, charismatic leadership. Yet the structure of Eisenstein's *oeuvre* is also that of a vicious circle writ large, a revolutionary cinema that refuses to stop evolving. After the triumph of *Potemkin* we see a descent into the formalism and ideological errantry that plagued Eisenstein's middle period, including the largely fruitless years in the United States and Mexico. The cycle begins again with the critical and popular success of *Nevsky* and *Ivan the Terrible, Part I* only to turn once more—in the evaluations of the cultural watchdogs—toward excess, "psychologism" and ideological error in *Ivan, Part II*'s satiric portrait of totalitarian masquerade (finished 1945, but not released until 1958). Read as a chronological narrative, the *gran recit* is a doctrinaire brief on Marxist history, from the confederation of feudal city-states in the premodern *Nevsky*, through the birth of the bourgeois state in the *Ivan* films, down to the dialectical exposure of class struggle leading to the "ten days that shook the world" (October 15–25, 1917). However, when we read the films according to the date of their release, what emerges instead is a tragic counter-narrative that begins with the birth of class consciousness and social revolution (e.g., *Strike*), giving way to the idealized union of collective action with strong, charismatic leadership in *Nevsky*, which in turn degenerates into the rampant state of paranoia of the *Ivan* films. Indeed the persistent contemporary analogies evoked by the later films set in the 13th and 16th centuries encourage just such a reading: in Eisenstein's *oeuvre* the macrocosm of Russian history from the Middle Ages through the present is repeated in the microcosm of the decades after the revolution, as Marxist dialectics gives way to Lenin's "revolution from above" and finally to the Stalin cult's reigning state of terror. Reading the seven completed films in that way allows us to see the surviving *oeuvre* as a grand tragedy of communism, the tragedy not of a particular hero but of the Soviet revolution itself.[1]

This notion of history as recurrence marks a crucial break with the revolutionary and utopian politics of Eisenstein's early films. The change in historiography is apparent when one compares the early silent to the later sound films, but it is seemingly born full-grown in Eisenstein's abortive project *Que Viva Mexico!* (1979). His description of the scenario (1931) delineates a series of shots that were actually filmed and transitions from the appearance of alterity to the discovery of an underlying unity and circularity:

> Death. Skulls of people. And skulls of stone. The horrible Aztec gods and the horrifying Yucatan deities. Huge ruins. Pyramids. A world that was but is no more. Endless rows of stones and columns. And faces. Faces of stone. And faces of flesh. The man of the Yucatan today. The same man who lived thousands of years ago. Unmovable. Unchanging. Eternal. And the great wisdom of Mexico about death. The unity of life and death. The passing of one and the birth of the next one. The eternal circle.... Living in the twentieth century but medieval in ways and habits.... Statues of saints that were erected on the sites of pagan altars. Bleeding and distorted like the human sacrifices that were made on top of these pyramids. Here, like imported and anemic flowers, bloom the iron and fire of the Catholicism that Cortes brought. Catholicism and paganism. The Virgin of Guadalupe worshiped by wild dances and bloody bullfights.[2]

Like many tourists Eisenstein's baggage arrives at the border crammed full of preconceptions, most evident perhaps in his introduction of the infamous *ius prima noctis*, which the film imagines as the cause of a popular uprising in a contemporary Mexico still "medieval in ways and habits."[3] Yet what is most striking about this formulation is that many years before *Nevsky*, when Eisenstein was perhaps at the furthest remove he ever achieved from Soviet control and censorship, he was already conceiving of human subjectivity, culture, and history in fundamentally archeological rather than exclusively revolutionary terms. While class consciousness and dialectical materialism are still essential features of Eisenstein's vision of Mexico, the dominant concern in his scenario as well as in the frames of film that survive is the composition of a transparent historical palimpsest.

Certainly colonial tourism and a benighted search for the primitive shadow Eisenstein's Mexican adventure, but there is also a real continuity between his vision of Mexico and the new philosophy of history that emerges upon the return to mother Russia. Indeed, I would argue that the Mexican adventure becomes the paradigm through which Eisenstein approaches nationalist history in the later films. With his subsequent failure to obtain a release for *Bezhin Meadow* (a film about cooperative agriculture), Eisenstein turns in *Alexander Nevsky* toward the collectivization of history itself in a decidedly un–Marxist inflection of nationality as an atemporal or synchronous reality that underlies even the most radical historical developments. As he assured prospective audiences:

> The theme of patriotism and national defense against the aggressor is the subject that suffuses our film.... When you read the chronicles of the thirteenth century alternately with current newspapers, you lose your sense of

the difference in time, because the bloody terror which the conquering Orders of Knighthood in the thirteenth century sowed is scarcely distinguishable from what is now being perpetrated in Europe [qtd. in Taylor 86].

Eisenstein's Teutonic Knights were "the ancestors of today's fascists" and his film "appears to be a contemporary picture" (*ibid*). He prepared to compose the scenario for *Nevsky* by reading medieval chronicles and Hitler's *Mein Kampf*. An early draft of the screenplay (1937) begins by quoting Hitler's plan that the German (re)conquest of Eastern Europe "travel by the same road, along which once went the knights of our orders" (qtd. in Nesbet 181). This expresses quite a pure nationalist historiography that, as we shall see, trenchantly enlists film in the war of medievalizing propaganda that pits Russia's thirteenth-century halt to the *Drang nach Osten* against Himmler's occult idealization of the elite SS as the perfected reincarnation of the *Ordensritter*. As has been recently demonstrated yet again, one of war propaganda's most crucial battles is for the possession of the past.[4]

Yet, to return briefly to the question of historiography in *Que Viva Mexico!* and *Nevsky*, the most obvious link between the two films is Eisenstein's fascination with the *danse macabre*.[5] His scenario emphasizes the salutary intimacy of Mexicans with death; their ability to laugh at — even "eat (confections of) death"— demonstrates, as his fellow Russian Bakhtin would argue, the potential of the carnival to suspend time and to expose the arbitrary, fleeting nature of worldly power. In *Nevsky*'s opening emblematic shots pose the shock of death (specifically the "death's head") as a horror that must be overcome. The scene comprises what Eisenstein had called in his teaching "a montage unit," here composed of four frames, followed by a transitional shot. These emblematic shots pause at some length (32 seconds) over the "debris" left by the Mongol invasion, collapsing time and identities much as medieval death imagery was designed to do. The first two shots survey the remains of the carnage from an objective distance, while the latter two tighten the focus to particular skeletal remains. The third shot in the sequence participates in the medieval tradition of macabre, specular humor: a close shot of bleached skulls shows one sporting the distinctive pointed helmet of the Rus and the other with shield still stubbornly couched under chin. That the dead are Russian and their killers Mongols was established in the prose of the title sequence, but of course the point of *memento mori* imagery is the ubiquity of its reference: "as I am so shall you be." Prokofiev's score plays over this bonefield, the theme that will be associated with the Germans throughout the film — a paradigmatic instance of the celebrated "vertical montage." Here the theme functions to generalize the *memento mori* imagery, providing the sound track to the silent screams of slack-jawed skulls.

The anamorphic border in Eisenstein's *Alexander Nevsky*.

The final shot employs the axial cut integral to Eisenstein's later theory of montage and which plays so extensive a role in *Nevsky*. On a hill the skeleton of a horse is picked over by crows, while the two human skulls have been relegated to the bottom right of the frame. These blurred, distorted skulls are in homage to the famous anamorphic stain in Holbein's *The Ambassadors*. Yet the perceptual process has been reversed: the skulls appear initially front and center without anamorphic distortion (in shot 3) and then are relegated to the blurry, peripheral foreground of the frame (shot 4), with the perspectival distortion produced by the axial cut in. As I will argue in more depth below, the extremes of the film frame create an especially charged border region in the politics and poetics of this film, imaging by turns entrapment and transcendence. Here, though, let us pause over the difference this anamorphic stain makes in the last shot of the opening montage unit.

Applying Lacan's comparison of the stain in Holbein's portrait to the function of *objet petit a*, Slajov Zizek reads the "Hitchcockian blot" as the "gaze of the other." He identifies what "sticks out" in the image as a "phallic element," which "opens up the abyss of the search for meaning." This phallic spot is the means whereby the picture is "subjectivized:" it represents "the point from which the picture itself looks back at us" (93). Eisenstein's anamorphic image also opens the field to further meanings and connotations, subjectivizing the distant past so that contemporary audiences are forced to confront its "relevance." The "gaze of the other" looks out from the historical frame at a Soviet audience for whom the skulls had a specific relevance: the SS, the "Order of the Death's Head," which Himmler claimed to be the reincarnation of the Order of the Teutonic Knights. The SS insignia, worn on their uniforms and rings, was the *Totenkopf* ("death's head").[6] The gaze of the other linked to death and insinuating itself as a subjectivized medieval mirror, interrupting the sightlines between the viewer and his or her object, is reiterated again and again in the film. Later Eisenstein quotes his own shot in a telling self-reference to *Que Viva Mexico!* in which skulls line the bottom of the frame, replaced in *Nevsky* with a line of the infamous (and inhuman) tank-like helmets of Knights: the new face of death. In both shots death heads limn a boundary between the viewer and the Catholic monks who are the putative object of the audience's gaze — a spatially significant representation of the menace *beneath* the civilizing mission of the Roman Catholic Church both in the Northern Crusades and in Mexico "to kill or convert" pagan peoples. These two-tiered shots analyze the Church in traditional Marxist terms as an obscene base upon which a diversionary superstructure is staged.

Nazi medievalism's fascination with the military orders of the Crusades was broad and deep. In the early 1930s the modern *Drang nach Osten* was already imagining the re-settlement of Russia and the former Prussian empire in the Baltic with what Höhne's classic study of *The Order of the Death's Head* calls "a sort of feudal peasant aristocracy" (295). Many have compared the SS to a state within a state, not unlike that granted to the Order of the Teutonic Knights in the Baltic by Honorius III and his successors. As Robert Koehl concludes:

> National Socialist historians, as well as Rosenberg and Himmler, gave a high place to the Teutonic Order. For them the essence of the Order was its elitism. It, too, was an elaboration of the war-band, the self-constituted league of fighting aristocrats.... It was in the Teutonic Order that the Hegelian synthesis of German pride and Christian humility was fused to create Prussiandom. The *Ordensritter* was a knight *sans peur et sans reproche*, not for himself, not for the Holy Church but for an Idea. That this Idea was not fully revealed to him, though it had something to do with the future and with Europe as a whole, was an advantage, not a drawback.... Himmler devised his *Schutzstaffel* or Elite Guard (SS) in the conscious effort to form a new pioneer-nobility for a feature German east [Kallis 273–4].

The manifest destiny of the Himmler elite was widely recognized throughout the complicated Nazi power structure. As Otto Hofmann conceded, "the

East belongs to the SS" (qtd. in Höhne 294). It was Himmler's responsibility to fulfill Hitler's dream to "form an Order, the brotherhood of the Templars around the holy grail of pure blood" which would "arrest racial decay" (Rauschning 226).[7] As I will explore in the next section, the battle lines between warring medievalisms are not simply reflected in general ways throughout Eisenstein's *Nevsky*; rather they are re-inscribed as a Manichean binary of warring ontologies represented in diametrically opposed styles of film.

The Open and Shut Films of *Alexander Nevsky*

Siegfried Kracauer's *From Caligari to Hitler* (1947) saw in German cinema between the wars the evolution of a worldview that had horrifying consequences for Germany and the rest of the world. In fact Kracauer analyzes what Frederick Jameson would later call a "political unconscious," including ideas about the impotence and suggestibility of the individual, the immutability of fate, and the hypnotic power of charismatic leadership. Kracauer would go on to champion cinema's capacity to document real life, yet the suspicion of historical and fantasy films in his later work, *The Theory of Film: The Redemption of Physical Reality* (1960), stems from the conclusions reached in the earlier book's survey of German cinema between the wars. Leo Braudy's popular *The World in a Frame: What We See in Films* (1976) adapts Kracauer's distinction between open and closed films in a considerably less tendentious approach to the categorization and analysis of authorial style in cinema. In closed films the frame demarcates the totality of the represented world, an artificial, often dream-like ontological construct from which we fear we may never awaken and in which dread, confusion and entrapment are to a great extent a function of the *mise-en-scène*. Open films, on the other hand, suggest the arbitrary, provisional, and temporary nature of the frame as a slice of life. These films are open to the wider world because what we see within the frame allows spaces, times, and actions to spill over the boundaries of the shot into realms of causation and consequence that the film itself doesn't contain.[8] Giles Deleuze's *Cinema* books (1986 and 1989, a decade after Braudy's work) would go on to narrativize this distinction as a historical transition from the movement image to the time image in post World War II auteur cinema. Yet Kracauer's reading of German cinema as being dominated by closed, claustrophobic frames teeming with entrapment, the occult, the erotic, and the capricious exercise of supernatural powers best characterizes the view of German cinema between the wars that *cineastes* in Europe and the United States gleaned from the works of admired directors such as Fritz Lang or F. W. Murnau. As cinema was increasingly nationalized and centralized between the wars, ideas about national character reflected in a national style of filmmaking became more deeply ingrained.

Whatever Eisenstein's personal problems with individual censors, he certainly understood that some portion of his difficulties had stemmed from an inability to integrate his distinctive style of montage with an increasingly hegemonic Socialist Realism. The recurrent charges of formalism, psychologism, and esoteric, personal imagery leveled against his films make sense only within the context of a Soviet national cinema policing the borders that separate it from American and West-European films. In trumpeting the advances of *Nevsky*, Eisenstein insisted that he knew what his problems had been over the course of the preceding decade and promised a film whose theme would be "patriotism and national defense against the aggressor" (Taylor 84). We note that there are really two related themes identified here: patriotism and the defense of a border. I will argue that there are also two quite distinct film styles in Eisenstein's *Nevsky*: an open, patriotic style characterized by expansive *mise-en-scène* and what I call *partisan camera*, which is chiefly reserved for the depiction of an evolving Russia in living contiguity with the present, and a closed, claustrophobic world of detached spaces and floating instants, rendered through artificial, tableau staging, which increasingly folds the paranoia and sadism of the Teutonic Knights in upon itself. The "closed film" within *Nevsky* is a scenic obscenity, dominated by fetish, surveillance, and literal representations of the "occult" nature of the proto–Nazis' secondary narcissism. But it ultimately falls victim to Eisenstein's bawdy and satirical sense of humor, now usefully redirected against a foreign enemy through Brechtian "distanciation." Such, I would argue, is the compromise inherent in the "rehabilitation" of Eisenstein's reputation and his style. My argument about *Alexander Nevsky*, then, is that open and closed styles characterize respective sequences in the film, as reality and surrealism vie for control of Russia. For example, the occupied city of Pskov is not only a "closed city" in Rossellini's terms, but it is also shot in a closed style, whereas Novgorod's "freedom" is expressed through an open style of cinematography.

Both styles are introduced in the Lake Pleshcheevo sequence that launches the film's diegesis. The sequence begins with a series of long takes, connected by axial cuts, depicting rural fishermen in an expansive, natural environment. The song celebrating the eponymous Nevsky's victory against the Swedes on the River Neva plays over the scene, but it is not clear initially whether the words are being sung by the medieval peasants or by a modern choir in a recording studio. The ambiguities of this "vertical montage" create a moment in which past, present, and future freely intermingle, in tune with the timelessness of peasants fishing a lake. The song about Nevsky's heroic past provides the background to (as well as the precondition of) the idyllic scene of peaceful peasant life, but it also looks forward to the wars to come. The "Viking" *drakkar* with its still un-planked transverses rhymes with the skeletons we saw in the *memento mori* frames, but the carved dragon prow is repeatedly associated with the stiff-necked Nevsky throughout the film. The ship, unlike the skeletons, represents the future under construction in the present, a telling example of what Deleuze calls a "time-image." Metaphors in the song are literalized as particular shots are put in vertical harmony with lyrics recounting the battle against the Swedes: "we chopped them up like matchsticks" (as the boys chop wood for the boat) and "we spilled our blood like water" (as the axial cut deepens our perspective to take in the lake). From the POV of the boys on the hill we see a Mongol slave caravan against a cloudy sky that was not present before. The arrival of the Golden Horde has brought a change in weather. A Mongol strikes one of the over-excited boys, provoking the kind of "Kino-fist" shock to the audience that Eisenstein's earlier cinema had advocated. The blow also seems to provoke a series of fast cuts and quick movements through the frame that characterized the director's earlier "kinetic," revolutionary style. Here though, as James Goodwin remarks, "class conflict quickly becomes a question of Russian patriotism" (165) enlarged to mythic proportions, which has less to do with revolutionary history than with Stalin's reclamation of heroic authoritarianism — his precursory "great men." Cut to Alexander still knee-deep in the lake, who complains that the racket is scaring the fish. As the Russian prince turns to quiet the ruckus, ripples radiate to the shore.

Alexander's movements are stylized and "expressive" to an extreme degree. His individual postures of hands on hips and arms folded make of his body a portable threshold, a human barrier that in contrast to the animated lion and tumbling monuments of earlier films repeatedly pose Nevsky as a living but immovable statue.[9] The fat and shiftless Mongol warlord is crammed within the internal frame of his palanquin, peering out from between its curtains. The palanquin itself tilts precariously on the hillside. When the chieftain finally emerges and offers Nevsky a bribe to join the Golden Horde, the shot reframes on the wispy-bearded Mongol and leaves the head of the towering Russian out of the shot, as Alexander refuses to be taken in. The landscape itself seems to impede every movement the Mongols make, while Nevsky stands impassively atop a hill, as he will later atop "Raven's Rock." The plasticity of the Mongol's expressions and glances also contrasts with Nevsky's lack of expression or movement — here as throughout the film he stands apart from those around him and maintains a stiff-backed, frontal relationship to the camera/audience. Throughout the film Nevsky speaks directly to the camera and hence directly to the modern Soviet audience as well. As the Mongols depart, Nevsky watches them from a POV that relegates the caravan to the extreme bottom right corner (the space of the anamorphic skulls in the opening shots of the film) as Nevsky himself ranks the Mongols beneath the Germans, who represent the greater, more immediate threat. In essence the unfinished ships, which repeatedly occupy the borders of the frame, serve as an objective correlative to Nevsky's patient resolution to take on the Mongols only after more pressing concerns have been addressed. These strategies will be complicated in subsequent sequences, but they establish the stylistic regime for everything to come.

The following sequences, up to the climactic "Battle on the Ice," alternate between open and closed styles. As the "last stronghold of a free Russia," Novgorod adheres to the parameters of the open style. A bit of business employing something akin to a match cut also defines the borders of the frame as the contested site of containment, reversals, and transcendence. The Lake Plescheevo scene ends with the dragon prow looming motionless at the left of the frame, and the following sequence in Novgorod begins with a long shot of that city from the harbor, seemingly and rather absurdly under attack from an animated dragon prow that menaces the city from the right. This manipulation of scale in wide lens and deep focus photography is a joke typical of the early Eisenstein. But the symbolism is also coded in a complex and telling way, indebted to his later theories of the multivalence and fluidity of the symbolic film image. The two dragons attacking from opposite directions clearly symbolize the larger geopolitical reality of the film in which medieval Rus found itself threatened from the East by the Mongols and from the West by the Germans, just as modern Russia was caught between Japan and Germany. Yet I have claimed that the dragon prows in the film are repeatedly associated with Nevsky himself; indeed, in a later scene wooden dragon prows decorate his bedroom! Of course that is not as contradictory as it first appears: the plot of the film turns on Nevsky's strategic reversal of containment, which lures the Teutonic Knights, like the infamous vixen, into a pincer tactic.

That the messenger has escaped at all to tell Novgorod the tale of the sack of Pskov perhaps looks forward to the ultimate failure of the Knights to contain the Rus. His bandaged eye recalls the famous shot of the wounded gaze in the Odessa Steps sequence of *Battleship Potemkin*— in Eisenstein atrocities wound the eye.[10] The film's subordination of the role of the Eastern Orthodox Church to exigent political realities is obvious in the shots of Olga strolling through the market toward the Church in answer to the bell's call, interrupted by the countervailing rush of the mob into the town square, spurred onward by a different bell clanging rapidly with the new message of present danger.[11] The wounded messenger is shouldered into the square by a wave of peasants who gush forth into the frame from behind the camera. This "rolling foreground" is another element of style politically motivated in the film; it again embodies what I am calling a *partisan camera* as the reservoir of kinetic Russian power, which the camera seems to release on cue like the breaking of a dam. In locating the source of this power on the side of the screen that contains the contemporary Russian audience, Eisenstein elicits an emotional identification and investment that intensifies the medieval/modern parallelisms of the film's storyline. The Cathedral as background in the scene at first participates in the top-heavy framing, which pushes the messenger off into that same lower right-hand corner. Eisenstein's artificial cathedral is literally that, an immaculate, whitewashed substitute that stood in for the sunken, stained original. Emotionally the cathedral creates an oppressive presence, especially as its sepulchral whiteness rhymes with the white cloaks of the Teutonic Knights. But the Church remains in this film where it began, in the background. The cathedral serves as a neutral screen on which are projected the call for justice made in this early scene as well as in Nevsky's final distribution of justice at the end of the film. There is little if any intimation that the German invasion represents an attempt by Roman Catholicism to bring back into the fold an Eastern Church deemed schismatic.

The cathedral becomes more obviously a neutral screen as a series of three axial cut-ins bring us closer to the messenger recounting the horrors Pskov under the German yoke — a speech that could not have failed to provoke more recent memories of the German occupation of the Soviet Union in the First World War. As the distance is closed by the axial cuts, the messenger's body movements and the horrors he recounts intensify. When he reports that the Germans are dividing the cities among themselves (even Novgorod, as they count their spoils prematurely), the shot cuts away to a distant perspective on the same axis, revealing a now thronging crowd that has thickened considerably during the interval of the speech. These axial cuts throughout the film remain the technique that opens a perspective onto the seemingly infinite resources inherent in the Russian landscape and its people. The Germans, as we shall see below, are typically viewed through close-ups and shot/counter shot, framed according to a theatrical staging that alienates the image from surrounding spaces and cut in a way that disorients — makes mystical and surreal — our sense of their (non)existence in space and time.

The disparity between the Novgorod sequence and the following sequence in occupied Pskov suggests Eisenstein's use of montage to embrace the juxtaposition of whole scenes and styles. Pointedly the Novgorod sequence contains no music, but in Pskov Prokofiev's score returns menacingly as the report of atrocities gives way to what is clearly a *staging* of the very acts of torture and land endowments described in the earlier scene.[12] The decision to recall Alexander at the close of the Novgorod sequence would logically be followed by the embassy to summon him so that the Pskov sequence seems an interruption, with very little dialogue and formal, tableau staging that makes it represent not so much an element of the plot as a floating fragment, a display of ideology without a human face posing for group portraits. This temporal disjunction operates like a flashback but also seems to function — as scenes featuring the Germans will repeatedly — to exclude, to set apart and essentialize German existence, partitioning it from the flow of chronological time and spatial relationships. This isolation, both cultural and psychological, is precisely the turn in German culture that Kracauer finds so ubiquitous in German films made after the First World War, films "that dissolved history into psychology" (1947, 54).

The sequence begins with a quick series of axial cuts that appears to parody those in the earlier scene: ridiculously the Knights stand guard over deserted structures they have gutted and reduced to smoking ruins. The cuts, though, quickly grow more severe. A shot in deep focus includes Pskov cathedral as a backdrop to the panoply of Knights and monks, the latter holding crosses as their knightly counterparts do spears. The place of the bell in the foreground left of the Novgorod shot is taken by a gibbet in the Pskov long shot, and the thronging square of Novgorod is answered by the hierarchical, ceremonial disposition of the Knights in Pskov arrayed around a bonfire and shot from behind the bound Russian prisoners in the center. Next we get *the first reverse shot of the film*, depicting the kneeling prisoners from the POV of the leaders of the Teutonic Knights and revealing the prisoners' containment within a circle that suggests some kind of ritualistic ceremony. However, the *mise-en-scène* is not simply or even primarily about *physical* containment: the camera stages a series of gazes that pose a cumulative menace. Eisenstein's penchant for *pars per toto* shot construction, his love of synecdoche and the hieroglyphic language of the film image, make this wordless series of shots speak volumes. Five successively closer shots stage the gradual revelation of a totalitarian gaze that interpellates its objects between the Church and the Teutonic Order. In the first of this series the Archbishop slowly raises his head to reveal a piercing, malicious stare beneath the bill of his (Latin Cardinal's!) omophoron.[13] The next shot from the opposing direction answers with a Knight's bucket helmet emblazoned with a cross, the cross beam of which provides thin slits through which he can see without being seen. The following image is a two shot of the famous "tank helmets" that seem an abstraction of the cross design, retaining only the two parallel, horizontal slits — as if what we have here is a trajectory from medieval, religious warfare to the impersonal mechanization of the modern battlefield — an effect intensified by the blurry line of soldiers dressed in identical armor which snakes out behind the two in the foreground.[14] The fourth in the series is another two shot of bucket helmets in which sightlines have been cut out in the shape of a crude cross. The crudeness of these incisions suggests runic inscription (the rune "+"—*naudiz, naudr, nyd* denotes "compulsion" or "distress"). Eyes and noses protrude grotesquely from the cross-shaped holes in a blatantly phallic pun. The final shot in this series, which depicts the Grand Master von Balk with his crowned helmet and bull's horns, is also the closest shot in this series. Echoing the cut out design of the cross visors, this helmet's opening is the most revealing of the face beneath and takes the shape of a chalice. The chalice of course refers to the Nazi propaganda quoted above of a holy grail that is in fact a pure German bloodline. This crackpot theory about the Grail as a sacred genealogy has re-emerged in the work of the writers of *Holy Blood/Holy Grail* and was adopted wholesale by Dan Brown in *The Da Vinci Code*, but none of these best-selling authors acknowledges the descent of his "discoveries" from the occult substratum of Nazi racism. In any event, there is something decidedly obscene about this final framing of the gaze. Perhaps this image answers the phallic joke of the helmets in the fourth shot with its grotesque vagina and giant clitoris functioning as a nose guard.

Yet the most important point I want to make here is how the increasing tightness of the shots and the gradual opening of the orifice of the gaze stage an increasingly disembodied and threatening look. Let us also note that the film produces something akin to J.R.R Tolkien's all-seeing eye of Sauron. Perhaps these near contemporaries, Tolkien and Eisenstein, refer obliquely to the infamous cold, dead stares cultivated by the SS and noted in many contemporary descriptions of them. More specifically both gazes have the apparently supernatural power to strike and debilitate all they look upon. Eisenstein, who early on theorized a visceral cinema that could produce physical shocks in its audience capable of altering their behavior in a Pavlovian manner, ends the sequence of shots we have been discussing with a long-delayed counter-shot wherein the gaze of von Balk causes women and children to cower and stumble backwards as if the glance itself had delivered a blow, in what is perhaps a visual pun on the Grand Master's name.[15] Later in the film von Balk will apparently deliver orders to his troops, like the Sauron of the recent Tolkien films, through a wordless telepathy, simply by turning his glance in their direction.

Throughout the sequence of the Pskov charnel house, the only thing that escapes the frame is the billowing smoke emanating from a variety of sources. The Master's gaze is briefly met by that of Vasilisa's father Pavsha, bound and on his knees, who raises his head in defiance beyond the containment of the shot only to bow down again in deference to the Archbishop's threat to punish the Novgorod rebels: "Whoever does not bow down to Rome shall be put to death." Finally goaded by Tverdilo, the collaborationist mayor of Pskov, Pavsha rises to his feet, renewing his defiance. But only in death can the people of Pskov escape the frame. Given the command for genocide, "Wipe them from the face of the earth," the Knights trample the prisoners under foot and their swords reach down out of the frame — efficient mass murder is concealed from view as its victims disappear. The white robes of the Knights make infants disappear too as they tear them from their mothers. Babies are baptized in fire, but as they are dropped into the flames, they too fall out of the bottom of the frame. Pavsha is strung up alongside a Church, his "passion" in contrast to the impassive stone saint chiseled on the wall behind him. In agony he calls out for Alexander, and his body tenses and expands diagonally across the screen, head and lower body exceeding the frame, until finally he collapses into a fetal position within its confines.[16] In the Pskov sequence the framing reinforces the seemingly magical power of the Teutonic Knights, which first contains the populace and then makes them disappear.

The Germans carry out the sack of Pskov with a contempt that suggests a trans-lingual pun: the massacre of the inhabitants is orchestrated with an efficiency and thoroughness emphasized by the cuts between various acts of atrocity and the strangely invisible character of its results. As Eisenstein's theory of montage developed, he increasingly explored the notion of *pars per toto* shot construction as well as the possibilities inherent in cinematic tropes like synecdoche, evident in the dragon prows discussed above. As David Bordwell puts it, "the Germans freeze gestures into blazons" (2005, 215). The framing and the cuts in the Teutonic sequences not only suggest the Kino-eye camera as the double of an oppressive, ubiquitous gaze; the cinematography and editing strategies also create a collage of images in which revelation and concealment, sadism, and fetish play an integral role. In the visor sequence I discussed above, crosses, tank grills, and grails stage gazes rendered perverse by obscurantism.

As Eisenstein knew well, Freud thought fetishism a symptom of castration anxiety and likened it to scotoma, a restriction of the field of vision. The "extraordinary case" that Freud cites in his famous essay on "Fetishism" turns on a German/English pun "Glantz auf der Nase" (shine on the nose), which the patient's unconscious mistranslates as "glance at the nose" (952–55). This pun is evident in the fourth shot of Eisenstein's series, where shiny noses dangle from cavities of the cross-shaped cutouts. For Freud men create fetishes out of the fear caused by the mother's lack of a penis, a lack which fetishists supplement by charging objects with erotic energy. Freud goes on to connect this "panic" with threats to structures of power, "when the cry goes up that Throne and Altar are in danger," which taps into fundamental anxieties about threats to masculinity itself (953). The final shot in the sequence of the Teutonic Master broadly hints at such gender panic. As the Master senses that he not only looks but is also seen looking, and Pavsha returns his stare, the Master removes his helmet, cradles it lovingly in his arms, and grabs one of the bull horns in his fist — a posture he maintains for the rest of the scene. His castration anxiety is well founded. Later in their duel Nevsky chops off this horn, and the blow which should not have phased the Master — since he himself is never touched — seems to sap all his strength, and he is quickly knocked off his horse. In casting the Knights as fetishists whose power is not only symbolized by but also contained within such talismans, Eisenstein perhaps suggests that their symbols really are magical just as the phallus itself is magical, but that only renders masculine power all the more vulnerable. Under the gaze of the audience the blond, long-haired Master's gender seems as unstable as the famous figure/ground diagram. Are we looking at a cup or a face?[17]

This slippage in the meaning and power of synecdoches, where a part renders vulnerable the integrity of the whole, becomes more broadly comic in later scenes. As the troops prepare to hunt the "Russian bear," the theatrical framing of the shot is a blur of white punctuated by a riot of crosses. When the troops hasten away, the three most important Teutonic Knights — the Master von Balk; Hubertus, the newly endowed prince of Pskov; Dietlieb, presumptive ruler of Novgorod — remain behind. Heralds scurry to take their places behind the three Knights but in their haste garble the heraldic symbolism. Eisenstein's use of heraldry is for the most part drawn from the Manesse Codex (University of Heidelberg Library MS Cod. Pal. Germ. 848), an early fourteenth-century MS illustrating the works of the *minnesingers* that features the eagle's talons, bull's horns, and the stylized horseshoes seen adorning the crests, shields and banners of Teutonic Knights in the film.[18] As the troops charge off to battle, the confusion of the three Knights who linger behind is evident. The Master in his horned helmet is in the center backed by a banner displaying the Teutonic Eagle at the intersection of a golden cross. To his left is Hubertus, whose crest is a claw of three talons — not four as Teutonic heraldry requires. To the Master's right stands Dietlieb whose crest mimics a truncated Nazi salute. The Master looks to his left and then to his right, seemingly disoriented: the trouble is that in the confusion the banners of Hubertus and Dietlieb have gotten reversed, and the Knights have no intention of going into battle before this mess is straightened out. The banner *supposed* to go behind Dietlieb depicts two hands, accompanying the single hand on his helmet, while that of Hubertus contains three crosses on a field of fleur-de-lis, matching the three claws on his helmet. Of course this slapstick, Chaplinesque confusion is also a fairly savage send-up of the Trinity, desperately trying to sort out the mystery of three-in-one and one-in-three before launching its crusade against the heretics. Each of these crest/talismans will be laid low, their meanings bathetically inverted in the fall of the Knights. I mentioned above the strangely debilitating castration of the Master's horn in the final duel. After he falls to the ground, his hand and arm re-enter the shot in mimicry of the Nazi salute, now functioning as a sign of surrender — a sign of helplessness echoed later as another Knight sinks through the ice.[19] As Ignat takes him prisoner, the tight shot on the Grand Master's helmet suggests that he himself is an insubstantial shadow, an empty suit of armor like the void behind the armor of Sauron in the prologue to Jackson's *Lord of the Rings*. When Dietlieb is brought low, his helmet's talismanic Nazi salute is transformed into a gesture beseeching a hand out, perhaps a backhanded reference to German penury after the First World War and its connection to the rise of National Socialism.[20] The claw on the helmet of a fallen Hubertus appears poised to latch on to the treasonous Russian monk, Ananias, just before he is caught, perhaps alluding as well to the torments that await the renegade monk in Novgorod, or in hell.

Eisenstein's great precursor film was Fritz Lang's *Die Nibelungen* (1924), and his response to Lang's theatrical, operatic film is twofold: stylization and parody.[21] The closed film of the Teutonic Knights in *Nevsky* alludes repeatedly to both Lang's claustrophobic, mystical *mises-en-scène* and also includes many obvious quotations, such as the Master's ambush announced as a "hunt" and the dressing of small boys in tank helmets to mimic similar shots of Lang's dwarfs. Eisenstein costumes his Tverdilo like Lang's Hagen, and again like Hagen Tverdilo finds a weak spot in the armor of his prey. In Lang Siegfried's weak spot is a function of his bath in dragon's blood and the catastrophic lime leaf, while the tragedy of Ignat (like Siegfried a blacksmith) is a euhemerized variation, the result of wearing armor too small for him. On the other hand, Eisenstein's open film of the Rus parodies the raging, self-destructive jealousies of Lang's love quadrangle with a Shakespearean comedy of marriage. We have Lang's paradigmatic *femmes*, the blond prize (Kriemhild/ Olga) and the raven-haired danger to men (Brunhilda/ Vasilisa). Like Siegfried, Olga's suitor Gavrillo returns home at the end of the film on a bier, but he soon revives and begins planning to live happily ever after with Olga. Vasilisa like Brunhilda is a match for any man, but unlike her Germanic counterpart she meekly agrees never to turn her fists against her future husband. Vasily first meets Vasilisa on the battlefield where she remedies the loss of his sword by giving him a large pole — a notably un–Brunhilda-like gesture, who refuses to cede the phallus to her emasculated husband. By invoking only to subvert Lang's closed, tragic film, Eisenstein evokes comparisons not only between films, but also between national cinemas and the differing fates of nations as a product of their collective consciousness.

The Battle on the Ice

The contradictory signification whereby excess is associated with containment and the precariousness of gender boundaries with the phallus is nowhere more evident than in the famous "Battle on the Ice."[22] The German vanguard is the most daunting of Eisenstein's fetishistic synecdoches, and the Rus await its charge with awed admiration: "The German Wedge!" Of course the wedge in mystical symbolism — as fans of *The Da Vinci Code* are well aware — is easily inverted to become a sign of the feminine. Nevsky's strategy, inspired by Ignat's fable of the rabbit and the vixen, requires that the Nazi wedge "stick deep;" only then, like the unfortunate vixen stuck between two trees, will its backside be exposed. Arguably the most gargantuan example of "queering" in the history of cinema, the white phalanx of knights penetrates deeply into the dark Russian force only to find itself assaulted from behind. In fact as filmed from above, the pincer tactic neutralizes the Teutonic invasion like an antibody surrounding a virus or like an embryo in a womb.[23] "Mother Russia" exposes the fear of castration inherent in the Germanic worship of the phallus — every penetration is a possible castration. Hence the chastity of the Warrior Monks is also exposed as the neurotic fear of the other that is ultimately femininity itself. This fear is embodied in the woman-warrior, Vasilisa, who is later celebrated as their most redoubtable foe. The cross-dressing Vasilisa follows what will become a familiar trajectory in later movie medievalism as she transforms from the Knights' victim (they kill her father, Pavsha) to their scourge. She is among the first of many such representations to encapsulate nationality, femininity, and the hidden, powerful resources of Nature "herself" within the patriotic image of the woman-warrior. Vasilisa is the direct ancestor of Antoine Fuqua's Guinevere and Peter Jackson's Eowyn.[24] I would argue that Vasilisa's fluid transitions back and forth across the gender divide present yet another example of the openness of the style associated in this film with the Rus.[25] Of course this openness is shown throughout the battle to be a function of the Russian natural landscape itself, out of which soldiers pop up like Jack-in-the-boxes from holes in ground to answer Nevsky's call to arms and into which the Germans are plunged as the ice gives way.[26] David Quint in one of the most powerful essays ever written on the film notes how *Nevsky* "comes self-consciously to terms with the literary genre" of epic by reversing the imperialist binaries of the Virgilian tradition (361). The Eastern, feminine, natural world absorbs the Western thrust of mechanized masculinity in what many have seen as an abiding characteristic of Russian nationalist identity. This national character proudly remembers the role of the landscape itself in the defeat of the medieval Crusaders, Napoleon, and finally Hitler (see Quint 363).

While we have insufficient space here to follow the many details of the Battle on the Ice and its aftermath, I do want to discuss a representative sampling from the war of film styles that structures this famous sequence. Two points in space serve to orient (or disorient) our attempts to follow the extended action sequences: Raven's Rock and the camp *cum* field altar of the Teutonic Knights. Roland Barthes thoughtfully drew connections between the *mise-en-scène* of Eisenstein's early films and the distanciation effects of Brecht's staging, stating categorically that "nothing separates the scene in epic theater from the Eisenstein shot (except that in Brecht the tableau is offered to the spectator for criticism not for adherence)" (in Rosen 173). While Barthes was speaking of the films of the twenties, the comparison with Brecht holds true for the closed style of *Nevsky* as well, particularly in the scenes depicting the Teutonic camp. Barthes also asks whether it follows from distanciation that "a tableau [is] then (since it arises from a process of cutting out) a fetish object?" The result in Eisenstein is a "cinema by vocation anthological, itself holding out to the fetishist, with dotted lines, the piece for him to cut out and take away ... like a lock of hair, a glove or a woman's underwear" (in Rosen 175). Employing Brecht's concept of the "social gest" (a sign or gesture which encapsulates a social reality), Barthes compares the "gest" to "a hieroglyph in which can be read at a single glance ... the present, the past, and the future; that is, the historical meaning of the represented action" (175). Such hieroglyphs are by their very nature complete and artificial, characterized by an excess that is integral to their significance; that is, they display an excess of significance, and this excess is itself significant. The excesses of the tableaux of the Knight's camp in *Nevsky* offer just such an asynchronous, detached hieroglyph of historical significance: duplication, stasis, and incongruity form a sign removed from time and space but containing a transcendent meaning.

The first of the five scenes set in the Teutonic camp features the heraldic confusion of the Knights discussed above. An *unheimlich* religious service is accompanied by music from an organist who seems to float on air, a shot only later related spatially to its context within the ceremony. (The pipe organ and bellows are yet another backhanded slap at opening shot of the forge in Lang's *Die Nibelungen*.) The acutely discontinuous space is later assembled through an axial cut, but unlike the axial cuts featured in scenes depicting the Russians that add elements to the *mise-en-scène*, here the cut back simply stitches elements we've already seen into a coherent (albeit staged and artificial) whole. The service is briefly interrupted; music and chanting stop, as the Grand Master launches into his exhortation to "hunt the Russian bear." But the music quickly resumes to accompany his oration, the "vertical montage" effectively collapsing all difference between worship and war. The Knights depart for a

The turncoat monks in the Teutonic camp of *Alexander Nevsky*.

nighttime ambush, and perhaps twelve hours pass in real time before we see the camp again. When we return to the camp, it is morning, yet in the shot *everything is exactly the same as we left it the night before.* The Bishop still stands upon the carpet cross, flanked on either side by pairs of monks in white who are in turn framed by the white tent and flanked by the organist, etc. The tableau is compulsively balanced and symmetrical, yet the inference here also seems to be that time has stopped or that like actors the monks have returned to their marks. As if on cue, the monks all move in unison, conferring a blessing upon the Knights now arrayed on the battlefield. We are never allowed to perceive any spatial relationship between the camp and the battlefield, though the two places are certainly some distance apart. However, the cut to the battlefield apparently shows the Knights responding to the monks' blessing, raising their banners in reply and preparing for the initial charge. Single chords struck on a piano also serve as sound bridge across the indeterminate expanse. The Knights then organize their forces set to the musical theme many of us first heard in *Jaws*!

As the tide of battle turns in favor of the Rus, we get a weirdly cacophonous bridge of screeching pipes and tambourines. This seemingly impromptu performance is also disjointed spatially, though it appears to be located somewhere between the battlefield and the camp. As the music bleeds over into the next shot of the camp, there is a suddenly frenzied and chaotic movement seemingly spurred by the cacophony. Horns within the camp then strike up a more deliberate tune as the chaos is brought under control. Monks in the foreground hurriedly arrange themselves and lift their crosses into the air, only to perform a quick-change trick, apparently trading their white robes for black ones. White flakes still cling to the fabric, suggesting that the black robes were tucked away in the snow bank. Perhaps the monks are mourning their dead, but more likely the turncoats no longer wish to be identifiable as warrior monks and have reclassified their status to that of non-combatants! In the long interval between the first scene in the camp and this one, the Master and the two princes have finally gotten their heraldry sorted out, just in time to depart rather tardily for the battlefield and the definitive duel between Nevsky and the Master.

A final scene at the Teutonic camp, split in two by crosscutting between the camp and the battlefield, shows Vasilisa's attack on the monks, who in a revealing bit of primitive *bricolage* turn their crosses into swords, but to no avail. Of course the irony resides in the "defamiliarization" this inversion of the cross represents; its literal use in this context exposes the violence implicit in the symbol as well as its ultimate impotence. Ignat chops down the tent pole, and the tent collapses. The rhymes throughout the sequence between the white tent decked with black crosses and the tunics of the warrior monks had posed the tent as the center of their totemic power. Its collapse suggests the striking of a set — the circus is leaving town — and connects the mysteries of the faith with the ephemeral nature of sideshow illusion, a distanciation fully complete when Ignat folds the tent of this portable, imperial Christianity. As Julia Kristeva remarks of Godard and Bresson: "It was probably necessary that specular fascination arrive at its peak of perfection in the cinema, so that both its dread and its seduction might break out in laughter and in distanciation. Without demystification, the cinema would be nothing but another Church" (in Rosen 242). As the Archbishop flees the Rus, he is juxtaposed with the beasts of battle, who already dine on the flesh of the dead. He slips, and his crosier slaps the ice, initiating the cracks that will submerge many of the Knights. Their fall through these chunks of ice is the final allusion to the jigsaw, "cut out" nature of their reality. While these sheets of ice are typically jagged, the last shot shows a Knight struggling unsuccessfully to use a piece of ice as a flotation device. When it flips over, drowning him, we recognize this slippery piece of real estate as a cut-out map of Russia.

The open style that characterizes our view of Eisenstein's Rus throughout the film and especially their victory in the Battle on the Ice depends upon the director/theorist's expanded notion of *pathos*. As Anne Nesbet explains, pathos denotes more than sympathy with characters on the screen, rather a recognition of oneself as part within the whole that composes a work of art and even the historical process itself (179–84). As an individual is to the collective, so too is a moment to time. Parts contribute to wholes as frames to a film, or moments to a life, but lives and films also play their parts in greater wholes. In *Nonindifferent Nature* Eisenstein insisted: "This experience of a moment of history is imbued with the greatest pathos and sense of unity with this process. A sense of being in step with it. The sense of collective participation in it. Such is pathos in life" (36). The Teutonic Knights are committed to an ideology that alienates them from the wholes of which they are a part. The closed frames, the talismans, the rage of this Order for order walls them off from the possibility of pathos, both theirs and that of the world at large. Nature in the Battle on the Ice is anything but indifferent. We could adapt Henry V's famous words in Shakespeare to read, "*Nature* fought for us."[27] After the defeat of the Teutonic Knights, Olga makes the elemental nature of the battle clear: "There are no more Germans! No more Germans, my dear ones! They were defeated! Spread to the four winds or sunk below the ice." But so, I would argue, does the camera itself fight on the side of the Rus, positioning its viewers within a collective perspective that elides differences in space and time.

In shots depicting the Rus, the back of the camera is the locus of the collective and the continuous, created by axial cuts and what Eisenstein called "a rolling foreground." The camera is not only ideologically but also literally and spatially on the side of the Russians. The positioning of this partisan, nationalist perspective not only elides historical differences and encourages what Lacan called "imaginary identifications," it also creates a seemingly infinite reservoir of patriotic energy. What is in effect a nationalist POV shot does not typically reverse its perspective to define the identity of who looks but rather animates the audience's gaze as collective action and tracks the line of sight as it overwhelms its object. In Pskov the frame centers on the Knights trampling their victims and stabbing bodies fallen beneath the shot. On Lake Peipus the peasant army remains out of the shot: makeshift weapons like grappling hooks enter the frame to pull the Knights from their horses. The Battle on the Ice is very much a war of horizontal and vertical lines. Eisenstein's camera tends to remain outside the fracas, casting the war in terms of its geometry. Yet the competing styles of these externally shot lines remain distinct, an intricate deployment of the difference between staging in depth and depth of field (on the distinction, see Bordwell 1997, 158–271). Staging in depth repeatedly emphasizes the size of the German army, yet without the use of deep focus. The result, as in the line of tank-helmeted soldiers I discussed above or in the Teutonic cavalry charge, is an extenuating line that blurs as it recedes from view. In stark contrast the Russian army is typically staged as well as shot in depth, and oblique camera angles use deep focus to the emphasize the Russian line as a substantial force of distinct individuals, all of whom remain in focus.[28] When the Knights charge, they push the Rus up against the camera, but the horizontal boundary demarcated by the partisan camera prevents them from advancing any further. In a number of what might be dubbed *internal wipes*, a line of white Knights is pushed from the frame by the dark lines of the Rus. A brilliant example comes in a shot that begins with the white Knights occupying the top of a hill. The camera unleashes a seemingly endless dark wave of Russian peasants, which undulates over the uneven topography and washes the Knights from the frame — an effect repeated *mutatis mutandis* a number of times.[29]

The centrality of Raven's Rock in the battle contrasts with the floating space of the Teutonic camp. The rock anchors the Russian space, orients our perspective, and serves as the boundary line where Nevsky determines to halt the Teutonic invasion.[30] Repeated shots personify and monumentalize the landmark. It is the site of yet another triad, with Nevsky in the center, echoing the three-pronged organization of his strategy and in stark counterpoint to the triad of Teutonic Knights with their superfluous and confused heraldry. The Rock jutting bolt upright from the ice rhymes with Nevsky's own posture, and he is repeatedly shown atop it. There is a kind of natural magic insinuated here as well, connected to pagan myths of giants bound in the ice, but the "magic" is chiefly the supernaturalism of "nonindifferent nature" in which landscape and character are parts of a unified field. In championing Japanese landscape painting, Eisenstein had insisted that: "Everywhere the emotional landscape turns out be an image of the mutual absorption of man and nature one into the other" (1987, 359). His later theoretical turn is the "pathetic fallacy" writ large in which Nevsky's stony resolve is an extension of the landmark, and the stone seems in the process of sculpting itself as his monument. The rock is not a magical talisman or synecdoche, but rather a natural and sympathetic extension of the resolve of Nevsky and his forces: evidence in Eisenstein's terms of the "ecstasy" which pathos creates by establishing continuities across space and time, between people and their environment, between art and its audience. Of course the rock is also a calculated signature for the director's eccentric conflation of monumentality and natural supernaturalism: *Eisen* (iron) + *Stein* (stone). Nevsky's own "expressive movements" in their aggressive frontality likewise establish a border that rather deliberately transcends time. In the final speech of the film, he turns to the camera to deliver the film's message directly to the future world of its audience: "He who comes to us with the sword shall die by the sword. On this stands Russia, and on this she shall stand forever." The reverse shot films his audience of Russian soldiers as an endless expanse, and the "Epilogue," in an extra-diegetic, editorial title sequence, reiterates the threat for audiences foreign and domestic, as the still shot of the army fades to black.

In the Middle

I have been arguing that Eisenstein's Manichean nationalism is structured according to a stylistic and ultimately ontological binary. Yet it may be useful to complicate this picture by asking whether *Alexander Nevsky* is also a dialogical film. Eisenstein's employment of two distinct film styles for the depiction of two distinct national worldviews is provocative. But in the traditional sense of Russia's geographical and historical placement as well as in Eisenstein's personal vision of his country's place, Russia stood in the middle of the world, a mean between East and West, between political and cultural extremes. At the time of the Crusades, the Eastern Church was represented and also at times chose to represent itself in this way, as a mean between the "Franks" and the pagan "Saracens." World War I reinforced this sense of Russian cultural identity as an embattled middle between the extremes of Germany and Japan, a worldview again confirmed in the tense years before the outbreak of the Second World War.

Along with Pudovkin's *Storm over Asia*, the historical films that most influenced Eisenstein's *Alexander Nevsky* were Fritz Lang's *Die Nibelungen* and D. W. Griffith's *Birth of a Nation*. Eisenstein was also a lifelong aficionado of Japanese *Kabuki* theater and studied Japanese intensively as a student, later employing the "hieroglyph" as metaphor for the language of film and adapting *Kabuki* styles of historical narration throughout his career. The poetics of *Alexander Nevsky* in its detailed evocation of recurrence and synchronicity is perhaps most indebted to the modernism of James Joyce's *Ulysses*, which Eisenstein dubbed "the Bible of the new cinema" (in Bulgakowa 80). More crucial still for our purposes is Eisenstein's early fascination with secret societies and the occult: in his twenties he became a member of both the Rosicrucians and the Freemasons, though luckily he managed to distance himself from these groups before their violent repression. The substantially more developed film culture of Germany, in its adulation of *Battleship Potemkin*, was directly responsible for Eisenstein's greatest success and also introduced the young director to the Western world—the beginning of a popular and critical respect outside of the Soviet Union that conferred upon Eisenstein an authority and a degree of invulnerability few artists in his country possessed. A decade after the release of his masterpiece the National Socialists in Germany were still touting Eisenstein's accomplishment: Ghering called for a "people's" epic cinema, comparing *Potemkin* with the *Iliad* and the medieval *Nibelungenleid*. In 1934 Josef Goebbels called for a "National Socialist *Potemkin*" (in Bulgakowa 65). With the signing of German-Soviet Non-Aggression pact in 1939, Eisenstein's film was pulled from release, and he began rehearsals to direct a version of Wagner's opera *Die Walküre*. Perhaps more fundamentally Eisenstein's authoritarian father came from a family of German Jews. The profound influence of another German Jew, Sigmund Freud, on the films of Eisenstein, often ridiculed by his Soviet detractors, also helped to determine the paths taken in Eisenstein's persistent explorations of his own psyche and sexuality, as well as his fascination with authoritarianism. See for instance Bulgakowa's discussion of the powerful effect on the early Eisenstein of the analysis of artistic personality in Freud's essay on Leonardo Da Vinci. Whereas Eisenstein noted in his journals his own repressed homosexuality, Bulgakowa quite provocatively characterizes the director as inhabiting a psychosexual middle, a "bisexual androgyne whose cult was celebrated in Russia at the beginning of the century among the Symbolists" (43). As Bulgakowa (99) recounts, the Germans the director met on his trip to Berlin in 1929 were struck by the fondness of this revolutionary Russian artist for "gay, lesbian and transvestite clubs" as well by his fascination with pornography. Eisenstein's enthrallment to the capital crime of homosexuality is abundantly evident in his depiction of the Teutonic Knights, who live in a closeted, homo-social world, which the director explores through a telling mixture of fascination and the distancing effects of crude humor. A widely circulated production still shows a Teutonic Knight astride a long pole that in horsy-back fashion reproduces the artificial, bared-device effect of unnatural, rhythmic movement in the shots of the cavalry charge: Eisenstein the director holds the pole in his fist (see Bordwell 2005, 28).

What I mean to suggest by this list of "influences" (which could certainly be extended) is Eisenstein's attraction to and investment in the alterity he so resolutely contains in this film. The doctrines of Mani as well as their sublimation within doctrinal Christianity insisted on the internal struggle between light and dark *within* each individual human being. We do Eisenstein a great disservice, I believe, if we treat his double style simply as a function of careerist exigency or the historical circumstances of the Soviet Union in the late 1930s. Nor are the open and closed styles of *Alexander Nevsky* simply a formal compromise between the differing tenants of national cinemas that arose following the First World War. As a theorist Eisenstein repeatedly observed how meaning itself resides in the middle, the product of often violent clashes between opposing views of the world. Such clashes occur at the microcosmic level of the montage of two shots, at the macrocosmic level of warring ideologies or historical forces, but also in the individual mind of the artist, which, as Freud had taught Eisenstein, was also a battlefield of forceful drives, cathexes, sublimations, and projections. *Alexander Nevsky* opposes the psychoanalytic and occult allure of German films with a more open style derived in equal part from the heroic individuality of American cinema as well as the Social Realist conception of history as a function of collective action. But these styles, as well as the worldviews they connote, are also tied to internal struggles waged within Eisenstein himself. I see Eisenstein's *Alexander Nevsky* as his most personal film, one reason perhaps that he repeatedly distanced himself from it. The expression of such internal conflicts, more than idiosyncratic habits of editing or shot construction, were and to some degree remain the defining sign of the *auteur*. The kind of nuanced approach to ideology, psychology, and style I'm advocating here has the benefit of precluding self-righteous verdicts on Eisenstein, such as that which John Aberth permits himself in *A Knight at the Movies* (107–121). Aberth is certainly right to insist that "the American Left has yet to come to terms with its toleration of fascism's mirror image: Soviet communism under Lenin and Stalin" (121), just as, we might add, Neoconservatism needs to be held responsible for its own investments in neo-medievalism (see Holsinger). Yet Aberth's "bottom line ... that *Alexander Nevsky* was part of an effort to justify the liquidation of millions of people" (119) is a peevish slur, not only made from the safety of hindsight, but lacking any sustained attempt to come to terms with the form or the sense of the film. Aberth can flatly dismiss the recent attempts of Bordwell (2005), Ian Christie (1993), Barry Scherr (1998), and Norman Cantor to revisit the way ideology is textured within the montage of sound and images because his own analysis is confined almost exclusively to quoted dialogue and press releases. As Herbert Engle (in LaValley and Scherr 169–192) notes, scenarios and screenplays were the most susceptible to ideological influence and preemptive self-censorship, yet the images themselves in concert with cutting and vertical montage open the possibilities of critique to a much greater degree because significance becomes in the completed film a function of texture and resonance. Also by failing to read Eisenstein's published writings and speeches within the contexts of the Great Terror of 1937 and by failing to note that Eisenstein's responses to such situations invariably included admixtures of subservience, self-promotion, and self-criticism, as well as irony and satire, Aberth misses the opportunity to sift historical and contemporary references with anything like the care they deserve.

It is true that Eisenstein chose the topic partly because so little was popularly known about Nevsky. He realized that he was creating what we would call today a "prosthetic memory:" "If I choose a fat actor, then Nevsky was fat.... Then and now, always and forever" (in Bergan 296). He knew his audience would be likely to identify Nevsky with Stalin, and he repeatedly encouraged this identification. But he also knew — and knew that anyone possessing even a passing familiarity with medieval history would know — that Nevsky had cooperated with his country's more dangerous enemy, the Mongols. Relations between the Soviet Union and Germany were a very volatile, unfolding situation when *Nevsky* was released. It was soon withdrawn upon the signing of the German-Soviet Non-Aggression Pact and then re-released in 1941 when Germany invaded the Soviet Union. Eisenstein's script called for Nevsky to be poisoned by the Mongols, a final sequence red-penciled probably by Stalin himself with the comment: "such a great hero must not die." The final sequences of the film, then, were to have shown Stalin's historical double carrying out as well as threatening to carry out violent repressions of his own people and subsequently dying rather ignominiously in his attempt to appease a foe bent on the colonization of Russia. Stalin/Nevsky's historical mission could only be completed by his descendents. The portrait of Nevsky is certainly a flattering one to Stalin, but it hints ironically at how the threat of foreign invasion sets the precedent for states of emergency in which disloyalty creates what Georgio Agamben calls the *homo sacer*, the victim of a blood sacrifice designed to purify the state. Having Tverdilo brought in wearing a draught collar and then having him torn apart by a frenzied crowd directly recalls the sacrificial image of the bull at the end of *Strike*. Eisenstein's critique is indirect because no other avenue of critique *in a censored film* was open to him. The last, un-filmed sequence also dared to imagine both the assassination of Stalin/Nevsky as well as the better days on the horizon *after* his passing. Stalin got the "joke," but made sure no one else would by canceling the scene. Both Eisenstein and his films are complex intersections of forces: aesthetic, political, ideological, as well as personal. Red baiting, leveled at socialist sympathies in contemporary, Western universities, can get on just as well without traducing Eisenstein or his films to service its agenda. The film remains an intersection of the old and the new, of East and West, coded in unexpected ways, politically, cinematically, as well as personally, allowing the film's Manichean allegory of national identities to embed a stubbornly personal ambivalence. "*Nevsky*'s self-conscious stylization," in Bordwell's view, offered an influential "option for the emerging genre of historical spectacle" (2005, 223). The remainder of this chapter touches on a number of films that exercise this option.

Aleksander Ford's *Krzyzacy*

Ford's *Krzyzacy: The Order of the Teutonic Knights* is one of the great treasures of movie medievalism and deserves to be better known outside of

Poland. Inside Poland it drew an audience of 30 million upon its release in 1960 and remains a beloved contribution to Polish national cinema. Ford adapted Henryk Sienkiewicz's Nobel Prize–winning (1905) novel for the screen, but he also adopted Eisenstein's strategies for a nationalist medievalism. The resulting film is a fascinating instance of adaptation where the *fabula* is provided by a novel and the *sjuzhet* by an imitation of an auteur's style. As in Eisenstein's film, *Krzyzacy* relies on binaries that are both stylistic and ontological. In Technicolor the color coding is if anything more extreme: Poles and Lithuanians are in living color, and the Teutonic Knights seem to exist in a separate movie shot in black and white. Yet the politics of Ford's film are anything but a simple replication of Eisenstein's nationalism. The occupation of the Polish kingdom by the Teutonic Order recalls not simply the Nazis, but also the rather tangled history of a modern Poland, which suffered from the Soviets as well as the Germans.

The Battle of Tannenberg (or Grunwald for the Poles) in 1410 was a larger and rather more decisive war than the one Nevsky fought on Lake Peipus in 1242. We remember that Chaucer's Knight crusaded "As wel in cristendom as in hethenesse" (I, 49), sat at the head of the table at Marienburg in "Pruce," and "reysed" in pagan Lithuania as well as in Orthodox "Rus." A few decades later the German forces at Tannenberg were still bolstered by seasonal crusading "guests" from France and England, even though Poland was not only part of "cristendom" but also distinctly *Roman* Catholic. This seeming contradiction is satirically belabored in the film in the person of the French knight de Loche, a guest of the Order fulfilling his vow to crusade against the pagans, who is troubled to find that his adversaries are not the "Saracens" he was led to expect, but rather fellow Roman Catholics.[31] The combined armies of the kingdom of Poland and the Grand Duchy of Lithuania inflicted an important though far from catastrophic defeat on the Prussian state of the Teutonic Order that halted the Order's imperial pretensions in the region and ultimately led to its demise.[32] The 200-year reign of the Teutonic Knights in Prussia was dealt a more decisive blow with the fall of the Marienburg fortress in 1457, though they fought on until the Order was secularized in 1525.[33] The twentieth century was to revisit the Battle of Tannenberg perhaps more intensely than any other medieval conflict. The German general Paul Hindenburg insisted that the 1914 defeat of the Russian empire also be dubbed the "Battle of Tannenberg," and German propaganda widely claimed this victory as revenge for the defeat of the Teutonic Knights half a millennium before.[34] A medievalizing election poster (1920) for the German National People's Party under the caption "Rettet den Osten" (Save the East) depicts a medieval Teutonic Knight being attacked by a Bolshevik and a contemporary Polish peasant.[35] The German monument constructed at Tannenberg in 1927 ultimately housed Hindenburg's remains, but it was demolished after World War II, and its stones were recycled for use in the "Grunwald Monument" fashioned thereafter to memorialize the medieval (1410) victory of the Poles. In the period of the German-Soviet Non-Aggression Pact (1939–1941) — the period that saw Eisenstein's *Alexander Nevsky* pulled from distribution — Germany and the Soviet Union invaded Poland. In the spring of 1940 the Soviet NKVD (later KGB) executed perhaps 21,000 Polish officers, intellectuals, priests, and boy scouts; a mass grave was discovered in forest near Katyn containing 5,000 victims, many posthumously clad in Polish uniforms.

Hence Aleksander Ford's imitation of Eisenstein's patriotic film is a less than sanguine acceptance of Soviet "influence" on Polish culture and sovereignty.[36] Indeed as a colonizing presence in Eastern Europe, Ford's Teutonic Knights often seem to foreshadow the contemporary USSR, the KGB in particular. Unlike the novel, Ford's film begins in a state of cold war, an uneasy truce between Poland and the Order, where "various bad things happen at the borders." Deliberately quoting Eisenstein's opening sequence, the beginning of *Krzyzacy* shows an occupying army on parade dragging prisoners of war in their train. The dauntless Jurgan of Spychow crosses their path, and a skirmish begins when one of the Knights lets fly a bolt from his crossbow. We never see the arrow find its mark: a jump cut shows a German survivor of the fight stumbling into a chapel of the Order where a few dozen Knights in white lie face down on the stone floor, silently embodying the Polish name for them, *Krzyzacy*. The claustrophobia and the formal staging certainly recall Eisenstein's closed style. The Knights jump to attention as the message that the whole Teutonic caravan has been slain spurs a Knight to ask the Master, Siegfried von Lowe, for permission to take vengeance. The Knight only gets three words out ("Father, Let us...") before another jump cut tracks a flame licking its way along a line of fuel set in a forest. We cut back to the chapel, where the growing blaze seems to be occurring in parallel with von Lowe's prayer.

As in Eisenstein there is an uncanny telepathy associated with the Knights where desires are transmuted immediately into action, collapsing time and space. The fire is scented first by the animals in the forest, and shots of frantic peasants are intercut with shots of fleeing animals. The film will go on to emphasize again and again the association of the Poles with the natural world. This sequence also introduces the blond love interest, Danusia, whose marriageable age is signified by the circle of maidens who dance around her in the forest. Her subsequent death in the film is only part of the larger Manichean struggle between the sterility of the celibate Knights and the natural regeneration connected to the survival of the Polish "race."[37] The Poles win this battle on the field, but more elementally in the survival against all odds of Danusia's suitor, Zbyszko, who is united finally with the dark-haired (Vasilisa-like) Jagienka at the end of the film.

The central figure in the "cold war" along the border is Jurand of Spychow, whose tragedy embodies the progressive closing of the world undertaken by the Teutonic Knights. The Knights kill his wife and kidnap his daughter, Danusia, holding her at the Teutonic castle in Ortelsburg where Jurand is summoned to recover her. His arrival at the brick fortress is a ritualized ordeal designed to divest this scourge of the Order of his humanity through an elaborately staged parody of contrition, confession and penance. A series of gallows marks the frontier of the Order, and Ortelsburg itself offers a concentric series of thresholds through which Jurgan must pass to regain his daughter.

The forced conversion of Jurand begins when he approaches a gate and sounds his horn in knightly fashion, expecting admittance. Kept waiting all day and into the night before the metal door, he is finally commanded to dismount, surrender all his weapons, exchange his armor for sackcloth, and wear his scabbard like a leash around his neck. Told to "humbly wait" until the gate is opened, Jurand spends the night in the snowy courtyard. Eventually a parade of flagellants issues from the gate behind him in an extended quotation of Ingmar Bergman's *Seventh Seal* (1957). It is the middle of the night and the nightmarish procession seems staged solely for Jurand's benefit as he kneels in the snow and crosses himself. Jurand is being initiated into the Teutonic form of Christianity through a sado-masochistic trial in which the Pole is forced "willingly" to play his part. The morning comes with Jurand lying facedown in the snow, having assumed the subservient posture of the Teutonic Knights we saw earlier. But his "conversion" is to that of domesticated animal. A guard kicks him awake, calls him a "dog," and leads him on his leash through a series of gates and doorways. When Jurand finally arrives for his audience with the Knights, he meets his apparent predecessor: a tame bear that is lead away on a leash. The council of the Knights is an elaborately staged and symmetrical scene that deliberately recalls the closed, theatrical *mise-en-scène* of Eisenstein's *Nevsky*, reinterpreted through the lens of *film noir*. A series of triangular brick arches accentuates the staging in depth, and low-key lighting makes the white uniforms of the Knights shine brightly, while Jurand stands before them as quite literally as a shadow of his former self. But these "Knights of the Virgin" orchestrate the most obscene of their parodies when they substitute a "half-wit" serving girl as the prize for Jurand's patience — a "mistake" later justified by the assurance that the Teutons never look closely at women. Ultimately Jurand is trapped like a bear in a net and confined to a prison cell of Chinese boxes, the smallest of which is a rigidly confining oubliette, shaped according to the model of Magritte's sitting coffins.

The Soviet NKVD and later KGB were fond of using such forms of eliciting "confessions" even though it was widely acknowledged that such tactics tended to produce false admissions — which was probably their purpose in the first place. Stress positions produce intense pain and disorientation by severely restricting movement and allow authorities to deny the use of torture.[38] Clearly the consignment of Jurgan to such a place of forgetting and the use of non-invasive forms of torture in the film are meant to recall Soviet practices — there is nothing like this in Sienkiewicz's novel.

However, with the death of the Master's adopted son, Rotiger, Jurgan's torture, which had effectively rendered him powerless, mute and blind, assumes a more terrifyingly literal form. As if in adherence to Matthew 5:28–9 and the strictures against slander (e.g., in Ezekiel), von Lowe has Jurand's right eye, right hand and tongue amputated, though like all torturers he proclaims Jurand's resistance a form of self-mutilation. Just as in Eisenstein the right hand becomes a fetishisized symbol of power and obedience when the Master places it as a totem in the casket of his defeated "son." The embedded placement of the duel between Rotiger and Zbyszko within the scenes of Jurgan's tortures suggests that torture is war by other means, exactly as Elaine Scarry maintains it always is. While certainly this form of what might be dubbed fetish warfare is thoroughly in keeping with the totemic fetishes of the Knights as portrayed in both Eisenstein and in Ford, we should not lose sight of the intimate connection of torture with religious paradigms of con-

Mechanical model shows a Teutonic Knight striking a Pole as the Knights lavishly entertain their Polish guests in *Krzyzacy*.

fession, penance, and conversion. As many critics have noted, there is a strange sameness about torture: strategies and tools used by the Inquisition are still employed throughout the world today. The persecuting society of the Middle Ages still dominated the officially agnostic world in which Ford himself lived, where heresy to a reigning ideology was punished by an enforced cycles of contrition, confession and penance. The tortures of Arab prisoners by the United States have also functioned in analogous ways: mockeries of Islamic doctrine and the deliberate violation of religious taboos suggest a benighted attempt at the forced "conversion" of prisoners. When Jurand finally returns home, he can only signal the identity of his torturers by crossing himself with his *left* hand, signifying "Krzyzacy:" the cross has been emptied of all meaning other than as a sign of criminality — not unlike the meaning of the American flag in many parts of the world today.

The film's most elaborate sequence occurs at a peace conference between the Poles and the Order at Marienburg, the capital of the Prussian state. The warrior monks throw quite a party, and Ford's signature use of extended, slow tracking shots from left to right takes in a seemingly endless array of excess. Acrobats and tumblers are everywhere, and tricks, sleights of hand, and mechanical models of Teutonic Knights furnish the endless but shallow *mise-en-scène*, itself a kind of parody of Da Vinci's "Last Supper." Dwarves on pulleys fly through the air to pour the wine as the Germans descend ever more deeply into their cups. Ford repeatedly deploys Hitchcock's famous device of obviously "hidden" cuts from *Rope* (1948) to string together a series of shots into an artificially constructed appearance of wholeness. Yet the quotation of this famous editing strategy is more than simple formalism. In Hitchcock's film the (intentionally poorly) hidden cuts call attention to the manufactured, staged nature of the reality being performed by two young men who have murdered their companion and then serve supper to his family and friends over the corpse, which they have neatly tucked away in a chest they employ as a buffet table. Ford's film suggests a similar relationship between a theatrically produced spectacle and the secret sadism that underlies it. Hitchcock's killers proclaim themselves Nietzschean supermen, and their banquet is a testament to that superiority. Ford's Teutonic *Übermenschen* likewise stage a banquet designed to showcase their superior culture and wealth. This shot, though, follows a glimpse into the basement beneath the hall where naked, "heretic dogs" slave on an assembly line, forging piles of weapons: diplomacy above, arms race below. By exposing the base of cruelty and repression which supports the impressive superstructure the Knights show to Poles, Ford rather archly calls to mind both the modern arms race as well as the false face of prosperity that the Soviet Union insisted upon showing to the outside world.

The climactic battle at Tannenberg is an extended homage to Eisenstein's battle on the ice of Lake Peipus, although the action sequences are filmed in a more realistic style. Here I would like again to focus on two particular elements: the structure of the battle as a whole and the final duel between the Order's Kuno Lichtenstein and Zbyszko's uncle, Macko. While there is much debate over how the actual battle unfolded, Ford's solution to the problem is thoroughly Eisensteinian: he relies upon a synecdoche whose imaginary power lures the Grand Master, Ulrich von Jungingen, into a catastrophic mistake. When the red banner of King Wladyslaw/Jagiello of Poland first falls to a small contingent of Germans, Jagiello himself is not there — many sources report that he directed the whole battle from a nearby hill, as indeed he does in the film. Like Eisenstein's Teutonic Knights, Ulrich's forces invest the fetish/flag with the powers of the signified; they absurdly disarm amidst the violence of battle and break into song to celebrate their "victory." Jagiello sends in three companies to recover the banner, which provokes Ulrich to commit all of his remaining cavalry — trampling their own infantry in the process — in the belief that the king is with the banner. The Knights charge down the hill in wedge formation, only to break up into a circle, flanking the Poles. Constructed here by stages is a series of concentric circles around the Polish King's banner, but of course the center itself is hollow since Jagiello himself remains on the distant hill — which Zizek would no doubt identify as a prime example of "the empty core of ideology." When Jagiello sends in his infantry, they in turn flank the encircled Knights. Here the cinematography directly employs Eisenstein's strategies. The Grand Master Ulrich von Jungingen appears trapped within an ever-tightening frame: we see him desperately hacking at invisible adversaries on all sides. Finally the "Poles" encircle him, and he is stuck from all sides by long pikes — the pikemen themselves never enter the shot. In the next shot the infantry, again in Eisensteinian fashion, gush forth in a wave of humanity that makes Ulrich disappear from the frame.

Ford's imitation combines the duel and the Battle on the Ice in a clever way. As the Teutonic Knights flee the field in the background, Macko and the Teuton Kuno meet to settle a private quarrel. The camera tracks their swordfight from left to right through a wood and onto a marshy bog. What had been a rather evenly matched contest goes quickly Macko's way because, though younger and slimmer, Kuno cannot keep his footing on the floating tufts of grass — in yet another example of a native landscape enlisting on the side of the good guys. Macko slams his shield, bearing the family device of the "blunt horseshoe," down onto the unbalanced German, who we are left to imagine sinks to his doom in the bog, though of course we never see his body sink, for that too takes place out of the shot. Ford returns to survey the field of carnage in an extended series of tracking shots from left to right, strung together as were the shots in Marienburg by "hidden" cuts. And in perhaps a final nod toward Eisenstein and Prokofiev's "vertical montage," kettledrums continue to sound the dirge even after the last in the line of Teutonic drummers falls dead. The corpses are left to litter the field while a host of German banners are piled at King Jagiello's feet in a final reduction of the power of the Teutonic Knights to their synecdoches. The last shot of the film is again a tracking shot, though this time from right to left, which expansively surveys the Polish landscape and reconnects the hero Zbyszko with the future of his country in the person of his bride-to-be Jagienka.

Frantisek Vlacil's *Valley of the Bees*

Though certainly less well known than *Nevsky* or even *Krzyzacy*, Vlacil's *Valley of the Bees* (1968) is arguably a better film than either of its predecessors. It is also a much smaller film which views the closed world of the Teutonic Knights from within, where the Knights are chiefly at war with themselves. Borders, self-denial, and a fear of nature in general and sexuality in particular define their lives. The story unfolds like a folk tale with its repetitions and parallels, yet these align under an abiding curse that pulls the diegesis inexorably toward Greek tragedy: *Virgin Spring* meets *Oedipus Rex*. As a boy Ondrej puckishly brings a gift to his (very) young stepmother's wedding, a basket filled with flower petals but lined with baby bats. The insult provokes his father to hurl him into a stone wall. When it appears Ondrej will die, his father promises to dedicate the boy to the Virgin should his life be spared. Ondrej is soon initiated into the Teutonic Order, but later as an adult he runs away after another monk, Rotigier, is executed for attempting

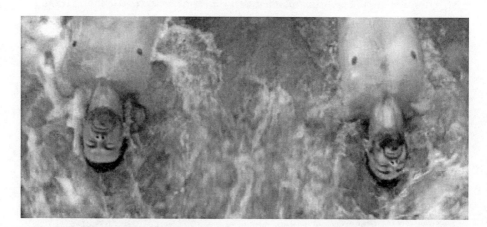

Armin (Jan Kacer) and Ondrej (Petr Cepek) chasten their wayward flesh on the cold shore of *Valley of the Bees*.

The phallic fishes in *Valley of the Bees*.

to escape the Order. Ondrej returns home and takes his dead father's place as the ruler of the small castle and as the lover and ultimately husband of his step "mother," Lenora. When his friend from the Order, Armin, arrives to take him back, Ondrej's refusal drives him mad with jealousy, and the misogyny everywhere apparent in the film reaches its seemingly fateful climax with Armin cutting the throat of the newly wed Lenora in her bridal chamber. Ondrej coldly avenges her death by loosing his hunting dogs on the Teutonic Knight. Yet strangely the last scene of the film shows Ondrej's return to the Order.

Such a bare paraphrase cannot do justice to this remarkable work but it is necessary because so few westerners have seen the film and it seldom appears even in extensive lists of medieval movies.[39] Vlacil's film in many ways was both the harbinger and the victim of the Soviet invasion of Czechoslovakia in 1968, where its devastating critique of colonialism and cultural repression cut too close to the bone for Soviet censors. In fact the film was widely thought to have foretold the Soviet backlash against the liberalization of the Czech and Slav Republics. Vlacil's Teutonic Knights live in the closed world that Eisenstein invented for them. Outdoors, repeated shots place them at shorelines or riverbanks; indoors, the tableau staging is a study in geometric foreclosures of space that pose natural light as a blinding sublime. The friends Ondrej and Armin begin their observance of Lent lying together on the beach where the freezing water of the sea crashes over their naked bodies:

> Armin: You'll feel a chill, then pain. Your lower body will be numbed, but your spirit will rise above your weakness and human wretchedness.
> Ondrej: Your hand feels as cold as if it were lifeless.
> Armin: Suffering is my way to God.

Later at their Lenten repast a long claustrophobic shot in deep focus shows the Knights lined up on either side of a long table, a lone, quite unappetizing fish on every metal plate. The shot construction poses the dead fish as penises, each lying lifeless and uncooked before the pelvises of the standing Knights. Armin's charity when he dumps his fish on Ondrej's plate is only one of many such gestures that hint at homosexuality, albeit one rigidly conscribed within regimes of self-denial and mortification of the flesh.

The trickster figure is the monk Rotgier who attempts to flee this Lenten mortification and return to his own lands. Ondrej finds him at the riverbank and Rotigier tempts the young man with the promise of wealth and a woman, suggesting they share Ondrej's horse in order to flee together. The suggestion of course is a broad parody of the Knights Templar emblem of poverty: two knights on a single horse. The river is seemingly the border between suffering and the earthly delights of physical pleasure; it is also the outermost limit of the Teutonic Knights' lands. Their side of the river is a sandy waste, but on the other side is a forbidden forest containing the stubborn remnants of paganism, which in the film's allegory perhaps represents the modern West. Paganism throughout is equated with the deadly mystery of sexuality. When Rotgier is finally caught, his expulsion from the Order includes an elaborate ceremony that deliberately recalls the staged symmetries of Ondrej's initiation as a Teutonic Knight. The formal staging is first shot from far above, the V-shaped pattern of the Knights doubled by a V-shaped sliver of light from above which separates Rotgier from his judges. In center in the dark is the renegade Rotgier, who watches chagrined as the Knights complete the ceremony of excommunication, blowing out and breaking their candles and turning their backs on him. A trap-door suddenly opens behind him, flooding the room with light, and Rotgier plunges into a courtyard several stories below where his corpse is mauled by a pack of dogs. This forced suicide of course damns the wayward brother's soul, but also absolves the Order from its own strictures against spilling the blood of a fellow Knight.

The lurid, noiresque pathologies of the film's final scenes at Ondrej's castle starkly pit heterosexual unions against homosocial bonds. Armin's fear and hatred of women is established in the middle of the film when a blind girl coyly asks what would happen if she touched him: "You would lose your hand." As a boy Ondrej brought his father's young wife a wedding gift was flowers and bats; Armin's wedding gift is the no less ill-fortuned one of sand from the Holy Land mixed with blood. As Lenora awaits her groom in the bedroom, slowly disrobing and anticipating the caresses of her new husband, Armin enters instead and opens her neck with a knife, splashing the bridal bed with blood. The eroticization of violence in the film is seemingly the product its no-way-out world, the only channel for passion this world of enforced homosocial misogyny leaves open to its postulates. Ondrej's revenge duplicates the Order's punishment of Rotgier, Armin also is fed to the dogs, but this uncanny repetition also seems to doom Ondrej too, rather than free him from the Order's influence. In the courtyard we watch Ondrej watching his friend being mauled as he himself slowly backs into the darkness. This fading into the black is itself a kind of suicidal resolution. When we next see him, he is back at the shoreline below the Order's castle, having returned, we imagine, to suffer a similar fate at the hands of the brothers. The cycle of repetition and return is made to seem inexorable. In many ways Ondrej's suicidal return to the Order is among the bleakest gestures in all of cinémedievalism because in coming full circle it makes the closing of the world complete. For Eisenstein and Ford the Teutonic Knights represent a pride that can be humbled and a threat that can be contained and overcome. Vlacil's Knights are no longer Nazi calques, but rather represent a contemporary Soviet Union where ideological control is much the equal of military compulsion. In Althusser's terms Ondrej is a subject who has been taught to "work by himself." The substance of this critique, however disguised in distant historical allegories, was quickly rendered moot. Vlacil's film was released in the Spring of 1968, a time when real if limited social change was finally coming to pass with the liberalization of restrictions on speech, the press, and travel. The Warsaw Pact countries — along with 2000 tanks — rolled into the newly federated Czech and Slav republics late that summer, as the Prague Spring was crushed.

Eisenstein's Manichean Medievalism under Globalization

Though many of the films discussed in the section are not explicitly about the Crusades, they do demonstrate the powerful influence and mutability of the *Nevsky* tradition in movie medievalism and fantasy. Perhaps the greatest film in the *Nevsky* tradition is in fact the work of a German director, Werner Hertzog, whose *Aguirre: The Wrath of God* (1972) translates the Eisensteinian binary of closed and open worlds to a Peruvian jungle, the immensity of which provokes delusions of grandeur among a contingent of Cortez's *conquistadores*. Delusions of grandeur quickly give way to paranoia as the Spanish journey ever deeper into the heart of darkness.[40] Hertzog's contribution to the *Nevsky* tradition begins just as we would expect, with a slave caravan winding its way through a forbidding landscape. Yet nothing except the landscape impedes their progress: they never encounter anything like the human boundary such colonizing forces meet in *Nevsky* or *Krzyzacy*, only a war of (grindingly slow) attrition. Hertzog gives us the attenuation of a crusading ethos in a new world without (apparent) borders, quite literally too large for European imaginations. In a brilliant re-interpretation of Eisenstein's closed, cut-out world, the Spanish contingent on their raft grow ever more detached from space and time and ultimately from reality. The raft is repeatedly filmed as a staged tableau, its occupants unmoving and impassive. They die one by one as the raft floats down river toward El Dorado, yet neither we nor they ever see whence the arrows protruding from their bodies have come. Hertzog's jungle is Eisenstein's "nonindifferent nature" with a vengeance, and just as in *Nevsky* and *Krzyzacy* the outside-the-frame is the anthropomorphized space of overwhelming natural forces. *Aguirre* is still very much a crusade film, and if its allegories reach forward to Vietnam, they still fundamentally depend upon the closed world of Eisenstein's proto–Nazis. In the immensity of the Peruvian forest, Aguirre's microcosm quickly assumes a bunker mentality where real and imagined conspiracies take their ineluctable toll. The last to survive, Aguirre stubbornly clings to a non-existent future where he and his nation of monkeys "will stage history as others stage plays." Aguirre's shrunken world is itself that stage, the fetish/frame that Barthes identified in the Eisensteinian theatrical *mise-en-scène*. His floating utopia stages with some precision the disastrous course of National Socialism.

With George Lucas' *Star Wars* saga (beg. 1977), the *Nevsky* tradition enters fully into the new configurations of Cold War Manichaeism, as historical analogy itself becomes pure fetish, disseminated across a fantasy space that freely generalizes mythic and cinematic quotation. Lucas revives the historical propaganda film within a very different climate. A globalizing fantasy pulls us away from national identities—and sovereignties—to imagine a world without borders where dark and light forces contend for universal supremacy as well as the souls of particular human beings. Citations of Eisenstein have become common currency in popular culture, so there is no need to detail them here. The "tank helmets" and the child-sized Storm Troopers dressed all in white refer with palpable nostalgia to the Manichean clarities of Eisenstein's vision. Yet these futuristic medieval Nazis, who inhabit the fantasy space of another galaxy existing "long ago and far away," collapse the nationalisms inherent in the *Nevsky* tradition completely. The Soviet empire is foreshadowed in the terms in which Eisenstein had cast the Nazis, as the successors of the Teutonic Knights. And the resistance to world domination is cast from another hallmark in the *Nevsky* tradition, Kurosawa's *Seven Samurai* (1954), such that the Japanese, foes of the Western axis powers in World War II, become the template for the spiritualized knighthood of Jedi samurai in a strange new world where the Japanese are allies of the West.

At the same studio (Twentieth Century–Fox), at the same time, and with similar designs on the essentialization of Eisenstein's nationalism, Ralph Bakshi turned out the animated masterpiece *Wizards* (1977). The post-apocalyp-

The rotoscoped Teutonic Knights in Ralph Bakshi's *Wizards*.

tic battle between good and evil, elves and mutants is a Tolkienian fantasy made for adults in which the elves' most daunting foe is cinematic archive itself. In both Lucas and Bakshi we see the wedding of Tolkienian fantasy to Eisensteinian style. The evil wizard Blackwolf turns the all-powerful eye of the movie projector against the innocent inhabitants of Montagar, reincarnating rotoscoped Teutonic Knights from Eisenstein's film who ride across the sky like clouds in a storm front. Eisenstein's sinister organist has a rotoscope cameo, as do the Bishop, the Teutonic Master, and the horn-blower who join forces with silhouettes of other baddies from *El Cid* and *Zulu* to attack the elves to the accompaniment of Prokofievian screeching pipes and horns. The rotoscoping goes beyond mere citation in order to stage something like a return of the repressed. The final battle for the most part pits these black silhouettes against cartoon elves, the animated battle occurring in front of a screen on which play back-projected images from *Alexander Nevsky* and other wars. As the tide begins to turn in favor of the elfish army, Blackwolf switches reels, projecting Leni Riefenstahl's Hitler from *Triumph of the Will* as well as the Luftwaffe and panzer divisions rotoscoped from *Battle of the Bulge*—a horror with which the elves simply cannot reckon. Only the destruction of the movie projector, like the ring of Sauron in Tolkien, can oversome this strangely disabling fear. With this "death of the cinema" the shadow creatures are frozen, and they fade away once "Hitler was dead again." For Bakshi the cinema archive is a kind of Mordor, a reservoir of fear where an evil magician splicing together medieval and modern Germans, Africans and Saracens creates mutant images. The archive phantasmizes the past, providing the backdrop against which present conflict takes place. Through the prosthetic memory of film the past threatens the future in a turn increasingly characteristic of American fantasy, collapsing all historical and national boundaries. Genuinely a product of the Cold War, *Wizards* presents the post-apocalyptic future as George Lucas saw the futuristic past and Ronald Reagan the film-mediated present, as an eternal, elemental struggle between evil and good empires. Bakshi's film pits Tolkien against Eisenstein, just as his contending magicians closely resemble a hobbit and Ivan the Terrible. Nationalist Manichaeism is subsumed within a global Manichean vision in which Eisenstein's film — as well as the Soviet Union, whose synecdoche it has become — has gone over to the dark side.

Peter Jackson's *Lord of the Rings* trilogy (2001–3) represents in many ways the culmination of this fantasy globalization of Eisenstein's stylistic binary. Certainly there is little space here to do justice to these splendid films. We must content ourselves instead with noting some of the ways in which Eisenstein's visual stylistics offered the filmmakers strategies for rendering Tolkien's Manichean world in strikingly visual terms. Obviously Eisenstein's "nonindifferent nature" is in many ways comparable to Tolkien's more intricate supernaturalism. Both "epics" grow out of an awareness of the disastrous toll mechanized warfare takes not only on human life, but also on the environment that supports it. In self-defense natural features of the landscape are animated (in both senses of the term) and infuse human allies with their resilience and chthonic influence. Recall the internal wipes in Eisenstein's film where peasant armies undulate over a hilly topography to overwhelm Teutonic Knights. In Jackson's version of the river episode in *Fellowship of the Ring* (2001), the flood morphs into a stampede of Magritte-like water stallions as it tramples down the ring-wraiths and washes them from the frame.[41] In the prologue the excision of Sauron's ring finger has the same disproportionate effect as does the castration of the Grand Master's bull horn: the giant warrior falls to the ground and sets off an apparent chain reaction that reduces his whole army to dust in the wind. Remember too Olga's words at the end of the Battle on the Ice: "There are no more Germans. They were spread to the four winds or sunk beneath the ice." When the ring is finally destroyed in the cracks of Mt. Doom, Sauron's artificially created armies again disappear in another broad allusion to Eisenstein, when a seeing-eye earthquake carefully traces fault lines around the Orcs and the earth collapses beneath their feet.

The most recent, most obviously post 9/11 contributions to the *Nevsky* tradition, *King Arthur* and *Pathfinder*, are especially revealing in their re-projection of this fantasy synthesis of the *Nevsky* tradition back onto a putatively historical screen. *King Arthur* leverages advances in the genetic mapping of the British Isles to pose the Battle of Badon Hill as the survival of a national identity coded in the DNA of the native Picts. The proto–Nazis here are Dark Age Saxons, led by Cerdic, who, like the Teutonic Master in Eisenstein's film, pursues a deliberate strategy of genocide against every "man, woman, or child" and executes one of his own soldiers for attempting miscegenation. "We don't mix with these people. What would that yield? Weak people, half people." Fuqua's film counters traditional Anglo-Saxonism with a British gene pool that was and remains distinctly "Woad," bolstered by seven Sarmatian knights who borrow their strategy from Kurosawa's samurai and their battle cry of "Rus!" from Eisenstein's Russians. But of course this attempt to invert the genetic fantasies of Nazi racism yields less a counter-narrative of national identity than the same dangerous concoction of race and nation: a Britain whose native Celtic stock adheres primarily in its female line, impervious to Germanic incursions.

The most elaborate set piece in Fuqua's film is his extended recreation of Eisenstein's Battle on the Ice, a scene I have discussed in detail elsewhere (Haydock 177–8). Here it suffices to remark that Fuqua not only takes a page from Eisenstein's production notes, seeding a summer valley with fake snow and filming tighter shots in studio water tanks, but he also if anything intensifies the supernatural pathos of the natives and their landscape. Eisenstein's Teutonic Knights plunge through the ice because their enormous cavalry is heavier; Fuqua's pedestrian Saxons are targeted by a miraculous crack that beats a beeline for their position and then explodes into dozens of fragments, a crack supposedly initiated by Dagonet chopping a hole in the ice fifty yards away! Marcus Nispel's *Pathfinder* (2007) pits Native Americans against a genocidal troop of Vikings who are also defeated by a nonindifferent Nature which first plunges many beneath the ice and then finishes off the remainder with an avalanche of snow called down upon them by a Viking foundling left behind on an earlier raid. The boy grows up among the Indians to become the eponymous pathfinder who ultimately employs his knowledge of the landscape to lead the Viking raiders to their doom.

Obviously the *Nevsky* tradition is alive and well in contemporary movie medievalism, but its mutation and survival through the Cold War and into the post–9/11 world poses questions that beg to be addressed. The kind of cultural work performed by the films of Eisenstein and Aleksander Ford was straightforward. Those films trace national identity from medieval battles fought against the Teutonic Knights and show in the Northern Crusades a distinct if distant mirror of contemporary conflicts. The fantasy projections of Cold War films like the first Star Wars trilogy, *Wizards*, and to some degree the recent films made from Tolkien's novel all participate in a war-of-the-worlds mentality in which specific historical analogies and national identities give way to a fully essentialized Manichaeism. In *King Arthur* and *Pathfinder* this generalization of the German menace fills the gap in the other hollowed out by political correctness. Indigenous populations (Picts and Native Americans) take the opposing place in the Manichean binary. Are these multiform proto–Teutonic Nazis (second-century Saxons and eleventh-century Danes) simply evidence of a post-historical, post-political Middle Ages, where historical analogy has been reified, cut off from all relevance to the present world, where analogy becomes a fetish, quoting, as it were, earlier historical analogies between Germanic peoples and the Nazis in a kind of self-consciously vicarious thrill, akin to Steven Spielberg's stylizations of 1940s adventure serials in *Raiders of the Lost Arc*? To some extent the answer is yes. The influence of Spielberg and Lucas is palpable in these supposedly historical films. Yet, whatever their pretensions to historical accuracy or possibility, and whatever their adherence to fantasy and action-adventure prototypes, the imaginary Germans of these films embody a threat from the East that political correctness since 9/11 has left largely unsubjectified. If we need a medieval threat from the East, bent on conquest and genocide, to embody an orientalist fear then what better stand-in for the "Saracen" than the proto–Nazi? In many pre–9/11 films set in modern times Arabs and Germans are interchangeable parts and can often be seen working in concert to terrorize "the West." The analogical vacuum produced by the terrorist attacks on 9/11 was initially filled by comparisons to Pearl Harbor, but an emerging analogue for the terrorists has become the Nazis and their "Absolute Evil." If the Crusades in popular imagination offer unflattering parallels to the contemporary clash of civilizations where the West was both the chief aggressor as well as the loser (e.g., *Kingdom of Heaven*), then simply *re-orient* the Germans as the embodiment of a perdurable Eastern menace and cast Britain and the United States not as fundamentally Anglo-Saxon peoples, but rather as indigenous cultures whose resistance comes to embody an enduring, vital separateness. There could be no more ironic example of what Slavoj Zizek calls "the empty core of ideology" where indigenous populations come to stand in for the "enduring freedom" beloved by those nations whose birth was the all but wholesale annihilation of those cultures now posed as their spiritual core.

Postscript

Though first to depart for the Third Crusade, the Holy Roman Emperor Frederick Barbarossa was among the last to arrive. On June 10, 1190, Barbarossa attempted to lead the German Crusade across the Saleph River. Either thrown from his horse into the river or trying to swim across in his armor or simply bathing to cool himself, Frederick was overcome by the cold water and by what some chroniclers identify as a whirlpool.[42] The German Crusade was effectively halted and never reached the Holy Land in strength, though Frederick's son did eventually bury his father's boiled bones in Acre. Saladin reportedly saw the accident as a divine deliverance. Certainly he was fortunate in not having to face the combined English, French, and German forces headed by the indomitable Barbarossa. In July of 1941 the Germans launched an invasion along almost the whole of the Eastern Front, covering an axis of some 1800 miles, which would ultimately become the largest and most disastrous theater of war in human history. The codename for this mission was "Operation Barbarossa." Indeed, given the Nazi penchant for myth-making, it could scarcely have been called anything else. Barbarossa's forces made up the first Order of the Teutonic Knights, and it was their mission of civilization against the "Slavic hordes" that the Nazis saw themselves repeating and fulfilling. But in Barbarossa's tragedy, his unfulfilled promise, there was always a strong element of bathos: that fatal tumble into the drink. The tradition begun by Eisenstein's film poses the Teutonic Knights as heirs to a rather bathetic repetition compulsion, a pride that continues to send the Germans out upon thin ice in film after film. But do not these almost hysterical repetitions in the fantasy history of recent American cinema betray a certain fascination with repetition itself? And don't these recent turns on Eisenstein's old Manichean strategies in the shadow of 9/11 suggest a growing ambivalence, an uncertainty about how history will view our role in the world? American troops are finding deserts every bit as "nonindifferent" as they once found rice paddies. Does our renewed fascination with Eisenstein's medieval Nazis, along with our nostalgia for the Manichean certainties of the Second World War, also suggest a certain growing unease with the other in ourselves, with our be(k)nighted missions of forced conversion, with our sense of glory and good will recklessly squandered? That is to say: does not the very recurrence of these medieval Nazis in seeking to confirm our Manichean view of the world threaten to render evil less absolute and the analogy itself more portable? By such means, I would argue, recent popular films trade on inferences they dare not assert.

Notes

1. The notion of a series of films that serves as an episodic historical narrative is a hallmark of Eisenstein's early conceptualization of cinema. Both *Strike* and *Battleship Potemkin* were originally to serve as entries in a seven part series.

2. The Kino Video reconstruction of the film (2001) excerpts this running shot description from an early autograph treatment that Eisenstein sent to his financial backer, Upton Sinclair. The treatment was published in *Film Sense* (251–55).

3. The fanciful use of *ius prima noctis* as an incitement to popular revolt is also prominent in a number of later medieval films such as *The War Lord* (dir. Franklin J. Schaffner 1965)

and Mel Gibson's *Braveheart* (1995). It is useful to compare the montage strategy, which Eisenstein outlines here but never edited, with the intellectual montage of *Strike* and *October*. The former emphasizes "typage" through the juxtaposition of human types and their animal counterparts, while the latter includes an extended montage sequence of deities from around the world. The notable difference between these two earlier films and *Que Viva Mexico!* is the almost complete lack in the Mexican film of the bald and bold satire that characterizes Eisenstein's earlier use of intellectual montage.

4. Contemporary battles over the meaning and applicability of medieval Crusades to contemporary interventions in the Persian Gulf have revived the Crusades as contested ground in a war of medievalizing propaganda. See Holsinger, Haydock (2008, 134–64), and Arthur Lindley (in Ramey and Pugh 15–30).

5. See Anne Nesbet's conclusion about the role of the Mexican adventure in Eisenstein's evolution: "Mexico was not just Eisenstein's psyche spread out horizontally, but could also serve as a kind of "exterior unconscious" for Soviet history as well" (151).

6. On the death's head ring (*Totenkopkbände*) and Himmler's medievalism see Höhne (149–154) and especially Lumsden (142–70), who calls the *Totenkopf* "the one emblem that endured throughout the history of the organization and became firmly associated with it" (142). This symbolism is wittily invoked in the climax of Steven Spielberg's *Indiana Jones and the Raiders of the Lost Arc*, where the fury unleashed by the opening of the Arc of the Covenant quickly incinerates the flesh of the SS officers and reduces them to literal death heads.

7. According to Hermann Rauschning, Hitler conceived of the SS in these terms in 1934. Hitler goes on to interpret Wagner's *Parsifal* as a quest for pure blood that would cure the corrupted blood of the sick king (Rauschning 227). For a recent discussion of Nazi Grail lore and its sources, see Barber (314–17). As Christopher Tyerman remarks, Hitler demanded Memel be a part of the Third Reich in March of 1939 on the justification that the Teutonic Order had settled it in 1252: "No part of historic Prussia was to be outside Greater Germany" (689).

8. See Noël Carroll's (2003, 281–302) careful dismantling of Kracauer's "medium specific argument" for photography as the essence of the cinematic in its capacity to express "the unstaged, the fortuitous, the indeterminate and endlessness" (283). Carroll rightly traces the source of such arguments to Lessing and rigorously refutes the premises upon which it is based. While Carroll's critique of Kracauer's film theory is certainly fair play, it fails to address the cultural and historical context in which this theory was conceived, as well as its influence. Kracauer's valorization of material reality over fantasy and costume drama cannot be separated from his experience of German cinema between the wars. In any event, Eisenstein's warring styles in *Alexander Nevsky* do suggest the embeddedness of film "ontologies" within nationalisms and ideologies.

9. Folded arms as a sign of resolution and resistance was first employed by Eisenstein in *Strike* (1925). Three workers superimposed over turning wheels fold their arms and the wheels stop, signaling the beginning of the strike.

10. Like the woman in *Potemkin* he is positioned at the bottom of a flight of stairs. And although the interval is extended, the carnage he has seen has forever affected his view of the world — a particularly literal example of the kind of effect the young Eisenstein hoped to produce by subjecting the Kino eye to a series of shocks that would alter the audience's perceptions.

11. A textbook example of "vertical montage" occurs here where changes in the rhythm of sound precede or lag behind changes in the image, which Eisenstein insisted was more aesthetically effective than cutting directly on tonal or rhythmic changes. See the essay "Synchronization of the Senses" in Eisenstein's *Film Sense* (69–112).

12. See Richard Taylor's cogent discussion of the film, and of this scene in particular, as "atrocity propaganda" (85–98). Originally this scene was to have been followed by one depicting a fight on Novgorod Bridge between opposing factions. According to Viktor Shklovsky the scene was dropped because Eisenstein's assistants, eager to comply with Stalin's request to screen the film, neglected to include the reel Eisenstein (asleep at the editing table) was in the process of cutting. Once the film received an enthusiastic thumbs up from Stalin himself, no one dared add the missing footage, which subsequently disappeared (qtd. in Eisenstein 1984, p. 107; missing scene screenplay, pp. 70–2). See my discussion of Timor Bekmambekov's re-imagination of this footage in the recent *Nightwatch* (2004) in Haydock (2008, 188–94).

13. The winking Archbishop clearly hints at the supposed conspiracy of the Vatican and

the Nazis. The medievalism and authoritarianism of Pius XI and Pius XII — so called "Hitler's Pope"—certainly did find common cause with the National Socialists' anti–Bolshevism. What the Church found useful in the Nazi movement was its stance against modernism, secularism, nationalism, and particularly popular revolutions such as that of the Soviets that threatened unity and order. Eisenstein's Archbishop calls for one ruler of the world, Rome, and his call would certainly have been chilling for a Soviet audience who feared a re-emergence of a medieval super-state. The *Reichkonkordat* between Germany and the Vatican was agreed in July 1933, the first treaty with foreign power signed by the Third Reich. A good recent account is James Carroll's *Constantine's Sword* (475–546). Carroll is unwilling to see the Church's sins as solely those of omission, concluding: "No. Nazism, by tapping into a deep, ever-fresh reservoir of Christian hatred of Jews, was able to make an accomplice of the Catholic Church in history's worst crime, even though, by then, it was the last thing the Church wanted to be" (476). A fuller sifting of the evidence, particularly that from newly opened Vatican archives, is Gerhard Besier's *The Holy See* and *Hitler's Germany*.

14. Indeed the close shot connected to a wavy line of "pilgrims" anticipates the famous shot in *Ivan the Terrible* where a line of suppliants in the distance echoes the curve of Ivan's profile.

15. As Bordwell (221) notes, this shot like others in the Pskov sequence is punctuated by Prokofiev's score. Indeed the "audiovisual montage" in this shot as well as those of the archbishop and Pavsha raising their heads to stare at their enemies suggests a kind of synaesthesia whereby we "hear" the defiance or menace of the gaze.

16. This failure of transcendence in the shadow of the church and under the watchful eye of an angel of stone was significantly quoted in the opening scene of Andrei Tarkovsky's *Andrei Rublev* (1966). For Tarkovsky the Eisenstein shot becomes an ironic image of Soviet art's failure to rise above the harsh censorship within which it was made. See Andrew Barratt, "In the Name of the Father: The Eisenstein Connection in Films by Tarkovsky and Askoldov " (in LaValley and Scherr, eds., (148–160) and Haydock (46–53).

17. Of course the Teutonic Order had very strict requirements about heraldic devices and beards — the latter were required and the former were confined to a single black cross (see Desmond Seward, *The Monks of War*, 107–8). Yet Eisenstein's design for the helmets and crests is drawn directly from medieval manuscript illuminations of the Teutonic Knights. The bull horn helmet of the Master comes from a thirteenth-century representation, the pot or bucket helmets are featured in a number of contemporary artworks, and the griffin claw crest is featured in the famous illustration from *Chansonnier Manesse* (see Urban 178–9).

18. The whole manuscript has been digitalized and is available at http://digi.ub.uni-heidelberg.de/diglit/cpg848/.

19. Certainly my discussion of fetishism emphasizes the Freudian meaning of the term as opposed to Marx's notion of "commodity fetishism"—as indeed does Eisenstein's film. Yet I find Laura Mulvey's attempts to unite these two notions of fetish through a focus on the denial of knowledge in favor of belief an intriguing formulation. Given the montage of the gods in *October*, I suspect Eisenstein would have likely agreed as well. See Mulvey, *Fetishism and Curiosity*, 1–18.

20. The Nazi salute talisman perhaps alludes directly to the opening parade in Leni Riefenstahl's *Triumph of the Will* (1935), where Hitler's own truncated salute is delivered with bent arm next to his head. Riefenstahl presents a number of close shots of Hitler's hand.

21. Kracauer's *From Caligari to Hitler* (93) suggests: "This Fate — conditioned story materializes through scenes which seem to be staged after decorative paintings from some by-gone era." Kracauer goes on to connect the ornamental *mise-en-scéne* of Lang's film with Nazi arrangements of public spectacles as mass ornament. Eisenstein had his first lessons in cutting film under the tutelage of Ester Shub in March 1924, as she reduced the two parts of Fritz Lang's *Dr. Mabuse, The Gambler* (1922) to a single film for domestic distribution in London. Eisenstein cut his editing teeth on a project that made readily apparent the differences between German and Soviet film cultures. On Eisenstein's work with Shab see Bergan (89) and Bulgakowa (45). In 1926 Eisenstein and his cameraman Eduard Tisse visited Lang's set for *Metropolis*. Eisenstein was soon planning a parodic retort that he called *The Glass House* (never filmed, see Bulgakowa, 63). Indeed Eisenstein's early career can be seen at least partially as an attempt to define his own cinema in contrast to Lang's successful UFA pictures.

22. Aberth (76–9; 107–22) and Urban (91–108) have succinct discussions comparing the film with the historical battle. For a fuller account of the Northern Crusades, see Christiansen.

23. The womb is common metaphor for montage in Eisenstein generally. See Rosemund Bartlett's intriguing discussion of the circle and line as significant shapes in Eisenstein's theory and films (ed. LaValley and Scherr, 65–76).

24. Quint (362) compares Vasilisa to "Virgil's Camilla, Ariosto's Bradamante and Tasso's Clorinda" and notes that "Eisenstein dramatized the worst psychic nightmares of the fascist enemy, who, as Klaus Theweleit has shown, characterized the Red Menace as an uncontrolled flood, closely identified with 'flowing non-subjugated women'" (363).

25. While he doesn't discuss *Alexander Nevsky* in any detail, Al LaValley's chapter "Maintaining, Blurring and Transcending Gender Lines in Eisenstein" offers a cogent introduction to the question (in LaValley and Scherr, 52–64).

26. Nina Tumarkin thoughtfully compares Nevsky's speech, "Arise O Russia," with the Soviet World War II hymn, "Sacred Battle:" "Rise Up, vast country/ Rise up to mortal battle/ With the Dark fascist power,/ With the accursed hoard./ Let noble rage/ Boil up like a wave!/ A people's war is going on,/ A sacred war./ As two opposite poles,/ So we differ from them./ We fight for light and peace, They — for the kingdom of darkness" (qtd. in Tumarkin 62). Barry P. Scherr notes that "the film's most successful scenes focus not on Alexander, but rather on the Russian masses, on shots of the earth and sky, and on aspects of Russian spirituality" (in LaValley and Scherr, 222).

27. Eisenstein's great precursor in this use of a nonindifferent nature is V. I. Pudovkin's *Storm over Asia* (1928), the culminating scene of which depicts the supposed descendent of Genghis Kahn leading a rebellion against British imperial forces in 1918 Mongolia. The modern British army is flattened by a storm blowing from the direction of the Mongol cavalry charge, constructed as a resurgence of "ancient strength." Pudovkin's use of the closing exhortation, which seems to come from the mouth of the central character as well as the director himself, is also the model for the patriotic exhortation at the end of Eisenstein's film.

28. In fact it is useful to compare Eisenstein's discussion of the war in heaven in Milton's *Paradise Lost* (as a "shooting script") with the montage of battle formations in *Nevsky*. Compare Eisenstein's quotation of the "Approach of the Host of Satan" with the shots depicting the Teutonic army in *Nevsky*: "Farr in th' Horizon to the North apeer'd/ From skirt to skirt a fierie Region, stretcht/ In battalious aspect, and nearer view/ Bristl'd with upright beams innumerable/ Of rigid Spears..." (Bk. VI, lines 79–83). And compare his quotation of Milton's description of the "Heavenly Host" with the shots of the Russian host: "with them rose/ A Forrest huge of Spears: and thronging Helms/ Appear'd, and serried Shields in thick array/ Of depth immeasurable" (Bk. I, lines 546–49; qtd. in Eisenstein 1970, 59). The difference between Milton's "innumerable" and his "immeasurable" is roughly the difference between staging in depth with and without the use of deep focus.

29. As a point of comparison with Eisenstein's use of crowds and mass action, note Kracauer's description of German cinema after the First World War in *From Caligari to Hitler*: "The mass scene typical of the Lubitsch films decomposed the crowd to exhibit as its nucleus "one single figure" who, after the crowd's dissolution, was left alone in the void. Thus the individual appeared as a forlorn creature in a world threatened by mass domination. Paralleling the stereotyped plot of all those pageants, this pictorial device treated the pathetic solitude of the individual with a sympathy which implied aversion to the plebian mass and fear of its dangerous power. It was a device that testified to the anti-democratic inclinations of the moment" (55).

30. This landmark as a sign of natural and national resistance to colonization is also borrowed from V. I. Pudovkin's *Storm over Asia*. In Pudovkin's motif the rock is topped by a tree, whose stubborn flourishing represents the stubborn quality of resistance and links it to natural growth.

31. The Order manipulated the belief that the Lithuanians were Saracens in order to attract Europeans to their seasonal *reisen*. As Eric Christiansen points out, "The contrast between the way the war was fought and the way the Order justified it became increasingly apparent after 1386, and by 1409 was one of the strongest weapons in the hands of Witold and Wladyslaw" (1/6). As Tyerman notes, after the conversion of Lithuania in 1386 "the *raison d'être* of the crusades and, some argued, of the Teutonic Knights' rule in Prussia and Livonia itself was called into question" (709).

32. French and English guest-crusaders stopped coming soon after Tannenberg with resumption of hostilities in the Hundred Years War. All foreign crusading in the region ceased after 1423 in the aftermath of the Council of Constance (1414–18). As Tyerman cleverly remarks, "It was difficult to persuade onlookers to regard Tannenberg as a Hattin-like defeat for Christendom, not least because it was not" (710).

33. For a cogent history of the Order from 1409–1525 and what he aptly calls "the withering of the crusade," see Christiansen (227–58). Tyerman points out that the Church abandoned the crusades in the Baltic "not necessarily because it was bad business, but because it had degenerated into at best a sham and at worst a lie" (721).

34. See Todd Kontje's chapter "The Nearest East" in *German Orientalisms* (177–224) and his discussion of "German prejudice against the Asiatic Slaves" and "Northern Saracens," i.e. the Poles.

35. See the reproduction of the poster in Turnbull (86).

36. Aberth notes that Ford fled to the Soviet Union upon the Nazi invasion in 1939 but ultimately turned his back upon Soviet Realism in favor of a "pre–Communist, native national history" (123) in a period when Poland was strengthening its independence from Moscow.

37. The Order's Grand Master, Conrad von Jungingen, was held as a martyr by his followers when he died, refusing to engage in therapeutic intercourse with a woman, which his doctor ordered as a cure for gallstones. See Christiansen (227).

38. These Soviet techniques became a crucial part of U.S. training in the program SERE (Survival, Evasion, Resistance, and Escape), which taught those likely to fall into enemy hands how to survive their ordeals, but ironically the tactics have recently been recycled as a guide to "noninvasive" methods of torture in the questioning of prisoners at Abu Ghraib and Guantánamo Bay.

39. Kevin Harty's superb encyclopedia *The Reel Middle Ages: Films about Medieval Europe* has no entry for this film nor does Paul Halsall's website "Medieval History in the Movies" at http://www.fordham.edu/halsall/medfilms.html. Facets Video released a DVD of the film in 2006.

40. Aguirre's signature phrase ("I am the wrath of God, who's with me?") perversely and revealingly translates the presumptions inherent in *"Deus hoc wult!"*

41. Though Jackson was initially reluctant to admit it, the river morphing into horses appears in Ralph Bakshi in his 1978 animated film *The Lord of the Rings* (and also in Tolkien).

42. The most plausible account and the one given in the Old French Continuation of William of Tyre reads: "The emperor set off to cross the river following the two knights and with a large number of people in front and behind. When he came to the middle, the horse on which he was sitting stumbled and he fell into the water. As a result of the heat that he had endured and of the coldness of the water into which he fell, he lost his strength and could do nothing to help himself. The veins of his body opened, and he drowned. His men were scattered around and were not able to do anything to save their lord" (Edbury 88).

BIBLIOGRAPHY

Aberth, John. *A Knight at the Movies: Medieval History on Film.* New York: Routledge, 2003.

Agamben, Georgio. *Homo Sacer: Sovereign Power and the Bare Life.* Palo Alto, CA: Stanford University Press, 1998.

Bakhtin, M. M. *Rabelais and His World.* Trans. Helene Iswolsky. Bloomington: Indiana University Press, 1984.

Barber, Richard. *The Holy Grail: Imagination and Belief.* Cambridge: Harvard University Press, 2004.

Bergin, Ronald. *Sergei Eisenstein: A Life in Conflict.* Woodstock, NY: The Overlook Press, 1997.

Bordwell, David. *The Cinema of Eisenstein, With a New Preface by the Author.* New York: Routledge, 2005.

———. *On the History of Film Style*. Cambridge: Harvard UP, 1997.
Braudy, Leo. *The World in a Frame: What We See in Films*. Chicago: University of Chicago Press, 1976.
Besier, Gerhard. *The Holy See and Hitler's Germany*. Trans. W. R. Ward. New York: Palgrave Macmillan, 2007.
Bulgakowa, Oksana. *Sergei Eisenstein: A Biography*. 1998. Trans. Anne Dwyer. San Francisco: Potemkin Press, 2001.
Carroll, James. *Constantine's Sword: The Church and the Jews*. New York: Houghton Mifflin, 2002.
Carroll, Noël. *Engaging the Moving Image*. New Haven: Yale University Press, 2003.
Christiansen, Eric. *The Northern Crusades*. New York: Penguin Books, 1997.
Deleuze, Gilles. *Cinema 1: The Movement-Image*. Trans. Hugh Tomlinson and Barbara Habberjam. Minneapolis: University of Minnesota Press, 1986.
———. *Cinema 2: The Time-Image*. Trans. Hugh Tomlinson and Robert Galeta. Minneapolis: University of Minnesota Press, 1989.
Edbury, Peter W. *The Conquest of Jerusalem and the Third Crusade: Sources in Translation*. Burlington, VT: Ashgate, 1998.
Eisenstein, Sergei. *The Film Sense*. Trans. Jay Leyda. New York: Harcourt Brace, 1970.
———. *Nonindifferent Nature*. Trans. Herbert Marshall. Cambridge: Cambridge UP, 1987.
———. *Two Films: October and Alexander Nevsky*. Ed. Jay Leyda, Trans. Diana Matias. New York: Lorrimer Publishing, 1984.
Freud, Sigmund. "Fetishism." *The Norton Anthology of Theory and Criticism*. Vincent B. Leitch, gen. ed. New York: Norton, 2001: 952–56.
Goodwin, James. *Eisenstein, Cinema, and History*. Urbana: University of Illinois Press, 1993.
Harty, Kevin. *The Reel Middle Ages: American, Western and Eastern European, Middle Eastern and Asian Films about the Middle Ages*. Jefferson, NC: McFarland, 1999.
Haydock, Nickolas. *Movie Medievalism: The Imaginary Middle Ages*. Jefferson, NC: McFarland, 2008.
Höhne, Heinz. *The Order of Death's Head: The Story of Hitler's SS*. New York: Penguin, 2000.
Holsinger, Bruce. *Neomedievalism, Neoconservatism, and the War on Terror*. Chicago: Prickly Press, 2007.
Kallis, A., ed. *Fascism Reader*. New York: Routledge, 2003.
Kontje, Todd. *German Orientalisms*. Ann Arbor: University of Michigan Press, 2004.
Kracauer, Siegfried. *From Caligari to Hitler: A Psychological History of the German Cinema*. 1947. Rev. ed. Princeton: Princeton University Press, 2004.
———. *Theory of Film: The Redemption of Physical Reality*. London: Oxford University Press, 1960.
Lavalley, Al and Barry P. Scherr, Eds. *Eisenstein at 100: Reconsideration*. New Brunswick, NJ: Rutgers UP, 2001.
Lumsden, Robin. *Himmler's Black Order: A History of the SS*. Gloucestershire, UK: Sutton Publishing, 1997.
Mulvey, Laura. *Fetishism and Curiosity*. Bloomington: Indiana University Press, 1996.
Nesbet, Anne. *Savage Junctures: Sergei Eisenstein and the Shape of Thinking*. 2003. New York: I. B. Tauris, 2007.
Quint, David. *Epic and Empire: Politics and Generic Form from Virgil to Milton*. Princeton: Princeton University Press 1993.
Ramey, Lynn and Tison Pugh, eds. *Race, Class, and Gender in 'Medieval' Cinema*. New York: Palgrave Macmillan, 2007.
Rosen, Philip, ed. *Narrative, Apparatus, Ideology: A Film Theory Reader*. New York: Columbia University Press, 1986.
Rauschning, Hermann. *Hitler Speaks: A Series of Political Conversations with Adolph Hitler on his Real Aims*. 1940. Whitefish, MT: Kessinger Publishing, 2006.

Scarry, Elaine. *The Body in Pain: The Making and Unmaking of the World.* Oxford: Oxford University Press, 1985.
Seward, Desmond. *The Monks of War: The Military Religious Orders.* 1970. New York: Penguin Books, 1995.
Sienkiewicz, Henryk. *The Teutonic Knights.* 1901. New York: Hippocrene Books, 1993.
Taylor, Richard. *Film Propaganda: Soviet Russia and Nazi Germany.* 2nd ed. London: Tauris, 1998.
Tumarkin, Nina. *The Living and the Dead: The Rise and Fall of the Cult of World War II in Russia.* New York: Basic Books, 1994.
Turnbull, Steven. *Tannenberg 1410: A Disaster for the Teutonic Knights.* New York: Osprey, 2003.
Tyerman, Christopher. *God's War: A New History of the Crusades.* Cambridge: Harvard University Press, 2006.
Urban, William. *The Teutonic Knights: A Military History.* London: Greenhill Books, 2003.
Zizek, Slavoj. *Looking Awry: An Introduction to Jacques Lacan through Popular Culture.* Cambridge, MA: MIT Press, 1991.

Filmography

Aguirre: The Wrath of God, dir. Werner Hertzog, 1972.
Alexander Nevsky, dir. Sergei Eisenstein, 1938.
Andrei Rublev, dir. Andrei Tarkovsky, 1969.
Battle of the Bulge, dir. Ken Annakin, 1965.
Battleship Potemkin, dir. Sergei Eisenstein, 1925.
Bezhin Meadow, dir. Sergei Eisenstein, destroyed by Soviet officials, 31 minutes from beginning and end of the film remain.
Birth of a Nation, dir. D. W. Griffith, 1915.
Braveheart, dir. Mel Gibson, 1995.
The Da Vinci Code, dir. Ron Howard, 2006.
Destiny, dir. Youseff Chahine, 1997.
Dr. Mabuse, The Gambler, dir. Fritz Lang, 1922.
El Cid, dir. Anthony Mann, 1961.
Flowers of St. Francis, The, dir. Roberto Rossellini, 1950.
General Line, The, alt. title, *Old and New,* dir. Sergei Eisenstein, 1929.
Ivan the Terrible, Part I, dir. Sergei Eisenstein, 1944.
Ivan the Terrible, Part II, dir. Sergei Eisenstein finished 1945, released, 1958.
Jaws, dir. Steven Spielberg, 1975.
Kagemusha, dir. Akira Kurosawa, 1980.
King Arthur, dir. Antoine Fuqua, 2004.
Kingdom of Heaven, dir. Ridley Scott, 2005.
Krzyzacy: The Order of the Teutonic Knights, dir. Aleksander Ford, 1960.
Lord of the Rings, dir. Ralph Bakshi, 1978.
Lord of the Rings: The Fellowship of the Ring, dir. Peter Jackson, 2001.
Lord of the Rings: The Two Towers, dir. Peter Jackson, 2002.
Lord of the Rings: The Return of the King, dir. Peter Jackson, 2003.
Metropolis, dir. Fritz Lang, 1927.
Nibelungen, Die, dir. Fritz Lang, 1924.
October, dir. Sergei Eisenstein, 1928.
Passion of Beatrice, The, dir. Bertrand Tavernier, 1987.
Passion of Joan of Arc, The, dir. Carl Theodore Dreyer, 1928.
Pathfinder, dir. Marcus Nispel, 2007.

Que Viva Mexico!, dir. Sergei Eisenstein, not completed, released, 1979.
Raiders of the Lost Arc, dir. Steven Spielberg, 1981.
Rope, dir. Alfred Hitchcock, 1948.
Sansho the Bailiff, dir. Kenji Mizoguchi, 1954.
Seven Samurai, dir. Akira Kurosawa, 1954.
Seventh Seal, dir. Ingmar Bergman, 1957.
Star Wars, dir. George Lucas, 1977.
Star Wars: The Empire Strikes Back, dir. George Lucas, 1980.
Star Wars: Return of the Jedi, dir. George Lucas, 1983.
Storm over Asia, dir. Vesevolod Pudovkin, 1928.
Strike, dir. Sergei Eisenstein, 1925.
Triumph of the Will, dir. Leni Riefenstahl, 1935.
Valley of the Bees, alt. title *Údolí Vcel*, dir. Frantisek Vlacil, 1968.
The War Lord, dir. Franklin J. Schaffner, 1965.
Wizards, dir. Ralph Bakshi, 1977.
Zulu, dir. Cy Endfield, 1964.

3. Now Starring in the Third Crusade

Depictions of Richard I and Saladin in Films and Television Series[1]

LORRAINE KOCHANSKE STOCK

As Adam Knobler argues, various post-medieval political/cultural regimes on both sides of the Atlantic evoked or appropriated the tropes, characters, and ideals of the medieval European Crusades, using these holy wars' imagery and ideology as a highly "portable memory of history."[2] Crusading ideology thus became a translatable cultural *lingua franca* employed to justify or further a variety of political and cultural agendas, including the justification of subsequent wars, whether religiously motivated or not. Knobler posits three aspects of Crusades lore — two positive and one negative — that inspired and promoted this nineteenth and twentieth-century *translatio studii*. The Crusades provided: 1. an originary "collective past" that helped to define developing symbols of European nationhood; 2. specific "heroes" of the Crusades, charismatic individuals "to whom nations, states, or political factions could point and who would provide such a rallying point for political and social action"; 3. "a negative image of the past about which the West should be ashamed" (Knobler 294). This last point was a backlash against nineteenth and twentieth-century imperialism, whereby crusading tropes were used "to indict current political circumstances directed against the Islamic world by Europeans" and (in the post–9/11 climate) by Americans. In this view of the Crusades, Western imperialism was constructed as "the direct linear descendent of medieval crusading against Islam," exemplified notoriously in September, 2001, when George W. Bush defined America's declared "war on terrorism" as a "crusade," an equivalence he later retracted because of the medieval Crusades' religious implications (Knobler 323).

In the same way that later historical figures, regimes, and ideologies tapped into the collective memory of the Crusades for assorted agendas, twentieth and twenty-first-century American and international filmmakers also reinterpreted the medieval Crusades as "distant mirrors"[3] of not only medieval history/myth, but also political events and especially wars waged contemporaneous with or just previous to production of their respective films or television series. These examples of what Nickolas Haydock dubs "movie medievalism" also registered for their immediate audiences current issues of sexuality, gender construction, orientalism, and various racial, religious, and misogynist "othering" that were less relevant to the medieval period that the films purported to represent than they were to morés developing throughout the century in which cinema became a major cultural force, and the emerging television medium even more "portably" delivered these constructions of past and present "history" into the homes of even larger audiences. My present purpose is twofold: to suggest the richness of the cinematic Crusades corpus, including sub-topics of "medieval cinema" (Ramey and Pugh) not typically labeled "the Crusades"; and to focus explicitly on Knobler's second trope of Crusading memory, the *heroes* who became rallying points around which were assembled political and cultural constructions of the Crusades as "distant mirrors" of events (especially wars) and issues in the cinematic age.

When Hollywood and international filmmakers create feature films or television series about the medieval European Crusades, they most often focus their cameras on the Third Crusade (1189–92), a strategy inspired by the charismatic pairing of well-matched antagonists, both constructed as "Warriors of God" (Reston) whom medieval chroniclers and modern historiographers have made into the "stars" of that holy war, England's King Richard I (nicknamed "the Lionheart") and the Muslim Saladin, Sultan of Egypt and Syria (Aberth 70). Not surprisingly, cinematic interpretations of these two compelling, almost mythic figures have varied widely, reflecting the contemporaneous political developments of the decades in which they were produced and the cultural expectations of the particular audiences for whom these educating entertainments were created. Moreover, films and television created after the mid-twentieth century participated in Knobler's third trope, the backlash-inspired enterprise of re-inventing the Muslim antagonists of the Christian Crusaders into more "politically correct" figures, thus neutralizing the "othering" effect of earlier "orientalism" (Said). I selectively survey (in greater or lesser detail) both iconic and less familiar films and television series that treat either Richard I, or Saladin, or the interaction of both heroes, concentrating, where possible, on scenes that provide fruitful intra-film evaluations.

The Robin Hood Legend as a Source for Crusades Cinema

Inventories of cinematic Crusades materials often overlook the myriad film and television treatments of the Robin Hood legend.[4] Late-medieval ballads about the yeoman "Robyn Hode" neither situate the hero in a particular century nor consistently specify the English king's reign during which he became a forester-outlaw.[5] Nevertheless, the popular image of Robin Hood became firmly associated with the Third Crusade in Sir Walter Scott's 1819 novel *Ivanhoe*, set in the twelfth-century reign of Richard I, whose extended Plantagenet family, Prince John and Queen Mother Eleanor of Aquitaine, became fixtures in the cinematic Robin Hood canon.[6] Although *Ivanhoe* takes neither Richard I nor Robin Hood physically to the Third Crusade, King Richard who, disguised as the "Black Knight," collaborates with Robin, Friar Tuck, and the Merry Men in the plot of *Ivanhoe*, became firmly identified as *the* Western hero of the Third Crusade, effectively the quintessential European crusader. Whether by "halo effect" or "guilt by association," the movies' Robin Hood too became connected with the Third Crusade. Most films or television series about the outlaw either place Robin *at* the Crusade or relate his post–Crusade adventures upon his returning to England and finding himself forcibly disinherited from his patrimony. Despite his financial and chivalric demotion, the Earl of Huntingdon (in some versions Locksley) remains a loyal subject of the absent King Richard, thwarting the plots against the crown by Richard's enemies, his usurping brother Prince John, the Sheriff of Nottingham, and Guy of Gisborne. Although in Robin Hood films Saladin is rarely named explicitly as the antagonist against whom the English army fights, Richard is usually an influential, if offstage presence, effectively the invisible "elephant in the room." It has become almost a cliché to have the cinematic Richard I make a brief obligatory appearance upon returning from Jerusalem or from imprisonment by Duke Leopold V of Austria, if only to pardon Robin and endorse his loyal comrade's marriage to the royal ward Marian at film's end.[7]

Douglas Fairbanks' 1922 *Robin Hood*: The Third Crusade as a Distant Mirror of World War I

Despite Richard's relegation to a walk-on role in many Robin Hood films, he plays a major part in Douglas Fairbanks' 1922 *Robin Hood*, one of the first popular culture vehicles to transport the twelfth-century English monarch and the gentrified Saxon outlaw-hero to the Third Crusade. This early film's depiction of Richard offers a baseline against which later characterizations may be compared. Despite its usual categorization as a "Robin Hood" movie, this silent film is almost as much about Richard's campaign in the medieval holy war as about Robin's expected benevolent activities on behalf of downtrodden Saxons.

Early on, after the Earl of Huntingdon wins a tournament against Sir Guy of Gisbourne, the last joust to be held before going to war, Richard promotes the victor to be "our second in command" in the impending "Holy Crusade," much to the chagrin of nefarious brother John and thug-like Sir Guy. Crusades tropes abound in the film, which devotes several scenes to the imminently departing troops whose "brave hearts ... smile through parting tears" as they bid farewell to courtly ladies, whose "eyes speak courage to their knights." Soon "o'er the kneeling hosts [of soldiers] the Bishop lifts his hand in benediction" as "for the cross that gleams upon his shoulder, each knight breathes a silent vow." Such pre-war blessings bestowed on imminent Crusaders are repeated in later films, especially Cecil B. DeMille's 1935 *The Crusades*, which presents Philip of France on the altar steps in a cathedral — his elaborate ermine-trimmed robes, signifying his royal position, fanning out around his kneeling body receiving the bishop's sanction of his participation in the Crusade.

In Dwan's film, costumed equally magnificently in their Crusader attire, Richard and Huntingdon depart the castle, followed by Richard's enormous army, about whom the caption announces: "And so the very flower of England's knighthood marched to its *high purpose*." Written by Fairbanks under the pseudonym Elton Thomas, these captions' language, evoking "olde merrie England," echo the diction of Scott's nineteenth-century romantic medievalism. Exceeding the customary romanticism of movie medievalism, the monumental scale and visual splendor of the *mise-en-scène* of Richard's 90-foot high, $250,000 castle set[8] as well as thousands of extras employed to convey the grandiose scope of Richard's army were lavish by silent film or even contemporary cinematic standards.[9]

However, such over-the-top visual effects represented more than "bread and circus" entertainment for the film's early audience. In 1920s America the sustained camera shot of the marching to Palestine of multitudes of "soldiers of Christ"— medieval pennons aflutter and white crusader crosses proudly displayed — visually evoked newspaper photos and newsreels of the mobilization of over sixty million European and American troops to another recently idealized but ultimately disillusioning conflict, the "Great War" of World War I, which had been propagandized as fulfilling a similar "high purpose." The First Crusade, intended permanently to regain the Holy Land from Muslim occupation for the safety of European Christian pilgrims, was supposed to be the last war necessary to attain that goal. Clearly for Dwan's audience the

Third Crusade resonated with the recent "War to End All Wars." Ironically the hindsight of history ruefully demonstrates how a medieval "War to End All Wars" did not deliver as promised. Arguably the many subsequent medieval Crusades succeeding the original one preached by Pope Urban II in 1095 have a place on a trajectory of wars leading ultimately to the current Iraq War.

Yet *Robin Hood* also offers a hopeful message: although the recent World War had been humanly and materially catastrophic, recapturing the glories of the past was still possible. In this sense the film's medievalism both reflected the past through a "glass darkly" mirror and proffered a "rosy-lensed" prophecy of the present's recuperation of the medieval Golden Age.[10] The film's initial expository captions, surrounding the establishing shots of medieval castle ruins, lament:

> So fleet the works of men
> Back to their earth again
> Ancient and holy things
> Fade like a dream...

Subsequent shots of the battered castle are explained: "Stately castles whose turrets pierced the sky have left imperishable record.... Though the storms of centuries have laid waste the works of men [,] their spirit soars on and poets make live again the days of chivalry." As each film frame of a ruined castle appears onscreen, mists (of time?) accumulate progressively until the final frame reveals a stately castle refurbished to its former, glorious medieval intactness. Does the film's romanticized medievalism promise the audience a similar renovation — that fields of red poppies will organically (and thus cosmetically) restore the battlefields of Flanders that so recently were scarred with trenches, corpses, and the exploded remnants of downed airplanes?

As the English troops journey toward Palestine, Richard approvingly remarks that Huntingdon is "the very backbone of the adventure," optimistically spurring the soldiers to march despite suffering "fevers" (Huntingdon calls them "passing ills") en route to battle. When Huntingdon receives a message from Marian reporting Prince John's perfidy in Richard's absence — exorbitant taxation, physical oppression, and executions of the king's loyal subjects[11] — he decides that if Richard knew, he would return to England to redress the injustice, with the result that "this Holy Crusade would fail." Huntingdon instead himself seeks Richard's permission to return, deferring his own promised attainment of the "Kingdom of Heaven" as a reward for fighting in the Crusade, a patriotic/spiritual sacrifice he makes to set England politically to rights. Misinterpreting his refusal to declare the purpose of his return — Richard assumes that desire for Marian motivates Huntingdon — the king impugns his second-in-command's loyalty and valor: "You! Turned chicken-hearted for a wench!" Upon Huntingdon's attempt effectively to go AWOL, Guy reports his desertion, demanding his execution for treason, reflecting the relatively high incidence of desertions by shell-shocked soldiers during World War I, for which the official punishment was execution. Richard instead orders Huntingdon incarcerated while he and the army progress to the Holy Land. Huntingdon and his squire escape and return to England, assuming the identity of Robin Hood and Little John, at which point, in most Robin Hood movies, the plot segues into the outlaw's career in Sherwood and Nottingham.

However, the next caption explains: "In far-off Palestine, Richard meets with victory and concludes a truce with the infidel," followed by a shot of Richard reviewing a parade of European troops victoriously riding horses through a vaguely oriental-looking, onion-domed city gate, followed by a company of turbaned "infidels"—perhaps prisoners of war—on foot. The next sequence establishes Huntingdon, now Robin Hood, forming his gang and wreaking havoc upon Prince John's tyranny in England, followed by further shots of Richard in Palestine. The film's plotline thus arcs back and forth from the typical Robin Hood outlaw narrative to the parallel plot of the Crusade. Perhaps more than any other Robin Hood movie, Dwan's *Robin Hood* equates in importance the Third Crusade plot with Robin's transformation from aristocrat to outlaw, which more usually develops *after* he returns from crusading.

Back in Palestine, to the soundtrack's ominous strains, Sir Guy attempts an unsuccessful assassination of the king in his tent, mistakenly stabbing Richard's fool, who always tried to "play the king" whether in Richard's chair or bed. Finding the corpse of his jester, Richard recognizes the knife as Gisbourne's. For the film's audience this nearly successful attempt on Richard's life would resonate with the successful assassination of Archduke Ferdinand that instigated the "Great War," concluded merely four years before. Next, in typically exaggerated silent movie body language, a messenger from England mimes the treacherous depredations of John back home, as Wallace Beery darkly glowers Richard's response. Hearing of the counter-insurgence of a "robber knight" named Robin Hood, Richard's gloom turns to joy as he intuits that Huntingdon loyally represents his interests after all, whereupon Richard returns to England to join Robin Hood in Sherwood, disguised as a "mysterious stranger." The masquerading king engages in another traditional Robin Hood film convention, a quarterstaff fight with Friar Tuck who, impressed with the outsider's valor, says, "With such strength — thou almost makst me think thou are Richard himself."[12]

The rest of the film delivers the usual Robin Hood plot points. Prince John captures Robin; lecherous Guy threatens Marian's virtue; the Merry

Men, accompanied by the mysterious stranger and his troops, storm the castle. Just as the arrows of John's executioners are about to pierce through Robin's chest, a shield bearing the Plantagenet triple couchant lions, placed there by a now-revealed Richard Lionheart, preserves Robin's life. Seizing John by the scruff of the neck, Richard physically others his sibling by depositing him outside the castle drawbridge, restoring order into his kingdom. He apologizes to Robin and the scene cuts to the wedding night of Huntingdon and Marian, another standard ending of Robin Hood movies, here handled provocatively.

Despite the film's romanticized and religious rhetoric — an expository caption sets the film in "Mediaeval ... England in the Age of *Faith*" and Prince John's desire to succeed Richard is identified as "unholy"— Wallace Beery, billed in the credits as "the *Lion-Hearted*," portrays Richard as a physically robust "man's man," given more to fleshly pleasures than to religious devotion. In nearly every scene of the film in which he appears, Beery is shown eating with gusto — a capon leg at the tournament, a roast peacock at the feast, a coconut (crushed in his hand) in his tent in Palestine, an apple while he reviews his troops' parade after the truce — and he is often presiding over a table laden with food, whether at home or at war. The caption identifying his character at the tournament characterizes him as "immortal, impulsive, generous and brave." Despite the fact that he earned his "lionheart" epithet as an adolescent for his skill as a military leader, the movie provides Richard with fewer opportunities to demonstrate bravery — he displays strength in Sherwood against Tuck, not in Palestine against Saladin — than an impulsive, irascible personality. A king often criticized by historians for spending a mere six months of his entire reign in England, Richard in this film does not wear the crown comfortably; at the tournament he removes it from his head, seemingly in weary irritation.

Rather, in its presentation of the king, *Robin Hood* illustrates the traditional and ongoing historiographical uncertainty about Richard's sexuality, revealing the uneasy continuum of relations between Richard I and Huntingdon, in scenes suggestive of the historical/mythical construction of Richard I as a homosexual.[13] Homosocial relations between Richard and his "favorite," the Earl of Huntingdon, verge perilously on the homoerotic as Beery's vigorous and perhaps excessively hearty Richard's gestures to Huntingdon after the tournament and at the feast — slapping and patting his body — seem *too* "hands on." Richard's presumption that Huntingdon's request for leave is motivated by desire for "the wench" suggests peevish jealousy. Moreover, Richard betrays latent insecurity about Huntingdon's new romantic attachment to Marian, with whom the Earl shared his final moments before departure for the Holy Land. Mobilizing his army, Richard summons his "second in command" by shouting "HUNTINGDON!"—an exclamation that he repeats significantly at the film's end. Ultimately, Dwan even destabilizes the hetero-normative convention of the king bestowing his blessing on Robin and Marian's marriage. The very last frames of *Robin Hood* display Richard I frantically pounding on the huge doors of Robin and Marian's wedding-night chamber—again shouting "Huntingdon!"—indefinitely delaying their marriage's physical consummation in the world of this film (see Stock and Gregory-Abbott).

Fairbanks' silent blockbuster *Robin Hood* was truly foundational. It inaugurated the cinematic construction of the charismatic figure of Richard I in a mainstream Hollywood vehicle. Its depiction of the Third Crusade as a speculum of the recent World War set a precedent for subsequent Crusades films. In the remaining discussion, I survey, in briefer compass, various branches of this film's cinematic family tree.

Richard I and Saladin Between the World Wars

Thirteen years after Dwan's *Robin Hood* first presented a cinematic Richard I to an international audience, Cecil B. De Mille's blockbuster "talkie" *The Crusades* paired Richard with his charismatic Third Crusade foil, Saladin. The screenplay by Harold Lamb, based on his own two-volume history of the Crusades,[14] still owes much to Scott's Crusades fiction, especially *The Talisman*. DeMille's epic creates an improbable, if entertaining, erotic triangle between the crusading Richard I (Henry Wilcoxen), his infatuated bride of convenience Berengaria of Navarre (Loretta Young), and his military antagonist-romantic rival, Saladin (Ian Keith). In byzantine plot twists Saladin saves Berengaria's life—she attempts suicide by exposing herself to Saracen arrows for the Crusade's and England's sake—and, after curing her arrow wound, he inveigles her into joining his harem. Throughout the film, Berengaria is often little more than a commodity, like her father's cattle and fodder, mutually traded "between men"—from father to royal husband, and then from husband to military foe/lover.[15] The fantasy of Saladin's otherwise implausible romantic desire for a European, blonde, Christian woman has some tenuous historical foundation in the negotiations for a proposed marriage between Saladin's brother al-Adil and Richard's widowed sister, Joan of Sicily.[16] The *mise-en-scène* in the shots of Saladin and Berengaria in his seraglio-like pavilion resemble illustrations from nineteenth-century translations of *The Arabian Nights*.

Adding another layer of sex/gender complication, *The Crusades* continues the tradition of Richard's ambiguous sexuality suggested in *Robin Hood*.[17] The blatantly irreligious Richard uses the Crusade as an excuse to avoid a dreaded marriage to Alice, sister of Philip Augustus of France. Alice, played by sultry Katherine DeMille (the director's daughter) as a hard-boiled *film noir* heroine transported to the Middle Ages, underscores Richard's palpable reluctance to marry her when she archly observes to the indignant Philip, "He's not an *ardent* suitor, *is* he brother?" Marriage to Berengaria is initially even less welcome, for Richard sends his sword, delivered by his jester-like minstrel Blondel, to represent him at their wedding ceremony, to Berengaria's humiliation and disappointment. Although DeMille later purports that Richard desires her, his ardor may be fueled more by her stubborn rejections of him from her bed than by love. Medieval chroniclers accused Richard of rape in the Holy Land and in Aquitaine, though the reliability of these sources is not airtight (see Gillingham). In the scenes between Richard and Berengaria in her tent, her fearful reluctance to allow her serving woman to leave her company (at Richard's insistence) and her invoking the protection of the thick bedposts of her four-poster — named for the Evangelists, Matthew, Mark, Luke, and John — signal her fear that Richard intends to claim, against her will, his conjugal right to her body as her husband, effectively raping her.

Richard I (Henry Wilcoxen), Berengaria (Loretta Young) and Saladin (Ian Keith) share water in Cecil B. DeMille's *The Crusades*.

Before Richard has a chance to make good on this threat, he is called to deal with an attack on the Crusaders' camp, preventing the consummation, whether voluntary or forced. Despite his late conversion and reluctant prayer to God to possess Berengaria at the close of the film, their marriage still remains unconsummated, mirroring the historical marriage engineered for Richard by his mother, Eleanor, which appeared to be one of political convenience, the spouses spending almost no time together.

Despite DeMille's protestation that he intended to portray the Muslim antagonists of the Franks as highly cultivated, not barbaric, throughout the film Demille orientalizes Saladin. This process begins with his gaudy entrance, which seems to deliberately invert the shot in Dwan's *Robin Hood* of Richard observing the triumphant English knights riding through the onion-domed gate of an Eastern city followed by walking oriental-costumed Saracens. In his revision of this scene, DeMille introduces Saladin riding a magnificent white Arabian stallion, preceded by a parade of drum-beating turbaned "Turks," the Eastern equivalent of Richard's horn-blaring heralds, and protected by black-skinned, bare-chested, scimitar-wielding Nubian guards dressed only in wide, metal-studded, leather sashes over skimpy leopard-skin loincloths. Saladin's own costume signs visually deliver to the audience the famed splendor of the Orient: flowing robes of luxury fabrics embroidered in precious metals, silken sashes horizontally criss-crossing an "X" on his chest, gilt and jeweled crescent pendants on his sash and turban, which is topped by a gold minaret-like spike. His troops are similarly if less richly garbed. Compared to the western crusaders — uniformed in utilitarian chain mail hauberks emblazoned with vertical crosses signifying their crusader identity on their tabards — the "Saracen" army and Saladin himself appear exotically feminized.

Saladin next appears on the ramparts of Acre, glowering down at the Crusaders' herald, who demands surrender of the city; Saladin responds by shooting the messenger with an arrow. Here his turban's minaret is flanked by twin golden crescents, forming horns, a costume sign that silently telegraphs his deviltry to the film's Western Christian audience. Saladin's next appearance is at the council of European kings to negotiate a truce, where he arrives on his white charger, again heralded by rhythmically-beating drums, wearing sumptuous fur-trimmed garments, a crescent-adorned breastplate, and a helmet — evoking "Egyptian Pharaoh" — topped by sabers and another crescent. He is announced as "Saladin the conqueror, Sultan of Islam," boasting, "There is room in Asia to bury all of you." When Richard commits the blunder of offering wine to "the infidel," Saladin politely reminds him, "We of the *true faith* drink no wine." Richard demands "A goblet of water for the King of the infidels." When Saladin's emir warns that the water may be poisoned, Richard's new bride Berengaria volunteers to taste Saladin's water, thus smoothing over her husband's diplomatic gaffe. Earlier she had observed, "They told me [Saladin] had *horns* like the *devil*. I think he's magnificent." As she departs the tent, Saladin's mutual attraction to her is obvious.

In his next appearance Saladin is disguised in Christian armor to pass undetected through Acre's gates to mobilize his army against the Europeans, a reversal of the usual "Richard disguised" motif in Robin Hood films. Acting on his infatuation with Berengaria, as he finds her wounded by one of his own men (who mistook her for a soldier because she too was "disguised" in Crusader garb in the "no man's land" between the camps), he abducts her to his Jerusalem palace, whose orientalized *mise-en-scène* suggests the luxury of Persian manuscript miniatures. There, fulfilling the movies' persistent association of the East with advancements in medicine, he cures her wound, professes his courtly love for her, and strikes a bargain: she must ransom herself (and her love) to him to spare Richard's life. If Saladin has been transformed from Oriental other to courteous lover, Richard has undergone a similar makeover, from unbelieving religious skeptic to hopeful convert, praying to regain his wife.

For all its typically DeMille, over-the-top spectacle, combining European military chivalry and Eastern exoticism, the film also employs medieval events to reflect America's post–World War I mood of isolationism and neutrality. Near the end of the film in a meeting between Saladin, Berengaria, and Richard in Saladin's tent, as a traditional peace-weaving bride, Berengaria performs the role of a "medieval League of Nations"; among the three characters, the word *peace* is articulated nearly a dozen times in the scene (Aberth 90–91). In their early cinematic representations of the "stars" of the Third Crusade, Dwan's and DeMille's films establish the stereotypes of Richard and Saladin that subsequent films would repeat and respond to during the rest of the century. The remainder of this essay outlines these developments.

The Cinematic Crusades and World War II

In mid-century a Robin Hood film, a popular television series, and a feature film based on Sir Walter Scott's novel *The Talisman* used the Crusades as a "distant mirror" of the recent Second World War and the Korean War. Walt Disney's 1952 *The Story of Robin Hood and His Merrie Men* and the mid–1950s television series *The Adventures of Robin Hood* used the Third Crusade to reflect changing gender roles resulting from the recent war, with interesting depictions of Prince John, the Queen Mother Eleanor of Aquitaine, and the monarch Richard, who is notably absent at the Crusade. As played by Joan Rice in *Story* and Bernadette O'Farrell in *Adventures*, the formerly "distressed damsel" Marian from Dwan's *Robin Hood* is now almost unrecognizable, depicted as a capable, almost tomboyish, cross-dressing equal to the Merry Men, out-shooting and out-scheming the male outlaws, even rescuing Robin from the distress of the Sheriff's prison instead of vice versa. It is as if Rosie the Riveter has time-traveled back to Sherwood Forest. For her part, in both vehicles a mature Eleanor, played by Martita Hunt in *Story* and Jill Esmond in *Adventures*, is shown actively running the kingdom in Richard's absence, collecting funds for his ransom from Austria, and consulting with the Archbishop of Canterbury and Chancellor William Longchamp about thwarting John's attempts to gain illegal control of Richard's crown. These 50s Robin Hood film projects mark the first cinematic appearance of Eleanor of Aquitaine. The Queen Mother's prominence in both vehicles surely reflects the iconic role of *Eleanor* Roosevelt in America during World War II. Both female characters in the mid-century cinematic Robin Hood legend reflected the expanding roles of British and American women during World War II (Stock and Gregory-Abbott 205–07). *Adventures* devoted at least two entire episodes to the motif of Richard's return to England in disguise, a theme explored earlier in Dwan's *Robin Hood*.[18] Saladin remains a distant, off-screen threat.

However, both Richard and Saladin were paired again in *King Richard and the Crusaders,* the 1954 Technicolor Hollywood film directed by David Butler, an outright adaptation of Sir Walter Scott's *The Talisman*. This historical romp further exaggerates Saladin's orientalism and use of disguise, extends his identification with healing by having the Muslim leader masquerade as Saladin's personal physician tending to the wounded Richard I, and repeats the motif of Saladin's being enamored of a western Christian woman — all reflecting Scott's nineteenth-century medievalism more than medieval chronicle. When he surreptitiously treats Richard's injuries with the "talisman" of Scott's title, Saladin, portrayed by blue-eyed Rex Harrison in brown face paint, becomes smitten with Richard's fictitious Euro-blonde cousin, Lady Edith Plantagenet, played by Virginia Mayo, whose buxom form is packaged in costumes with built-in 1950s bras looking like twin ice cream cones.

Instead of the handsome, vigorous Henry Wilcoxen of DeMille's 1935 film, a gray-haired, avuncular George Sanders plays Richard, a return to Wallace Beery's mature monarch from *Robin Hood,* perhaps reflecting recent mature national leaders on both sides of the Atlantic, Winston Churchill and Dwight Eisenhower. To be sure, Berengaria accompanies Richard to the Holy Land, but Sanders seems to appreciate her even less than Wilcoxen did Loretta Young in *The Crusades*. When she enters his sick-tent, Richard grumpily says of his simpering queen, "Who is that wailing she-cat?" and seems relieved when she proposes that she and Edith make a pilgrimage for Richard's recovery. This Richard has a healthy (and mutually felt) respect for his Muslim adversary. They chivalrously agree upon a truce until Richard's recovery, after which the entire Crusade's outcome will be determined by single combat between Richard and Saladin, a dramatic, if historically unlikely conceit.[19]

In this 50s film there is less othering of the Muslim antagonist than of the Scotsman Kenneth (played by Lawrence Harvey). Victim of the traditional medieval stereotyping of the inhabitants of Celtic border countries like Wales and Scotland as Wild Men and barbarians, Kenneth the Leopard-Knight from Scotland, whom Richard thinks too ignoble to marry his Plantagenet cousin Edith (they are already sweethearts), is the real other to the "self" of England, not the noble and courtly Saladin. Although Butler's *King Richard* demonstrates far less religious devotion motivating the Crusade than does DeMille's film, this secularization does not preclude anti-war sentiments proclaimed by Mayo's Edith, who has the lead female role. Voicing the audience's fatigue about the recent Second World War and the briefer, though less popular Korean War of 1950–53, which added several hundred thousand more casualties to those of World War II, Edith admits: "I'm beginning to despise war. The dread, the wondering each time you ride away if you'll come back among the living." And to Richard she adds, "War, war! That's all you ever think about, Dick Plantagenet! You burner, you pillager!"

The orientalizing of Harrison's hilariously miscast Saladin ultimately demeans the great military leader. At least Ian Keith's exotically garbed Saladin exuded *gravitas* when he traded insults with the impetuously callow Wilcoxen's Richard. The phony-looking face paint, the powder blue, sequined lamé Aladdin robes and turban, the harem of gaudy belly dancers, and his gleeful labeling of the European Crusaders as "Frankish lobsters" ultimately trivialize (and feminize) Harrison's Saladin. Western cinematic constructions of the Eastern other were due for a paradigm shift, and that shift occurred nine years later in a presentation of the Third Crusade from the Arab viewpoint.

Youssef Chahine's *Saladin*

In 1963 Egyptian director Youssef Chahine produced an antidote to such Euro- and Christo-centric constructions of the Crusades in his remarkable film *Saladin*, whose Egyptian title, *El Naser Salah el Dine*, makes a punning political reference to one of the most important political figures in modern Arab history, Gamal Abdel Nasser, President of Egypt (1954–70). Chahine's film blatantly encourages drawing parallels between Saladin, the twelfth-century Egyptian sultan who led Muslim armies against the colonizing European

Crusaders, and Nasser, a figure who promoted Arab nationalism by inspiring anti-colonial, pan–Arab revolutions in several Middle Eastern nations and who industrialized modern Egypt. By dramatizing Saladin's call for the unification of Muslim states prior to the Third Crusade in a stirringly exhortative nationalistic speech early in the film (the historical Saladin actually rose to power by subjugating various Arab groups), Chahine distorts history just as much as previous Hollywood films had done, but this time in pursuit of a different agenda: portraying Arabs as peaceful and innocent victims of Western self-aggrandizement and colonialism.[20] In response to how earlier Hollywood versions of the Crusade misrepresented history, Chahine's film filters the Third Crusade through the revisionist lens of the Muslim/Arab point of view.

Chahine earned his status as an "auteur" director by learning his craft during a "golden age" of emerging world cinema, having been exposed to Hollywood film techniques (and movies like Dwan's *Robin Hood*, DeMille's *The Crusades*, and Butler's *King Richard and the Crusaders*) when he studied acting and directing in the late 1940s in California at the Pasadena Playhouse. Returning to Egypt in the early 1950s, he was exposed to and influenced by Italian neorealist directors such as Vittorio De Sica and Roberto Rosselini. He also no doubt encountered DeMille doing location shooting in Egypt for his blockbuster biblical epic *The Ten Commandments* (1956). Further, the influence of Russian filmmaker Sergei Eisenstein's "discontinuity editing" or "montage" technique is particularly striking in Chahine's depiction of a key early scene in the film,[21] Reynald of Châtillon's brutal, unprovoked attack of a caravan, a deliberate violation of the truce between Crusaders and Muslims, which precipitates Saladin's execution of Reynald discussed below. Although historically the caravan Reynald attacked probably consisted of merchants, in Chahine's version of events they are religious pilgrims to Mecca, whom Reynald ruthlessly slaughters in contempt of their religious devotion. The historical Saladin traditionally insured the safe passage of pilgrims of all faiths, and Reynald's brutal disregard of the mutual agreement to respect pilgrims, according to Chahine, motivated Saladin's routing of the European armies at the 1187 battle of Hattin.

Victory at Hattin was accomplished partly by the Muslims' barring the Franks from access to a source of water in the intense July heat and partly by trapping them in the valley between the twin hills of Hattin, surrounding them on all sides. After the battle victorious Saladin summoned the Frankish leaders — Guy de Lusignan the Latin King of Jerusalem, Reynald de Châtillon, and Balian of Ibelin — to his tent, where Saladin offered iced water to quench the thirst of Guy, whom he respected. After drinking, Guy inadvertently passed the water to Reynald without Saladin's authorization. Saladin executed Reynald, beheading him with his own sword, as much for the audacity of drinking without the offer of the sultan's hospitality as for his reckless and selfish violation of a truce.

This important event in Saladin's career not only demonstrated his tactical acumen, but also revealed his personal character. A comparison between Chahine's and Sir Ridley Scott's interpretation of the same "historical" moment in his 2005 *Kingdom of Heaven* underscores the Egyptian director's almost hagiographical revision of his title character. Chahine's version takes place not in a desert tent, but in what appears to be Saladin's palace; the shot's *mise-en-scène* is highly elaborate and luxorious, reminiscent of interiors of the Hagia Sophia in Constantinople. Upon hearing the Franks cry, "Water, we want water," a stately and excessively courteous Saladin, proclaimed "the liberator of Jerusalem" and solicitous about whether the prisoners have been offered water, remonstrates, "Have you no mercy? Give them water at once." The sultan's edict is read, granting equality between Muslims and Christians and safe passage to Jerusalem for Christian pilgrims. How could Saladin be any fairer to the defeated? The camera cuts to the captive Franks, worrying about their ultimate disposition, whether prison or execution, and one of them acknowledges, "When an Arab gives you water, it means he has given you your life." As Guy humbly kneels to their generous captor, thanking Saladin in the name of Christ, Reynald rudely interrupts "the old fool" Guy's gesture of respect, demanding, "Where the hell is that water?" When a servant pours a pitcher of water into Guy's goblet, Reynald rushes over, seizing the entire pitcher, greedily slaking his thirst. Frowning his disapproval at this breach of etiquette, Saladin, played by Ahmed Mazhar, reminds Reynald, "You drink the water, yet it's against our will. You're used to quenching thirst with blood," an allusion to Reynald's blood lust at the ambush of the pilgrim caravan. Reynald impetuously boasts, "Had I my sword, no one would dare talk to me this way." When Saladin instructs them to provide Reynald a sword, despite his staff's disapproval and offer to kill him on the spot, Reynald proudly taunts that he fights "only an equal, a king," challenging Saladin to personal combat. The sultan swears that Reynald will be slain by "a lowly servant of God."

There ensues a two-minute scene that seems to extend much longer, shot from constantly changing camera angles in a series of medium shots, close-ups, panoramic shots, giving a sense of the vast space commanded by the sultan, and from high overhead, dwarfing the personal combatants in their *agon*. Chahine blocks (really choreographs) the scene as an athletic ballet on a stage, watched by the audience from high in the balcony of a theater. Throughout Saladin wields his sword in one hand, the other held behind his back. The cowardly Reynald employs both sword arm and free hand, flailing his arms, cutting down a chandelier over Saladin's head to purchase himself some advantage, and he cheats by picking up a handy battle-ax. Wielding two weapons against Saladin's lone sword is an unfair fight, violating the rules of chivalry. As they "dance" around the amphitheater-like space, Saladin forces his opponent's hand over the flame of a candle. Crying out from the burn, Reynald drops the ax, whereupon Saladin seizes his fairly gained advantage and runs Reynald through with his sword, proclaiming, "If I could punish him for all his crimes, I'd kill him a thousand times over." Chahine cuts to an extreme close-up of Reynald's face, his dead eyes staring and blood trickling from his formerly boastful, now-stilled mouth, a visual echo of the close-ups of the faces of the slaughtered victims of the caravan ambush.

Chahine's presentation of Reynald's "execution" rewrites a key scene in DeMille's film, wherein the boorish Richard first offers wine to Saladin, then is forced to permit his young wife to assure his military adversary, who has come to talk terms for peace, that the water, substituted for wine in deference to Saladin's religious practices, will not poison him. Ironically, for Saladin in DeMille's Western film, Frankish water portends the possibility of treachery and death. For the Franks in Chahine's film, the offer of water by an Arab insures the preservation of life. Starting with the granted request for water, the sequence also is calculated to recall an earlier scene in Chahine's film in which Saladin's astute military strategy of infiltrating the Crusaders' camp and sabotaging the Franks' water supply leads to dramatic close-ups of empty water jugs and thirsting Franks, in their hot chain mail, sweltering sluggishly in the merciless, broiling sun.

Historically the Europeans' loss of their water source aided Saladin's victory at Hittin, but Chahine's version credits Saladin for cleverly planned military espionage and creates dramatic irony in the post-battle summit of the leaders, who still thirst after the battle and are offered water by the gracious victor, enhancing Saladin's largesse and magnanimity. Although Reynald's arrogance invites what historically was his execution, in Chahine's staging of events his death is not an execution at all, but the losing of a chivalrous man-to-man challenge, with Reynald trying to cheat his way to winning and Saladin defeating him through justly employed fighting skill. This approach rewrites Crusade history, privileging Saladin's chivalry and almost saintly benevolence toward his most hated enemy.

Saladin's killing of Reynald in fair hand-to-hand combat could not be more different from Ridley Scott's depiction of the same event in the 2005 film *Kingdom of Heaven*. More closely adhering to actual historical events, but exaggerating the impassive brutality of Saladin's retaliation, Scott portrays Reynald's death as a bloody, vengeful execution. In the scene leading up to the execution in Saladin's tent, as the Franks trudge in the blazing sun and dust toward the debacle at Hittin, Scott shows a shot of Reynald, played by a grizzled Brenden Gleeson, taking a slug of water and then wastefully pouring the rest of the bottle over his hauberk's shoulders. A series of quick intercut shots reveal: Saladin's Muslims giving their war cry, "God wills it"; the Franks marching to their doom; Balian (Orlando Bloom) and Tiberias (Jeremy Irons) on a distant rampart "sensing" disaster; the aftermath of the carnage as Muslims pick valuables off the mountains of European corpses; Saladin (Ghassan Massoud) returning to his tent to refresh himself with a goblet of ice. He proffers the goblet to Guy (Marton Csokas), who hesitates, then passes it to Raynald, who gruffly pronounces, "I drink water for what it is" and downs the ice, grunting in satisfaction. Scott creates a series of quick intercuts between close-ups of Reynald's and Saladin's faces before Saladin ominously states to Reynald, "I did not give the cup to you," to which Reynald has the grace to admit, "No, Milord." Only several frames later, after being offered a sword and a meaningful glance by his factotum Nasir, with lightning speed, Saladin whips out his own dagger and swiftly slices it through Reynald's jugular, his slit throat gurgling and spattering blood on Guy's impassive face. After passing his sword across his face as if to bat away a fly, Saladin exits the tent to finish the job. Reynald would die anyway from such an extreme wound, but Saladin heaves the sword through his neck, decapitating him while Reynald is still alive and aware of his demise. Were this Chahine directing, the audience would be led to surmise that the decapitation was a mercy killing, literally cutting short what might have been a lingering, painful death. But Saladin's grim, purposeful demeanor and his quizzical statement to the stunned Guy, "A king does not kill another king; why are you not close enough to a great king to learn by his example?" underscore how deliberate was this execution. The scene's gory violence is over the top, almost surreal. The spurting blood, the gurgling death throes, and Reynald's severed head impaled on a stake attracting buzzards and discovered by Tiberias and Balian as they survey Hittin's aftermath are elements in a slasher horror movie. They are ironically undercut by the peaceful ecclesiastical music in the soundtrack. Scott pulls out all the stops to show how ruthless Saladin could be, though his Saladin also comes across as fair-minded. It is a balanced portrait, while Chahine's is entirely biased in favor of demonstrating what a chivalrous figure Saladin was. However, for the sake of what anticipates our contemporary "political correctness," Chahine's Saladin *must* be perceived as magnanimous for, intentionally constructed as an analogue of Egypt's president Gamal Abdul Nasser, Chahine's Saladin is less a medieval military tactician than a figure in a political allegory about Nasser's championing of Egyptian nationalism and pan–Arab unity against the combined colonialism of Britain, France, and Israel in the Suez Crisis of 1956.

The Third Crusade, the Vietnam War, and 1970s Robin Hood Cinema and Television

In the 1970s two cinematic Robin Hood vehicles, among the gloomiest versions of the greenwood legend ever filmed, coincided with the recently concluded and disastrous Vietnam War, one of the most unpopular wars in American history. Once again the Middle Ages as "distant mirror" metaphor seems to be operating two or three years before Tuchman coined the term. Suitably the 1975 BBC TV mini-series *The Legend of Robin Hood*, directed by Eric Davidson, features a glum, almost dour Robin Hood played by Martin Potter. Robin is surrounded by the usual suspects and their internecine Plantagenet feuding: Richard, who is preparing to embark on the Crusade; John, who is preparing to abscond with the kingdom; Queen Eleanor, who again plots with Longchamp to insure Richard's maintenance of his crown. The Third Crusade is a sustained subplot alongside the usual Robin Hood plot points. Interestingly this version of the legend is unusual for being gritty and realistic — no spangled green tights for this Robin. The six-part series is also period authentic, one of the very few cinematic treatments of Robin Hood that ends with the hero's death, which also concludes the original late-medieval ballad *A Gest of Robyn Hode*, wherein after a lifetime of adventures Robin is murdered by his kinswoman, the Abbess of Kirklees Abbey, who was meant to heal him of some undisclosed ailment. Instead, with the help of her lover she kills him by excessive (and definitely non-therapeutic) phlebotomy. Perhaps bloodletting was considered too strong for the possibly squeamish television audience, because, though this series' Robin dies at the hands of a nun, she happens to be Guy of Gisborne's sister avenging Robin's killing of Guy. Nearly all other examples of Robin Hood cinema conclude with Robin and Marian riding off into the sunset of an indefinitely long life together. Here Robin and Marian are denied that happy ending.

Considering the national and international mood about the just-concluded Vietnam War, we may guess it perhaps not coincidental that the only feature film in which Robin dies was released one year after this television series. In Richard Lester's 1976 *Robin and Marian,* all the usually youthful greenwood characters are middle-aged or old. Robin, played by the mature Sean Connery, who is described in James Goldman's screenplay as "close to fifty" (59), is returning to Sherwood weary and disillusioned after twenty years of following Richard I around the Holy Land during the Crusade and more recently attending him in Southwestern France, where Richard was subjecting the run-down, deserted Chaluz Castle, part of his Aquitaine fiefdom, to siege warfare by a mangonel he has lugged back from the Holy Land, catapulting rocks at a castle sheltering only women, children, and a crazed, half-blind old man. The Lionheart, played by Richard Harris, is attempting futilely to extract a treasure, a gold statue that doesn't exist, from a castle that will yield nothing to him except a valueless rock abandoned in a turnip field. Goldman's stage directions describe Richard as "a hero gone wrong. Still vigorous and powerful, he had become a feverish and driven man, decayed and dangerous.... Richard who was known and feared for fits of rage, looked taut and angry" (63). Richard has evolved a long way from the burly, food-loving Wallace Beery, from the vigorous, young Henry Wilcoxen, from the suave-mannered George Sanders, from the swarthily stolid Hamdi Geiss in Chahine's epic. When Richard is told that the treasure doesn't exist, he petulantly orders Robin and his soldiers to attack the castle anyway, even if it means killing, as Robin reminds him, "just children and a mad old man." Robin refuses, reasoning, "I've followed you for twenty years. I fought for you in the Crusade. I've fought for you in France. Show me a soldier and I'll fight him for you now. But I won't slaughter children for a piece of gold that never was." Richard again orders Robin to attack the children and Robin refuses, whereupon Richard orders Robin and Little John (Nicol Williamson) to be placed in Chaluz's jail and Richard's attack of the castle's inhabitants, mostly children, is undertaken by him and his soldiers. By his own admission he "killed them all this afternoon." Meanwhile, the mad old man, shouting, "Lionheart, you are a pig!" hurls an arrow at Richard and wounds him in the shoulder, a wound that proves ultimately fatal.

Having escaped from Richard's imprisonment once again (an echo of Dwan's *Robin Hood*), Robin and Little John assess what Richard has become. John insists, "He's our king." Robin argues, re-evaluating his adoption of the Crusade," I took him for a great King. There we were in Sherwood, robbing abbots, giving pennies to the poor. It didn't seem like much compared to rescuing the Holy Land. I wonder sometimes if we ever should have left," and then about Richard, "I don't know him anymore. I don't know the man."

When Robin and John are led to visit the dying Richard, Harris gives a tour de force performance as an angry king who has lost control of everything: the loyalty of his favored soldier Robin; the love of his famous mother about whom he pouts, "She'll be eighty soon, the bitch. I've sent for her. You think she'll come?"; his control over England, for he admits his brother, John Lackland, will get "all the lands now. Christ! Why did I have no children? Never gave a damn for England; never there." When Richard threatens to "carve" Robin as punishment for his disloyalty, his reach for his iconic sword proves beyond his grasp, and he collapses into Robin's arms. The homosocial/homoerotic relationship between Richard and Robin introduced in Dwan's 1922 *Robin Hood* is reprised here as Richard dies, cradled by Robin, addressing him as if a lover, "You couldn't leave me, could you?" When Robin shakes his head, Richard utters his dying words, "What will you do now, Jolly Robin, now I'm dead?"

Harris's portrayal of a demented Richard anticipates the construction of similarly mad American military leaders in the Vietnam War in Francis Ford Coppola's 1979 *Apocalypse Now*. Robin returns to Nottingham and Sherwood after two decades of absence expecting everything to be just as he left it, everyone welcoming him with open arms, and he is puzzled and stunned that his homecoming is not welcomed, nor his military service in the Holy Land particularly valued by a mature and independent Marian (Audrey Hepburn), who has gotten on with her own life in Hood's absence, taken the habit, and trained as an herbalist. As she simply explains to the perplexed Robin, "I like my life." Robin feels he and his valor are redundant (this 1970s movie Marian, a product of feminism, no longer needs rescuing). His frustration and bafflement mirror the feelings of Vietnam veterans who were not cheered as returning heroes, as in other wars, or who returned to wives who no longer wanted them.

Also like some Vietnam vets, Connery's Robin ruefully re-evaluates and devaluates his own service for God, king, and nation when he later recounts to Marian the atrocities he witnessed at the Third Crusade:

> On July the twelfth, 1191, the mighty fortress that was Acre fell to Richard. That's his one great victory in the Holy Land and he was sick in bed and never struck a blow. And on the twentieth of August, John and I, we stood there on the plain outside of town and watched while every Moslem left alive came marching out in chains. King Richard spared the richest to be ransomed. Then he took the strong for slaves. And then he took the children, all the children, and had them chopped apart. When that was done, he had the mothers killed and then, when everyone was dead — three thousand bodies on the plain — he had them all eviscerated so their guts could be explored for gold and stones. The Churchmen on the scene, and there were many, took it for a triumph and a bishop put his mitre on and led us all in prayer.... You ask me if I'm sick of it?" [Goldman 107]

Connery's disillusioned account of what Robin witnessed in the *Holy Land* under Richard's command suggests that Goldman's script was merging chronicle accounts of the genuine depredations committed against innocent Muslims during the Third Crusade with accounts of the atrocities committed against civilians, women, and children in the My Lai massacre. Once again the Crusades proved a dark mirror of a twentieth-century war. The movie ends with Robin's death, produced by his old sweetheart Marian, who uses her acquired knowledge of herbal medicine to poison both herself and her lover. Although Lester's *Robin and Marian* is one of the most poignant and literate Robin Hood films ever made, it bombed at the box office for killing off a hero that audiences did not want to see die. Nevertheless, the film faithfully chronicles the mood of its era, when wars like the Crusades or the perplexing Vietnam conflict seemed just not worth the waste of human life.

The Third Crusade and the Persian Gulf War of 1990–91

Once again illustrating the pattern that movies evoking the Crusades provide a distant mirror of contemporaneous wars, I suggest it is hardly coincidental that a highly anticipated summer blockbuster adventure film about a long ago war waged by a coalition of European nations and states in the Middle East should be produced in the midst of another war conducted in that geographic region, the Persian Gulf War waged by a similar world-wide coalition against Iraq in 1990–91. In June 1991 *Robin Hood: Prince of Thieves* opened with a lengthy introductory sequence placing an almost unrecognizably grubby Kevin Costner, playing English Earl Robin of Locksley, in a Muslim jail. The movie's opening exposition situates the plot in the now familiar Richard I–Robin Hood association: "800 years ago, Richard the 'Lionheart,' King of England, led the Third Great Crusade to reclaim the Holy Land from the Turks. Most of the young English noblemen who flocked to his banner never returned home." The movie tells the story of one who did. Locksley's stereotypically villainous and sadistic Muslim captors—a return to the racial essentialism of the Arab other—force Robin to endure for five years horrible conditions and the threat of physical maiming as a prisoner of war, in which he demonstrates "English courage." His improbable escape, evoking the openings of *Indiana Jones* movies, thrusts him into an initially uneasy but growing friendship with Morgan Freeman, playing the Muslim Azeem, easily the best thing about the film. Aside from the pairing evoking countless other Hollywood "buddy" movies, Azeem also functions as a not very Eastern looking, yet orientalized, if "politically correct," stand-in for Saladin. In fact this is the first Robin Hood movie involving him at the Third Crusade in which one may say that Saladin (or a reasonable surrogate) plays a part. Released a year after Costner's hugely successful, also "politically correct" treatment of another cinematic "other," Native Americans, in 1990's *Dances with Wolves*, *Prince of Thieves* struck many medievalists, including me, as "*Dances with Wolves* goes to Sherwood Forest." By being shown practicing his religion—facing Mecca to pray daily, refusing to drink ale for religious principles while in the camp of the copiously imbibing Merry Men, articulating the voice of reason countering Robin's impetuosity—Azeem becomes a "neutralized" alter ego of the bloodthirsty Arab jailers seen earlier in the film, participates in Knobler's third premise, that the medieval Crusades presented "a negative

Azeem (Morgan Freeman) among the merry men of Sherwood Forest in Kevin Reynolds' *Robin Hood, Prince of Thieves*.

image of the past about which the West should be ashamed" (and for which they needed to apologize). The characterization of Azeem presents such an apology for previous cinematic essentialism of the Muslim other.

Yet in its arch political correctness, it creates its own stereotypes. Azeem follows Robin from the Crusade back to England with the obligation of saving the outlaw's life in return for Robin's saving his back in Jerusalem. The casting of a popular African-American actor as an Arab neutralizes the stereotypical orientalizing of Muslims or Saladin in earlier Hollywood films about the Third Crusade. At least Freeman, unlike Rex Harrison in *King Richard and the Crusaders*, did not have to wear face paint to look like an Eastern person of color. Nevertheless, Freeman's Azeem also capitalizes on the way previous Hollywood Crusades films orientalized the Arab other by acknowledging the reputation medieval Arabs/Muslims had for skills in medicine and science, for translation (and thus preservation) of the medical writings of the ancient Greeks, and in the practice of hygiene and sanitation superior to that of the West. Azeem saves the life of Little John's wife by delivering her baby in a difficult breech birth, and he uses a telescope, an invention of which the sometimes-cloddish European Robin seems ignorant and suspicious, to view their adversaries when he and Robin first return to England. Here we see an evocation of the various earlier films in which Saladin plays the role of physician to Richard or Berengaria or encourages and supports scientific discovery (as in Chahine's *Saladin*).

In his 1993 *Robin Hood: Men in Tights*, along with just about every other convention of Robin Hood feature films, Mel Brooks lampoons Azeem's scientific knowledge in the far stupider, but street-smart character Ahchoo (played by Dave Chapelle). Brooks also parodies the obligatory late-in-the-film entrance of King Richard when Scots actor Patrick Stewart trumps Sean Connery's uncredited appearance as Richard I in *Prince of Thieves* by appearing at the last minute to bestow the very unmaidenly Maid Marian to Robin in marriage and by laying on an even thicker Scots accent than that of Connery. Is the casting of these Scots actors to play the Anglo-Norman Richard a reverse othering of Richard's othering of the Scottish Sir Kenneth, the real ethnic other of Sir Walter Scott's *The Talisman* and its film adaptation *King Richard and the Crusaders*? For that matter, although Richard's "Englishness" is emphasized in all the Robin Hood and Crusades movies, as Duke of Aquitaine, son of the originally French Eleanor, and possibly lover of French Philip Augustus, Richard should have represented the other "other" to the native Saxons whom Robin Hood championed against the oppressive Normans in many Robin Hood narratives and films. Reynolds's *Prince of Thieves* and Brooks' parody of it present a series of Russian nested dolls or Chinese boxes of otherings! Although Richard I remains marginalized, and Saladin is only ghostly represented by his stand-in Azeem, for its evocation of the Third Crusade in the prison escape sequence *Prince of Thieves* deserves a place in the canon of films that depict the interface between the crescent and the cross in the Crusades as a distant mirror of the contemporary Gulf War.

Postscript: The 21st Century Iraq War and the Crusades

The distant mirror of the Third Crusade continues to reflect contemporary political history. The 2006–07 BBC television series *Robin Hood* features: a Robin of Locksley returning from the Third Crusade with a case of post-traumatic stress syndrome; a Muslim woman, Djaq, joining the Merry Men; an episode referencing Saladin's famed "Assassins"; a still-absent Richard whose claim to the English throne Robin must defend against the machinations of the flagrantly cruel Sheriff of Nottingham and the Heathcliff-like Guy of Gisborne. As in the 1922 *Robin Hood*, Guy still wickedly desires a considerably feminized Marian, who gives outlawed Robin a run for his money in her role as the Night Watchman. The series is engaging, even if sometimes with tongue planted firmly into cheek, with parallels between the Third Crusade and the current Iraq War. In cinematic versions of these medieval events, Richard and Saladin represent much more than their original medieval historical avatars.

NOTES

1. A version of this paper was presented March 29, 2008, at "Remembering the Crusades: Myth, Image, and Identity," the 38th Annual Conference of the Center of Medieval Studies, Fordham University. I thank the organizers for structuring a stimulating, focused, interdisciplinary conference and the audience for their enthusiastic reception of my argument and their provocative questions at the session on Saladin. Special thanks go to Geraldine Heng, who recommended my paper to one of the editors of this volume.

2. Knobler (294) discusses appropriations of crusading mythology in the development of nationhood in France, Spain, Russia, Ethiopia, Great Britain, Bulgaria, and Egypt.

3. I use the term as did Barbara W. Tuchman in her "glass darkly" comparison between the "calamitous 14th century" and post–Vietnam War America.

4. At the 2004 Biennial World Conference sponsored by *Film & History*, whose theme was "Film and War," I co-presented (with Candace Gregory-Abbott) the paper, "Serving the Cause at Home: Women in Films about the Crusades," liberally using examples from the Robin Hood canon. The audience of interdisciplinary medievalists who used film to teach medieval history and literature were skeptical, then delighted, at the wealth of Crusades material in a film corpus they hitherto ignored as fictive romantic swashbucklers. I myself first learned about the Crusades, Richard the Lionheart, the other Plantagenets, and Robin Hood by watching the long-running mid–1950s television series, *The Adventures of Robin Hood*, produced by Hannah Weinstein in England for British and American juvenile or family audiences.

5. On the development of the Robin Hood legend from medieval ballads through movies and television, see Knight, 1994 and 2003.

6. To varying degrees film versions of Scott's *Ivanhoe* present interestingly creative depictions of Richard I, Prince John, and Queen Eleanor. See Richard Thorpe's *Ivanhoe* (1952) or even better Stuart Orme's BBC TV/A&E miniseries *Ivanhoe* (1997), whose adapter, Deborah Cook, invented extra concluding material about the dysfunctional Plantagenets. For similar delving into Plantagenet domestic psychodrama see Anthony Harvey's 1968 film of William Goldman's 1966 play, *The Lion in Winter*, and a 2003 television movie directed by Andrei Konchalovsky. All versions deal with Richard before he embarks on the Third Crusade. Richard, John, and Eleanor figure prominently in Ken Annakin's *The Story of Robin Hood and His Merrie Men* (1952) and in various episodes of the television series *The Adventures of Robin Hood* (1955–58).

7. See *The Adventures of Robin Hood* (1938), directed by Michael Curtiz and William Keighley, starring Errol Flynn as the "fluently treasonous" Earl of Locksley, and *Robin Hood: Prince of Thieves* (1991), directed by Kevin Reynolds, starring Kevin Costner as Locksley. Ridley Scott's 2005 *Kingdom of Heaven* continues this tradition by having Richard make a brief appearance on his way to the Third Crusade, meeting Balian of Ibelin after he has returned from Jerusalem at the film's end.

8. Aerial photos of Robin Hood's castle set at Pickford Studios reveal its realistic size, literally towering over and dwarfing the actors and extras. The sets for the Crusades scenes are equally lavish; Richard's camp pavilion resembles a towering castle made of cloth.

9. *Robin Hood*'s *mise-en-scène* compares favorably with recent Crusades blockbusters like Ridley Scott's 2005 *Kingdom of Heaven*, whose huge scale and graphic effects were realized through computer graphics manipulation, a technology not available in 1922. The effects paid off, as the New York premiere of *Robin Hood* drew over 100,000 people and the movie grossed over $5 million for Fairbanks' studio (Aberth 2003, p. 164).

10. Aberth argues that this film's romanticism "was probably what the people wanted in the aftermath of the most destructive war to date in the modern world." (Aberth 2003, p. 166).

11. Aberth notes that graphic scenes of these depredations in the film reflect "the brutality of the Great War" (Aberth 166).

12. Richard's using disguise to reenter England secretly is a convention in Robin Hood narratives and films starting with the king's impersonation of a monk and disguised combat with Robin Hood in the late 15th-century ballad *A Gest of Robyn Hode*, continuing with Richard's impersonation of the "Black Knight" in Scott's *Ivanhoe* and to most Robin Hood films featuring Richard.

13. For varying interpretations of chronicler Roger of Hovedon's evidence that Richard

had a sexual relationship with Phillip Augustus of France, based on the fact that they slept in the same bed, ate from the same dish, and Phillip loved Richard "as his own soul," see Brundage 1974, pages 88 ff, 287 ff.; Boswell 231–32; Jaeger 26, 129, 133; Reston 67. Movies such as the versions of *The Lion in Winter* (1968, 2003) directly allude to Richard's preference for men.

14. Harold Lamb, *The Crusades* (1930–31). DeMille hired Lamb as scriptwriter and as historical consultant overseeing the film's historical authenticity.

15. This relationship resembles other examples in "movie medievalism" of what Eve K. Sedgwick terms "triangulated desire" or the trafficking of a woman "between men," such as occurs between Arthur, Guinevere, and Lancelot and Mark, Isolt, and Tristan. Although such triangulated desire occurs frequently in medieval literature, Sedgwick only starts her chronological survey of the motif with Shakespeare in the Early Modern period.

16. As early as the late Middle Ages, romance writers tended to romanticize this paragon of chivalry into a courtly lover of Western women. See Castro (1954), Heng (2003), and Kontor (2004).

17. Space does not permit expansion of this theme here. I analyze this aspect of *The Crusades* in a forthcoming essay, "'He's not an ardent suitor is he, brother?': Richard the Lionheart's Ambiguous Sexuality in Cecil B. DeMille's *The Crusades*," to appear in *Queer Movie Medievalisms*, ed. Tison Pugh and Kathleen Coyne Kelly (Ashgate).

18. In the first series of *The Adventures of Robin Hood*, Marian, Eleanor, and Richard were each accorded their own eponymous episodes: "Maid Marian," "Queen Eleanor," and "Richard the Lionheart."

19. This historically unfounded idea is so appealing that a *bas de page* miniature of the 14th-century *Luttrell Psalter* depicted a dark-skinned Saladin jousting against the English king.

20. The scope and complexity of the myriad plots and subplots of Chahine's film, which deserve a separate discussion, preclude lengthy analysis of the entire film here. For detailed analysis of the film's political aspects, artistic merits, cinematic influences, and questionable historicity see Halim, Aberth, and Ganim.

21. This scene is thoroughly analyzed by Aberth, Ganim, and Halim.

BIBLIOGRAPHY

Aberth, John. *A Knight at the Movies: Medieval History on Film*. New York: Routledge, 2003.
"A Gest of Robyn Hode." *Robin Hood and Other Outlaw Tales*. Ed. Stephen Knight and Thomas Ohlgren. Kalamazoo, MI: TEAMS Middle English Texts, Medieval Institute Publications of Western Michigan University, 1997.
Boswell, John. *Christianity, Social Tolerance, and Homosexuality*. Chicago and London: University of Chicago Press, 1980.
Ganim, John M. "Reversing the Crusades: Hegemony, Orientalism, and Film Language in Youssef Chahine's *Saladin*." *Race, Class, and Gender in Medieval Cinema*. Ed. Lynn Ramey and Tison Pugh. New York: Palgrave Macmillan, 2007: 45–58.
Gillingham, John. *Richard the Lionheart*. London: Weidenfeld and Nicholson, 1978.
Goldman, James. *Robin and Marian*. New York: Bantam Books, 1976.
Halim, Hala. "The Signs of Saladin: A Modern Cinematic Rendition of Medieval Heroism." *Alif: A Journal of Comparative Poetics* 12 (1992): 78–94.
Haydock, Nickolas. *Movie Medievalism: The Imaginary Middle Ages*. Jefferson, NC: McFarland, 2008.
Heng, Geraldine. *Empire of Magic: Medieval Romance and the Politics of Cultural Fantasy*. New York: Columbia University Press, 2003.
Jaeger, C. Stephen. *Ennobling Love: In Search of a Lost Sensibility*. Philadelphia: University of Pennsylvania Press, 1999.
Knight, Stephen. *Robin Hood: The Complete Study of the English Outlaw*. Oxford: Blackwell, 1994.

_____. *Robin Hood: A Mythic Biography*. Ithaca and London: Cornell UP, 2003.
Knobler, Adam. "Holy Wars, Empires, and the Portability of the Past: The Modern Uses of the Medieval Crusades." *Comparative Studies in Society and History* 48.2 (2006): 293–325.
Kontor, Ann. "The Bold and the Beautiful: A *Cortois* Saladin." Chimères 28 (2004): 73–82.
Lamb, Harold. *Iron Men and Saints and the Flame of Islam* (2 vols). Garden City: Doubleday, 1930–31.
Lewis, Bernard. "Saladin and the Assassins." *Bulletin of the School of Oriental and African Studies, University of London* 15.2 (1953): 239–245.
Ramey, Lynn T. and Tison Pugh, eds. *Race, Class, and Gender in "Medieval" Cinema*. New York: Palgrave Macmillan, 2007.
Reston, James, Jr. *Warriors of God: Richard the Lionheart and Saladin in the Third Crusade*. New York: Doubleday, 2001.
Said, Edward W. *Orientalism*. New York: Vintage Books, 1978.
Scott, Sir Walter. *Ivanhoe*. 1819. New York: Barnes & Noble Classics, 2005.
_____. *The Talisman*. 1929. New York: Dodd, Mead & Co., 1943.
Sedgwick, Eve Kosofsky. *Between Men: English Literature and Male Homosocial Desire*. New York: Columbia University Press, 1985.
Stock, Lorraine K. and Candace Gregory-Abbott. "The 'Other' Women of Sherwood: The Construction of Difference and Gender in Cinematic Treatments of the Robin Hood Legend." *Race, Class, and Gender in Medieval Cinema*, ed. Lynn Ramey and Tison Pugh (New York: Palgrave Macmillan, 2007). 119–214.
Tuchman, Barbara W. *A Distant Mirror: The Calamitous 14th Century*. New York: Alfred A. Knopf, 1978.

Filmography

Ivanhoe, dir. Richard Thorpe, 1952.
Ivanhoe, BBC/A&E miniseries, dir. Stuart Orme, 1997.
King Richard and the Crusaders, dir. David Butler, 1954.
Kingdom of Heaven, dir. Ridley Scott, 2005.
Robin and Marian, dir. Richard Lester, 1976.
Robin Hood, dir. Alan Dwan, 1922.
Robin Hood, BBC Television series, dir. Matthew Evans *et. al.*, two seasons, 2006–07.
Robin Hood: Men in Tights, dir. Mel Brooks, 1993.
Robin Hood: Prince of Thieves, dir. Kevin Reynolds, 1991.
Saladin, dir. Youssef Chahine, 1963.
The Adventures of Robin Hood, dir. Michael Curtiz and William Keighley, 1938.
The Adventures of Robin Hood, ITV television series, 4 seasons, dir. various, 1955–58.
The Crusades, dir. Cecil B. DeMille, 1935.
The Legend of Robin Hood, BBC television mini-series, dir. Eric Davidson, 1975.
The Lion in Winter, dir. Anthony Harvey, 1968.
The Lion in Winter, dir. Andrei Konchalovsky, 2003.
The Story of Robin Hood and His Merrie Men, dir. Ken Annakin, 1952.

4. SaladiNasser

Nasser's Political Crusade in El Naser Salah Ad-Din

PAUL B. STURTEVANT

> "We must always be aware of the fact that Saladin's very real achievements—the victory at Hittin and the conquest of Jerusalem—had already been formed into a myth during his lifetime and this obliterated Saladin's personality and deeds. Only on rare occasions is the non-mythical Saladin discernable."
> Yaacov Lev, Saladin in Egypt p. xii

Salāh ad-Dīn Yūsuf ibn Ayyūb, known to the west as Saladin, is something of an unlikely hero for the Arab world. Since his death in 1193, his legend has seen a meteoric rise from the relative obscurity in which it languished for centuries to that of the most iconic Muslim hero of the Crusades. Since the renaissance of his legend in the nineteenth century, Saladin has been a constant figure in popular culture. Saladin is by far the most popular Muslim leader who fought the Crusaders in the Holy Land to appear in film. Additionally, many films which have depicted (as their main plot) the Crusades in the Holy Land have included Saladin as a character.

Be it Hollywood, British, Continental or Middle-Eastern, his seems *the* story worth telling. Whether he is coolly seducing Richard the Lionheart's wife (in an Orientalist fantasy *par excellence*) in *The Crusades* (1935) or replacing an overturned cross in *Kingdom of Heaven* (2005), his character remains a constant, if static, presence: static because the legend of his magnanimity and nobility have expanded beyond what his biography can contain to the point where he is never shown to change or develop as a realistic character. Instead, his representations in popular culture, particularly in the West, tend towards the hagiographical, with Saladin existing as a moral benchmark against which the Crusaders rarely measure up. His character is limited to being a predictable part of the background scenery upon which the main action takes place. His legend is ripe with juicy irony: an "infidel" who is more chivalric than the flower of Western chivalry that he opposes. Kaiser Wilhelm the Second, who famously laid a wreath at Saladin's tomb on his tour of the Holy Land in 1898, called the Sultan "a Knight without fear or blame who often had to teach his opponents the right way to practice chivalry" (Aberth 70). As Yaacov Lev argues, this oft-repeated interpretation evolved over time from the one created during his lifetime into the 'Saladin myth' still articulated today.

Although Saladin was considered a relatively magnanimous and noble leader by both Eastern and Western medieval sources, the myth that grew around him after his death was solely Western. In the years immediately following his victory over the Third Crusade in 1192, Saladin was, predictably, demonized by Western authors. But in the early thirteenth century an anonymous French poet penned *L'Ordene de Chevalerie*.[1] At first the author presents the sultan in a manner typical of the day: "He had the name Saladin / To that many by this great king / To the people of our faith / The Saracen often did great damage / By his pride, by his contempt" (lines 20–24).[2] But as the story progresses, Saladin undergoes a conversion, not to Christianity, but to the Western ideal of chivalry. Upon converting, Saladin frees the captive protagonist of the tale and sends him on his way loaded with coin. After this turning point Saladin gradually was used as a stock heroic figure in medieval European epic and romance tales, and he even takes a rare place reserved for "virtuous pagans" in Limbo alongside Plato and Socrates in Dante's *Inferno* (Canto IV, line 129). This Western tendency cast Saladin as the "only noble infidel" and the "worthy adversary" of Richard Lionheart. Unsurprisingly those parts of his biography that did not fit into this mould and the portions of his life in which he was not interacting with the Crusaders are omitted from the legendary treatment. The legend is interested in Saladin as an archetype rather than Saladin as a man.

The most influential depiction of Saladin in Western culture is Sir Walter Scott's 1825 historical novel *The Talisman*. Scott presents a revisionist (at least for its day) interpretation of the Crusades. The Crusaders are portrayed as scheming fanatics who invade and savage a superior, noble, peaceful Saracen culture. Saladin, as re-presented by Scott for a new "modern readership," is the magnanimous and chivalrous King of the Muslims, a man of whom "no greater name is recorded in Eastern history" (Scott 88). Saladin's generosity and nobility are emphasized by his gifts to Richard Lionheart when the Crusader-king takes ill: "Saladin, to whom none will deny the credit of a generous and valiant enemy, hath sent this leech hither with an honourable retinue and guard, befitting the high estimation in which El Hakim [the physician] is held by the Sultan, and with fruits and refreshments for the King's private chamber, and such message as may pass betwixt honourable enemies" (103–4).

Scott inflates the courage and generosity of Saladin (and casts him as a qualified physician) when it is revealed that the leech is actually the Sultan in disguise. Cast as a physician, Saladin is no longer just a warrior-king, but also an amalgam of the positive iconic qualities of the East in the eyes of the nineteenth-century West: erudite, wealthy, educated, technologically advanced. In the world of *The Talisman*, Islamic culture during the Middle Ages is so advanced that every king is a qualified physician. With *The Talisman* Scott set the legendary interpretation of Saladin's moral character that has endured since.

When the legend of Saladin gained popularity in the Middle-East during the nineteenth century, it was taken directly from these Western sources. Despite having more than one sympathetic biographer during his lifetime, Saladin, after his death, "was ignored for centuries in the Middle East" (Hillebrand 593). But over the course of the nineteenth century, "with western Christians once again intruding into the *Dar al-Islam*, intent on rewriting the past politically and historically, Arab Christians and Muslims found little to challenge the western construct of the Crusades as precursors of current events and attitudes" (Tyerman 2005, 202). As the Western Christian interpretation of Crusades began to take over, "news of [Saladin's] glowing reputation in Europe percolated into the Middle East" (Hillebrand 593). This glowing image has since supplanted nearly all other Muslim characters in Crusading history in the East, eclipsing even those considered by medieval Muslims to be far better foes of the Crusaders: Nur Ad-Din and Baybars (Hillebrand 593). After the Second World War, as Middle Eastern states like Egypt and Syria struggled for their independence from England and France, Saladin began to be specifically appropriated as an anti–Western figurehead for those movements and regimes who defined themselves by their opposition to the West. This ideology fuels the Egyptian epic film *El Naser Salah Ad-Din*. The film appropriates Western ideological structures in order to create a propagandistic portrait equating Saladin with the Egyptian President Gamal Abdel Nasser.

Released in 1963, *El Naser Salah Ad-Din* is unique in that it is the only successful attempt by the filmmaking industries of the Middle East to portray the events of the Crusades.[3] Critics have praised it as "perhaps the most important epic film in Arab cinema" (Massad 81), and it has helped, in part, to launch the career of one of the Middle East's best-known and most highly regarded directors, Youssef Chahine. *El Naser Salah Ad-Din* wears its politics plainly on its sleeve, causing many to argue that the film functions as little more than government-sponsored propaganda.

This chapter will explore the political terrain of 1963 Egypt, the allegory of the film, and how the ideology of "crusade" was constructed and revised by politician and filmmaker alike to promote a political agenda. It will focus on the three core tenets of Nasser's political ideology discernable within the film: secularism, pan–Arab unity, and opposition to colonialism. Furthermore, it will examine the film within the context of the socio-political milieu which, though not part of Nasser's political rhetoric, informed various episodes within the film, especially with regard to the treatment of Jews, non–Arabs and women. It will particularly compare the film with the reality of the Crusades as evidenced by recent scholarship and examination of the medieval sources. Examining the film in this context is not a way of lambasting the film for being "historically inaccurate," but a way of throwing light on what sorts of sources the filmmakers used and how their interpretation of history is shaped by the overall political thrust of the film.

Many films use propaganda in that they try to change the perceptions of the public or to influence their behavior (particularly spending behavior). Garth Jowett and Victoria O'Donnell's definition of propaganda focuses upon the aspect of intent: "*the deliberate*, systematic attempt to shape perceptions, manipulate cognitions, and direct behavior to achieve a response that furthers the desired intent of the propagandist" (6). The key difference between *El Naser Salah Ad-Din* and other films is intent: while other films may promote agendas as a matter of course, this film was produced, in part, by the Egyptian government. It intends to allegorize the actions and ideology of their administration in a heroic light and to bestow upon them a historical precedent.

However, it is difficult to gauge the extent of the direct influence of the government upon the film. In 1963 the Egyptian state completed its takeover of the film industry by establishing the National Cinema Council (Samek 12–15). Fawal says the film was "heavily supported by Nasser's regime" (158), and Maureen Kiernan notes the political allegory required to attain public funds: "the project conformed very nicely with the political focus of state film production at this particular historical moment.... So in this instance, the political parallels suggested in the script, as presented to the National Film Board and to Chahine, were effective in securing funding" (137). Though the extent to which the state directly controlled the political messages in *El Naser Salah Ad-Din* is unclear, the film does not deviate from its staunch support of the Nasser administration's ideals.[4]

The politics of 1963 visibly influenced how the filmmakers (including the aforementioned National Cinema Council) wished to have their recent and distant past understood by the public.[5] To the Egyptian public of 1963, the Crusader Kingdom of Jerusalem during the years following the First Crusade was comparable with the recently established nation of Israel. Ibrahim Fawal notes, "In both cases, the perception was that under the guise of religion, a sacred Arab city was descended upon by waves of outsiders who, unprovoked, proceeded to dispossess the rightful owners and inhabitants and to wreak havoc in their life" (159–60). Additionally, for Egyptians, the Revolution of 1952 (which ended the British occupation of the country and ousted the monarchy in favor of a military leadership) and, more recently, the nationalization of the Suez Canal in 1956 had become symbols of national pride, representing their victory over those same "waves of outsiders." These victories parallel the victories of Saladin: his reconquest of Jerusalem in 1187 can be interpreted as an ousting of western occupation and restoring indigenous rule similar to the Revolution of 1952. Additionally Saladin's victories over the Third Crusade can be interpreted as a successful resistance to an attempt by Western imperialists to re-establish their hegemony over the Middle East, like the Suez Crisis of 1956.[6] *El Naser Salah Ad-Din* argues that the catalyst necessary to replace the failures at the end of the First Crusade with the successes at the end of the Third was a strong leader, one capable of uniting the people, inspiring heroism, and defeating his foes either through battle or diplomacy. In the twelfth century Saladin filled this role. The film argues that Nasser fills this role as a new incarnation of Saladin by giving a deific representation of Saladin a recognizably Nasserite ideological bent.

The filmmakers are not subtle about the equation of their contemporary political situation and their political interpretation of perceived Crusade history. As Joseph Massad notes: "Historical epics are not simply used by Chahine to illustrate historical events, but as a lens on the present. In this sense, his epics emerge more as national allegories" (81). The film presents the events surrounding the Third Crusade as a cipher for the political events of 1963's Egypt. The influence of Nasser's cult of personality, political ideology, and aspirations are present in the film, wrapped in the classic Hollywood historical epic genre.

The Cult of Saladin

The manner in which a heroic character is represented in a historical film shows not only what sort of values the hero was reputed to have, but what values are deemed heroic in the eyes of the filmmakers. In *El Naser Salah Ad-Din* understanding the construction of Saladin's heroic qualities is the key to interpreting the film's historical context, since the film is a propagandistic attempt to equate the heroic actions and qualities of Saladin with Gamal Nasser. Nasser, as figurehead of the Egyptian revolution, president for life, and architect and ruler of the United Arab Republic, propagated a growing personality cult that was fed by pervasive propaganda. *El Naser Salah Ad-Din* is atypical of Nasser's propaganda campaign; it is one of the only historical cinematic propaganda efforts (in direct contrast to the pervasive photographic presence of the president), and the allusion linking Saladin to Nasser was not widely exploited or repeated in the media.

Unlike in DeMille's *The Crusades* (1935), where the audience is asked to understand and ultimately identify with King Richard's redemptive journey from childish braggart to penitent true believer, the hero of *El Naser Salah Ad-Din* is the stuff of legends: beyond reproach and without flaw. The audience is not asked to identify with Saladin, since he is so noble, moral, and virtuous; they are asked either to worship him or to aspire to be like him (if such a thing could be even possible). The film does not attempt to present a complete biography of Saladin, but rather the legendary excerpts which have given him his heroic status. The film excises anything which might potentially paint the man in an unpleasant light, which amounts to the first half of his military career. It begins at a positive moment in the life of Saladin: 1187, before his decisive victory of Hattin, before his conquest of Jerusalem, before successfully stymieing the Third Crusade. It skips the uncomfortable portions of Saladin's life in which he rebelled against his lord Nur al-Din and, through guile or siege, had managed to conquer Egypt, Syria, and many of its environs. It skips over all of Saladin's setbacks and losses. It does not continue to Saladin's peaceful death, which occurred soon after Richard returned to England, but instead ends triumphantly with Saladin, standing tall, thanking God for his victories after Richard's departure, in spite of the fact that Saladin's real death would make ample cinematic fodder. Saladin was grievously ill during his fight against the Third Crusade and died shortly after the final truce was brokered. This story could easily be spun into a narrative of a hero giving his life for his cause. Additionally, according to the poet Baha' al-din Zuhair, when his treasury was opened to prepare funerary arrangements, it was found to be empty because Saladin had given so much to charity. Whether that is reliable or apocryphal, it would certainly have made an appropriate end to the film. But Saladin's death is omitted, possibly in deference to the Saladin-as-Nasser metaphor—propagandists would likely be opposed to seeing their heroic Nasser-figure dead. So this Saladin does not falter, does not fail, and will never die: more icon than man. The title itself reflects this desire. *El Naser Salah Ad-Din*, aside from a punning visual reference to whom the film is *really* about, translates into either "The victorious Saladin" or "Saladin Victorious." Here, the film clearly states its purpose: to show the Saladin of legend having come out victorious over Egypt and Syria and finishing with his victory over the Crusaders. *El Naser Salah Ad-Din* does not present a narrative arc or the development of character, only a meteoric rise because of innate, unfaltering, superhuman virtue.

In the film Saladin's only thought is for his people. He weeps for the lives of his soldiers, and his motives are those of a altruistic uniter: "My dream is to see the Arab nation united under one flag ... hearts united and free of hate."[7] He is willing to lay down his life to preserve his people's reputation as noble and virtuous, saying, "Our [the Arabs'] good reputation is more important than my life." This idea concurs with Nasser's projected public image as a selfless, humble uniter (Nutting 6). Nasser's public image was enhanced when he tried to abdicate power in 1953 and 1967, only taking it back when public outcry demanded that he do so (and after oppositional elements had been purged from the government). Saladin is also shown to be humble and pious, praising God in the final scene with "Thanks, O Lord, you have made your servant victorious. By your will alone we have vanquished the enemy." He is shown as religiously sensitive and tolerant to a fault, inviting the Crusaders into Jerusalem for Christmas and deciding to stay his armies on that night, even when an attack would have been to his advantage. This scene attempts to construct a historical pedigree for Nasser's secularist policies and his opposition to fundamentalist religious movements in his country (Ajami 41–43). The conflict of the film's Crusade (and, to the viewer, the conclusion of the entire narrative of the Crusade) is ultimately resolved not by the blood of the warriors, but by the magnanimity and pacifist diplomacy of Saladin. Through Saladin's constant drive for peace, for which he even puts his own life at risk, Richard Lionheart's pride, and symbolically the pride of the entire Crusade, is broken. Saladin gets the final word, instructing Richard to "tell all those in Europe that war is not always the solution." When this statement comes from Saladin, it shows wisdom and restraint from the commander of a superior and victorious army. However, in 1963 the military roles were reversed, and in this context it becomes a pacifist plea for restraint to those who could have destroyed Nasser's Egypt during the revolution of 1952 and the Suez crisis of 1956. During the revolution Nasser was renowned for promising the safety of the British colonials and their property, a politically savvy move that decreased the threat of British intervention. In 1956, when his country was defeated militarily by France, Great Britain, and Israel, Nasser diplomatically courted the sympathy of the United States and Soviet Union, achieving a diplomatic and relatively peaceful resolution to the crisis in which Egypt's control of Suez was restored.

The film imbues Saladin's character with the nineteenth-century Western medievalist's image of the refined gentleman-knight, further proof of the far-reaching influence of Sir Walter Scott's *The Talisman* on the popular history of the Crusades. Here he is fierce in battle, but unflinchingly honorable, flatly rejecting and exposing the treachery of Conrad de Montferrat with the words, "We don't fight over a patch of land, we fight over moral and spiritual value.... [T]he Arabs will see that a defeat with honor is better than a dishonorable victory!" Saladin is shown to be an expert strategist during his victory at Hattin, a scientist (complete with laboratory in his tent), and a doctor when, in a scene invented by Sir Walter Scott, he risks his life to infiltrate the tent of Richard in order to heal him. Though this last example is taken directly from *The Talisman*, it indicates a larger historical trend started in the nineteenth century which argued that the Crusades were a conflict between the sophisticated and scientifically advanced culture of the Arabs and the brutal, barbaric, and fanatical Crusaders. As in *The Talisman* the cinematic Saladin himself embodies all the positive qualities ascribed to the Arabs within this paradigm. That is neither a unique perspective nor even an iteration of Occidentalism; it is an Eastern re-appropriation of Western ideology recycled to promote a pro–Middle East, Nasserite ideology.

Nasserism

Three main facets of Nasser's political ideology are entwined with the Crusade narrative throughout the film: ideologies of anti-imperialism, anti-capitalism, pan–Arab nationalist unity. Each has distinct ramifications in the context of how these ideologies employ and impact on the crusade narrative.

One of the ways in which the film allegorizes its political climate is by constructing the Crusaders as congruous with the imperialist, capitalist European nations against which Nasser defined his regime: "Colonialism tried every means to weaken the Nationalists and to weaken the Arab Identity, and still to divide us through the creation of Israel as a tool of colonialism" (Nasser 1956). Both are desirous only of the "riches of the East," and ready to violently defend their interests. For example, the character 'Issa makes a speech that, though directed in the film to the Crusader-knight Louisa, functions also as the filmmakers' plea in favor of Arab self-rule and against the imperialism and capitalism of the Western powers:

> Jerusalem has always been an Arab land. We shall prove that we can rule it in peace and respect. You would rather follow those who turn their religion into a trade, to turn the holy places into markets in which to swindle the poor, pay for your blessings. The money goes into Europe's coffers; anyone who poses a threat to those profits faces fire, war and death: blackmail in the name of the Holy Scriptures.

'Issa's words frequently ring true, since (save Richard) every leader of the Crusade in the film is motivated by the promise of wealth. All of the evil deeds perpetrated by the Christians, from Reynaud's assault on the pilgrim caravan to the Third Crusade itself, share this motivation. Many Crusades scholars have exploded the traditional myth that the Crusades were populated with disenfranchised younger sons seeking their fortunes; instead, those who went frequently were already wealthy and were required to sell vast tracts of land to finance their journey. Nearly all of those who returned had been impoverished (Riley-Smith 81–105).[8] The "riches of the East"[9] which are promised to the Crusader kings (especially to the King of France) are a fabrication, a product of the fantasy of the wealthy and exotic Orient common to the Western imperialist imagination.

In contrast, Saladin is portrayed as a socialist warrior-revolutionary fighting against the opulence and greed of the wealthy imperialists. His simple military camp and the functional, often monochromatic dress he and his men wear are juxtaposed against the opulence and extravagance of the Crusaders. In one of the opening scenes, hordes of stick-wielding Arabs in peasant dress run in angry waves towards the camera, while Saladin's stoic face is overlaid on the action, calmly observing with an approving face. The peasant dress of the Arabs is in direct comparison to the armor and ostentatious gilt surcoats of the Crusaders. Whereas in *The Crusades* this same paradigm created a moral binary based upon "civility," where the more lavish dress of the Crusaders implies their civility as opposed to the Muslims' shirtless barbarity, in *El Naser Salah Ad-Din* virtue is defined by modest poverty. In one notable scene the filmmakers depict, as part of the background to a Crusader encampment, fire breathers, acrobats, and dancing harem girls all lavishly costumed in jewel-tone satin. These figures provide visual shorthand for the perceived contemporary Western attitude towards the "exotic" Oriental: by placing them in the Crusaders' camp, the filmmakers portray the twelfth-century European kings as modern Western tourists, ignorant of true Middle Eastern culture in favor of their collective fantasy. This scene exposes the absurdity of Western "orientalism."

However, in spite of the film's portrayal of the corrupted motives of the leaders and nations behind the Crusade, the film is somewhat sensitive in its depiction of the motivations of the individual, ordinary Crusaders. In one particularly poignant scene, Saladin visits and tends the wounds (again employing the M.D. bestowed upon him by *The Talisman*) of some of the Crusaders he has captured and learns about their lives: one is a mercenary, one a poor sword maker, one a Knight of the Temple, and one with whom he spends more time is a "peasant from Normandy." Saladin has great sympathy for the man, telling him he should "plant fields instead of sowing grief," evoking the familiar Christian trope of beating swords into plowshares. The filmmakers are making an interesting statement, both about the Crusaders and about their modern lives. In both enterprises, the filmmakers posit, there are ordinary people whose motives are suspect (the mercenary) and those whose motives are pure if misguided (the Knight of the Temple). In addition to the suspect and the pure, there are those, more poignantly, like the peasant: thrust into the conflict against their will and suffering just as much from the evil of their leaders as their opponents do. This portrayal is a profoundly sensitive estimation of the myriad motivations of those participating in Crusade. It preaches tolerance, humanizing the average soldier of the Crusades and thus by extension the imperialist nations against which the movie defines itself politically.

The Crusade-as-imperialism narrative is overtly represented through the visual medium as well as the dialogue. In one telling scene a group of bronzed Arabs is shown bare-chested and slave-like, pulling siege towers at the head of the Crusading army, a clear allegory for those Arabs who, in the pan–Arabist's eyes, remained in oppression in 1963; it echoes Nasser's words: "imperialism is the great power laying round the whole region a siege" (1959, 64). These towers are shown as hulking, indestructible technological behemoths, impervious to the weapons of the Arabs (until ultimately conquered by Arab ingenuity). They contribute to the larger allegory, posing the Crusaders as a seemingly unbeatable, technologically advanced, imperialist war-machine like those against which Egypt fought in 1948 and 1956. The scene ends as the caravan of siege equipment is ambushed by Saladin's cavalry, and an Arab slave cries out in praise of Saladin just before the camera cuts away.

Even the colors of the uniforms represent the imperial powers: the French are attired in blue, the soldiers of the Kingdom of Jerusalem in white, the English in red. In the group scenes solid bands of the three colors are lined against one another, creating visual congruities with the modern flags of England and France.[10] The use of the symbol of the cross in the visual composition is also striking. Each Crusader uniform and banner bears a cross, usually two or three of them. In group scenes the screen fills with hundreds of crosses. This imagery visually coheres the disparate Crusader groups into a single oppositional force: they are representatives not only of medieval and modern imperial nations, but also specifically of Christians who are homogenized by their religion. The crosses, however, are corrupted. Rarely shown in their proper configuration, they are frequently turned ninety degrees left or right (making them look more sword-like), or at times they are inverted, betraying the Crusaders' (and by extension imperialists') religious bankruptcy. Even though they profess their religion proudly on their clothing, it is twisted by their imperial greed.

Secondly, although the army is ostensibly Christian, the only character who evokes Christian imagery (usually limited to allusions to the Mount of Olives) as justification or motivation for Crusade is Richard. Richard's portrayal as an honorable man amongst zealots and thieves has little to do with history and demonstrates another influence of Sir Walter Scott's *The Talisman*. King Richard and his men are the only ones whose surcoats are blazoned with a single upright cross, denoting Richard's pure motives and uncorrupted religion. This myriad of crosses implies that in spite of their apparent unity as Christians, the Crusaders (and, by extension, their modern imperial counterparts) are fundamentally fragmented between those who use the cross as an empty symbol, a tool for personal gain and oppression, and those whose piety is real and whose motives are pure.

Blood Is Thicker Than God

El Naser Salah Ad-Din is unique among Crusade films because it defines the East not through religion, but through ethnicity. Whenever anyone, Western or Eastern, speaks of the group opposing the Crusaders, they specifically use the modern ethnic term *Arab*. This locution shows the influence of Nasser's ideals of pan–Arabic unity on the film's Saladin. On February 1, 1958, Egypt and Syria joined together to form the United Arab Republic. Even though the union collapsed three years later,[11] Fawal asserts that this "did not affect the people's love for him [Nasser], for they blamed it on others" (158). Nasser himself blamed the failure of the Republic on "Treason, which was endorsed and supported by reactionaries and endorsed by agents of colonialism, and also endorsed by the leadership of the Baath Party who endorsed and signed the document of separation because it was felt that they might have a chance in the spoils of secession" (Nasser 1963). Direct parallels between Nasser as United Arab Republic and Saladin as Sultan of both Egypt and Syria would be obvious to Egyptian audiences of the time.

However, this link is spurious. Unlike the Saladin of the film, the real Saladin did not conquer Syria and Egypt in a quest for ethnic unity, but at the head of a hostile army. Saladin's rule of Egypt was, arguably, as much a foreign invasion as the Crusaders' rule of Jerusalem; he solidified his power over Egypt only after defeating and deposing the indigenous Fatmid rulership. Interestingly Saladin's conquest of Egypt also had religious ramifications as Saladin was a Sunni whereas the defeated dynasty was Shi'ite; Shi'ites were subsequently purged from Egypt's government. Saladin then proceeded to conquer Syria in a rebellion against the lord, Nur Ad-Din, under whose banner he had conquered Egypt. Neither was the army he led Arab, but, as Lev relates, "Maqrizi [the Mamluk-era Sunni historian] is very explicit about the ethnic composition of the new army created by Saladin in Egypt; it was made up of Kurds and Turks" (150). Saladin's army was a highly paid professional force consisting nearly exclusively of heavy and light cavalry similar to the military system of Nur Ad-Din, Saladin's erstwhile master; it was certainly not composed of peasant revolutionaries as is depicted in the film.

So, despite the fact that neither Saladin himself nor his army was Arabic, this film strives to forge an ahistorical link between Saladin and the Arab people as a secular (or, at least, multi-religious) cultural-ethnic group. In the film Saladin is never overtly described as an Arab, except in his occasionally-used title "Sultan of the Arabs." This identity is instead implied by his frequent references to the Arabs as "my people," even though the historical Saladin was not an Arab, but rather a Kurd.[12] This conflation of ethnicities is related to Nasser's ideology of the pan–Arab state, which promoted the idea that "the real bonds of ... unity and development could not come from the world-wide believers in Islam but had to stem from Arab nationalism" (Heikal 26). In fact the film specifically depicts Saladin's army and the populace of the region to be like the Egypt (and greater Arab community) of 1963: religiously diverse but ethnically unified. Saladin's chief general, 'Issa, is pointedly and repeatedly shown to be an Arab Christian more pious than the Crusaders, whom he rebukes with the charge: "I am a better Christian than you. I believe that taking what is not mine is an unforgivable sin; my belief in justice is the basis of my faith."[13] Saladin's legacy as a *mujahid* is downplayed as a direct result of Nasser's secular politics and both Nasser's and possibly Chahine's, opposition to the burgeoning Islamist movement.[14] Saladin is never shown to be specifically Muslim, always referring to himself only as "a lowly servant of God and of the Arabs." Though in this piece of dialogue God takes priority, throughout the remainder of the film Saladin focuses on the latter. He does not specifically fight for Islam, never refers to the war as a *jihad* or calls himself (or is called) a *mujahid*, and goes so far as to say that "Islam and Christianity condemn bloodshed, yet we will fight if necessary *to defend our land.*" Similarly, counter to the explosion of crosses seen on the screen in group shots of the Crusaders, no crescents are seen in group shots of the Arab armies. Though it is true that Saladin's armies were not solely composed of Muslims, the fact that Islam seems to have been so thoroughly purged of his force and his rhetoric, especially in stark contrast to the cross-laden visual portrayal of the Crusaders, is obviously more a statement about religious politics of 1963 than those of 1191. Nasser himself conjured this image of unified, multi-religious struggle against colonialism and Crusade in his speech marking the unification of Egypt and Syria in 1958: "Safety motivated the region to unify and join forces when they were intimidated by European colonization, with its attempt to use the cross to cover ... to veil its acquisitive ambitions behind the mask of Christianity. The meaning of this unity had a pointed significance, when Christianity in the Arab East participated in the resisting of the Crusaders side by side with the hordes of Islam" (Nasser 1958).

Ultimately, the film aims to polarize the conflict of the Crusades, expanding it from a prolonged feud between religions and cultures into a battle of monolithic binary opposites; those who would rape and pillage a land to fill their coffers in the empty name of religion are juxtaposed against those who would unite their diverse ethnic group to defend the land they claim to be theirs. By setting the defining characteristics of each side of the conflict in this way, the filmmakers dictate their audience. They imply who has the right to take the heroic figure as one of their own and to whom the film should speak. Ideologically this audience includes only ethnic Arabs, bound together by their blood, and excludes those like radical Muslims or Christians who would seek to define people by their faith or those of the varied other ethnic groups of the region.

I Need a Jew

Not entirely surprisingly this religious inclusivity within the Arab forces does not seem to extend to the Jews. Jews were a very real presence in the Holy Land at the time. Saladin himself even famously employed Moses Maimonides, the greatest Jewish physician of the day, amongst other Jewish physicians in his retinue (Meyerhof 444). Within this context, in addition to the fact that Chahine's films frequently meditate on the question of Jewish-Muslim relations and are known for a variety of sympathetic Jewish characters, John Ganim asserts that: "The missing Jewish presence in *Saladin* thus requires explanation" (55). The story of Moses Maimonedes' employment by Saladin may have inspired the episode in *The Talisman* in which Saladin, in disguise, heals Richard. It likely inspired the aforementioned scene in *El Naser Salah Ad-Din* where Saladin sneaks into Richard's camp amidst an anti–Muslim rally in order to heal him. But ultimately the scene of Saladin-as-healer seems more an iteration of the recurrent influence of *The Talisman* on the film than any sort of clever injection of a Jew into the film. Rather than ascribing Jewish qualities or narrative functions to existing characters in the film, it seems more appropriate to examine why Jews may have been excluded from the film altogether.

I find it more feasible that any governmental interests would not have been comfortable with a Jewish presence in the film, particularly a sympathetic one. Though Chahine certainly would not have shied away from such a depiction, the government's staunchly anti–Zionist stance might have resisted any character that could lend a historical precedent to a Jewish presence in, and thus claim to, Jerusalem. However, without information from the people involved in the making of this film, this possibility cannot be taken beyond conjecture. As opposed to Chahine's other films, which engage with and tackle controversial and taboo social problems such as religious intolerance, homosexuality, and racism, *El Naser Salah Ad-Din* is gloriously uncontroversial. It is not an examination of society as it is, but rather a governmentally vetted image of how society should be wrapped in a commonly accepted historical legend.

El Naser Salah Ad-Din is certainly not alone: no other film that depicts the Crusades in the Holy Land, even the liberal-minded *Kingdom of Heaven* (2005), has any Jewish characters.[15] It is possible that this tradition was born of the Hollywood epic genre's requirement for narrative simplicity.[16] And the Jews are not alone. In a black-and-white legend of the epic struggle between Christendom and Islam, there exists little room for those who do not fit neatly into that paradigm: Jews, Copts, Syrians, Armenian or Greek Christians, or those who were the products of the many intermarriages which straddled ethnic and sometimes even religious lines. Additionally, by homogenizing the indigenous peoples of the Middle East into a single Arab ethnicity, the film sacrifices the presence of all other ethnic groups (both medieval and contemporary) within the *Dar al-Islam* on the altar of narrative simplicity and pan–Arab polemic; Turks, Kurds, Bedouins and black Africans, among others, are all ignored. Further, the sectarian divide in Islam lies completely unaddressed. While it may have seemed cumbersome to represent all these various ethno-cultural and religious groups in the film, *El Naser Salah Ad-Din*'s obsession with ethnic identity, coupled with its tacit refusal to acknowledge anyone but the Arabs, represents a political attempt to construct a fictional memory of the Crusades where Arab contributions outstrip all others. So by omitting any Jewish presence, *El Naser Salah Ad-Din* is operating both within the socio-political constraints of its time and within the pre-established ideological purview of the Crusade cinema genre.

Female Morality and Interracial Relationships

El Naser Salah Ad Din also sets itself apart from many other Crusade films by its depiction of women as lovers *and* fighters. The female characters in the film, Virginia and Louisa, take up arms and join the Crusaders in the battle of Hattin and during the battles of the Third Crusade. While that may seem anachronistic and more a function of the recruitment policy of the Israeli army than an accurate depiction of crusading armies, the truth may be more complex. Some Western chroniclers acknowledge that women, particularly noblewomen, accompanied their husbands on the Third Crusade, yet none of the Western sources depict them taking up arms. On the other hand, Muslim chroniclers 'Imād al-Din and Bahā' al-Din both explicitly relate stories of "many female knights among the Christians, who wore armour like the men and fought like men in battle, and could not be told apart from the men until they were killed and the armour was stripped from their bodies" (Nicholson 337–38). These accounts may themselves be politically motivated, seeking to cast the Crusaders as weak or morally dubious, but whatever the motivation, their account remains.[17]

These two female characters take up opposite poles of the typical angel/harlot binary of female morality. Virginia,[18] the vain, avaricious black-widow of Reynaud, instigates the entire Third Crusade on false pretenses, spinning tales in Richard's court of "Christian children dying of thirst ... [and] priests fleeing into the desert," which had been shown in the previous scenes to be patently untrue. She is a seductress and a harlot, shown wearing shockingly low-cut sheer gowns while seducing the leaders of the Crusade into betraying Richard. In the truly apropos conclusion Virginia is disfigured by being crushed beneath a falling siege tower as the ultimate karmic punishment: finally, her mangled face reflects her soul. Her beauty mangled, she confesses her crimes to Louisa and as a reward is strangled by one of the men she manipulated — the filmmakers' warning to all women who seek to gain power by manipulation.

Louisa is the female Crusader who, after deceitfully wounding 'Issa, repents from her life of war, becomes a nurse, is tried for saving 'Issa's life, and at the concluding moments of the film decides to stay in Jerusalem to marry him. She serves as the angelic counterpart to Virginia; her virtue is in her tolerance, her peacefulness, and even her chastity. During her trial Conrad de Montferrat and Virginia chastise her by saying:

> No one except Louisa denies that Saladin is anything but a savage. "Saladin has been generous with his promises," "Arabs are not barbarians," "it is not shameful to deal with them." She no longer has the sacred hate in her heart! She gave her Christian body to an Arab, forgetting the war and that we will not win if we don't hate them!

Louisa becomes a Joan of Arc figure, her virtue highlighted by the evil of those accusing her. Her tolerance and love is superior to their "sacred hate." Furthermore, the audience knows that the accusation that she has given her body to an Arab is untrue, but the fact that it is used as a weapon against her not only reinforces her sexual purity, but also reflects the contemporary idea that a woman's morality is determined primarily by her sexual integrity.

The relationship between Louisa and 'Issa fulfills two of the generic requirements for the Hollywood historical epic: the romance and the happy ending. The structure of the romance, however, is reversed from that in *The Crusades*. In this case the woman must give up her pride and lose everything before accepting the pure, noble love of the man. This scenario is played out both in politics of gender and ethnicity. When the audience first sees Louisa, she is at Reynaud's side, not only as a warrior, but as a captain of the Templars.[19] Clad in armor (but wearing uniquely feminine headgear), she is clearly identifiable as female in man's costume, perhaps a reference to the Israeli

Defense Force's mixed-gender conscription, particularly because Louisa's uniform is light blue and white (as opposed to the usual Templar red cross on a white field), the colors of the Israeli flag. After her life is twice spared by 'Issa, Louisa gives up her life as a warrior and assumes a more traditional female role: nursing the injured. In the scene where she nurses 'Issa back to health in the Crusader hospital, she is visually congruous with the rest of the *mise en scène:* all of the other medics are women; she looks, and is dressed, exactly like the rest of them, and the color of her dress matches her environment. Though the visual statement of her comfort in the hospital could represent a gesture towards history, as women commonly took roles as nurses during the Crusades (Nicholson 335–49), the lack of men and the visual incongruity of her in warrior's garb makes more of an antifeminist statement about the role of women in combat.

Even though the narrative presents a tolerant face with regard to race politics, it has its limits. For example, in the conclusion of the narrative of 'Issa and Louisa, the European woman is finally won over by the Arab man. She stays and lives with him and, ostensibly, joins his people. Since their dialogue frequently involves polemical debates about the Crusade (and by extension modern conflicts), the construction of their union, with Louisa abandoning the West and joining the Arabs, is meant to show the moral superiority of the Arab arguments, culture, and even ethnicity. Even though their ethnicity differs, however, their religion does not: the Christian 'Issa marries the Christian Louisa. The film may show multi-ethnic relationships (possibly as a nod to the contemporary reality of the multi-ethnic families of postcolonial Egypt in 1963), but inter-religious marriage is still taboo. Though the relationship between 'Issa and Louisa is controversial in that it is multi-ethnic (especially in light of the ethnic conflicts which are rife through the rest of the film), Louisa's anti-feminist angelic morality and the couple's religious congruity allow the audience to accept not only the generic romantic happy ending, but also the superiority of Saladin's, the Arabs,' and thus, Nasser's politics.

The Question of *Orientalism*

Edward Said's provocative work *Orientalism* proposed a new theory of the relationships and power structures constructed by the Imperialist West in its dealings with those places in the East it colonized and conquered and about which it fantasized. A film such as *El Naser Salah-Ad Din*, which portrays so intimately the struggle between East and West, would seem particularly suited to analysis in light of Said's thesis. However, can *El Naser Salah-Ad Din* be considered an Orientalist film, or is it, as some have argued, an "antidote" view of the Third Crusade? Surely having been made by Egyptians it cannot be considered to be Orientalist in the same way that famous Hollywood fantasies of the East like *The Sheik* (1921), *The Lives of a Bengal Lancer* (1935), or *The Crusades* (1935) are.[20] But all the same the filmmakers of *El-Naser Salah Ad-Din* did not break fully with the Western fantasy of the exotic East: the fantasies of the riches of the East, the trope of the Middle-Eastern man who seduces the European woman (though this time, instead of exoticism and eroticism, his tools of seduction are political rhetoric), the scenes of nubile acrobats and fire breathers remain, even if they live alongside scenes of medieval Muslim peasantry (albeit being crushed by a mailed boot). The placement within the film of scenes that depict stereotypical Oriental fantasy is important, however, as those stereotypical images are always associated with the Crusaders. The Crusaders lust after and cling to the Eastern jewels. Theirs is the camp of with the *Alladin*-esque circus acts. In associating the Crusaders with the despised Oriental fantasy propagated by Western popular culture, they further associate the Crusaders with the hated colonial presence.

Due to the stereotyping of the Westerners, can this film be argued as Occidentalist, just as *The Crusades* is Orientalist? The fantasies of the East are coupled with equally fantastical depictions of Europeans and Europe. Surely the casting of Hamdi Geiss (in a shocking red wig and whitened face) as Richard Lionheart is just as lamentable as the casting of either Ian Keith or Rex Harrison as Saladin (in *The Crusades* and *King Richard and the Crusaders* (1954), respectively). I don't know whether this casting was done in *El Naser Salah Ad-Din* with an ironic proverbial wink and a nod, as a clever send-up of the Hollywood habit of casting white actors and making them up to look Middle Eastern (which is likely to be as accurate and offensive as blackface).[21] It is equally likely, however, that it was merely done due to the practical difficulties of casting a recognizable Egyptian actor not only able to pass for a Plantagenet king of England, but also fluent in Arabic. This academic discourse raises a broader question of identity: how much of *El Naser Salah-Ad Din*'s fantasy can be attributed to the Western orientalist picture of the East, and how much is authentically Egyptian? Chalking all of it up to Western influence, no matter how well couched in academic language, is an orientalizing act in itself, and it condescendingly strips the filmmakers of their creative agency.

You Need a Montage

Much has been made by critics of the film's use of montage. Occurring during battle scenes or scenes of massacres, montage sequences are used, according to Privett because "he [Chahine] did not want these audiences, who he presumed would include, among others, both Muslims and Christians, to be so outraged that fighting would erupt in the theatre. So he made the scene[s] rather abstract" (see under "Saladin"). In the longest montage in the film, the slaughter of the Arab caravan by Reynaud de Chatillon, the filmmakers use a quick-cut montage of about forty shots to create a non-mimetic impression of a large massacre. They used intermixed shots of weapons, faces, avaricious Crusaders clad in black examining their plunder, weapons meeting bodies and a rapidly circling wheel of white cloth splattered with red paint, and they interposed red, white, and black fills to represent a great slaughter.

In terms of color symbolism, red, white, and black would have been deeply symbolic to the Egyptian public, as they were the colors of flags of both Egypt (from 1952–1958) and the United Arab Republic (1958–1972). White symbolized the future of Egypt after the 1952 revolution, red, the bloodshed of the revolution, and black the oppression of monarchy and colonialism. The scene's colors become an index for the audience, representing a reversion from the white of the *hajj* garments of the pilgrims, through the deepening red of the blood on the white, and ending with stark shots of black fabric, signaling that moment as the genesis of imperialist oppression (Smith 361). Color symbolism makes the ideological argument that the origins of Western imperialism, from under which Egypt has just emerged, can be found within the actions of the Crusades. Nasser himself wrote in his *The Philosophy of the Revolution*, "If the Crusades marked the first dawnings of the Renaissance in Europe, they heralded the beginning of the ages of darkness in our country" (1959, 39). It is doubtful that medieval Egyptians would have agreed. Egypt remained central to the Ayyubid dynasty founded by Saladin and the Mamluk Sultanate which dominated the region for the next three hundred years.

Despite the claim by Chahine that the montage was constructed to prevent fights in the theatre, the question remains why the scene even exists in the first place, as it seems to be entirely a historical fabrication. In spite of Viola Shafik's assertion that "[k]eeping with historical facts, it [the film] narrates that the Arab troops and their leader accept and tolerate the presence of Christians in Jerusalem and all the other contested cities while the crusaders commit bloody massacares among Muslim civilians," this pervasive image of "Arab moderation as opposed to European bloodthirstiness" (Shafik 2007, 43) is more a reiteration of the polemicist's image of Crusade and the novels of Sir Walter Scott than of medieval reality. As Tyerman argues, "One of the odder myths concerning the Middle Ages is of intolerant Christendom corrupting tolerant Islam" (2006, 228). Though the First Crusade infamously culminated in a mass-slaughter of the people of Jerusalem, regardless of creed or color, by the Crusaders in 1099, life in the Outremer afterwards was typified by varying degrees of tolerance for outsiders. In the Crusader states policies and attitudes towards non–Christians varied from locality to locality, ranging from limited integration and cooperation to relatively peaceful apartheid. Though "[t]o portray Outremer as a haven of inter-communal, still less interfaith, harmony would be absurd" (Tyerman 2006, 227), to portray it as a land where Christians butcher Muslim civilians as a matter of course, as *El Naser Salah Ad-Din* does, is equally absurd.[22] Similarly, as opposed to the image of a benevolent, tolerant Muslim society, non–Islamic communities living under Islamic rule were treated largely the same way: disenfranchised, taxed, and sometimes enslaved, but largely unmolested.[23]

The exception to this rule was Reynaud de Chatillon.[24] Medieval chroniclers recount Reynaud de Chatillon (perhaps the most universally loathed Crusader recounted by both Eastern and Western sources) violating a truce with the Muslims by capturing mercantile caravans and even conducting piracy on the Red Sea to fill his pockets. However, his *modus operandi* did not extend to slaughtering unarmed Muslim pilgrims for fun or profit as *El Naser Salah Ad-Din* depicts. The very fact that Reynaud de Chatillon was so universally loathed emphasizes the fact that his behavior was considered abnormal by those on either side of the conflict.

Later sources such as the *Old French Continuation of William of Tyre* conflates one of Reynaud's raids against a Muslim caravan in 1186 with a report of Saladin subsequently reinforcing a caravan of pilgrims returning from Mecca that included Saladin's sister (Edbury 29). The oft-repeated (if entirely fictional) scene of Reynaud attacking this caravan of pilgrims and either capturing or killing Saladin's sister emerges. This conflation may have influenced the filmmakers' decision to depict Crusaders assaulting pilgrims (and may be a window into the kind of sources the filmmakers were using for their research).[25] But, if the filmmakers' intention was to dull the inflammatory edge of the scene by shooting it in a non-mimetic way, why did they depict the Crusaders as attacking religious pilgrims at all, when Reynaud's assaults were against merchants? And why did he depict a slaughter, when in reality those merchants would have been held captive (as dead men collect no ransom)? Why fabricate something so inflammatory and then offer a stylistic retraction? Perhaps the filmmakers are trying to have it both ways: much like horror films, they have established all the tension of a horrific act, but cut away at the last moment in order to keep the act itself unseen so it can play itself out more powerfully in the imagination of the viewer. This technique also serves to support the film's "reality effects." In a their use of a technique similar to the horror film cut away from the action, the filmmakers suggest that the reality they depict is too horrible to be seen. In other words, by visually arguing that the slaughter is too horrible to be shown as it truly was, the film argues that the "reality" they cannot depict was unimaginably horrifying.

Though the film is claimed by some to be an antidote perspective to the familiar European view of the Crusades present in *The Crusades*, *King Richard and the Crusaders*, or *The Talisman*, it does not seek to present an equitable account. Rather than breaking the paradigm of stereotyping and vilification, it merely reverses it. *El Naser Salah Ad-Din* is not an antidote; it is retribution.

Conclusion

By the conclusion of the film, the image of Saladin as a medieval Nasser figure is confirmed; he is humble, selfless, pacifistic, and tolerant, while fiercely fighting for Nasser's ideal of pan–Arab unity, secularism, and anti-colonialism. It has little to do with the historical reality of 1191 or 1963 and much more to do with the construction of an image that the filmmakers felt would resonate with the contemporary Egyptian public. But this lengthy analysis ultimately leads to the question: did it work? Did the propaganda of the film have its desired effect, or any effect beyond entertaining its audience? The unfortunate answer is that it is very difficult to tell. The film did not seem markedly to affect the popularity of Nasser positively or negatively, as he reigned until his death in 1970 and is still lionized by certain sectors of the Egyptian populace.[26] Furthermore, the association between Nasser and Saladin did not seem to take significant root. Saladin (the man or the film) was never mentioned in any of Nasser's many speeches or in any of his books.[27] Though his image was ubiquitous in Egypt during his reign, Nasser was never visually associated with Saladin, and no statues or public works of art depicting Saladin were erected in Egypt during Nasser's regime. Though Saladin did not become associated with Nasser, he has been claimed by a succession of Middle-Eastern leaders, all wishing to cast their actions in a heroic light, most recently (and ironically) Saddam Hussein.[28] The film's overriding interpretation of the Crusades as a precursor of Western imperialism has remained, though the perceived imperialist enemy has shifted from European nations to the United States. Since the Iran-Iraq conflict of the 1980s, Saladin's status as a heroic symbol of Pan-Arab unity has also been challenged within Muslim society along broadly sectarian lines. As Mohamed El-Moctar argues:

> In today's Sunni and Shi'a memories about Saladin, there is little room for complexity or ambiguity. For Sunni Muslims his idealism and sincerity are beyond any doubt. He is the unifier of Islam, the liberator of Jerusalem and

the ultimate example of piety, courage and selflessness. For the Shi'a Muslims, Saladin is no more than a selfish adventurer and a traitor who compromised with the Crusaders, destroyed the most meaningful empire in Islamic history (the Shi'a Fatimid Empire) and betrayed the trust of his political leaders and his people [2].

With all that being said, *El Naser Salah Ad-Din* was certainly not a failure. It is still regarded by critics as a rare achievement in Middle Eastern cinema, and it enjoys a continuing popularity in the region. Its political connotations, though their original reference point is gone, are not entirely lost. While Egypt has changed markedly since 1963, and Nasser's vision of socialist, multi-religious, pan–Arab Unity has largely come to naught, *El Naser Salah Ad-Din* is still played annually on the state-controlled TV channel in Egypt on the national holiday celebrating the birthday of President Mubarak.

Notes

1. Roy Temple House offers this dating in his edition of *L'Ordene de Chevalerie*, but gives no reason for his conclusion other than "It seems reasonably certain that our original poem dates from very early in the thirteenth century, although all the known MSS. Are somewhat later." No subsequent scholarly editions, and no translations from the original Old French, of this poem have been done (House 34).

2. "Il ot a non Salehadins / A icel tans de che bon roi / Fisent aus gens de nostre loi / Sarrasin souvent grant damage /Par lor orgueil, par lor outrage." My translation. (House 4).

3. In 1941 the Lama brothers of Egypt made a film entitled *Saladin*, but the film was a financial and critical failure, due in no small part to the fact that it shamelessly bootlegged footage from *The Crusades* (1935) (Fawal 156).

4. It is possible that more light may be thrown on this question by exploration of Egyptian governmental archives or by interviews with the filmmakers. Mr. Chahine died on July 27, 2008.

5. It is unclear to what degree this film was influenced by its director, Youssef Chahine, as he was brought onto the project as a replacement director when Ezzeldine Zulfiquer fell ill. For this reason (and more generally because of the collaborative and evolutionary nature of film production) I reject the typical auteur theorist's concept that this film is a product, primarily, of its director. Instead of referring to this film as "Chahine's," I refer to the filmmakers as a collective unit.

6. The Suez Crisis is commonly known in the Arab world as the "Tripartite Aggression" and is also denoted by any of the following names: the "Sinai War," the "Suez-Sinai War," the "1956 Arab-Israeli War," the "Second Arab-Israeli War," the "Suez Campaign," or the "Sinai Campaign." The Israeli operation during the conflict was called "Operation Kadesh," and the Anglo-French operation was called "Operation Musketeer." A monograph with further references on the Suez Crisis that examines a broad range of primary source documents is Gorst and Johnman's.

7. All of my quotes from the film are from the English subtitles given on the video. I do not know how well these subtitles render the original Arabic dialogue.

8. For a fuller discussion of the motivation and financial ramifications of undertaking crusade, see Riley-Smith and Chapter 2 of Tyerman (2006).

9. In the film the riches of the East, as represented by a chest of obviously-fake gold coins, jewels and strings of pearls, are seen twice, first when Reynaud de Chatillon gloats over them after looting them from the pilgrims he slaughtered. Afterwards, the king of France gloats lustfully over them as they are offered to him as an enticement to embark on the crusade. It is possible that the obviously-fake jewels were used to expose the absurdity of the orientalist myth of the wealth of the East. Equally possible is that these were simply the best props available to the production company at the time.

10. In one montage the Crusade soldiers in blue and white (possibly a reference to the flag of Israel) are intercut with shots of waves crashing. Then soldiers in red run through the ranks, as if they were blood in the waves, and the blood of the battle forms an icon of the imperial nations.

11. Egypt kept the name "United Arab Republic" until after Nasser's death in 1971, even though all other nations had seceded from the union by 1961.

12. Identification with Saladin was most recently used to bolster Saddam Hussein's image, making use of the fact that they were both raised in Tikrit. This is particularly ironic because Hussein is infamous for his genocidal campaign against the very ethnic group, the Kurds, of which Saladin was a part (Tyerman 2005, 209).

13. Not only can 'Issa be viewed as a representative for the Christian minority of Egypt, but possibly also as a mouthpiece for the director, who is a member of the small Egyptian Catholic minority.

14. The Islamist movement has tried to claim Saladin as the prototype of a *mujahid* (jihad struggler). However, his dedication to jihad was not universally accepted by his contemporaries; some saw his actions as "manipulating Islam to win power for himself" (Lyons and Jackson 365–366).

15. There are some extras in group shots in *Kingdom of Heaven* which may be depicting Jews, but it is difficult to say with certainty. There are certainly no Jewish speaking characters.

16. Although *The Talisman* does not contain any Jewish characters, Jews are frequently referred to: twice in chapter two, three times in chapter eight, twice in chapter eighteen, once in chapters twenty and twenty-two.

17. Some Western sources deny that women participated in the Crusade *at all*. These instances can also be regarded as politically-motivated invention.

18. Virginia has no direct historical parallel but descends rather from the works of Tasso and Ariosto. She may also represent a satirical reference to the Virgin and thus a verbal representation of the moral disparity between word and action among the Crusaders. The character could also be read as a lampoon of the Christian ideal of female virtue.

19. Whether or not women fought in the Crusades, it is well known that the Templars forbade women to join their ranks.

20. For more on interpreting Hollywood films such as these through the lens of Orientalism, see Bernstein and Studlar *Visions of the East*.

21. The seminal work on Hollywood blackface, particularly in the context of the racial politics of Jewish actors dressing in blackface, is Michael Rogin. *Blackface, White Noise*.

22. Here Tyerman is possibly taking a jab at *Kingdom of Heaven*, released a year before his book, which portrayed the Outremer as just such a haven of communal and interfaith harmony.

23. Christopher Tyerman's chapter "East is East and East is West: Outremer in the Twelfth Century" in *God's War, A New History of the Crusades* provides a thorough examination of intercultural relations in the years between the First and Third Crusade.

24. Reynaud de Chatillon is alternately spelled in the sources Reynaud, Renaud, Reynald, Reynold, Renald or Reginald of Chastillon.

25. A scene in *Kingdom of Heaven* depicts Reynaud capturing and killing Saladin's sister in a manner described by these latter sources.

26. With that being said, Nasser's legacy is certainly not universally positive today, though he is remembered more fondly among the rural and urban working class.

27. Searches on the extensive Nasser Digital Archive, http://nasser.bibalex.org/, turned up no results in speeches or correspondence ever mentioning Saladin.

28. Darkly ironic because, while on one hand Saddam tried to claim Saladin's legacy, on the other hand he is known for ordering the extermination of hundreds of thousands of Kurds.

BIBLIOGRAPHY

Aberth, John. *A Knight at the Movies: Medieval History on Film*. New York: Routledge, 2003.

Ajami, Fouad. "On Nasser and his Legacy." *Journal of Peace Research, Vol. 11 (1)* (1974): 41–49.
Bernstein, Matthew and Gaylyn Studlar. *Visions of the East: Orientalism in Film.* London: I.B. Taurus & Co., 1997.
Dante. *The Inferno.* Trans. Robert Hollander and Jean Hollander. New York: Anchor, 2002.
Edbury, Peter W. *The Conquest of Jerusalem and the Third Crusade: Sources in Translation.* Burlington, VT: Ashgate Publishing, 1998.
El-Moctar, Mohamed. "Saladin in the Sunni and Shi'a Memories." Paper presented to the "Remembering the Crusades: Myth, Image and Identity" conference, Fordham University, New York, March 29–30, 2008.
Fawal, Ibrahim. *Youssef Chahine.* London: British Film Institute, 2001.
Ganim, John M. "Reversing the Crusades: Hegemony, Orientalism and Film Language in Youssef Chahine's *Saladin*." *Race Class and Gender in "Medieval" Cinema.* Eds. Lynn T. Ramey and Tison Pugh. New York: Palgrave McMillan, 2007: 45–58.
Gorst, Anthony and Lewis Johnman. *The Suez Crisis.* Oxon: Routledge, 1997.
Heikal, Mohamed. *Nasser: The Cairo Documents.* London: New English Library, 1973.
House, Roy Temple, ed. *L'Ordene De Chevalerie; An Old French Poem.* Chicago: University of Chicago Libraries, 1918.
Hillebrand, Carole. *The Crusades: Islamic Perspectives.* Edinburgh: Edinburgh University Press, 1999.
Jowett, Garth S. and O'Donnell, Victoria. *Propaganda and Persuasion.* London: Sage Publications, 1999.
Kiernan, Maureen, "Cultural Hegemony and National Film Language: Youssef Chahine." *Alif: Journal of Comparative Poetics. No. 1. Arab Cinematics: Toward the New and the Alternative* (1995): 130–152.
Lev, Yaacov. *Saladin in Egypt.* London: Brill, 1999.
Lyons, Malcolm Cameron and Jackson, D.E.P. *Saladin: The Politics of the Holy War.* Cambridge: Cambridge University Press, 1982.
Massad, Joseph. "Art and Politics in the Cinema of Youssef Chahine." *Journal of Palestine Studies* 28.2 (Winter 1999): 77–93.
Meyerhof, Max. "Mediaeval Jewish Physicians in the near East, from Arabic Sources." *Isis* 28.2 (May 1938): 432–460.
Nasser, Gamal Abdel. *The Philosophy of the Revolution.* Buffalo: NY: Economica Books, 1959.
_____. "Address by President Gamal Abdel Nasser in the field of the Syrian People's Congress occasion of the tenth atheist revolution, 7/22/1963." Gamal Abdel Nasser Digital Archive, *http://nasser.bibalex.org/Speeches/browser.aspx?SID=1050,* (accessed 04/22/08).
_____. "Address by President Gamal Abdel Nasser on Revolution Day IV in Alexandria 'The speech nationalizing the Suez Canal,' 7/26/1956." Gamal Abdel Nasser Digital Archive, *http://nasser.bibalex.org/Speeches/browser.aspx?SID=495,* (accessed 04/22/08).
_____. "The speech of President Gamal Abdel Nasser in the nation on the occasion of the Declaration on the foundations of unity between Egypt and Syria, 2/5/1958." Gamal Abdel Nasser Digital Archive, *http://nasser.bibalex.org/Data/GR09_1/Speeches/1958/580205.htm,* (Accessed 04/22/08).
Nicholson, Helen. "Women on the Third Crusade." *Journal of Medieval History* 23 (1997): 335–49.
Nutting, Anthony. *Nasser.* London: Constable, 1972.
Privett, Ray. "Three Films from the Middle East." *JUSUR, The UCLA Journal of Middle Eastern Studies Online,* 2004, *http://www.isop.ucla.edu/cnes/jusur/article.asp?parentid=15504,* (accessed 08/17/06).
Riley-Smith, Jonathan. *The First Crusaders 1095–1131.* Cambridge: Cambridge University Press, 1998.

Rogin, Michael. *Blackface, White Noise: Jewish Immigrants in the Hollywood Melting Pot.* London: University of California Press, 1998.
Rosenstone, Robert. "History in Images/History in Words: Reflections on the Possibility of Really Putting History onto Film." *The American Historical Review*, Vol. 93.5 (December, 1988): 1173–1185.
Samak, Qussai. "The Politics of Egyptian Cinema." *Middle East Research and Information Project Reports* 56 (April 1977): 12–15.
Scott, Sir Walter. *The Talisman.* 1825. Doyleston, PA: Wildside Press (no date).
Shafik, Vida. *Popular Egyptian Cinema: Gender, Class, and Nation.* Cairo and New York: American University in Cairo Press, 2007.
Smith, Whitney. *Flags Through the Ages and Across the World.* New York: McGraw Hill, 1975.
Tyerman, Christopher. *Fighting for Christendom: Holy War and the Crusades.* Oxford: Oxford University Press, 2005.
_____. *God's War: A New History of the Crusades.* London: Penguin, 2006.

Filmography

The Crusades, dir. Cecil B. DeMille, 1935.
King Richard and the Crusaders, dir. David Butler, 1954.
Kingdom of Heaven, dir. Ridley Scott, 2005.
The Lives of a Bengal Lancer, dir. Henry Hathaway, 1935.
El Naser Salah Ad-Din, dir. Youssef Chahine, 1963.
The Sheik, dir. George Melford, 1921.

5. "La geste que Turoldus declinet"
History and Authorship in Frank Cassenti's Chanson de Roland

Lynn Ramey

The medieval epic known as the *Song of Roland* was never concerned with faithfully recording history. Scholars date the poem to about 1100, but the story ostensibly tells of Charlemagne's crusades in Spain, which took place in the late eighth century. One of the greatest conquerors in history, Charlemagne forayed into Spain to reclaim land from Muslims who had come earlier in the century and met with one of his very few encounters with defeat. He took Pamplona, but his siege of Saragossa failed, and he left Spain without any real victory. On his way through the pass between France and Spain, he was attacked by other Christians, very likely Basques, and lost some of his men.

From this small amount of historical information, stories were told and retold, changing and expanding on this moment in history. By 1100, the Oxford version of the *Song of Roland* presents us with a tale of treason, intrigue, pride, and punishment. Recast in moralistic terms and cloaked in nascent nationalism, the epic has Charlemagne conquer virtually all of Spain, and only through trickery and the treason of a Christian can the Muslims claim any victory—the annihilation of Charlemagne's rear guard, including his nephew Roland. Christian-on-Christian violence, the historical Basque attack on the rear guard, takes on a good versus evil, Christian against Muslim struggle of literally epic proportion. Charlemagne emerges from the conflict in control of all of Spain and as protector of Christian truth. Deforming the past served Christian French society of 1100 well, as the *Song of Roland* could be used to encourage Christians to take up Urban II's 1095 call to Crusade in the Holy Land.

When French director Frank Cassenti chose to make a film he entitled *La Chanson de Roland* during the 1970s, he, too, eschewed any attempt at faithfully recording history. Cassenti admitted that he was drawn to the Middle Ages because, as a key period far removed from our own, the setting allows us to understand our present (Desrues "Entretien" 15)[1] Cassenti, as director and screenwriter, aimed for a "subjective reconstruction of History that resonates with our present" (Bertin-Maghit 112).[2] What we find in Cassenti's *Chanson de Roland* is a personal exploration of what it means to be an author and, more important, what the role of an author is in righting societal wrongs. Charlemagne's crusade into Spain becomes Cassenti's own crusade against racism and injustice in 1970s French society. By first examining Cassenti's conception and construction of the author, we will then be in a position to understand how he arrives at the point where he can claim that the film is a remedy for the racism found in the medieval epic (Bertin-Maghit 109).

Cassenti's *Chanson de Roland*

The film tells Roland's story within a frame tale involving thirteenth-century pilgrims en route to Compostella. The pilgrim party has some semi-professional actors and a jongleur, appropriately named Turolde, who tells Roland's story when the pilgrims stop their trek each evening. As the pilgrims wend their way toward the shrine of Saint James, they perform and dine at the home of a minor nobleman, where the topic of conversation is a peasants' revolt in a neighboring county. The next day, the pilgrims encounter a group of fleeing peasants, who travel alongside the pilgrims for several days. This encounter touches the pilgrims, and when the peasants part ways with the pilgrims, the pilgrims' spiritual leader tries to convince the peasants to make their own journey to Compostella. The peasants refuse, and upon parting ways the peasants quickly perish at the hands of a much better armed group of noble-class horsemen seeking revenge. Oblivious to the plight of the peasants, the main group of pilgrims continues on, while the actor who plays Roland and two of his companions head north to join another peasant revolt in Flanders.

History and the Storyteller

The Oxford version of the *Chanson de Roland* ends with the famously enigmatic line, "Ci fait la geste que Turoldus declinet" (fol. 72r) [Here ends the *geste* that Turoldus has written]. Much critical ink has been spilt over the exact meaning of the verb *declinet*, which is not commonly used in Old French to indicate either copying or writing of texts. Whatever the exact meaning of *declinet*, this phrase appears to be some sort of authorial signature at the end of this foundational monument of French literature, but it is a signature that leaves us with many questions about the role of a medieval author and the status of texts like the *Chanson de Roland*.³ Is the text primarily a written artifact of an oral performance, or is it a written product of an individual author, perhaps Turoldus? In examining that question, the role of Turoldus comes under scrutiny: was he a mere scribe or a creative genius? The answers to these questions, forever lost, are less important than the consideration of what it meant to be an author in the Middle Ages, when many texts contained no indication of who wrote them and refer specifically to long oral traditions as their narrative lineages.

While the implications of the word *declinet* are unclear, the term *geste*, generally thought to be the record of a historical event, is equally unclear. History and story are indissociably intertwined in the word *geste*, for as Margaret Burland writes, "a fundamental trait of the *geste* is that it expresses a society's consensus about events in its collective history" (34). A true *geste* is told and retold, changed each time by the need of the present story-telling society to understand its own history in a different way. In 1978 Frank Cassenti stepped into this long line of re-tellers of the *Chanson de Roland*, offering his own cinematic revisioning of France's past while reflecting the needs of his own society to understand its collective history, particularly concerning its tumultuous history of Christian-Muslim conflict. A modern-day Turoldus, Cassenti adapts this 1000-year-old story as a complex web of historical events taking place in the eighth, twelfth, and thirteenth centuries, but with clear relevance for twentieth-century France. From this mesh of meanings a preoccupation with the storyteller's role emerges with striking questions about authorship that echo those asked of medieval texts, but that are immediately relevant to debates about post–New Wave, *auteur*-oriented filmmaking in France.

The narrative structure of the film is layered, as the twentieth-century audience watches the story of a thirteenth-century pilgrimage where the pilgrims entertain themselves and their hosts by acting out an eleventh-century epic that recounts a purported episode from the eighth-century life of Charlemagne. The film has an omniscient narrator who speaks at times with a voice-over, explaining everything from the previous lives of the pilgrims to the future fate of certain members of the pilgrim party. This narrator, the audience discovers, is not the Turolde who directs the Roland performance, but rather the unnamed "clerc" or clerk who writes the story of Roland as told by Turolde in addition to the histories of the pilgrims and the people they meet. This multiplicity of authorship serves to enhance the status of the anonymous author in the Middle Ages, but it also underlines the notions that no story has a single author and that all stories result from many interactions between authors and audiences, past, present, and future. In one scene the clerk sits writing, surrounded by the children of the pilgrim party. Curious, the chil-

The clerk (Pierre Clémenti) inscribes both the stories of peasant children and those of noble heroes in Frank Cassetti's *Chanson de Roland*.

dren ask what he is doing, and he explains that his writing is recording their stories, along with the *Chanson de Roland*. The children are surprised to hear that he is writing about them as well and that the clerk puts their stories on equal footing with those of Roland and Charlemagne. This idea that all stories are worth telling and that there is nobility in even the everyday life implies an egalitarianism that is certainly not reflected in the textual record that comes down to us from the "real" Middle Ages. It does, however, reflect Cassenti's notion of the author, as he gives even greater screen time to the story of the everyday lives of the thirteenth-century pilgrims than he does the legendary lives of the heroes of the epic *Chanson de Roland*. The importance of the author who tells all stories returns at the end as Turolde is killed in the violence between peasantry and nobility, but the story continues as the clerk finishes not Roland's story, but the story of Klaus and the other pilgrims.

The cinematography and mise-en-scène serve to support this hierarchical structure of the narrative, as the pilgrim and epic stories are filmed very differently. The pilgrim story is shot with a mobile camera, bringing the audience into the frame along with the pilgrims. The point of view is often that of a fellow pilgrim, so that as we move along the route with the same perspective as the pilgrims, we watch the performance as would a medieval audience member seated on the floor of the castle, and we see what the peasants see as the armed noble classes bear down upon them on horseback. On the other hand, the epic sequences generally begin with a camera movement toward a darkened or black area in the story time present, which serves as a fade to the epic frame. The epic story is filmed much more statically with long shots and a theater-like setting for the players. Though we know that the pilgrim actors have very little in the way of costuming or props, the epic frames transport the viewer to a liminal dream or fantasy space where the actors are clean and impeccably dressed, unlike their filthy thirteenth-century counterparts who are clad in rags. While we see the "horses" of the thirteenth-century performance are really simply a performer knocking together two round objects, in the epic frame the horse and weaponry are quite real. The pilgrimage is filmed with a more realistic color palette, and while it is often raining during the pilgrimage, there are also warmer, brighter colors both in the daytime scenes and in the campfire scenes. The epic portions are filmed with no indication of weather, creating a rather cold, uniform world with a slightly blue, and therefore cold, tint, which further adds to the feeling that even the epic battle scenes are shot on an indoor stage. These cinematographic choices serve to bring the audience closer to the "real" story of the pilgrims while distancing the viewer from the legendary story of Roland.

One of the most striking changes that Cassenti makes to the epic is his refiguring of the Ganelon-Roland conflict. In the Oxford Roland, the literary version commonly read and studied, Ganelon is the archetypical traitor, while Roland figures as an almost Christ-like hero whose martyred body is lifted directly from the battlefield to heaven by an angel. In Cassenti's version Roland's excessive pride and predilection for violent conflict are figured more darkly, giving Ganelon a moral upper-hand as he makes his plea for peace with the Muslim armies. In the opening scene two Muslim horsemen, apparently messengers, approach the Christian army, which stands watching on a hill. No threat could be construed from their approach or demeanor, particularly as they are vastly outnumbered and carry no visible weaponry. Roland makes a gesture to archers standing beside him, and one of them fatally shoots one of the messengers. The other messenger cries out in Arabic, while the archbishop Turpin, speaking to the camera in a voice that could not be heard by those around him, tells the remaining "pagan" to go and tell his king that God is helping the Christians and that Charlemagne will prevail. Charlemagne, expressionless, watches the drama unfold in front of him. Roland, then, from the first scene is cast as a maverick who unilaterally makes significant policy decisions, turning what could have been a moment of reconciliation or détente into heightened conflict. Cassenti's lighting makes evident Roland's ambiguous nature by shooting Roland with sharply contrasting

Shadows on the faces of Olivier (Pierre Clémenti) and Roland (Klaus Kinski) make manifest the ambiguity of Roland's actions.

shadows falling across his face for the entire scene, as he encourages Charlemagne to continue his fight against the Muslims.

Cassenti sets the thirteenth-century plot in parallel with the epic plot, as during a court feast the pilgrims hear about local peasant uprisings. Discussion of this "treasonous" behavior on the part of the peasantry creates tension between those who sympathize with the plight of the hungry underclasses and those who declare social roles as immutable and sacred. To release the tension the pilgrims are called on to perform a *geste*, and they pick up where they had left off in the *Chanson de Roland* story: the moment of Ganelon's treason. As Thierry, the pilgrim who plays Ganelon, plays the scene, his dislike for Roland is entirely motived by his dislike of Roland's pride and warmongering, which creates a sympathetic connection with modern audiences. The transition back from the epic plot to the pilgrimage plot occurs when Ganelon who, upon convincing Charlemagne that there will be no trouble and that Roland should lead the rear guard, collapses against a wall. As Ganelon falls, there is a cut from a distant shot showing all the players to a close up on Ganelon. At the moment of the fall and the cut, we find ourselves abruptly back in the present of story time, where Thierry has literally collapsed in playing the role of Ganelon. Klaus rushes to Thierry's side and explains to onlookers that "he could never play the moment of Ganelon's treason." This inability to betray, even in the interest of peace, further heightens the audience's perception of Ganelon as heroic traitor. His treason tears him apart, but since it is done for the right reasons, the audience is led to understand his motivation and forgive him.

Cassenti as Auteur

In choosing the *Song of Roland* as subject for a film, Frank Cassenti was faced with the daunting task of putting on celluloid a story known to all French; as France's first recognized literary work, for some this epic goes so far as to define the very historical notion of Frenchness. The *Chanson de Roland* has been a staple of the French educational system since Joseph Bédier's 1922 edition. One might expect Cassenti to film such a monumental work in a "epic" way, and the difference between Cassenti's version and a typical "epic" treatment is worth consideration. Surely one of the hardest film genres to define is that of the "epic" film, encompassing such examples as *Ben Hur, Gone with the Wind, The Ten Commandments,* and more recently, *300* and the *Star Wars* films. Some of these films are adaptations of literary works, but none comes from literary epics *per se,* and there is little that links these films with one another. Among those who espouse film genre studies, epic is one of the most despised and ignored genres, Vivian Sobchack tells us, often seen by criticsas overly extravagant and distasteful (298). One scholar advances a definition of epic film that would include high production costs, a cast of many, and multiple crane shots. Decidedly this was not the direction that Cassenti took.

Cassenti's Roland came to fruition a decade after the last of the great Hollywood historical epics, which reached their peak in the 1950s and 60s. As he struggled with the problem of how to tell Roland's story, Cassenti did not have the option of emulating the high budget Hollywood films that one might imagine would befit France's founding epic. French cinema of the 1970s was largely in a state of crisis, and elaborate sets with casts of thousands were not an option for this relative newcomer to French cinema. The crisis of French cinema found its way into the film, according to Cassenti.[4] Cassenti turned another direction, seeking not to make an epic film, but rather setting out to understand the epic in order to film it. While the *Song of Roland* had been part of the national intellectual fabric for fifty years, it had recently returned to center stage as the topic of heated academic debate, because of Paul Zumthor's *Essai de poétique médiévale,* published just a few years before Cassenti began work on his film. This nexus of filmic generic evolution with advances in knowledge of oral composition gave birth to a unique version of the *Song of Roland.*

Cassenti confronts the issues of history, authorship, and even genre. In a scene found toward the opening of the film, two "authors" of the *Roland* present their work. The first speaker is Turolde, the jongleur, who incarnates Cassenti's vision of Turoldus of the Oxford *Roland*. Turolde introduces a leper to Klaus, the actor playing Roland. When the leper asks who is playing Olivier, the film cuts to a man identified only as a young troubadour who knows how to read and write. This anonymous writer explains his work to a group of children.

Cassenti has thus cast Turolde as storyteller; elsewhere in the film he is said to tell Roland's story better than anyone else, but Cassenti does not see him as an author of the epic — he serves more the roles of casting and production manager, as well as screenwriter. Turolde finds his acting crew along the route, at one point convincing a priest to allow a condemned man to come with the pilgrims in order to expiate his sin, when in fact Turolde has heard that the man is an excellent actor and wants him in his *Roland*. Negotiating for favorable terms for the troupe, Turolde ensures that his players are fed at each stop in return for their work. At one point in the film, Klaus comments that Turolde has managed to eat an entire family's food for a week in return for one performance, and the viewers are well pleased with their trade. Turolde has a flair for the dramatic as he sets the scene for the epic each evening, tossing smoke-producing material into the fire for an almost magical effect. Acclaimed as the best storyteller, Turolde makes no claim to individual authorship, but rather celebrates the creative genius of retelling an old story in a new way.

Turolde's job is complemented by the work of the unnamed, literate troubadour who writes the story not only of Roland, but also the story of each of the contemporary pilgrims. As he explains to the children, he is telling their story as well as that all the pilgrims: their parents, Marie the former prostitute, the ex-slave from Africa, and many others. This vision of the author has the troubadour inserting contemporary concerns into the medieval text. The story he writes spans generations, linking the eighth-century Charlemagne with the thirteenth-century pilgrims. Cassenti seems to have merged Joseph Bédier's *Legendes épiques* thesis of the pilgrim route theory of epic origins with the notion of oral transmission. Following the oral-formulaic theory of the origin of the *chansons de geste*, this particular Roland was recreated orally until a literate individual trained in oral-formulaic composition wrote it down. Cassenti did his homework on this film: the oral-formulaic theory of epic composition was fleshed out during the 60s and 70s. According to this theory the *Song of Roland* and other epics could well have been told orally for generations, but at some point a scribe wrote a version of the song that he heard. The unnamed young man who plays Olivier, unlike the "writer" proposed by most epic composition theorists, is not a cleric, but rather a troubadour.

Cassenti embodies in this literate troubadour a different conception of creativity that finds resonance in the 1970s. Making the writer a troubadour gives him far more creative control over Roland's story. The troubadour and Turolde become a team in which both are the "authors" of the text, indispensable to the creation of the story. For Cassenti this notion of performative authorship corresponds to and refigures notions of authorship in film. The French film industry had grown increasingly corporatized following World War II, with most films being large productions with increasing input from financial backers, following the Hollywood model. The role of the director in making films had decreased in importance from the earlier French model of the art house film, where creative control lay mainly in the hands of the director. The French New Wave group that grew out of the *Cahiers du cinéma* in the 1950s put the question of filmic authorship at the center of critical attention, placing a much greater importance on the director's role. In *auteur* theory the director is a true author, as a literary author is, exercising full control over his or her work. François Truffaut, a key member of the *Cahiers du cinéma* and New Wave groups, illustrates this model of *auteurship* perfectly in his film *Day for Night*, in which Truffaut himself plays the director who acts as chief of casting, editing, and cinematography, acting coach, and even semi-spiritual, decidedly paternalistic, head of the family of actors. A creative visionary, the director incorporates into the film some of the crises that arise on the set. Tensions between pairs of actors find their way into the film, infusing it with an energy and uniqueness that would not have emerged in a more structured, corporate, capitalistic view of filmmaking. During the filming there is little separation between the actors and the characters they play; fiction and life reflect and reform each other in inevitable and often painful ways.

Cassenti's *Chanson de Roland* is a presentation of a theory of *auteur*-ship that modifies the New Wave take on the *auteur*. The thirteenth-century production of the *Song of Roland* is depicted as a joint creative effort, with essential roles being shared between Turolde and the literate troubadour. Between the two of them, they tell a universal story, one that links the eighth-century story of Ronceval with the thirteenth-century peasant revolt. Of all genres the epic has perhaps the least clear authorial lineage. Cassenti tells little of the story of Roland, relying on common knowledge of the epic; he focuses instead on the mass creation of a legend. He begins the film with a short scrolling narrative that reads:

> In 778 Charlemagne's rear guard was massacred by Basque looters in the pass of Ronceval. Of these facts, memory has only conserved the legend of the storytellers who sang of Roland and Olivier's prowess in order to make the

people forget their great misery. Because the imaginary and the fantastic were a part of the real, pilgrims, en route to Saint James of Compostella throughout the 12th century, identified with the heroes of the past in their martyrdom, forgetting for a time the real causes of their suffering. Of history, we only retain its legends.

As an exemplar of the notion that only legends remain of history, the film the parchment pages that the literate troubadour has so carefully inked with the pilgrims' story are dramatically destroyed during an attack on the group. We know, of course, that the story will eventually make its way to the page, but not this time and not with the story of these same thirteenth-century pilgrims. Following the vagaries of *mouvance*, this particular version will not reach the present day, but elements of the story surely will. Cassenti himself opts to tell not *the* story of Roland, but the story of how Roland became a legend and how Roland-like qualities are appropriate in other places and times.

These universal values are explicit in the two characters of Olivier and Roland. Olivier, the troubadour/writer, is the wise but more prudent of the two, even in the thirteenth century. The thirteenth-century Klaus, who plays Roland, acts bravely and with conviction, but like Roland must ultimately meet a tragic fate. Whereas Roland takes a doomed stand against a vast Muslim army, the thirteenth-century Klaus, upon hearing of the peasant rebellion, abandons his journey to Compostella, leaving the pilgrimage party to aid the rebels. The epilogue tells us that Klaus dies in Flanders fighting alongside the peasants in this noble but equally doomed affair. Klaus, who abandons the role of Roland in order to follow the rebellious peasants to the north, holds the key to understanding the film's take on the importance of struggle:

> The meaning of the film is a reflection on the representation of the History, myth and social role that the actor plays who acts in a Historical role. It's about a Historical actor who realizes that he is in the service of a certain ideology — that of death, of dominant orders — and who puts himself in the service of another ideology — that of revolt and of life"[5] [Bertin-Maghit 114].

In telling the *Song of Roland* in this manner, Cassenti has captured an essential part of epic composition, at least through his optic of notions of history and the epic genre. While we might have expected a huge, elaborate, corporate-financed story with a cast of many, in short an epic film to tell an epic on film, what we have instead is a personal interpretation of the creation and societal importance of epic. For Cassenti an epic is a story that makes people forget their miseries, a story for which they will gladly give up their food for a week in exchange. But ultimately more important, perhaps, it also inspires them to action, teaching them about the valor inherent in a struggle against all odds.

Creating an Ideology and History in 1970s France

The 1970s marked a turbulent period for Muslims in France. Following World War II many of the Algerians who had fought on the side of the Allies expected to become full-fledged members of the French nation. They had understood that if they fought for France, then they would become citizens and not the colonized underclass. While the French government made some concessions, full equality was neither granted nor perceived. In part due to the devastation of the French work force in the two World Wars, the French government actively encouraged immigration, particularly from North Africa. The massive wave of immigration resulted in conflict and misunderstanding between "old" and "new" French citizens. Meanwhile, the push for decolonization and France's initial resistance to granting Algeria its independence eventually resulted in armed conflict. Though the Algerian War officially ended in 1963, Algerians and North Africans encountered a backlash of sentiment in France for at least a decade. Hastened by the economic crisis of the early 1970s, anti-immigrant feeling culminated in the 1974 official end to immigration in France.

In good post–New Wave fashion, Frank Cassenti approached the *Chanson de Roland* not as a literary adaptation, but rather as an opportunity to film his own history and to rewrite History to make it relevant. Just as the scribe in the film tells the story of his contemporaries, Cassenti tells the story of his generation. Film critics seemed to sense the political leaning of the film, but they almost universally saw it as a response to the defeat that year of the French Communist Party in the general elections.[6] Cassenti denied this purported impetus, noting that he had begun the film years before. In an interview Cassenti states that he was motivated to make the film to address the racism of the *Song of Roland* (Bertin-Maghit 112). Born into a French-Jewish family in Morocco, he moved to Algeria as an adolescent. When Cassenti studied the *Song of Roland* in school, he felt the racist dimension of the text and made a connection between "fascist" Roland's imperialistic war and the wars of colonization (112).[7] Cassenti says no more about racism, but the film treats the Christian-Muslim conflict in a wholly different manner than the medieval epic does. The majority of the film plot has a notable absence of Muslims. The film begins with two lone Muslim horsemen coming to deliver a message to Charlemagne, and Muslims are present at the final battle. The felonious attack that Roland instigates on the messengers shows that the source of the conflict is in fact Roland, justifying the massacre that occurs later in the film. Just as the unarmed messenger is shot by Roland's archers, Roland does not die from blowing the horn as he does in the epic, but rather from a rain of arrows whose parallelism amounts to poetic justice.

Cassenti's work is marked by the pervasive influence of Frantz Fanon, a thinker and compatriot whose work could not have been unknown to the Algerian Jew. Following the publication of the *Wretched of the Earth* in 1961, Fanon was inextricably linked to the notion that change, a break with the past, could only be effected through violence and revolution:

> For the last can be the first only after a murderous and decisive confrontation between the two protagonists This determination to have the last move up to the front, to have them clamber up (too quickly, say some) the famous echelons of an organized society, can only succeed by resorting to every means, including, of course, violence [3].

Furthermore, for Fanon this change could only come about through a revolution led by the rural underclasses, or peasantry: "[the peasantry] has nothing to lose and everything to gain. The underprivileged and starving peasant is the exploited who soon discovers that only violence pays"(23). The *Chanson de Roland* ahistorically creates this same conflict within the confines of thirteenth-century France. True change in the miserable conditions of the medieval underclass, filmicly marked by the filthy and colorless world the peasants inhabit, can only take place through a rejection of the fascist legends of the past, as embodied in the character of Roland. The dinner discussion between the players and their noble hosts refers to the peasant uprisings and the problem of the peasantry not knowing "their place." Like Fanon, who dwells long on the pitfalls of religion in avoiding necessary violence, Thierry accuses organized religion in the exploitation of the underclasses. Cassenti claimed to be challenging the monolithic history of the past, refiguring Roland as a fascist nationalist and Klaus, realizing this, chooses a different path (Desrues "Entretien" 18). Klaus joins the peasant revolution and will die, but through his sacrifice and that of his fellow peasants, a history more meaningful than legend will be forged. While the underclass plays a privileged role in Cassenti's film, the communist link with the recent defeat of the PCF, while appropriately coincidental, does not replace Cassenti's own view that the film means to combat the fascism and racism that he finds inherent in contemporary French policies toward Muslims. The violence of the underclass in the film is generalizable, referring to the right of any oppressed group to take arms to bring about permanent change.

Klaus' ultimate sacrifice to free the European peasantry ranges far from the medieval oral poems that told of Roland's death at the hands of the Christian Basques in the service of Charlemagne. This recasting of the epic is oddly appropriate as it inverts exactly what "Turoldus" did when he changed the

Basque attack on the rear guard to a story of Muslim on Christian violence. Cassenti returns the conflict to one of Christian on Christian, class on class, erasing what he perceived to be the racism of the medieval epic. The virtual absence of Muslims in the story points out that real Muslims have very little to do with Western crusading ethos. In retelling the Song of Roland, Cassenti reminds the viewer of the uncomfortable truth: Crusades to Spain and the Holy Land have much more to do with internal Western social crisis and conflict than with a desire to see the establishment of truth and justice.

Notes

1. "C'est dans la mesure où il constitue une époque charnière que le Moyen Age m'a intéressé avec toujours la perspective de travailler sur l'Histoire, d'aller le plus loin possible dans la mémoire de mes contemporains pour leur donner à voir leurs origines historiques et culturelles en établissant sans cesse le parallèle avec la société dans laquelle ils vivent."
2. "Une reconstruction subjective de l'Histoire qui entre en résonance avec notre présent."
3. The long history of debates surrounding the authorship of this particular epic is beyond the scope of this paper, but see Burland for a discussion and further bibliography.
4. "Ce qui m'intéresse c'est de parler du présent et dans ce présent il y a ... la difficulté de faire des films," Hubert Desrues, "La Chanson de Roland: entretien avec Frank Cassenti," *Image et son: revue de cinéma* 328 (1978): 19.
5. "Le sens du film est une réflexion sur cette représentation de l'Histoire, du mythe et du rôle social que joue l'acteur interprète de l'Histoire. Il s'agit d'un acteur de l'Histoire qui prend conscience qu'il est au service d'une certaine idéologie; celle de la mort, des ordres dominants et qui va se mettre au service d'une autre idéologie, celle de la révolte et de la vie."
6. See Hubert Desrues, "La Chanson de Roland," *Image et son: revue de cinéma* 331 (1978): 102. and Jean-Pierre Oudart, "Le P.C.F. et la mode rétro: La Chanson de Roland," *Cahiers du cinéma* 295 (1978): 50–51. and Jean-Pierre Bertin-Maghit, "Trois cinéastes en quête de l'histoire: entretien avec René Allio, Frank Cassenti et Bertrand Tavernier," *Image et son: revue de cinéma* 352 (1980): 116.
7. "L'épopée de Roland et de Charlemagne a marqué ma scolarité en Algérie, où dans le contexte de la guerre, j'ai ressenti la dimension raciste du texte. Il était difficile de ne pas faire un rapport entre la guerre de Roland, ses visees imperialists et la guerre colonialiste."

Bibliography

Bertin-Maghit, Jean Pierre. "Trois cinéastes en quëte de l'historie: entretien avec René Allio, Frank Cassenti et Bertrand Tavernier." Image et son: revue de cinéma 352 (1980): 108–17.

Burland, Margaret Jewett. *Strange Words: Retelling and Reception in the Medieval Roland Textual Tradition*. Notre Dame, IN: University of Notre Dame Press, 2007.

Delorme, Christian. "Le dialogue islamo-chrétien en France." *Histoire de l'islam et des musulmans en France du Moyen Âge à nos jours*. Ed. Mohammed Arkoun. Paris: Albin Michel, 2006.

Desrues, Hubert. "La Chanson de Roland." *Image et son: revue de cinéma* 331 (1978): 101–02.

_____. "La Chanson de Roland: entretien avec Frank Cassenti." *Image et son: revue de cinéma* 328 (1978): 15–19.

Fanon, Frantz. *The Wretched of the Earth*. 1963 Présence Africaine. Trans. Richard Philcox. NY: Grove Press, 2004.

Oudart, Jean-Pierre. "Le P.C.F. et la mode rétro: La Chanson de Roland." *Cahiers du cinéma* 295 (1978): 50–51.
Sobchack, Vivian Carol. ""Surge and Splendor": A Phenomenology of the Hollywood Historical Epic." *Film Genre Reader III*. Ed. Barry Keith Grant. Austin: University of Texas Press, 2003. 296–323.
Turoldus? "La Chanson de Roland." c. 1100. May 18 2008. <http://image.ox.ac.uk/show?collection=bodleian&manuscript=msdigby23b>.

Filmography

La Chanson de Roland, dir. Frank Cassenti, 1978.

6. Agenda Layered Upon Agenda
Anthony Mann's 1961 Film El Cid

KEVIN J. HARTY

The myopic geopolitical view we may hold today can easily lead to a misreading of Anthony Mann's 1961 film *El Cid*[1] as somehow prescient of the world post–9/11.[2] The film's opening rant by Herbert Lom's head-to-toe black-garbed Ben Yussef is a screed worthy of the Taliban or El Qaeda:

> "...The Prophet has commanded us to rule the world.... Burn your books. Make warriors of your poets. Let your doctors invent new poisons for our arrows. Let your scientists invent new war machines, and then kill! Burn!"[3]

Mann's 1961 film is multilayered, but its politics are distinctly the politics of the late 1950s and the early 1960s, of the Cold War, and not of today's war on terror. And multilayered may not accurately reflect the nature of the film's politics. Indeed, everyone associated with the film — and that group includes a much greater cast of characters than might be immediately apparent — seems to have multilayered agendas.[4]

Such political agendas seem appropriate to a film about a historical figure who through the centuries has been used to advance a continuing series of often conflicting agendas. The historical Don Rodrigo de Vivar (d. 1099) was a mercenary and solider of fortune whose checkered career included service to, and conflict with, both Christian and Moorish masters. Ian Michael in his introduction to the standard bilingual edition of *The Poem of the Cid* edited by Hamilton and Perry calls him an "outlaw" (1). Eventually Don Rodrigo carved out a portion of the much divided Spain of his day as his own kingdom (nominally held in the name of Alfonso VI) with Valencia as its capital. He would die there peacefully in his sleep, succeeded by his wife, Jimena (or Ximena) of Oviedo as ruler until the city was besieged by Moorish invaders from North Africa, abandoned by Jimena, and burned by Alfonso in 1102.

The history of Don Rodrigo would soon enough become the stuff of legend, and the legend the stuff of myth. Much of the poem's modern reception has benefited from the lifelong dedication to the poem's unique manuscript[5] and the legend of the eponymous hero by the late Hispanist Ramón Menéndez Pidal, who served as an advisor to Mann's film.[6] Within a century of Don Rodrigo's death, his deeds were transformed and expanded into a body of literature that would find its synthesis in the three-part Castilian epic known as *Poema de Mio Cid*, itself preceded by a Latin chronicle the *Carmen campidoctoris*. It is in this literary tradition that the Cid joins company with the likes of Roland, Siegfried, Beowulf, and Arthur as a figure whose destiny and that of his country are inextricably linked. Further, this literary tradition would merge chivalric chronicle with chivalric romance in Mann's film to advance the legend of a man torn between his love for his wife and his love for his country — both framed by a monomaniacal loyalty to his king or to the idea of the Spanish kingship.

The legend surrounding the Cid continued to grow throughout the Middle Ages in epic and shorter poems,[7] and that legend became enough of the fabric of Spanish literature that it found its way into the opening chapter of *Don Quixote* — where the Cid is praised as a champion, but less so than Amadis of Gaul the Knight of the Two Blazing Swords — and more prominently in the Golden Age of Spanish literature in Guillén de Castro's *Las Mocedades del Cid* written around 1600, which in turn became one of the sources for Pierre Corneille's 1636 tragicomedy, *Le Cid*. Important for a number of reasons, not the least of which that it represents the first non–Spanish treatment of the legend of the Cid, Corneille's play continued the role of that legend as a political flashpoint, celebrating as it does Spain's national hero at a time when Spain was at war with France as part of the multiple conflicts that would comprise the Thirty Years' War. Corneille's play would lead to the enmity of and eventual censorship by Cardinal Richelieu as well as a public debate by pamphlet about the merits of the play.[8] Corneille's play, with its emphasis on the tortured love affair between the Cid and Chimène after he kills her father, would in turn become the unlikely source for Anthony Mann's 1961 film.[9]

One of the many, multi–layered agendas of Mann's *El Cid* may be the strangest. Samuel Bronson had set up shop in Spain in the 1950s, creating at the time a mini–Hollywood in Spain.[10] Previous practice had been for American film companies to come into Spain to make one picture and then leave. Bronson had other ideas, and he was aided in his efforts by a consortium that certainly proved politics makes strange bedfellows. In addition to setting up permanent studios in Spain, Bronson hit upon a unique way of financing his films with backing and bonafides from Pierre du Pont. Bronson pre-sold the distribution rights to his film country by country — and in the case of *El Cid* hired an international cast to ensure his film's popularity globally, so that he had ample working capital in hand to finance a series of projects.[11]

Spain's nonbelligerent status during the Second World War was in reality rather a lopsided neutrality. Spain had been aided by both Germany and Italy during the Spanish Civil War, and the country had a huge financial debt to Germany for that aid as the Second World War began. Franco's sympathies lay with Germany, and especially with Italy, but he was also dependent upon the Allies for oil and other resources. At the end of the war, Spain, in part because of its war stance and in part because of the continuance of Franco's repressive dictatorship, became a pariah state, virtually ignored by the victorious allies, who poured massive amounts of aid elsewhere into Western Europe to rebuild the infrastructures of allies and former foes alike.

With the outbreak of the Cold War the American government began cautiously and covertly to reassess its posture toward Spain, and Bronson's filmmaking efforts in Spain became a key element in that reassessment. In the 1950s and 1960s with its economy still devastated from the Civil War of the late 1930s, Spain found itself starved for hard currency and had in turn frozen what few American assets still remaining in the country. Bronson's films provided the basis for what was in effect an elaborate money-laundering scheme carried out with the combined blessing of both Madrid and Washington. Bronson was granted an exclusive license to import oil into Spain, while at the same time the State Department and the Spanish government encouraged American Express and the Hilton hotel chain to expand tourism opportunities.[12]

Its other agendas notwithstanding, *El Cid* would eventually prove an elaborate and effective travelogue for Spain. Indeed visits to the set during filming almost became a side tourist industry for Bronson and company. Crowds gathered at each day's shooting, and the chance to rub elbows with a panoply of international stars associated with the film in Madrid's new hotels and restaurants provided a much needed boost to the local economies and to the country's tourist industry as Spain suddenly became a highly desirable and affordable destination for American travelers.[13]

So eager was the Spanish government to encourage these efforts that no request by Bronson and company for assistance in their filmmaking efforts was considered inconsistent with Spain's national welfare. For the making of *El Cid* three thousand Spanish soldiers and 1500 mounted Madrid police were seconded to Bronson for a measly $2.00 a day (plus lunch)—a fraction of what extras would have cost back in Hollywood. Village and city life and routines were regularly interrupted to accommodate shooting schedules; telephone and electric poles and wires were taken down to provide unobstructed vistas; and the doors of cathedrals and castles were thrown open to serve as backdrops for the film's different sets. Bronson would before and after the shooting of *El Cid* have virtual carte blanche in Spain when it came to making films, but with Mann making the Spanish national literary epic (albeit by way of a French tragicomedy) into a film, he was assured of getting everything he wanted or needed to produce an epic film as well.[14]

Tied into this national agenda was a more personal agenda for Franco himself. *El Caudillo*, as Franco was known, variously saw himself as a bulwark against godless communism, savior of the nation, and protector of Spanish heritage. More particularly he saw himself as a modern day Cid who would unite Spain and protect her from the forces internal and external who threatened to tear her apart.[15] Franco had himself appointed regent for the weakened monarchy, and while he publicly scorned the pretender, Don Juan, he mentored his son Don Carlos for the throne and as his successor. Like the Cid Franco saw his loyalty to the idea of the monarchy, albeit his decidedly personal view of the monarchy, rather than to any particular monarch.

In Mann's film — which Franco's regime officially certified as an endeavor in the "Spanish national interest" (Rosendorf 275) — Heston's Cid is blindly loyal to whoever is rightful king — Ferdinand, Sancho, and finally Alfonso — no matter how venal or disloyal to him they may be. When Heston's Cid, unlike his historical counterpart, refuses the crown of Valencia for himself, claiming it instead for Alfonso who had recently thrown the Cid's wife and children into his dungeons, the Cid's Moorish ally Moutamin (Douglas Wilmer) voices what must have been a common unspoken sentiment among the troops amassed in Valencia: "would that so noble a warrior had so noble a king."

Charlton Heston as the title character in Anthony Mann's 1961 film *El Cid* (from the collection of the author).

Heston himself commented extensively on the Cid's heroic qualities in a radio interview contemporary with the film's release and included on the two-disc edition of *El Cid*. According to Heston the Cid had the rare "willingness to take responsibility for the men who followed him," and Heston further considered the Cid's fellow travelers to be Churchill, Gandhi, and Andrew Jackson (whom Heston had twice played on screen),[16] all of whom had an "unfailing view that ... [they were] right," while recognizing "the need for action" to confront obstacles and difficulties. In an age where no one accepts responsibility for his or her own actions, Heston opined that the Cid — and his other heroes — accepted "responsibility for a whole people."

Thus the Fascist Franco and a wary State Department teamed up to support a film starring an actor whose personal politics would only become more decidedly right wing, produced by the Jewish but Vatican-approved Samuel Bronstein — a cousin of Leon Trotsky who had fled Russia in 1918[17] and who would for a time have the financial backing of one of the scions of American wealth, Pierre du Pont — written by blacklisted Hollywood writers forced to work anonymously because of their alleged previous Communist sympathies: agenda layered upon agenda layered upon agenda. But *El Cid* wears none of these agendas on its sleeve — to mix a metaphor.

The film opens by pitting a fanatical anti–Christian menace from the infidels in East against the civilized West. The Cid's role is clearly messianic: indeed he literally takes up Christ's cross at the beginning of the film when he rescues a charred crucifix from a village set to the torch by Ben Yussef. In a later scene once he has been reconciled with the Cid, Count Ordonez (Raf Vallone) is crucified on a St. Andrew's cross by Ben Yussef, who in the one scene in the film in which he shows his full face then plunges a knife into his Christian prisoner's chest. But the Cid is no ideologue: he seeks to build bridges with Spain's Moors whom he sees as allies and brothers in a common war against the invading other: Ben Yussef's forces which threaten to destroy the film's version of Western civilization.

The Cid unlike Alonso offers no blanket condemnation of the world of Islam. He finds allies among some of the Moorish kings of Spain and traitors among others, most notably Frank Thring's Al Kadir. Indeed *El Cid* contains scene after scene of betrayal. Christian betrays Christian, and Moor betrays Moor. The Cid is accused of treason for not turning over his Moorish prisoners to the king — he wishes to make them allies in his fight for Spain again Ben Yussef. Chimene sees the Cid's killing of her father in a duel as a betrayal of their love. Alonso (John Fraser) and his sister Urraca (Genevieve Page) betray their older brother Sancho (Gary Raymond) and send him to his death. Any number of characters shift their allegiances, most notably Count Ordonez, multiple times in the film. Spies and traitors lurk everywhere, and even the Cid cannot always be sure who is on his side and who is not. Mann's film is then more than reflective of the American global political paranoia of the times in which it was made.

At the same time *El Cid* looks in part to a less fraught future with its plea for tolerance. The Cid can at one point find truer friends among the dark-skinned Moorish kings than he can in his own king, Alonso. If Spain is to be saved, it will require those with ethnic (if not quite racial) and religious differences to unite. The barbarians are at the gates, with Ben Jussef and his troops as less than subtle stand-ins for Nikita Krushchev and his allies. Ben Yussef's rants find a real life parallel in Krushchev's (in)famous "performance" during the fall 1960 meeting of the United Nations General Assembly when he pounded his shoe on the desk and threatened "to bury" the West. Both Krushchev's armies and Ben Yussef's hordes threaten to bury their enemies and destroy all for which they stand.

El Cid is not always successful in juggling its many agendas, especially since a great deal of the emphasis in the film is on the at first mercurial love affair between Chimene and the Cid. Loren and Heston were famously ill-matched in the film, according to Heston because she was jealous that he was paid substantially more than she for the film.[18] And Mann's film clearly combines a love story and an adventure–laden epic to show a conflict in the title character between love and honor that reflects a leitmotif of the original poem, if not the historical record.

Mann's *El Cid* is clearly the product of its time. It is a star vehicle for Charleton Heston who had already played larger-than-life characters in *The Ten Commandments* and *Ben Hur*— the Cid's encounter with and kind treatment of a leper recalls Ben Hur's meeting with his leprous mother and sister before they are cured by Christ. *El Cid* reflects a continuing concern for the red menace, and it nods in the direction of the American civil rights movement, coming down clearly on the side of inclusiveness. Behind the scenes global politics involving the American and Spanish governments at the highest levels were at work in the making of Mann's film. But somehow all of these agendas seem appropriate for a film that on a basic level simply represents yet another stage in the ever shifting legend of the Cid from historical outlaw to mythic figure. His contemporary the Moorish historian Ibn Bassam, who detested the Cid, nonetheless wrote of him that "this man, the scourge of his time, by his appetite for glory, by the prudent steadfastness of his character, and by his heroic bravery, was one of the miracles of God."[19] Neither Arthur, nor Roland, nor Beowulf, nor the most famous medieval outlaw, Robin Hood, can lay claim to such an epitaph.[20]

NOTES

1. *El Cid*, directed by Anthony Mann, produced by Samuel Bronston, from a screenplay by Philip Yordan and Frederic M. Frank (nominally) and by (the black-listed) Ben Barzman and others (actually) for United Artists, 1961.

2. The research for this essay was supported in part by a generous summer travel grant

from La Salle University's Leaves and Grants Committee and from the Office of Dr. Richard A. Nigro, Provost.

3. Book burning and anti-intellectualism are, of course, hallmarks of religious fanaticism. For another cinematic example of such activities and attitudes in the world of Islam, see Youssef Chanine's 1997 film *Al-Massir* (Destiny).

4. Invaluable sources for information about Mann's film are the commentary and other extras on the 2008 two-disc deluxe edition of *El Cid*. Some of the commentary on the two-disc edition is indebted to Rosendorf, *The Life and Times of Samuel Bronstein, Builder of "Hollywood in Madrid."* Rosendorf and Bronstein's son provide the running commentary about the film on the disc.

5. Biblioteca Nacional, Madrid, MS. Vitr.7-17, which is in very poor condition. For details of the manuscript and the careless ways in which is has been handled in the past, see Michael, pages 14–16.

6. Pidal's work on the poem dates from 1908 when he began to publish his three-volume *Cantar de Mio Cid: Texto, Gramática y Vocabulario*. The third volume was published in 1911, and the entire work was revised in 1944–1946 and reprinted again in 1954–1956. Pidal subsequently published a facsimile of the poem's manuscript in 1961. As important as Pidal's work on the poem remains, it is clearly a product of a historiographical method and approach now no longer held in favor. When faced with a decision between supporting Spanish nationalism or adopting historical objectivity or neutrality, Pidal more often than not opted to do the former. See Michael's introduction to the bilingual edition of the poem, as well as Richard Fletcher, *The Quest for El Cid* and *M. J. Trow, El Cid, The Making of a Legend*.

7. For the early literary pedigree of the Cid, see Michael 1–19.

8. Corneille's play occasioned the most celebrated public literary quarrel of the seventeenth century and eventually involved Richelieu and the French Academy, whose intervention in the so-called *querelle du Cid* was seen by some as a betrayal of its very charter. See Jouhaud 123–126 and 304–307, Merlin 239–268, Merlin-Kajman 169–187, and Shoemaker 160–163, 187–188, and 213–214.

9. Philip Yordan's team of largely blacklisted writers (notably Ben Barzman) turned to Corneille's play as the basis for the film — or at least for those parts of the film that chronicle the love affair between the Cid and Chimene after originally coming up with a script from which no one was willing to begin shooting. The library of the French embassy was opened on a weekend so Barzman could get his hands on a copy of the play. See the commentary by Barzman's widow on the two-disc version of the film. For further on the blacklisted Barzman's involvement with *El Cid*, see Norma Barzman 306–334.

10. See Rosendorf's dissertation and the commentary on the two-disc version of *El Cid* for further elaboration on what follows.

11. See Rosendorf 242–246. Du Pont would later turn on and ruin Bronson, who died nearly penniless (see Rosendorf, 314–324).

12. See Rosendorf 219–267. Along the way the Jewish Bronson also managed to secure the blessing of the Vatican in general and of Pope John XXIII in particular for his cinematic endeavors.

13. On the two-disc edition see the extra features "Hollywood Conquers Spain" and "Samuel Bronstein: Epic Journey of a Dreamer."

14. *Ibid.*

15. For a brief overview of Franco's highjacking of the legend of the Cid for his own purposes, see Trow 215–220.

16. In *The President's Lady* (1953) and *The Buccaneer* (1958).

17. See "Samuel Bronstein: Epic Journey of a Dreamer."

18. On the at times testy relationship between Heston and Loren, see "Radio Interview with Charleton Heston" and Heston's two volumes of memoirs: *The Actor's Life: Journals, 1956–1976* and *In the Arena: An Autobiography*. At one point Heston seems to have complained that Loren smelled from eating too much garlic, a complaint that she took to be an anti–Italian slur. In the latter volume Heston seems more intent on forgiving and forgetting.

19. Quoted by Fletcher (185).

20. Though compare Twain's comment (page 329) about Joan of Arc at the end of his novel about her: "she is easily and by far the most extraordinary person the human race has ever produced."

Bibliography

Barzman, Norma. *The Red and the Blacklist: An Intimate Memoir of a Hollywood Expatriate*. New York: Thunder's Mouth Press/Nation Books, 2003.

El Cid (two-disc deluxe DVD edition). The Miriam Collection. Hollywood, CA: The Weinstein Company, 2008.

Fletcher, Richard. *The Quest for El Cid*. New York: Oxford University Press, 1989.

Hamilton, Rita, and Janet Perry, trans. *The Poem of the Cid* (with an Introduction and Notes by Ian Michael). New York: Penguin Books, 1975, 1984.

Heston, Charlton. *The Actor's Life: Journals, 1956–1976*. New York: E. P. Dutton, 1978.

———. *In the Arena: An Autobiography*. New York: Simon and Schuster, 1995.

Jouhaud, Christian. *Les Pouvoirs de la Littérature: Histoire d'un paradoxe*. Paris: Gallimard, 2000.

Merlin, Hèléne. *Public et Littérature en France au xvii ͤ siècle*. Paris: Les Belles Lettres, 1984.

Merlin-Kajman, Hèléne. *L'Excentricité Académique: Littérature, institution, société*. Paris: Les Belles Lettres, 2001.

Rosendorf, Neal Moses. *The Life and Times of Samuel Bronstein, Builder of "Hollywood in Madrid": A Study in the International Scope and Influences of American Popular Culture*. Ph.D. Diss. Harvard University, 2000. Ann Arbor, MI: University Microfilms, 2008.

Shoemaker, Peter W. *Powerful Connections: The Poetics of Patronage in the Age of Louis XIII*. Newark, DE: University of Delaware Press, 2007.

Trow, M. J. *El Cid, The Making of a Legend*. Phoenix Mill, England: Sutton, 2007.

Twain, Mark. *Personal Recollections of Joan of Arc*. Mineola, NY: Dover, 1896, 2002.

Filmography

El Cid, dir. Anthony Mann, 1961.

7. *El Cid*
Defeat of the Crescentade

TOM SHIPPEY

In several ways the story of Rodrigo Diaz, El Cid, is entirely characteristic of the medieval legends appropriated by virtually all European nations during the nineteenth-century epoch in which national identities were either consolidated or created.[1] Like the stories of the Nibelungs, or Count Roland, or Beowulf, it derives much of its authority from a medieval poem of uncertain date, the *Poema de Mio Cid*. Like *Beowulf* the *Poema* exists in only one manuscript, and while in both cases the manuscript can be dated (in the case of the *Poema* to approximately 1350), the poems themselves may be much older than the manuscripts.[2]

As with the *Chanson de Roland*, and indeed most of the medieval legends of Europe, there is no doubt that the *Poema* is based on historical events, though they have been much distorted in the process of transmission. As with the legends of King Arthur, the medieval figure who has achieved longest and most lasting recognition in the modern world, the most prominent source — in the case of El Cid, the *Poema*, in the case of Arthur, Geoffrey of Monmouth's *Historia Regum Britanniae*— is surrounded, preceded, or corroborated by a number of other medieval sources, the most important of which for El Cid is the Latin *Historia Roderici* (see Fletcher 1991, 92–104).[3] As with King Arthur again, but unlike either Beowulf, or Roland, or the Danish legends of Hrolf Kraki, El Cid retained a presence in popular imagination into the modern period through a sequence of later epic poems, ballads, and chronicles, which continually added motifs to the story, sometimes eclipsing the earlier versions. This complication naturally provided much material for modern scholars, both those attempting to strip out non–authentic accretions and those arguing that the accretions must have had some basis in reality. Finally, the historico-legendary figure most resembling El Cid in the English-speaking world is probably King Alfred the Great: both men Christian champions who fought for the Church against, respectively, Islamic Moors, and Viking pagans, these latter in both cases originally invaders but by the time of the heroes increasingly bent on permanent conquest of the whole of Britain or Spain. Both men could be seen as launching a *reconquista* in which the invaders were absorbed into a new polity to be the foundation of modern states. And in both cases modern revisionist attempts to play down the role of Alfred or El Cid in nation-formation have been met, to say the least, with dogged or angry rebuttal even from scholars: in these and some other cases the medieval legends are still alive, still functional.

This last fact clearly both imposed constraints on and offered opportunities to Anthony Mann in his task of making the 1961 movie *El Cid*.[4] Recent movies about King Arthur have shown how producers and scriptwriters can ring variations on a traditional story whose essential elements are still fairly well-known, but no longer nationally sensitive: Arthur must be in some sort of triangle situation with Lancelot and Guinevere, but this problem may be resolved by the death of Arthur (Jerry Zucker's *First Knight*), or by the death of Lancelot (Antoine Fuqua's *King Arthur*), or left as in medieval accounts but excused and palliated (John Boorman's *Excalibur*). Since the legends of the Cid were in the 1960s effectively unknown to English-speaking audiences, Mann in a sense had a freer hand in dealing with them, but nevertheless took relatively few liberties. It is significant that the historical adviser to the movie was the famous, indeed pre-eminent Spanish scholar Ramón Menéndez Pidal, whose book *La Espana del Cid* was first published in 1929 then repeatedly re-edited and updated almost until the author's death at the age of 99 in 1968. It is accepted up to the present day as a field-dominating work of scholarship (Pidal 1929, trans. Sunderland 1934). For all its scholarly weight, however, Pidal's was at the same time a work strongly marked by the passions and requirements of the author and his own historical context. Writing in and for a nation which by the early twentieth century had lost colonies, including Cuba and the Philippines, and which appeared to be in permanent decline, Pidal was concerned to provide Spain with a Christian and chivalrous heritage in which it could take permanent pride. At the same time he wished to reinforce the idea of Spain as a natural and national unit, overriding the strong fissiparous tendencies that continue well into the present day in demands for independence, or autonomy, from the Basque country, from Catalonia, and from Galicia (of which Pidal was himself a native), pressures which were to show themselves much more forcefully within a few years of Pidal's book in the Spanish Civil War.[5] One major motif of Pidal's work was the presentation of El Cid as above all a Castilian, from the political and linguistic heart of modern Spain, the keystone of the national arch. In modern times the presentation of King Alfred as dedicated not to the preservation of his own kingdom of Wessex, but to the creation of an England not yet in being has followed very similar lines. One might sum up by saying that a persistent modern requirement of historians has been to prove that modern nations are natural units, which always have or always should have existed.[6]

That was part of Pidal's world-view and was accepted apparently without challenge by Anthony Mann. One major effect on the film was to present a clash between religious loyalty (Christian/Islamic) and loyalty to the idea of the nation of Spain, firmly resolved in favor of the latter. The opening voice-over, in scene 3, "Spain 1080," puts it straightforwardly by declaring that the Cid, "Spain's greatest hero ... rose above religious hatreds and called upon all Spaniards, whether Christian or Moor, to face a common enemy who threatened to destroy their land of Spain": note the repetition, "Spain ... all Spaniards ... their land of Spain." [7] The same voice-over makes it clear that the enemy is the outsider ben-Yusuf, from Africa, and avoids all suggestion that he might have been called in, as in fact he was, by his Spanish co-religionists. The theme of potentially divided loyalties has of course become startlingly more relevant in the present day, when — to give only one example — there is considerable political unease over the readiness of British-born citizens of the UK to carry out terrorist attacks like the London bombings of July 2006 on what might be thought to be their "home country" in support of international Islam. Issues of loyalty, and of multicultural integration within a national state, have become once more a European preoccupation.[8] In this respect Mann's film was in a sense innocent, even prelapsarian. In it "Spaniards" may fight among themselves, but only the most corrupt or terrorized put faith above nation; indeed, the only such case of which we see anything is the hedonistic governor of Valencia, al-Kadir, and he is thrown over his city walls by his own people. The political scenario presented is, then, Mann's or Pidal's mid–twentieth-century one, distanced both from the much more threatening twenty-first-century present and from the eleventh-century past, as far as this latter can be reconstructed.

Very largely as a result of the work of Pidal, the basic historical data concerning El Cid's eleventh-century Spain are not in much doubt, far less so, indeed, than is the case with any of the European heroes mentioned above with the exception of King Alfred. Rodrigo Diaz richly deserved his nickname of *campeador*, or *campi doctor*, "master of the (battle)field." His career consisted of an unbroken string of victories. In 1063, when he was probably about 20, he fought for King Fernando of Castile at the Battle of Graus, when King Ramiro of Aragon was killed. He is said to have subsequently won a couple of single combats and became *armiger*, or guard-commander, to Fernando's son King Sancho, transferring his service after Sancho's death to his brother King Alfonso. In 1079, while acting as Alfonso's envoy to Seville, he became involved in fighting with Alfonso's envoys to the rival kingdom of

Granada and took important prisoners, including one Garcia Ordoñez, who becomes a major figure in Mann's movie. In 1082, this time acting on behalf of the Moslem ruler of Zaragoza, al-Mu'tamin (another important figure in the movie) he defeated and captured Count Berenguer of Barcelona. Two years later he defeated King Sancho Ramirez of Aragon, once again taking many prisoners. In 1090 he was to defeat Count Berenguer a second time. However, El Cid's most important victories came in the last decade of his life, when he took Valencia by siege in 1094 and very significantly defeated the hitherto all-conquering Almoravide army of fundamentalist Islamic invaders from North Africa at the battle of Cuerta, 14th October 1094, repeating the feat at Bairén in 1097. He died peacefully in Valencia on 10th July 1099, just five days before the Christian armies of the First Crusade stormed Jerusalem. It is tempting to contrast El Cid with the Crusaders, to point out that he was much more consistently successful militarily, that his defeat of the Almoravides had more lasting effects than the brief Crusader occupation of Outremer, and that one reason for his success was his ability to form reliable partnerships with Moslem allies, all of which would seem to make him a much more acceptable role-model than Godfrey of Bouillon or Richard Lionheart for the twentieth and twenty-first centuries.[9] At the very end of Mann's movie El Cid is summed up as "one who lived and died the purest knight of all."

There are of course difficulties in squaring this last view with the historical data, and coming to a balanced appraisal of El Cid's career has been a preoccupation of scholars for some decades. At the same time, the historical difficulties and the complications of legend presented what must have been a very welcome opportunity for Mann's scriptwriters.[10] A movie which merely ran through the list of engagements summed up in the paragraph above would be at best lifeless, a mere military vita. What the movie makers needed was something personal — not least, something which would bring in a female lead and some element of sexual tension — as well as a strong theme which was not merely strategic or tactical, plus a striking moral. Furthermore, these three drives, to personalize, thematize and moralize, had to be done in a way that remained compelling and comprehensible to a mass audience. Jeanine Basinger has suggested that the basic structure of the movie can be summed up as "eight movements around a recurring pattern of Action, Decision, Ordeal, Heroic Reward" (Basinger 161, with supporting diagram 162–3), and this pattern is certainly visible in terms of action. I would suggest, however, that there is also a pattern in terms of conflict and that the conflict can be seen as a set of interlocking triangles in which two characters/sets of characters are repeatedly set against a third. (There need be no suggestion, of course, that Mann or his scriptwriters deliberately set out a diagram of triangles on a chart: the "eternal triangle" is such a narrative universal that it frequently imposes itself on any sequence of events, while it may be that Hollywood, for cultural reasons connected with its primary Anglo-American target audience, finds the device especially convenient.)

In making *El Cid* Mann seized on three major legendary additions to the Cid's career, which correspond roughly to the three requirements outlined just above. The last of these to appear is the most obvious and the least complicated in terms of plot. One of the most famous shots in the history of film comes in the last scene of *El Cid*, as the hero, dead, but strapped into his saddle, keeps his promise to his troops by riding through the gates of Valencia to lead the charge against ben-Yusuf and his Almoravide besiegers. As he does so, carrying a white banner and mounted on a white horse, the rising sun catches his armor and turns him into a figure of light, like an angel. This scene was, apparently, not planned, but a "happy accident of location filmmaking" (Basinger 173), and it provides a strikingly symbolic ending to the movie, signalled also by a withdrawal from the characters' speaking or cheering to a detached voice-over. As the White Knight rides out while his black-clad enemies scatter in panic, the voice-over comments from the long perspective of modernity, "And thus the Cid rode out of the gates of history and into legend," or, one might well say, into myth: it is a pure good-and-evil ending, with a strong element about it of resurrection (from the Cid) and of triumph over death (in the shape of the black-caped faceless Yusuf, last seen being trampled down like the dragon under St. George or Satan under St. Michael in traditional Christian iconography).

Taking up a much greater part of the movie is what I would describe as the "personalizing" addition, the domain of Sophia Loren as El Cid's wife

"And thus the Cid rode out of the gates of history into legend." Charlton Heston as the angel of light in Mann's *El Cid*.

Chimene, which takes up most of scenes 6 through 18 as numbered in the DVD version, or almost a third of the whole (13 scenes out of 44).[11] This component goes back not to the *Poema*, nor the *Historia Roderici*, but to the late medieval ballad tradition mentioned above, in particular the poem *Las Mocedades del Cid*, "The Cid's Juvenile Exploits." It brings together two familiar motifs, the idea of the *enfances* of a hero (nowadays we would call it a "prequel") and the "Romeo and Juliet" motif of love obstructed by feud and by the requirements of honor. For several centuries this was probably the most familiar part of the Cid legend, having been popularized by Pierre Corneille's classic French drama *Le Cid* (1635), which very clearly, and typically, opposes the demands of *l'amour* and *la gloire* in what Anglophone audiences are all too likely to feel is an overly schematic way. Briefly the story is that Don Gormaz, father of Chimene, has insulted Don Diego, father of Rodrigo (not yet "El Cid").[12] In view of his father's age Rodrigo takes up the quarrel and is forced to kill Gormaz. Chimene is then obliged by family loyalty to override her love for Rodrigo and seek vengeance by appealing to the king. A judicial duel is arranged and won by Rodrigo, and the king overrides Chimene's scruples (and satisfies her real wish) by ordering her to marry the victor. Mann essentially follows this story-line, but he makes several changes to enable him not to lose sight of his central "thematizing" element.

The first change appears at the root of the quarrel between Diego and Gormaz, that Rodrigo has been accused of treason for — at almost the very start of the movie, scenes 4 and 5 — sparing the lives of high-ranking Moorish captives and releasing them on receipt of a pledge never again to attack King Ferdinand's kingdom. Don Gormaz, in his role as king's champion, presses the accusation, though it was first made by Garcia Ordoñez (a historical character, see above). Don Diego resents the accusation and is publicly gauntleted by Gormaz. Rodrigo demands an apology, but in private, and with every effort not to humiliate Gormaz, and has it refused (again with an elaborate show of respect). He kills his prospective father-in-law in the resultant swordfight. At this point, however, politics enters the movie again, for King Ferdinand is challenged by King Ramirez of Aragon to settle the disputed possession of the city of Calahorra by a judicial duel. Having just killed the king's champion, Rodrigo insists that no one has a better right than he to take his part. The duel, then, is a political matter, not something sought by Chimene, though the two issues are fused by Chimene's very public gift of her black favor to the Aragonese champion before the duel, counterbalanced by the gift of her favor to Rodrigo by the Castilian princess, Urraca.

Urraca, like her brothers, was a real historical character, but Mann makes her a key figure in what I have suggested is a system of character-triangles. Historically King Fernando had three sons, Sancho, Alfonso, and Garcia, among whom his kingdom was divided on his death in 1065. Mann has eliminated Garcia and replaced him by the princess Urraca. In the movie Urraca is clearly attracted to Rodrigo and only too happy to see the marriage between him and Chimene broken off. In shots of very obvious symmetry we see the two women watching the duel, with Urraca provoking Chimene by asking whom she wants to win. Since Chimene has handed over her favor, she is forced to reply for the Aragonese champion Martin, at which Urraca says cattily that she hopes to be forgiven for taking the opposite view: "After all, we would lose a city." But the city of Calahorra is clearly only a secondary consideration for her. We then have one romantic triangle: Chimene — Rodrigo — Urraca. A second, however, is formed by making it clear that Garcia Ordoñez admires Chimene and like Urraca would be happy to see her marriage with Rodrigo prevented. In three scenes after the duel for Calahorra, Garcia proposes to Chimene that he should ambush and kill Rodrigo, and she agrees; Rodrigo demands Chimene from Ferdinand as the price of his victory and new role as king's champion (to the evident displeasure of Urraca). The ambush takes place, but fails, for Garcia to be captured, confess his guilt, and be spared by Rodrigo because "I want no more blood on my marriage."

If Mann were following the Corneille version, that would be the end of that plot-strand, but a modern audience demands that love should be the result of a personal decision, not a fiat from royalty. We have trouble with the idea of a woman being awarded, so to speak, as a prize for service. The movie accordingly has four successive scenes (15 through 18 in the DVD numbering) which center entirely on the Rodrigo-Chimene relationship and which end by leaving that relationship unresolved. In the first their highly formal marriage is taking place in a cathedral, but at the moment when it is up to Chimene to say "Volo," "I will," she hesitates and stands silent, while a mob of well-wishers forces its way into the cathedral. Her final assent seems to have been created by social pressure. In a dialogue after the marriage, she confesses to Rodrigo that she knew of Garcia's plot to kill him — which in fact he knew already, Garcia having tried to taunt him with her connivance — and while Rodrigo has already forgiven her, he realizes that some wounds are too deep to heal. The marriage remains unconsummated, Chimene retires to a convent, and the "personalizing" element of the movie's plot seems to have reached an impasse.

At this point Mann picks up a loose end and begins to develop the main themes of the movie: on the personal level, loyalty; on the national and cultural level, *convivencia*, religious and cultural tolerance learning to live together. This latter is of course a theme of major importance for the modern Western world, and it has only grown more so in the decades since *El Cid* was produced.[13] A model for it has long been thought to be Moorish Spain in the centuries between the original Islamic conquest and the eventual Christian reconquest. During much of this time Islamic rulers governed largely Jewish and Christian populations in the greater part of Spain without attempting forcible conversion; the period is remembered also as a Golden Age for science, literature, learning, medicine, and even mathematics. It is often pointed out that many modern words like *alcohol, algebra,* and *cipher* are derived from Arabic through Spanish intermediaries, while the European "twelfth century renaissance" owed much of its inspiration to the work of Moslem Spanish scholars such as the astronomer Arzachel (al-Zarqali, 1028–87) or the philosopher Averroës (ibn-Rushd, 1126–98).[14] Mass audiences for Anglophone movies cannot be expected to know that, but Mann makes the point right at the start, in the movie's first scene (see further below), before seeming to drop it. The revival of this theme some one-third of the way through the movie, however, enables him to resolve the personal crisis left hanging, to bring in one last legendary motif to the story, and to deal with what after all are some major difficulties in the presentation of the real-life Cid as a *chevalier sans reproche*, "the purest knight of all," a man faithful unto death and even, as the movie's last scene so memorably asserts, beyond it.

One uncomfortable fact which emerges even from the very brief account of the *campeador*'s life given above is that most of his victories were gained over fellow–Christians. He fought the King of Aragon and the Count of Barcelona for the King of Castile (Christian against Christian). He fought fellow Castilians on behalf of a Moslem ruler. Only in his two great victories against the Almoravides did he fight unequivocally for Christian against Moslem, and there is a strong suspicion among modern scholars (not shared by Pidal) that in his culminating conquest of Valencia he was not fighting for anyone at all, only for himself. He was, in short, a successful mercenary soldier in an ethnically and religiously confused situation who would fight for anyone at all if it suited his own advantage. No hint of any of that is allowed to enter *El Cid*. Mann gave front-and-center position to a grave and unexplained question hanging over El Cid's career, so far left unmentioned in this essay: his reaction to the murder of King Sancho, his relationship with King Alfonso. Both this issue and the issue of religious loyalties and *convivencia* mentioned above are dealt with once again by a kind of "triangulation."

The murder of King Sancho never has been solved, and no doubt never will be. On the death of King Fernando in 1065, his dominions were divided between his three sons, Castile, Leon, and Galicia going respectively to Sancho, Alfonso and Garcia. Garcia was rapidly eliminated by his brothers and sent into exile in Seville. Alfonso was also defeated by his brother Sancho in successive battles in which Rodrigo Diaz "bore the king's royal standard," and he likewise went into exile in Toledo, at which point Sancho appeared to have reached his goal of reuniting his father's domains. In 1072, however, Sancho was murdered in unexplained circumstances in the frontier town of Zamora and replaced as king by his brother Alfonso. On the ancient principle of asking who benefits from a crime, it seems obvious that Alfonso bore some and possibly total responsibility, while early sources almost all agree that some sort of treachery was involved. The Cid, however, loyal servant and *armiger* of Sancho, transferred his loyalties and became the loyal servant of Alfonso. Or did he? The doubt as to whether this was truly heroic behavior was felt so early that even in medieval times it had to be excused by yet another addition to the legend, the story that Rodrigo extorted a public oath from Alfonso that he had no part in his brother's murder, and Rodrigo refused him fealty till the oath was sworn (Aberth 133). Modern historians put no credence in the story — with the exception of Menéndez Pidal, who made it a major part of his presentation of the hero, and he saw much of the rest of his hero's life in terms of a long struggle between a loyal and upright servant and a guiltily ungrateful king. Pidal's interpretation does something to explain Alfonso's repeated exiling of El Cid in 1081 and again in 1089, with a very temporary reconciliation in 1086. Rightly or wrongly, this circumstance was taken over by Mann, and it energizes the greater part of the movie.

The movie-triangle in this case consists of Sancho, Alfonso, and Urraca, all three introduced successively in the movie's first big ceremonial scene when Rodrigo is accused of treason before King Ferdinand. Sancho and Alfonso are quickly opposed to each other: Sancho favors giving Rodrigo the duel for Calahorra, but Alfonso opposes it. Urraca's sympathies are divided, for while she tends to side with her younger brother Alfonso, Rodrigo fights the duel for her, wearing her favor, and the city is granted to her personally as a result, but then his loyalty and eventual marriage to Chimene acts as a further provocation. This tension drops to one side while the Rodrigo-Chimene-Garcia Ordoñez triangle takes center-stage, but is revived (in scene 19) by the death of King Ferdinand. Speeding up a process which in fact took some six or seven years, Mann shows Sancho refusing to follow his father's wishes and divide his kingdom, followed by the two brothers' engaging in a dagger-duel, won by Sancho, who spares his brother's life on the intervention of their sister Urraca, but then sends him off to prison in Zamora. In one of the less well-motivated plot twists, El Cid turns up to rescue Alfonso en route, telling the escort, "What you do is against God's law," so that Alfonso is diverted to his sister's stronghold in Calahorra. Sancho comes after him, is murdered by treachery outside the gate of Calahorra, and dies in Rodrigo's arms. Rodrigo demands an oath of innocence from Alfonso, insists on it despite Urraca's attempt to force intervention by Chimene, and eventually forces Alfonso's hand down on the holy book while he swears (falsely) that he had no part in the murder and calls down a curse on himself if he lies. Not surprisingly, in view of the humiliation involved, Alfonso responds once he has received the Cid's fealty by sending him into exile, as we know in fact he did.

What happens then is in a sense the pivotal sequence of the movie (scenes 26 through 32, but in particular the mysteriously unexplained scene 27). In these seven scenes the personal crisis between Rodrigo and Chimene is resolved; the (anachronistic) theme of national unity is asserted; Rodrigo as El Cid begins to take on superhuman, or supra-individual status, no longer a man, but a figure of destiny, not free to act personally. He reaches reconciliation and consummation with Chimene, indeed, only to have fulfilment almost immediately annulled. At the start of the sequence, Rodrigo has been stripped of his possessions and sent into exile with a further ban on anyone assisting or accompanying him. Riding alone he comes on a place where three crosses stand, and he is there accosted by a hooded figure: a leper, who says, "I thirst." Rodrigo dismounts and gives the leper his flask. At this point the leper says he recognizes him: "There is only one man in Spain who could humble a king and would give a leper to drink from his own pouch." The leper blesses him and leaves. Coincidentally — but one cannot help thinking *post hoc, propter hoc*— Chimene catches up with Rodrigo and declares her love for him. A little girl then tells them that her father has said that they will lose their hands for helping Rodrigo and that "there are eyes everywhere." But her father also says that soon it will be dark, and no one will see the lovers take shelter in his barn for the night. Giving water to the leper leads to statements of love and affection from Chimene and also from the little girl, representing the common people. But who was the leper? He says his name is Lazarus, by tradition the name of the Wandering Jew, and his request functions as a test of the kind that in fairy-tale leads to change of fortune. The three crosses also suggest powerfully a kind of divine sanction on Rodrigo's life and mission, as does the cross prominently carried by the leper.[15] Life and mission are, however, then immediately separated: in the barn where they consummate their marriage, Rodrigo and Chimene decide to make a new life for themselves alone. But when Rodrigo opens the barn door in the morning, he finds an army assembled, demanding — to Chimene's dismay — that he lead them. "Why?" she asks, and the answer is "For Spain." It is the duty of El Cid to make up for Alfonso's failures as a ruler. Rodrigo and Chimene have to accept that there is no hiding place where they can, to use the modern phrase, just "be themselves."

At this point the movie declares an "Intermission," at the end of which years have passed. El Cid is now older, bearded, and scarred. The theme of *convivencia* now takes over, once again in a kind of triangulation. Considering matters historically once more, we may see the most important event in the life of El Cid (viewed with hindsight) was the arrival in Spain of the Almoravide invaders. They came from a fundamentalist Islamic sect, emanating from far in the south, indeed, on the other side of the Sahara desert, at the end of the great Arab trade-route into West Africa. As King Alfonso extended his rule over one Moslem-Spanish city after another, one of the threatened petty governors of Andalusia asked the Almoravide ruler of North Africa, Yusuf, to come in and save them from Christian domination. He brought a huge army from North Africa and defeated Alfonso at the battle of Sagrajas, 23rd October 1086. Yusuf then retired, leaving the Moslems of Spain to their own affairs, but he was called in again three years later, this time taking over a string of Moslem cities (Granada, Seville, Cordoba) and defeating Alfonso again in 1091. During this period Alfonso recalled El Cid from his first exile (1081–6), but banished him again in 1090: in both his defeats Alfonso lacked the services of his most famous and successful general. This whole whirl of events is hard to follow or fully explain even by modern historians, and it would have no interest for a modern mass audience. What Mann did was to simplify events (one exile, not two, one reconciliation, deletion of the Cid's many campaigns against other Christian rulers) and to set up a clear opposition between two extremes, with two medial terms — a political structure which (no doubt coincidentally) parallels the symmetrical Urraca-Rodrigo-Chimene, Rodrigo-Chimene-Garcia patterns of the movie's romantic plot.

One polarity is of course the Almoravide ruler Yusuf, who appears however in only four scenes out of 44: at the very start, at the very end, and in two pivotal scenes (respectively numbers 3, 46, 21, 42). The first scene has Yusuf angrily addressing the wavering and moderate Moslems of Spain with their reputation for tolerance, scholarship, and civilisation — in a word, *convivencia*. Yusuf tells them that will not do:

> The Prophet has commanded us to rule the world. Where in all your land of Spain is the glory of Allah? When men speak of you they speak of poets, music-makers, doctors, scientists. Where are your warriors? You dare call yourselves sons of the Prophet? You have become — women! Burn your books! Make warriors of your poets! Let your doctors invent new poisons for our arrows! Let your scientists invent new war machines! And then — Kill! Burn! Infidels live on your frontiers — encourage them to kill each other. And when they are weak and torn, I will sweep up from Africa, and the empire of the One God, the True God, Allah, will spread, first across Spain, then across Europe, then — the whole world!

The speech is full of signposts for modern audiences, with the urge to world-domination, the rejection of the arts of peace, and the view of technology as only useful militarily, all things about which Western viewers in the 1960s (and indeed any period since) needed no further prompting.[16] The Yusuf Crusade, or rather Crescentade, gets off to a poor start, however, as a Spanish Moslem raiding party has its leaders captured by Rodrigo, who then releases them on receipt of a pledge not to attack again and in spite of strong urging from all sides to hang the prisoners. This scene shows Rodrigo's first act of magnanimity, and in the movie it is entirely successful. Moutamin, lord of Zaragoza, remains Rodrigo's faithful ally afterward. We accordingly have a first opposition set up between Yusuf and Rodrigo, with a medial term in Moutamin, who changes sides from the former to the latter.[17]

That act leads to the accusation of treason and the Gormaz-Chimena sub-plot detailed above, but Moutamin does not return to the action until scene 14, where he functions only as unexpected rescuer from the Garcia ambush. His next significant appearance is not till immediately after the "Intermission," when El Cid proposes to Alfonso — now aware of the threat from Yusuf— that Christians and moderate Moslems should make an alliance. The proposal is haughtily refused by Alfonso, but El Cid and Moutamin form their alliance anyway, the one saying, "You'll make a Muslim of me yet, my lord," the other replying, "We have so much to give to each other — and to Spain." This time the opposition set up is between Moutamin and Alfonso, with Rodrigo turning (back) from the latter to the former. Nevertheless, on this occasion the split is not a terminal one. While Yusuf is last seen being ridden down by the forces of moderation, Alfonso is not finally rejected: El Cid makes a point of conquering Valencia for Alfonso, not for himself, refuses a joint appeal to take the crown by Moutamin and Garcia Ordoñez (representing Moslem and Christian, respectively), and in the end gets his reward in a penultimate scene (no. 45) in which Alfonso manages to break free of his intransigent sister Urraca and appears to beg for forgiveness. It is true that the war cry at the end has been altered from "For God, Alfonso, and for Spain"— the version proclaimed by El Cid in scene 43 — to "For God, the Cid, and Spain," shouted as his dead body leads the troops in their final attack.[18] But (rather oddly) the curse which Alfonso pronounced on himself in scene 25 appears to have been forgotten by the end. Perhaps the difference felt by Pidal and promoted by Mann is that Yusuf, the Islamic bigot, is presented as African/alien, while Alfonso, the Christian bigot, is Spanish/native: in this movie patriotism trumps faith.

No viewer could fail to see the overall moral, which is that tolerance and co-operation will master bigotry and that good men of all faiths can and should come together against fanatics, all very welcome — much more sensible than the postulates of many medievalist movies.[19] A connected premise is the power of magnanimity, which Rodrigo displays repeatedly, sometimes successfully, sometimes not. He frees his Moorish captives at the start (success) and humbles himself to Count Gormaz to try to avoid combat (failure);

he kneels to Alfonso after humiliating him (failure) and gives water to the leper (success). He repeatedly shows his loyalty to Alfonso (eventually, if rather unconvincingly, a success) and, in one of the more dramatic scenes, uses his catapults to shoot bread into the starving city of Valencia to demonstrate to its citizens that their true enemies are not the Cid and his besiegers, but their guzzling rulers like al-Kadir who protract the siege for their own advantage (success). And though the academic habit of marking medieval movies on their closeness or otherwise to what is thought to be historical fact is not to be encouraged, one has to say that, with due allowance for the problems of compressing many confusing campaigns into a three-hour showing, Mann's *El Cid* manages to get a great deal of history across without too serious alterations. But, and finally, how does it rate as a movie?

Probably most people remember it as a star vehicle for Charlton Heston and Sophia Loren, one of Heston's most famous roles. Some reviews called the acting "wooden," and there is some force in that criticism. (I would add that the casting was not entirely successful, with Andrew Cruickshank particularly miscast as Count Gormaz: ever-increasing standards of physical development in actors have left him quite implausible as king's champion or indeed champion of anything. No one would give odds against Charlton Heston in their duel scene.[20]) Nevertheless, woodenness may not be too serious as a criticism in this case.[21] One of the main developments in the course of the movie is to see the individual in Rodrigo Diaz being swallowed up by the demands of the role, or the legend, of El Cid, and this development reconciles more successfully than most too deeply held but contradictory beliefs of Hollywood movies: on the one hand that heroes are larger than life, John-Wayne–style colossi immune to doubt and fear, but on the other hand that heroes are just guys, that it is open to all of us to be or become heroes.[22] Some movies, like Peter Jackson's *Lord of the Rings* trilogy, deal with this problem by separating out the requirements: Aragorn, Legolas, Gandalf in one category, Sam and Frodo in the other. *El Cid* manages to show not only a development, but a reluctant and compelled development from one to the other, with only two, or perhaps three, "mythic" moments: the leper scene, where the mythic element comes from the hooded leper, never clearly seen; the "angel of light" shot at the end, when as the voice-over says that the Cid is making the transition from human/historical to legendary/mythical; possibly the sequence in scene 42, where Rodrigo's enemy Garcia Ordoñez, won over by Rodrigo's magnanimity, has been captured and crucified by Yusuf, but nevertheless proclaims his belief that the Cid will never die, rather like the Good Thief crucified beside Jesus. The movie manages, in short, to raise its stylistic level at some moments without forfeiting credibility, a considerable achievement.

However, and I will end by speaking personally, the skill which I find admirable in Mann's direction is the way in which themes and strands of plot are kept going without entirely taking over on the one hand or disappearing from memory on the other. The movie starts with what one may call the Yusuf strand. It is then suppressed by the "losing Chimene" strand, which at the same time introduces the potential conflict between Sancho and Alfonso. This latter strand is allowed to take the foreground in such a way as to (apparently) resolve the former, while reviving the threat from Yusuf, but it is tied off in the center of the movie by Rodrigo's transformation into El Cid and by the aging and change of appearance after the "Intermission." Personal and political are then combined once again in the dealings between Alfonso, Chimene and Garcia Ordoñez, the latter's role steadily increasing. The movie then gathers pace with repeated confrontations along the same strip of beach outside Valencia in scenes 39–40, 42–43, and 46, interspersed with the slower indoor scenes as El Cid refuses the crown (41), refuses the operation which may save his life (44), and makes his farewells to Chimene and Alfonso (45). Many years ago, as a schoolboy working on the French classics, I expressed a characteristic Anglo-Saxon discontent with Corneille's *Le Cid*, on the grounds that it was deplorably short of action, to which my teacher replied, writing it on my essay several times in capitals and red ink, "CONFLICT IS ACTION." That is no doubt true, but I retain a strong feeling that it helps to have both: Anthony Mann combines the two requirements well. The movie of course projects a series of modern credos on to its medieval material: tolerance is good, unity is good, a nation is the most important focus of unity, it can include diversity (in short, *E Pluribus Unum*). It puts forward one notable reversal in the opening-scene statement that progress and civilization are by no means Western prerogatives, though this apparent liberalism is made easier by the fact that for once the scenario involves imperialism directed *against* a Western nation, not practised by it. Possibly its most important moralistic element is its reluctance, not shared by other medieval movies, to proceed from *Ein Reich, Ein Volk* (very much part of the movie's metastatement) to *Ein Führer*: Heston's El Cid memorably projects reluctance, indeed refusal, to accept the "supreme leader" role.

Notes

1. See for instance: Quint, *Epic and Empire* (1993); Geary, *The Myth of Nations* (2002); and Frantzen, *Desire for Origins* (1997).

2. The single extant manuscript of the *Poema* suffered a great deal from the attentions of nineteenth century editors. It resides in the Biblioteca Nacional (Madrid, Spain) as MS Vitr. 7–17. The scholarly text is Smith (1972). More generally accessible is Smith (2006). A reliable and widely accessible bilingual edition is Hamilton and Perry (1984).

3. For a sampling of chronicle sources in translation see Barton and Fletcher.

4. Cited here from the 2-disc DVD version released by Genius Products and the Weinstein Company, with digitally re-mastered sound and picture, and an introduction by Martin Scorsese (2008).

5. Colin Smith highlights and commends this element in Pidal's work in *Menéndez Pidal*, contending that "myth-making is part of the job of the imaginative historian" (qtd. in Winkler (1993, 94). The Reconquest was formally called a "Crusade" in the late eleventh century. General Franco's propaganda during the Spanish Civil War dubbed the effort to oust Republicanism "our crusade" (*nuestra cruzada*), which as O'Callaghan contends "was an appeal to the medieval tradition of a crusade," suggesting "a religious struggle against the forces of godless communism" (2003, 19). John Aberth (2003, 135–47) perhaps tends to overstate the concessions of Pidal and of the film to Franco's fascist medievalism, though he also makes clear how much semi-official assistance the producer, Samuel Bronston, received from the Spanish authorities and local labor. He comments, "*El Cid* was most definitely *not* a Hollywood production" (125).

6. See for instance MacDougall (89–106).

7. John Aberth's (125–47) extended discussion of Pidal's influence on the film in general and on Charlton Heston in particular (whom he interviewed about the film) is extensive and convincing. Aberth holds Pidal responsible for the film's completely untenable depiction of the Cid as a self-effacing uniter of the Spanish into a single nation. The film also follows Pidal's biography of the Cid in interlacing material from later ballads to fill out the portrait offered by *El Poema de Mio Cid*. However, as Aberth demonstrates, it is the portrait of the Cid as a capable if ruthless mercenary who accepted the crown of Valencia not for his sovereign but himself (which emerges in the *Historia Roderici* and in contemporary Arab sources) that has won the day in modern scholarship.

8. According to Slavoj Zizek, Samuel Huntington's popular thesis of a "clash of civilizations" must be modified to address the fault lines within both Western and Middle Eastern societies between religious fundamentalisms of all sorts, on the one hand, and the pursuit of material wealth, on the other: "the 'clash of civilizations' [...] must be rejected out of hand: what we are witnessing today are clashes *within* each civilization" (41).

9. And hence comes perhaps Ridley Scott's elevation of a re-imagined Balian of Ibelin to a Cid-like paragon of religious tolerance in the years before the Third Crusade in *Kingdom of Heaven* (2005). Muslims and Christians had been fighting one another as well as living peacefully together in the Spanish peninsula for four centuries before the First Crusade. Still, as Pidal insisted long ago, Papal bulls from the mid-eleventh century onward cast the Reconquest of Spain in language which anticipates that of the Council of Clermont in 1095 — or in Pidal's terms "a crusade before the crusades." Indeed, Pope Urban II's letters on the attempted reconquest of Toledo and Tarragona suggest that his grants of indulgences throughout Europe to those willing to fight in Spain were a prelude to his later policies in the East. As O'Callaghan concludes: "In seeking the genesis of the First Crusade one must look to these Spanish antecedents" (32).

10. Story by Fredric M. Frank; screenplay by Philip Yordan, Fredric M. Frank, and Ben Barzman.

11. There are 48 numbered scenes in the DVD version, but four of these — two each at start and end — consist of sound-track and credits. Scene 3 as numbered is thus the opening scene of the movie itself, scene 46 the final one.

12. Here and subsequently I use the forms of names as given in the film, though these regularly differ in the many different versions of the legend. For instance, the heroine's name is typically given as "Jimena," though the film adopts Corneille's "Chimene." In one case I distinguish the historical King Fernando from the movie's King Ferdinand.

13. See Maria Rosa Menocal's famous book, *The Ornament of the World* (2002), which makes a widely influential plea for this "culture of tolerance" (*convivencia*) in medieval Spain (see also Fletcher, *Moorish Spain*).

14. See Menocal, and David Levering Lewis *God's Crucible: Islam and the Making of Europe, 570–1215*.

15. In the first scene of the film, Rodrigo shoulders an ornamented cross and carries it from the ruins of a burning cathedral. Martin M. Winkler suggests "this symbolic act points to the future sacrifice of his life for the cause of Spain" (95). Winkler also suggests a number

of interesting parallels between *El Cid* and the cinematography of Anthony Mann's westerns and films noir.

16. Aberth suggests that "Yusuf is a kind of medieval Osama bin Laden figure, out to turn the clock back to a pure, fundamentalist version of Islam unsullied by a corrupt and decadent Western civilization" (145). Compare Yusuf's contempt for Andalusia's advanced civilization with the Muslim intolerance that the philosopher Averroës experiences in Chahine's *Destiny* (1997). Though Chahine's earlier film *Saladin* (1963) cast its hero in ideal terms (comparable to the presentation of El Cid in Mann), thereby holding an attractive mirror up to the regime of Egypt's Nasser, his later film *Destiny* pillories Muslim fundamentalism and suggests its culpability in the decline of Arab culture.

17. Just after the speech by Yusuf just above, Moutamin (behind Yusuf's back) is the only one of those addressed not to raise his arms and bow in token of obedience, though his show of defiance here does not explain why he has been burning Christian villages in the next scene. Jack G. Shaheen's influential reference work, *Reel Bad Arabs* (184–5), suggests the film "misleads viewers into thinking the Muslim god is different from the Christian god" (184), and quotes Jusuf saying: "This will be more than a battle. It will be our God against yours" (185) in his characterization of the film as anti–Arab. Such a judgment is not sustained by a careful viewing of the film; it is only Ben Jusuf who makes this mistake. Yet the attribution to Jusuf of western confusions of which no Muslim — medieval or modern — would be guilty is a fascinating instance of projection. The Muslim fundamentalist speaks the language of western Islamophobia.

18. Anthony Mann claimed that his reading of the "chronicles" contained "the greatest ending I'd ever read ... I started with the ending" (qtd. in Winkler, page 100).

19. This is also the message of Youssef Chahine's *Destiny* and Ridley Scott's *Kingdom of Heaven*.

20. Points such as this tend to minimize Hunt's argument that Charlton Heston in *El Cid* plays up to male narcissism in a homoerotic way. Hunt quotes some admiring reviews of Heston's physical appearance (68), and characters, for instance Chimene and Urraca, do gaze at him admiringly. but Heston is always fully clothed, and Hunt has to concede that, unlike Kirk Douglas in *Spartacus*, he is "not literally crucified" (73).

21. In his brief Introduction to the DVD version, Martin Scorsese remarks that "There's something truly monumental about Heston at his greatest" and adds that "the reported tension [between Heston and Loren] added rather than detracted from the performances, giving it a certain level of formality that's right for the material."

22. The opening voice-over already quoted, scene 3, "Spain 1080," declares, "he was a simple man, who became Spain's greatest hero."

Bibliography

Aberth, John. *A Knight at the Movies: Medieval History on Film.* New York: Routledge, 2003.
Barton, Simon and Richard Fletcher, ed. and trans. *The World of El Cid: Chronicles of the Spanish Reconquest.* New York: Manchester University Press, 2000.
Basinger, Jeanine. *Anthony Mann.* Boston: Twayne, 1979.
Fletcher, Richard. *Moorish Spain.* Berkeley: University of California Press, 1992.
_____. *The Quest for El Cid.* London: Oxford University Press paperback edition, 1991.
Frantzen, Allen J. *Desire for Origins: New Language, Old English and Teaching the Tradition.* New Brunswick, NJ: Rutgers University Press, 1990.
Geary, Patrick J. *The Myth of Nations: The Medieval Origins of Europe.* Princeton: Princeton University Press, 2002.
Hamilton, Rita and Janet Perry, trans. *The Poem of the Cid: A Bilingual Edition with Parallel Text.* New York: Penguin Books, 1984.
Hunt, Leon. "What Are Big Boys Made Of?: *Spartacus, El Cid* and the Male Epic." *You Tarzan: Masculinity, Movies, and Men.* Ed. Pat Kirkham and Janet Thumim. London: Lawrence and Wishart, 1993. 65–83.

Lewis, David Levering. *God's Crucible: Islam and the Making of Europe, 570–1215.* New York: Norton, 2008.
MacDougall, Hugh A. *Racial Myth in English History: Trojans, Teutons, and Anglo-Saxons.* Montreal, Canada: Harvest House, 1982.
Menocal, Maria Rosa. *The Ornament of the World.* New York: Little, Brown and Company, 2002.
O'Callaghan, Joseph F. *Reconquest and Crusade in Medieval Spain.* Philadelphia: University of Pennsylvania Press, 2003.
Pidal, Ramón Menéndez. *La Espana del Cid* (1929). Trans. Harold Sunderland, *The Cid and his Spain.* London: J. Murray, 1934.
Quint, David. *Epic and Empire: Politics and Genetic Form from Virgil to Milton.* Princeton: Princeton University Press, 1993.
Shaheen, Jack G. *Reel Bad Arabs: How Hollywood Vilifies a People.* Gloucestershire, UK: Arris Books, 2003.
Smith, Colin, ed. *Poema de Mio Cid.* Madrid: Catedra, 2006.
_____. *Poema de Mio Cid.* Oxford: Oxford University Press, 1972.
Winkler, Martin. "Mythic and Cinematic Traditions in Anthony Mann's *El Cid.*" *Mosaic* 26.3 (1993): 89–117.
Zizek, Slavoj. *Welcome to the Desert of the Real.* London: Verso, 2002.

Filmography

Destiny (alt. title *al-Massir*), dir. Youssef Chahine, 1997.
El Cid, dir. Anthony Mann, 1961.
Excalibur, dir. John Boorman, 1981.
First Knight, dir. Jerry Zucker, 1995.
King Arthur, Antoine Fuqua, 2004.
Kingdom of Heaven, dir. Ridley Scott, 2005.
Lord of the Rings, dir. Peter Jackson, 2001–2003.
Saladin (alt. title *An-Nasr Salah ad-Din*), dir. Youssef Chahine, 1963.
Spartacus, dir Stanley Kubrick, 1960.

8. Nobody but the Other Buddy

Hollywood, the Crusades, and Buddy Pictures

E. L. RISDEN

Given the odd but continuing cultural capital of Western notions of the Crusades, Hollywood has made relatively few films about them and fewer still that deal with them problematically rather than resolving lingering issues with something less than a Keatsian negative capability. Western popular culture often seems little to understand the impact of the Crusades on either Middle East or West, and politicians blunder into such embarrassing nomenclature as "Operation Infinite Justice," or they fail to realize that to Islamic nations military occupations — or, rather, "police actions" — look like little more than contemporary attempts to reignite long-abandoned Crusades, to gain religious, political, and economic control of land and resources to which they have no right. Such contemporary political language revives a continuing echo of an enormous medieval blunder. Our films tend to support notions of Western right and cultural superiority, but weakly and with a twist common to postmodern thought, a limited attempt to acknowledge or sympathize with and even befriend the "Other," not to his or her advantage, but merely to show that even the "heathen" can fulfill a role in our self-understanding or "self-actualization." That Other may seldom popularly serve as hero or protagonist, but may assume a semi-laudatory role as "sidekick" or buddy, from which he can help, cajole, or praise the Western hero toward the achievement of his more nominally worthy adventures.[1]

Buddy films, unlike Crusades films, have flourished. From the days of Gabby Hayes to *Butch Cassidy and the Sundance Kid* to *The Lord of the Rings*, Hollywood has never ceased to exploit the potential of matching heroes with consultative, complementary, or comic others both to highlight character and to enable the movement of plot — and often bluntly to reinforce notions of class, gender, or race. The notion of "buddy" may suggest sameness, but such an explanation seldom plays out in texts. The buddy may serve in a role ranging from servant to double to wholly other (*The Lord of the Rings*, for instance, highlights both Sam as buddy to Frodo and Gollum as both anti–buddy or, for a time, Other buddy), depending on the protagonist's needs and the buddy's background.[2] Buddy films complicate plot and character with war, romance, quest, or crime, but they typically exploit a main relationship to show how one "subordinate" helps a protagonist solve a problem or achieve a goal or reach a realization.[3] Naming or visualizing the buddy as Other allows the viewer to accept as more important the course or fate of one character without feeling guilty about having given short shrift to the nominal sidekick who, as Other, makes fewer demands on our sympathies. However, that pattern can also either raise or subordinate troubling issues of race or gender.[4]

In this chapter I'll examine three films that employ both medievalism — the revival or revision of medieval history, arts, or motifs by later authors — and the buddy motif, one whose fable occurs pre–Crusades, one during the Crusades, and one post–Crusades: *The 13th Warrior, Kingdom of Heaven*, and *Robin Hood, Prince of Thieves*. Each film, built largely of fantasy-adventure rather than with any conviction of faithfulness to history,[5] develops a narrative that places Western European heroes (or heroes-in-the-making) either in the Middle East or into conjunction with Middle-Eastern influences, where they confront an Arab "genius" (in the Latin or Renaissance sense) who assists them in gaining knowledge or developing or proving character. What they gain through that experience or contiguity enables them to complete their missions, enhancing their heroic status and permitting them a potentially more peaceful future. The buddy may serve as necessary teacher or companion or complement, commentator or foil, or source of a test or of experiential knowledge, but in each case, despite productive contiguity, he remains "Other" because of his ethnicity and faith — such a limited relationship seems the best we Westerners can accommodate. The desire to connect with and approve of the Arabic Other (often nascent and occasionally significant in late medieval and Renaissance epic/Romance characterizations of Saladin and echoed in the modern world) ends short of any serious cultural integration and barely touches admissions of the possibility of equality: the fables tend, though not exclusively, toward unfortunately patronizing conclusions (a narrator may hint, "You're a better man than I am, Gunga Din," and not mean it).[6] Western culture remains unwilling to cross the line that wipes out otherness (or at least tepid with respect to it), perhaps because of a continuing fear of an Islamic threat to Western notions of security and superiority, even as we hint darkly at the fact of medieval Islamic cultural superiority. And with the real and continuing if not constant threat of terrorism, with the promise of more from extremists, looming as a defining political issue of our time, any diffidence seems unlikely to disappear. But an analysis of the films must precede such serious conclusions.

Significantly the film set in a time before the taint of the Crusades, *The 13th Warrior* (released, notably in 1999, two years before the horrors of 9/11), gets the closest to a recognition of fundamental equality — and it even hints at Arabic cultural superiority. It also breaks the norm in that it sets the Arab character as protagonist or point-of-view character, though in the quest to the North he serves as helper rather than leader to his Norsemen/Viking friends, who need his assistance to defeat a dangerous, even overwhelming enemy (another sort of Other even less savory to Western thought, a kind of pre–modern human or Neanderthal). Of course those Westerners with whom the Arab bonds are not Christians, but "heathen" Norse: he follows monotheism, they polytheism, so in a sense his religious capital trumps their European appearance in Western eyes. Ibn Fadlan hasn't the jolly fatalism of the Norseman, but he can read and write, which they can't (though their leader shows an aptitude to learn), and he has cleanlier habits. The world of the film allows for no permanent allegiances, but it does permit temporary productive alliances with strong emotional connections.

In *Kingdom of Heaven*, our "during the Crusades" sample, Nasir cannot get too close to his Christian counterpart, since they fight on opposite sides of the continuing conflict between Muslim and Christian culture, but we see a clear mutual appreciation and mutual desire to show mercy (some viewers perceived the film as almost anti–Christian and pro–Islam, problematic for Americans particularly in a post– 9/11 world). Neither in fact expresses a desire for any continuing exchange, though each exhibits kindness towards and admiration for his Other. Battle lines limit the development of friendship while allowing hints that, in other circumstances, it might well flourish. That theme in some ways defines the movie: characters are continually looking for allies or friends, usually in all the wrong places, while possible useful and even appreciative allies lie outside their sphere of contact or interest. Even the "baddies" have loyal friends, but they turn out to cause more trouble than do enemies. Balian has learned that lesson by the end of the story, when he rejects Richard's companionship — the English king could not have done him any good, and for all his heroism he will accomplish little but harm in the Holy Land.

Robin Hood takes up post–Crusades issues. The Arab Azeem may help Robin escape from a Middle-Eastern prison (though Robin actually releases Azeem from his chains), and he may help Robin with avunculur advice and occasional swordsmanship. But the relationship never reaches anything the audience may seriously accept as equality: he may fill the role of buddy, but subordinate buddy, serving Robin's interests. The Crusades have changed the world seemingly irrevocably, with the establishment of battle lines that resist the assuaging effects of time or even friendship. Timing makes all the difference: pre–Crusades adventurers can make friends; the time of the Crusades allows mutual appreciation, but not friendship; the post–Crusades period permits assistance from the Other in a pinch, but no clear admission of lingering equality: the Other buddy must serve, not create his own space in the Christian world, and he serves largely because the "good Christian" has done him a kindness first.

Like *Beowulf*, from which it ultimately derives, *The 13th Warrior* engages the famous Anglo-Saxon notions of Northern heroism, and the film does so in a similar medieval context, more like that of the original than we dare hope from contemporary fiction or cinema. For my purpose here the film provides a perfect example of the possibility of West meeting East on more even footing in a pre–Crusades world. A pretty fair rendering of Michael Crichton's *Eaters of the Dead*, it follows the adventures of Ahmed Ibn Fadlan. Exiled via an embassy assigned to remove him from the comforts of his own more civilized land into the dangers of the uncivilized North, because he attempted indiscetions with the wife of a wealthy friend of his caliph, Ibn Fadlan finds himself in a position in which he must join a group of Norsemen who undertake a quest to save a settlement attacked by an unmentionable night terror. He joins them not by choice, but because a seeress appoints him as the necessary "thirteenth warrior" whom they need for their quest to succeed — in this case the "lucky number" despite his foreignness to his newly acquired comrades. The Norsemen tease him about his habits, his small horse, and the way he grinds their heavy longsword into a light, swift scimitar. But the Arab proves his worth with skillful riding, by rescuing a child as the enemy attacks, through his continuing loyalty to their mutual cause, and by canny advice as they plan and execute their own attack. He learns their language and sense of humor swiftly and deftly and proves himself invaluable, just as the seeress had predicted.

The Arab and Crichton's Beowulf character, whom he named anagrammatically and unfortunately *Buliwyf* (which would make him etymologically a cow instead of a bear — the other characters in the film pronounce his name "Bull-vie"), win each other's admiration, Ibn Fadlan by teaching Bullvie about writing, and Bullvie by proving a quick study and learning how to read (or at least copy) it. In fact mutual admiration grows throughout the story (not just with Buliwyf, but with most of the Norsemen) as the Norse continually exhibit their cheerful, indomitable courage, and Ibn Fadlan demonstrates his ability to adapt, think, and react adeptly in a pinch. The exile/outsider makes himself an insider, and a useful one at that. His exotic foreigness does not inhibit, and may even help, his finding a beautiful lover, and his intelligence makes up for the fact that he hasn't the physical size of his comrades.

There the themes of *The 13th Warrior* emerge: while the Norsemen enter battle with good sense and grim resolve, they lack the perspective that the Arab provides, that of someone who can see through their superstitions and prejudices and by means of his learning and reason help them understand what they need to do to incapacitate their bloodthirsty Neanderthal enemies. Ibn Fadlan refuses to submit to the numbing addiction of violence that defines the Norsemen's way of life, but he does help them win. More like *The Lord of the Rings* and *Robin Hood* than *Kingdom of Heaven*, *The 13th Warrior* foregrounds a hero who does not exceed those whom he helps in courage, commitment, and skill (though he does in intelligence and perhaps passion), but who instead willingly follows what the course of events dictates to him. He does the best he can, enjoying himself as he may, to return home to write his story at the end of his adventures, a story that, Crichton hints, may have become for its host culture one of its greatest literary products. Like Frodo, Ibn Fadlan may have the least (though not little) martial skill among the companions, but like both Frodo and Balian he lacks neither courage nor resourcefulness nor the desire to understand and help others. Like Balian and Robin he returns from a kind of banishment and, more like Bilbo than Frodo, to an apparently quieter life than he might have chosen. More like Beowulf than Frodo, he can and will fight at need, and he finds sexual love among his adventures, winning the heart of the beautiful Norsewoman, though probably by his exotic gentleness rather than by any little-hero-lost characterization.

As with Frodo, the smallest wins the day, but not without his stalwart companions fighting at his side. The Arab bears not so great a burden as does Frodo, and his world doesn't ask that of him; who but Tolkien would place the weight of the world and the responsibility of saving it upon the shoulders of one retiring fellow with a heart as large and fragile as love, a body as small and yet resilient as that of a perfect child, and the clarity of spirit of a sacrificial victim ready to accept a task he knows he must but can't complete? Ibn Fadlan's pluckiness, perception, and opennesss make him the perfect buddy for difficult adventures, and while the Norse think of him more as a little brother, they learn not to patronize him and to appreciate the differences in his culture and his religion. As Frodo is essentially pre–Christian, Ibn Fadlan represents the cultural intermixing possible before the Crusades, but perhaps not afterwards. The West has struck no blows, and the Middle East has therefore not felt obliged to simmer and counter. The "Arab" has become not Other buddy but protagonist.

Early in the film the Norsemen actually save the Arab without particularly intending to do so: banished to a mission in the North for sexual indiscretions, Ibn Fadlan is attacked by Tartars, whom the appearance of the "Viking" ship drives off. He must learn discretion as they must broaden their understanding of manliness: he risks his life to save a child they believe beyond saving as the Wendel attack. Ibn Fadlan, too, must gain a degree of tolerance. As he learns their language, he first comes to understand their insults and returns them tit for tat; they respond not with violence, as he might fear, but with appreciation for his linguistic abilities and for his willingness to participate in their repartee, which he realizes only then is simply a game. Having made his own prayer before the final Wendel attack, he joins in theirs as well. Upon his departure, when Herger, one of his better friends among the Norsemen, bids him well and hopes that his one god will offer him sufficient protection, Ibn Fadlan can accept the Norsman's adherence to a polytheistic worldview and forbear criticsim in the name of that friendship. Friendship and mutual service support mutual survival, and difference or Otherness need provoke no serious conflict. When they work together, the Norsemen defeat their "monster" (another Other far more dangerous to them than the helpful if originally hardly willing Arab), and the Arab achieves his mission in the North. Yet such success in film holds true fully only for the age before the Crusades, and even then it cannot last: each "other" returns to his own world.

Kingdom of Heaven in many ways wanted to become a buddy film, but stopped itself at each such leaning. An illegitimate son, Balian gains the comradeship of his father and his father's knights only briefly (as a result of his having killed a priest who stole a cross from his dead wife's body), until his father's death and the shipwreck on his arrival in the Middle East separate him from any remaining comrades. Balian gains and loses comrades throughout the film, until his final alliance with Sybilla as the film ends. He forms something near to a friendship with Baldwin IV, but that relationship has obvious and immitigable limits, drawn by both Baldwin's status and his leprosy. The point on which I believe I can connect it to the other films that comprise this discussion comes in Balian's limited but pointed meetings with Nasir, one of Saladin's generals. Before Balian can gain his bearings in the Middle East, he is attacked by two Arabs, one of whom intends to take Balian's horse. Balian manages to subdue them, killing the more violent, sparing the other, whom he believes to be the servant of the man he killed. Balian releases the survivor, Nasir, and offers him a horse, no small gift in that time and place and perhaps the means to his survival in dangerous lands. Despite custom he releases Nasir from the servitude into which defeat in battle has nominally rendered him: neither man had wanted the fight in the first place. Nasir proclaims to Balian, "Your quality will be known among your enemies before ever you meet them, my friend"; he expresses a friendship despite their lim-

"Your quality will be known among your enemies before ever you meet them, my friend." Nasir (Alexander Siddig) admires Balian's generosity in Ridley Scott's *Kingdom of Heaven*.

ited and violent interaction based on his perception of Balian's generosity, gentleness, and inherent good character, as well as his own willingness to accept as a friend a possible enemy.[7] In this case shared character, a perception of goodness, suggests a sufficient ground for friendship, something deeper than appreciation for a good deed.

Later, when Balian is taken prisoner during the defense of Kerak — a battle he knew hopeless, intending only to allow the citizens to time to reach protected ground — Nasir emerges not as another man's servant, but as one of Saladin's top generals. Nasir requests that Saladin spare Balian as Balian once spared him. He repeats the phrase about Balian's quality, Balian recognizes him, and one of the important but understated themes of the film emerges: these two peoples can and should be friends, based on their ability to discover in one another mutual, appreciable ideas of virtue and goodness. They often fail — despite such qualities in many of their leaders — because of the tendency for evil men to gain military power and use it to commit robbery and murder on a vast scale. And they often fail in the world of this film explicitly because of the acquisitiveness and violence of Crusading Christians.

As the film draws toward its close, once Balian has surrendered Jerusalem to Saladin, he and the other Christians are permitted to leave the city unharmed and free of the slavery that, again, defeat might have inflicted on them. As they walk from the city, Nasir finds Balian and returns an old favor, more as though to a friend than to a defeated and pitied enemy: he gives Balian a horse, which will make his journey much easier and his survival more likely, and wishes him peace. To help Balian accept the gift, Nasir obviously understates its value, claiming it not a very good horse, one he doesn't wish to keep anyway: an act of good will in a verbal construction designed to help Balian save face. Despite their limited interaction, the story suggests that these two characters could and should, through mutual sympathies, have become friends, had their world only permitted it. The idea of the possible but impermissable bond has greater power than any other idea in the film; while Nasir fights for faith and country, Balian, though nominally he does so as well, in fact does not: he fights for conscience, for a sense of personal redemption, to protect the Christians from the abuses wrought by their own bad leaders, and for the hope that a peaceful Christian presence in the Holy Land constitutes something worth fighting for (despite his own lukewarm spiritual convictions). The story "should" have evolved into a buddy film, the open and generous members of opposing cultures (each Other to the other) establishing a friendship based on a sense of mutual value and on having established a desire if not yet a pattern to do each other generous turns. Sadly the politics of that world obstruct any such a trope. Nasir assists Saladin to his victory, and Balian finds a sense of redemption in the good he has accomplished plus romance with Sybilla, with whom he returns safely to Europe. But continuing peace, let alone friendship, with the Other must remain a wish rather than a fact: back in France, as the film draws to a close, King Richard meets Balian, searching for the now-famous defender of Jerusalem, hoping once again to return the Holy Land to Christian control. Balian declines to accept a new war, calling himself merely a humble blacksmith; that humility has little value in his world, beyond of course what it does for him. A continuing friendship (even if one could have developed with Richard, with honest give and take—history records Richard as a gallant and able soldier, but a dubious ally), were it possible with someone in a position to *end hostilities*, would have accomplished much more. Balian may at last achieve the peace that Nasir has wished him, but Nasir will not: his land will remain, if not successfully retaken, at best under siege.

Robin Hood takes up our post–Crusade friendship: while Crusades would continue after Richard's, they would accomplish nothing but great harm. But for Robin and Azeem, a crusade to free Nottingham and Sherwood of its notably (and comically) evil sherrif replaces any desire to free the Holy Land from one perspective or another: their Middle Eastern Crusading/defending days have ended. Robin and Azeem have the freedom of friendship, but one that begins and continues through a sense of duty—though the interaction of the characters suggests that they find some pleasure in it as well. The plot clearly turns the Arab into the Englishman's sidekick: he brings devotion, worldly advice, and exoticism to Robin's new and unexpected quest to regain his heritage, his good name, his future, and a new bride.

The story begins with Robin and his fellows imprisoned in the Holy

"Our fighting days are done." Robin (Kevin Costner) and Azeem (Morgan Freeman) shake hands on Dover Beach in Kevin Reynolds' *Robin Hood: Prince of Thieves.*

Land. An opportunity to escape arises, and Robin takes it. A chance to free Azeem, a Muslim but a fellow prisoner (in difficulties, as with Ibn Fadlan, for indiscretions with a woman) arises, and Robin asks, "Why should I?" "For pity's sake," Azeem replies. One of Robin's colleagues objects to freeing a Moor, but Azeem offers to show them the way out, and he immediately makes himself indispensible with good advice. When one of Robin's friends dies in the escape, Azeem urges Robin on: "Come, my friend, make his sacrifice an act of honor." When Azeem asks Robin why he freed him, the best Robin can do in response is that no one should die in such a place, "whatever blood is in your veins." The offer of friendship comes from the Moor; the Christian's act, the film suggests, is one of mercy. At Dover beach Robin asks Azeem to free himself of his vow and return home to his family, but Azeem believes that he owes his debt not only to Robin, but also to his family and to Allah. "No man controls my destiny," he asserts, "especially that one who attacks downwind and stinks of garlic"—as with Ibn Fadlan our Muslim character has as great a sense of honor as any Christian and a greater sense of cleanliness, sympathetic to a modern audience if not a medieval one. Azeem even insists that in England he pose as Robin's servant (which by his vow he has made himself): "In your country am I not the infidel?"—enough wisdom, almost, for a sense of superiority, yet he walks behind Robin thereafter.

When they arrive at Sherwood Forest, and the foresters resist sharing with a Moor, Robin asks if English hospitality has changed so much that a man's friend cannot gain welcome. One of the locals observes that Azeem is a "savage"; Robin agrees, but adds, "no more than you or I." Azeem has by that time gained what I must call an incomplete equality: Robin nominally allows Azeem equality with himself, but Azeem remains bound to Robin to return the debt of his life, which Robin saved in prison. However, Robin pursues his own good, not Azeem's, which would require too true an exhibition of friendship for Western tastes. Azeem has technology, a small telescope, that befuddles Robin, clearly a symbol for his (and his culture's) ability to see farther and better. He makes gunpowder for the attack on Nottingham. And he has medical knowledge: he attends the birth of Little John's wife's baby. "You truly are a *great one*," Robin says, acknowledging Azeem's Arabic name, and one gets the sense that a better, or at least more innovative, story would have focused on Azeem more fully if not instead of on Robin. Unlike the English, Azeem will not touch alcohol, and he proves superior to most English warriors, a "credit to his countrymen," as Robin unfortunately calls him, since he has fought "better than twenty English knights." For all that, Azeem hardly reaches equality. Robin's catapult fires them together over the gate, and after Robin kills the Sherrif, Azeem kills the witch Morianan, fulfilling his vow to save Robin's life, but Azeem follows Robin's orders, a sidekick at last, helping Robin regain his lands, bring peace, and win his love. We know nothing of Azeem's future, a shame since the script jests at scars that never felt a wound, and perhaps without an author's intention reinforces stereotypes that in the long run the Other doesn't matter, beyond what he can do for the "real" hero. The post–Crusades Christian world allows for no more than that, and *Robin Hood, Prince of Thieves* makes no pretensions of supplying it.

In that sense *Robin Hood* plays with us the most cruelly of all three films: it hints at true friendship and equitability before taking it away: the Other adds a new and appealing element to Robin's quest for home and the rehabilitation of his father's name. But Azeem must either return home to his own affairs or remain forever an outsider among the English, at best an Other buddy: he will find no lasting sympathies for his Islam or his dark skin, despite the fact that he has willingly played the servant and saved his friend's life.

None of these films troubles itself with history, though each derives at least in part from historical allusions — even Robin Hood stories, built around ballads, retain a desire for the return of an idealized, lion-hearted king. Movies of course respond to and (in some ways) dictate popular taste, and because movie making as a business takes place in a political environment, movie makers (like artists of any sort) may respond in any number of ways to contemporary politics and prevailing public sentiments. After 9/11/2001 Western, especially American, perceptions of Middle Eastern history gained an immediacy they had lacked; Bill Maher was reportedly fired from his late night talk show for claiming that, whatever we called the terrorists who wrought such horrible and horrifying acts, we could not call them, as the President insisted we must, "cowards." Public outcry after the Twin-Towers attack varied from calls for vengeance to pleas not to link all Muslims with terrorism. Some critical responses have suggested that *Kingdom of Heaven* went too far in the opposite direction, depicting Muslims as honorable and Christians as horrors, yet the film before its release had elicited from some quarters a Muslim outcry against it, probably from an assumption that it would do the opposite.[8] *Kingdom of Heaven* distorts what we know of the times to cast a kinder light on Muslin participants in the defense against the Crusaders. But Christian writers have too easily forgotten that Muslims were defending their homelands and that Christian invaders committed atrocities of enormous magnitude — against Christians and Jews as well as Muslims — including the slaughter of the inhabitants of Jerusalem at the conclusion of the First Crusade, when, one commentator said, the streets ran ankle-deep in the blood of civilians sacrificed to unsatiated Crusader battlelust.

Few audience members expect historical accuracy from films, and filmmakers often enough take it upon themselves to reconstruct (rather than interpret) the past after their own fashion in the name of entertainment and occasionally polemic. All three films that I discuss in this chapter deal to a greater or lesser degree with prejudices, of West against Middle East and vice versa. They suggest to us the possibility of alliances and friendships, but they also express our persistent difficulty in reaching a balance point of equality and equitability. We continue to lionize and romanticize the deeds of heroic knights, while at the same time feeling both drawn to and repelled by the possibility of a friendship that seldom if ever really existed and that neither side may yet feel sure it wants. The recurrence of the friendship motif in film adaptations of Crusdades stories may suggest subconscious fear even more than subconscious desire: one day we will all awake to the realization of what, in our even greater desire for warfare, we have lost.

Notes

1. The idea of the Other has gained increasing philosophical attention since Hegel's consideration of consciousness and separateness in *Phenomenology of Spirit*, and it has elicited a large and varied literature — the reader will find many beside these few I will mention. Emmanual Levinas's idea of the *Infinite Other* presents the problem as a psycho-linguistic struggle with something interminable, indeterminable, and superior to ourselves (see *Totality and Identity*). Julia Kristeva explores a psychoanalytic approach to horror in *Powers of Horror: An Essay on Abjection*, which addresses not only the problem of meaning that comes from the loss of distinction between self and other, but also other issues of marginalization and exile. In *The Second Sex* Simone de Beauvoir critiques the cultural problem of woman as "minority " as outside the culturally favored male perspective. Recently Queer Theory has expanded on such ideas.

For some application of feminist issues to film study see the chapter "The Woman's Film" in Molly Haskell's *From Reverence to Rape*. Michel Foucault's *Madness and Civilization* considers the rise and development of the idea of confining the "unreasonable." Garcin in Jean-Paul Sartre's *No Exit* decides, "Hell, it is Others." Most pertinently for my essay, Edward Said in *Orientalism* discusses the othering by Western Europe of everything that to them was eastern, including the Middle East, but particularly anything Islamic. Medieval Europe saw Islam as "a fraudulent new version of ... Christianity," and for them Muslims came to represent "terror, devastation, the demonic, hordes of hated barbarians" (59). An especially pernicious reading of the Crusades descends later explicitly, Said argues, from Chateaubriand, who asserted that the Crusades constituted not so much an aggression as the raising of questions of freedom, abolishing (by the West, of course) cults and slavery (172). An interesting book on film history, *Unlikely Couples: Movie Romance as Social Criticism*, by Thomas A. Wartenberg, deals not specifically with ideas of Others or buddies, but with how films (and their audience and critics) deal with "mismatched" unions, either by class, race, or sexual orientation. For an illuminating novelized-history counterpoint to Western Crusade narratives, see Amin Maalouf's *The Crusades Through Arab Eyes*, particularly the crisp epilogue. For histories of the Crusades see: *The Crusades: A History*, 2nd ed.; *The Oxford Illustrated History of the Crusades*, ed. by Riley-Smith; *A New Concise History of the Crusades*, by Thomas F. Madden; *The Crusades: Essential Readings*, ed. by Madden; *God's War: A New Concise History of the Crusades*, by Christopher Tyerman; *The Chronicles of the Crusades: Eye-Witness Accounts of the Wars Between Christianity and Islam*, ed. Elizabeth Hallam; and *Arab Historians on the Crusades*, ed. and trans. Francesco Gabrieli.

2. Ironically Gollum unintentionally saves not only Frodo's life but also the whole quest at the edge of the abyss inside Mount Doom, and the "Other buddy" saves the life or lives of Western cohorts in each of the films I discuss in this chapter.

3. A brief review of buddy films — an impossibility because of their prevalence in all forms — directs us rather to our favorites or those that best define the genre from our own experience than to any absolute necessities. A multitude of interesting film pairings appears immediately. For Butch and Sundance we can parallel *Thelma and Louise*. For the Lethal Weapons series we have *The Defiant Ones*. For *Wild Wild West* (in both cinema and television incarnations) we have *Charlie's Angels*. For *Stand by Me* we have *Now and Then*, for *Bill and Ted* (or *Dumb and Dumber*) *Romy and Michele*, *The Full Monty* and *Calender Girls*, *Twins* and *Big Business*, *The Lemon Sisters* and *Mystic Pizza*, plus Bing and Bob on the road, *The Odd Couple*, *Some Like It Hot*, *The Deer Hunter*, *First Wives Club*, *The Blues Brothers*, *O Brother, Where Art Thou*— since one may go on at great length, I leave additional possibilities, including television series, to the reader.

4. See particularly Donaldson, *Masculinity and The Interractial Buddy Film*.

5. Siegfried Kracauer asserts that "historical films ... obstruct the affinity of the medium for endlessness.... [T]he world they show is an artificial creation radically shut off from the space-time of the living" (*Theory of Film: The Redemption of Physical Reality*, page 78). Films naturally follow the logic of their medium, and the suggestion of friendship provides a useful means to draw viewers into the visual and motive text. Kracauer observes later how the Hollywood "star system" contributes also to the viewers' connection to the film, how it "provides variegated models of conduct, thus helping ... pattern human relationships": the presence of the stars offers continuing relationships for the viewers, and we can easily believe that characters will quickly make friends with those played by our "friends," the stars of our choice (99). We also know that film serves, as Nöel Carroll explicitly states, as "an agency of ideological manipulation," and that aspect of cinema has afforded a "central preoccupation of film studies in the United States" for some time (275). He adds, in the context of film as of any textual source, "The rhetorician exploits what is common or familiar in order to gain the assent of the audience" (282) — what better means to familiarity than friendship, the safe sort of "buddy" connection that allows polemic without pugnacity, or even pugnacity that turns to devotion? Implied friendship diffuses any worry about "difference" or "otherness" to ease the audience toward a thematic realization.

6. In an interesting exception, *The Wind and the Lion* (1975), Berber chieften Raisuli gains respect, admiration, and almost love from the kidnapped Eden Perdicaris (they do at least become chess-buddies) and her children and at least appreciation from Teddy Roosevelt (perhaps because he opposes the Bashaw and is played by James Bond–Sean Connery).

7. The use of a locution such as "my friend" creates an interesting problem. Should we take it as a phatic utterance, much as we often use "How are you?" or "Good morning," not for any particular content, but as a social space-filler? Does Nasir use the term ironically, particularly since, had the situation been reversed, we don't know whether he may have killed Balian, a nominal invader in his land? Or should we understand it literally, since we do sometimes make friends quickly and in unusual circumstance? It does draw the viewer into the friendship as well, since our meeting with the two characters together is no less brief than their own; as interested voyeurs we too become "friends" with the characters, invested in the course of their adventures, their causes and outcomes. I read that usage as fully intentional and thematically important to the film.

8. The film ignores, for instance, that Saladin executed perhaps thousands of Christian prisoners after the Battle of Hattin in 1187 (though Richard did the same with Muslim prisoners after the Battle of Acre), and after the Siege of Jerusalem he released only the Christians who could pay ransom — he sold into slavery as many as 15,000 others. Yet he was notable among his own people for generosity, for instance leaving behind insufficient wealth for his own burial: he had given nearly all of it away. A famous story, apparently orgininally from the 12th Century biography of Saladin by Behâ Ed-Din, tells how when King Richard was ill in his camp, unable to fight or lead, and his physicans could not help him, Saladin sent fresh fruit and snow to ease his suffering. See *The Life of Saladin: Saladin, or What Befell Sultan Yusuf Salah ed-Din, 1137–1193 A.D.*, page 379. Steven Runciman also recounts this story in Volume 3 of his famous *A History of the Crusades* (*The Kingdom of Acre and the Later Crusades*, page 72.) Other stories tell of a closer relationship, even a friendship, between Richard and Saladin's brother, Saif ed-Din or al-Adil (see for instance Runciman, pages 59 and 63, where the author records that one of al-Adil's sons actually received the belt of knighthood).

BIBLIOGRAPHY

Beauvoir, Simone de. *The Second Sex*. NY: Knopf, 1953.
Behâ Ed-Din. *The Life of Saladin: Saladin, or What Befell Sultan Usuf (Salah ed-Din, 1137–1193 A.D.)*. Trans. C. R. Conder. London: Palestine Exploration Fund, 1897.
Carroll, Nöel. *Theorizing the Moving Image*. Cambridge: Cambridge University Press, 1996.
Donaldson, Melvin. *Masculinity and the Interracial Buddy Film*. Jefferson, NC: McFarland, 2005.
Foucault, Michel. *Madness and Civilization: A History of Insanity in the Age of Reason*. NY: Vintage, 1988.
Gabrieli, Francesco, ed and trans. *Arab Historians on the Crusades*. Berkeley: University of California Press, 1984.
Hallam, Elizabeth, ed. *The Chronicles of the Crusades: Eye-Witness Accounts of the Wars Between Christianity and Islam*. London: Weidenfeld and Nicolson, 1989.
Haskell, Molly. *From Reverence to Rape: The Treatment of Women in the Movies*. NY: Holt, Rinehart, and Winston, 1974.
Hegel, Georg. *Phenomenology of Spirit*. 1807. Trans. A. V. Miller. NY: Oxford University Press, 1979.
Kracauer, Siegfried. *Theory of Film: The Redemption of Physical Reality*. NY: Oxford University Press, 1965.
Kristeva, Julia. *Powers of Horror: An Essay on Abjection*. Trans. Leon S. Roudiez. NY: Columbia University Press, 1982.
Levinas, Emmanual. *Totality and Infinity*. Pittsburg: Duquesne University Press, 1969.
Maalouf, Amin. *The Crusades Through Arab Eyes*. Trans. Jon Rothschild. NY: Schocken Books, 1985.
Madden, Thomas F., ed. *The History of the Crusades: Essential Readings*. Malden, MA: Blackwell, 2002.

_____. *A New Concise History of the Crusades.* Lanham, MD: Rowman & Littlefield, 2006.
Riley-Smith, Jonathan. *The Crusades: A History.* 2nd ed. New Haven: Yale University Press, 2005.
_____, ed. The Oxford Illustrated History of the Crusades. NY: Oxford University Press, 2001.
Runciman, Steven. *A History of the Crusades (The Kingdom of Acre and the Later Crusades).* Vol. 3. Cambridge: Cambridge University Press, 1954.
Said, Edward. *Orientalism.* NY: Vintage, 1978.
Sartre, Jean-Paul. *No Exit and Three Other Plays.* NY: Vintage, 1949.
Tyerman, Christopher. *God's War: A New Concise History of the Crusades.* Cambridge: Belknap, 2006.
Wartenberg, Thomas. *Unlikely Couples: Movie Romance as Social Criticism.* Boulder, CO: Westview Press, 1999.

FILMOGRAPHY

Kingdom of Heaven, dir. Ridley Scott, 2005.
Robin Hood, Prince of Thieves, dir. Kevin Reynolds, 1991.
The 13th Warrior, dir. John McTiernan, 1999.
The Wind and the Lion, dir. John Milius, 1975.

9. Medieval Times

Bodily Temporalities in The Thief of Bagdad *(1924),* The Thief of Bagdad *(1940), and* Aladdin *(1992)*

KATHLEEN COYNE KELLY

> *Shalimar [Mary Ann Mobley] to Johnny Tyronne [Elvis Presley]:*
> *"When you cross the mountains of the moon into our country,*
> *Mr. Tyronne, you will be stepping back two thousand years."*
> Harum Scarum *(Gene Nelson, 1965)*

> *[I]t is impossible to ignore the dear delights of fraud and*
> *deception, the hourly pleasure taken by some minds*
> *in finessing through life.*
> Sir Richard Francis Burton[1]

In one of his forewords to *The Book of the Thousand Nights and a Night (Alf Layla wa-Layla),* Sir Richard Francis Burton excoriates previous translators for their "extreme of licence" that

> succeeded in producing a branchlet of literature, the most vapid, frigid and insipid that can be imagined by man,—a bastard Europeo-Oriental, pseudo-Eastern world of Western marionettes garbed in the gear which Asiatic are (or were) supposed to wear, with sentiments and opinions, manners and morals to match; the whole utterly lacking life, local colour, vraisemblance, human interest. From such abortions, such monstrous births, libera nos, Domine![2]

Burton's ambition in his translation was to restore what English translator Edward Lane had suppressed: an uncensored text "as the Arab would have written in English," as Burton put it.[3] Of course Burton took his own licenses; his version of *vraisemblance* was shaped by his personal desires: iconoclastic, sexual, and imperialist. Edward Said, while critical of what he sees as Burton's imperialist and nationalist impulses (and Burton's notes to his translation of the *Nights* surely testify to his bigotry and racism), nevertheless offers a sympathetic and nuanced analysis of a man who, better than almost any of his contemporaries, was able to enter into the cultures that he encountered in the Muslim Middle East:

> All of [Burton's] vast information about the Orient, which dots every page he wrote, reveals that he knew that the Orient in general and Islam in particular were systems of information, behavior, and belief, that to be an Oriental or a Muslim was to know certain things in a certain way, and that these were of course subject to history, geography, and the development of society in circumstances specific to it [195].

Said credits Burton with a poststructuralist sensibility: by understanding that human behavior is culturally contingent, Burton was the better Orientalist for it — though still an Orientalist.

Reading Burton and Said together (and keeping in mind their respective *oeuvres*, including Said's controversial memoirs) underscores what we already know about the debates over ownership of the discourses and narratives that construct the Middle East. Burton, at war with his Victorian Englishness, wants to identify elsewhere and does so by confidently counting on his own experiences and expertise. Said, equally at war with his Westernness, wants to identify with home, or "home," and does so by attempting to wrest the predominant, if not dominant, discourses away from mainly occidental Orientalists and to return them to whom they "belong"— fraught as that ownership is in the Middle East, among Christians and Jews and Muslims, between Palestinians and Israelis, between Sunnis and Shi'ites.

In his foreword Burton seems to recognize and therefore condemn the European desire to rewrite *The Arabian Nights* to fit Western tastes and mores, as if the cultures of the Middle East have no integrity of their own — quite Saidian of him. Burton "know[s] certain things in a certain way" enough to know that the *Nights* were skewed West when they were previously rendered into French and English. His interest (albeit often prurient in the extreme) in "local colour" indicates that he understands cultural difference and the pleasures and imperatives in getting that difference right; still (inescapably imperatively) such interest objectifies and exoticizes its subject. Both Burton and Said struggle with the unremitting problem of representation.

The tales that comprise *The One Thousand and One Nights*, often called *The Arabian Nights*— a title asserting cultural provenance as much as, in the West after Burton, it conjures a titillating exoticism — have been translated and re-represented once more, into a new medium: film, beginning with Georges Méliès' 1905 *Arabian Nights (Le Palais des Mille et Une Nuits)*. What Burton says about his predecessors can be applied easily enough to most of the Hollywood films that follow Méliès (an important precursor film) and that are based (directly or indirectly) on *The Arabian Nights*.[4] In this essay I focus on just three: the silent, black-and-white *The Thief of Bagdad: An Arabian Nights Fantasy* (Raoul Walsh, 1924), starring Douglas Fairbanks as the unnamed Thief; the swashbuckling *The Thief of Bagdad: An Arabian Fantasy (in TECHNICOLOR)*[5] (Alexander Korda,[6] 1940), with Sabu as Abu the Thief; the animated Disney film *Aladdin* (Ron Clements and John Musker, 1992), famous for the voice of Robin Williams as the virtuoso blue Genie. It is not my purpose to critique these films for their representations of the medieval Middle East and its customs and peoples, for others have done so, particularly with respect to Disney. As one scholar puts it: "To say that *Aladdin* is racist is merely to state the obvious."[7] Instead, I read the representation of what I call the heroic male body in each of these films, and I frame such representations as a temporal problem, since several times overlap and interplay: the Middle Ages; the time of each film (with its chronological, genealogical relations); the time *in* each film; the time we inhabit as we watch each (or any) film; our time, now. (While I do not take up the time of 9/11 explicitly, it ticks away throughout. For a long time to come, we will be post–9/11 in much of what we do as individuals, as scholars, and as citizens.)

Douglas Fairbanks had made almost forty films before he produced and starred in *The Thief of Bagdad*, including the popular swashbucklers *The Mark of Zorro* (1920), *The Three Musketeers* (1921) and *Robin Hood* (1922). Stripped to the waist in many scenes in *Thief*, the hyperbolically handsome Fairbanks makes the most of his athletic body. By virtue of Fairbanks's celebrity, his body was already known and recognized; an overdetermined signifier, it belonged (and belongs) in the public domain. On the other hand, John Justin, who made his film debut in the 1940 *Thief*, was not as well known as Fairbanks. In *Thief* Justin also appears bare-chested, but he is delicate, even scrawny, with a pilous moustache and a plummy delivery. Disney's Aladdin originates as code: his body is a digitized construct. Aladdin is voiced by teen star Scott Weinger, and his features are based on Tom Cruise in his *Top Gun* persona. Thus Fairbanks, Justin, and Weinger and Cruise by way of quotation (and Cruise signifies more than Weinger, as we shall see) offer very different cinematic masculinities.

Johannes Fabian in *Time and the Other: How Anthropology Makes Its Object* takes anthropologists to task for a locational presentism, as it were: too often, he argues, the anthropologist situates herself or himself in the "here and now" and the peoples under study in the "there and then." The Saidian (and post–Saidian) historical relationship between the West and the East can be productively recast in the temporal terms that Fabian describes: the West is always "here and now," and the East "there and then." And the *there* and *then* is, inevitably, predictably *medieval* (note the rhetoric of post–911 constructions of the Middle East, as in, for the most famous example, George

W. Bush exhorting Americans to a "crusade"). *The Thief of Bagdad: An Arabian Nights Fantasy*, *The Thief of Bagdad: An Arabian Fantasy*, and *Aladdin* exist in a timeless space in popular culture, for they are no longer confined to their original runs in theatres (a spatial limit as well), but exist in clips on YouTube and in special edition DVDs. As such these films (as all films now do in the digital realm) exist in what Bakhtin calls "great time:" "Works break through the boundaries of their own time, they live ... in *great time* ... [and] their lives there are more intense and fuller than are their lives within their own time."[8] *Aladdin* may be described as *out* of time: while it has received a good deal of attention, both popular and scholarly, for its resonances with the 1990–91 Gulf War, many of the users who leave comments about the film on the Internet Movie Data Base (IMDb) either ignore or neglect its 1992 release date and interpret *Aladdin* in the context of the war on Iraq. The two *Nights* and *Aladdin*, along with other Western films that draw upon *The Arabian Nights,* persist in the cultural imaginary as depictions of the Middle East *now*; such films, of course, depict a Middle East that never was, but are the result of Hollywood's version of "license."

There is enjoyment to be had in Hollywood's taking license and in viewing the two *Nights* and *Aladdin* in a state of temporal (and spatial) confusion — looking into an imaginary past with *anticipation*— and I locate my own pleasure in contemplating a set of impossibilities in each film: "body," "heteromasculinity," "whiteness," and "Arab." Such things are not impossible *in time*— we *make time* in order to make them intelligible and possible, forgetting our own complicity in constructing a coherent linearity.

In what follows I work through the films chronologically (mindful of thus making a commitment to linearity), for each film motivated the next while morphing into something different from its predecessor; thus, there is also a kind of cinematic *mouvance* to enjoy as one follows the timeline. I trace out the collapse and confusion of medieval and medievalized time and space as it is written on the body in a medium in which embodiment is also, and always was, a supplement — Derrida's contradictory something extra that completes (that is, enhances presence), but also demonstrates the impossibility of completion (that is, dramatizes absence). The cinematic body is always a present absence that arouses desire and, because it is once-removed from experience, is symbolic or metonymic; therefore (following Freud and Lacan) the cinematic body can never satisfy desire.

The cinematic body is never a historical, real body, but always a fantasy. What happens, then, when such a fantastical body is called upon to stand in for a body in other and other*ed* times and places, fantastical in themselves? The pleasures of spectatorship may be intensified and also fragmented, especially for viewers who come to films such as the 1924 *The Thief of Bagdad*, the 1940 *The Thief of Bagdad*, and the 1992 *Aladdin* not in a timely fashion — that is, not at the moment in which they premiered (which privileges chronology and a narrative of reception), but in moments dictated by another sort of time altogether: DVD time, which, as I have suggested, not only breaks with chronology, but also offers its own variations on time because the viewer can slow down and speed up, skip some episodes and re-watch others. Moreover, because it has come about that the film itself is no longer enough, viewers can also *supplement* their pleasure with DVD "paratexts" of outtakes, director commentaries, games, and "documentary" materials.[9]

In addition to contributing to the feeling of temporal displacement that underpins these three films, the bodies of Fairbanks/Thief, Justin/Ahmed, and Cruise/Aladdin, because they are either American or English, also contribute to a sense of disorientation: each actor substitutes for an othered, Arab body. Burton's notion of *vraisemblance* is hardly a value in the two *Thief* films and *Aladdin*. Profit certainly is. Hollywood has a long history of casting famous American and European stars as African, African American, Arab, East Asian, South Asian, and Native American heroes and casting supporting actors by race and/or ethnicity to emphasize and exploit said race and/or ethnicity.[10] Minstrelsy furnishes an analogue to the many films with Middle Eastern settings and story lines in which American and European actors and actresses are given lead roles: consider the French Claudette Colbert as Cleopatra or the Bronx-born Tony Curtis as an Arab prince.[11]

Eric Lott in *Love and Theft* argues that minstrelsy in America offered a safe site for whites to experiment with blackness. Lott's title is intended to capture what he calls the "mixed erotic economy of celebration and exploitation,"[12] and such is the case in orientalized fantasy/adventure films with *de rigueur* trailers that offer to take the viewer on "a magic carpet ride" to some exotic and romantic locale. As the trailer for the 1940 *Thief* puts it, viewers will be transported to Bagdad, "that ancient land of mystery, romance, thrills, and excitement." (Mystery and romance always exist there and then, not here and now.) What is being loved in the three films is, to follow Lott, an opportunity to play Arab, but what they steal is Arab-ness, the prerogative to describe and determine what Arab-ness is. To play Arab, I would argue, assets the supremacy of whiteness. Moreover, putting *on* blackface or "Arabface" or harem pants or other exotic dress (relatively speaking) means that one can take it *off*: one can go *back* (temporally and spatially). Still there is danger in such play: as Kaja Silverman puts it in her discussion of T.E. Lawrence, "imitation repeatedly veers over into ... identification."[13] That is precisely what the three films under consideration work hard to prevent by funneling spectatorship into certain grooves that privilege white, heterosexual masculinity, and they subsume other positions by foregrounding the very act of imitation or masquerade. (This is not to say that the discourses of the films are monologic or bulletproof; there is much room for a queer reading of all three films, for example.) Such assertions raise questions about spectatorship and ethnic and/or racial identity. Some ethnicities are, depending on time and place, constructed in opposition to whiteness. "Arab" is the pertinent case in point, for while the U.S. Census Bureau classifies "Arab" as "white," it is not necessarily always perceived and/or experienced as so, but may be described and/or felt as an ethnicity or as a race.[14] In Valentino's *The Sheik* (George Melford, 1921), for example, the abducted Lady Diana Mayo (Agnes Ayres) is consistently referred to as "white" and as a "white woman." The so-called difference between her and Sheik Ahmed Ben Hassan is thus emphasized, and, I would suggest, the appearance of difference contributes to the exotic and erotic *frisson* that a Western audience might experience: Valentino, after all, is chiefly responsible for what is now a cliché.

In the three films viewers are offered the security of pretend, identifying as both white and Arab simultaneously. In each of the three films, our heroes — the made-up, burnished Fairbanks, the pale, effete Justin, and the ochre-colored Aladdin — are clearly distinguished from other "Arabs," almost always darker in skin tone and often represented as menacing villains, blundering Keystone-Cops soldiers (the African slaves and guards in the two *Thief* films are particularly egregious), or extravagantly-dressed, avaricious merchants and nobles — this last stereotype affords opportunities for class critique. Thus, one might argue, there are no bodies at all in these three films, for they never existed in any time or place.

The idea of a body and the phenomenon of temporal and spatial disruption or displacement that both constitutes and cancels said body nicely resonates with (to return to Burton) the history of the text of *The Arabian Nights*. *Text* is a word woefully inadequate to describe the manuscript tradition of *The Arabian Nights* and the tales of Aladdin that came to be incorporated, in more than one sense, within that tradition. It is worth dwelling on this history because the history of the ur–Aladdin tale, "The Story of Aladdin and the Magic Lamp," is itself a substitution, an anomaly in the space-time continuum. Collections of fabulous and folk tales were first preserved in manuscript in the tenth century, and *The Arabian Nights* may have had its origins in these now-lost collections; at least the approach of gathering tales together within a frame tale survived. The stories in *The Arabian Nights* had their immediate origins in the Arab Middle East, but some can be traced ultimately to Persian and Indian sources, Arabized during transmission. All the tales reflect, as Husain Haddawy, eminent translator of and commentator upon the *Nights*, puts it, "Islamic hegemony, a homogeneity or distinctive synthesis that marks the cultural and artistic history of Islam."[15] By the thirteenth century *The Arabian Nights* coalesced into a definitive or "original" text, but it and a copy made a few generations later are now lost. The Syrian branch of the textual tradition (which may to go back to the fourteenth century) is considered to be closest to these lost texts; the Egyptian branch, on the other hand, proliferated in the seventeenth century and continued to produce what Haddawy calls "poisonous fruits" — that is, spurious additions and refinements — through the first part of the nineteenth century.[16] In the nineteenth century many printed editions followed, and, like earlier redactors, editors seemingly driven by a principle of completeness made many additions, rearrangements, and interpolations to offer exactly one thousand and one tales.[17]

"Aladdin and his Magic Lamp" first appears in a French translation by Antoine Galland. It is the first version of *The Arabian Nights* in a European language, and, let me emphasize, it marks the first time the tale of Aladdin is found in *any* language. (Galland published twelve volumes of the *Nights* between 1704 and 1717.) Galland, who says that he heard the tale from one Hanna Diab, chose to add the tale to his translation even though no such tale existed in any of his Arabic manuscripts. However, "Aladdin and his Magic Lamp" *is* found in two Arabic manuscripts dated *after* Galland's translation; it appears that the tale was translated from French back into Arabic not once, but twice, with enough changes the second time around that it was thought to be not a variant copy, but an analogue. Burton would use the French-into-Arabic manuscripts for his own translation (with additional interpretive commentary on the erotic passages that he retained).[18] Hence Burton, so sure that he was finally giving the West an "authentic" *Arabian Nights* (along with John Payne, who also translated the *Nights* with the tale of Aladdin in 1882), unwittingly perpetuated a fraud begun in the West and imposed on the East *about* the East. The history of *The Arabian Nights* and the tale of Aladdin is a case study in the supplement: like all great stories, *The Arabian Nights* and the story of Aladdin spurs a desire for origins (the Arthuriad being a useful parallel) that can never be fully satisfied.

Moreover (again, like Arthurian legend), the story of Aladdin proliferates, morphs, and takes new directions precisely because of its indeterminate (but overdetermined) origins. While I don't want to push the analogy too far, it is useful to read the history of the transmission of *The Arabian Nights* as a series of colonizations (true also of that tale about that legendary king of the Britons, now co-opted by American interests and Hollywoodenizations). Cinematic versions of Aladdin's adventures recapitulate the history of the textual versions in that the East is made into a fungible product.

The Thief of Bagdad: An Arabian Nights Fantasy (1924)

> "The Thief of Bagdad" is the story of the things we dream about:
> a tale of what happens when we go out from
> ourselves to conquer Worlds of Fancy.
> —Attributed to Douglas Fairbanks,
> Prefatory to the Souvenir Book

Seventy-three years after his last film, Douglas Fairbanks, Sr. (1883–1939), persists as a Hollywood icon. He and wife Mary Pickford were the first Hollywood celebrity couple; together they promised that anyone could obtain wealth, success, and fame (and later divorce). Like Valentino (1895–1926) Fairbanks made his reputation in dashing, romantic, swashbuckler pictures; however, while Valentino played the brooding, dangerous lead, Fairbanks brought a Chaplinesque humor to his portrayal of romantic heroes. For many in Hollywood the Italian-born Rodolfo Alfonzo Raffaelo Pierre Filibert Guglielmi di Valentina d'Antonguolla was too ethnic, too exotic, too effete. Valentino, in fact, was held responsible for a general "degeneration into effeminacy," as an editorial of the day railed.[19] On the other hand Fairbanks, who did almost all of his own stunts, was perceived as projecting a healthy masculinity—more important, an *American* masculinity.[20]

D.W. Griffith sourly said that Fairbanks had "a face like a cantaloupe," an insult that nevertheless captures Fairbanks' perceived wholesomeness.[21] Richard Corliss describes Fairbanks in this way:

> He played heroes from foreign cultures (Robin Hood, Zorro, D'Artagnan, the Thief of Bagdad), yet he was always an American abroad, showing the Old World how to win the fair maiden, cure each injustice.

Corliss, following Griffith, also says:

> Doug's full-moon face and double chin made him a long shot for movie swoondom; and in closeup his stage-bred gestures looked like cheerleader antics. All he had was it—the gorgeous muscularity and infectious brio that made folks want to pay to see more. His exuberance turned out to be the key to a genre Doug virtually created: the adventure comedy.[22]

Fairbanks certainly turns *The Thief of Bagdad* into an adventure comedy, and his thief is indeed a cheerleader. The constraints of silent film put a heavy burden on the language of the body, of course, for much must be conveyed by gesture and facial expression. The silent *Thief*, true to genre, often compels Fairbanks into larger-than-life melodramatic postures of which he takes full advantage. For example, at one point, Fairbanks/The Thief smells food cooking and lifts his head, exaggeratedly sniffing like a dog and then rubbing his stomach in hyperbolic circles. As in many other silent films, the camera

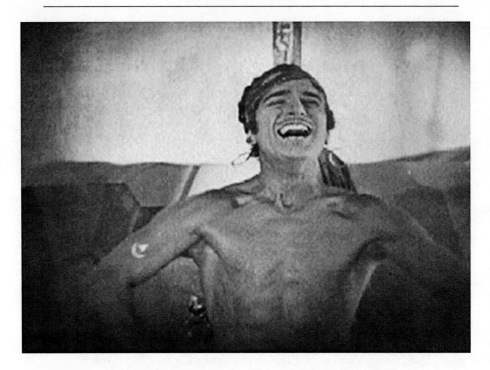

The Thief (Douglas Fairbanks) exhalant in *Thief of Bagdad* (1924).

in the 1924 *Thief* often functions like a spectator at a play, as figures often march "on" and "off," entering into one side of the frame of the camera and then departing through the other. The feeling of a stage set in *Thief* is reinforced by the extravagant props such as the gigantic pots that Fairbanks somersaults in and out of. The marketplace is obviously shot in a studio; the ground is really a highly polished floor. This fact is not an oversight; rather, the marketplace is intended to be recognized and enjoyed as a fanciful set. As the Souvenir Book for the film says, "when a thing is photographed, it is given substance and reality. This was overcome by building acres of glazed floors, which reflected the buildings, gave gleaming high lights ... [and] destroyed the reality of solid foundations."[23] At one point Fairbanks/The Thief begs for alms on as he lies on his back on this floor, raising up his arms and legs at the same time. We appreciate his well-muscled abdomen as well as his stylized, balletic pose. In another scene Fairbanks makes a graceful headstand in order to shake the coins that he's stolen out of his hair.

Fairbanks is no moon-faced cantaloupe in *Thief*; rather, he is lean and chiseled. We can see the planes of his face and the muscles over his ribs. He wears a scarf tied around his head, large hoop earrings, and harem pants that are cut tight over his lower torso and that then float out to be gathered at the ankle. His chest and feet are bare; his eyes are heavily made up. Fairbanks does not smolder as does Valentino; rather, Fairbanks is a laughing boy who vogues his way through the film.

Gaylyn Studlar in "Douglas Fairbanks: Thief of the Ballets Russes" argues convincingly that Fairbanks deliberately manipulates the aesthetics of dance in his portrayal of the Thief and that one can discern the influence of Vaslav Nijinsky as the Golden Slave in The Ballet Russes' production of Rimsky-Korsakoff's *Schéhérazade*, which caused quite a scandal when it premiered. Léon Bakst's costumes and sets for the ballet shocked audiences for what they saw as an orientalized homoerotic decadence, and Bakst's work certainly influenced William Cameron Menzies in his subsequent designs for *Thief.* The result, says Studlar, is that Fairbanks, "an exhibitionistic male performer," is "potentially compromised in his manhood by every visual element of the production: setting, costume, and movement."[24] Fairbanks' body signifies on several levels against such visual elements. Other male characters in *Thief* are lavishly overdressed, bedecked in elaborate turbans, embroidered sashes, and ropes of pearls and other jewels. Even the horses and mules that the other characters ride are overdressed. Most are bearded, and none is handsome. All contrast with Fairbanks' smooth half-nakedness. (See the photograph opposite, which shows the Thief as he has just outwitted merchants in the marketplace after stealing a rich man's purse, and note the white tattoo on his arm, a Hollywood per-version of the Islamic crescent and star.)[25]

Slaves (and most are Africans — rather, African Americans playing Africans) and minions are shirtless and/or bare-chested as well, so Fairbanks' revealing dress also registers his marginalized position in Baghdad's society. At one point the Thief steals clothes so that he may impersonate a suitor for the Princess and enter the palace. The Thief is costumed relatively simply in comparison to his rivals, all of whom could have stepped from a medieval morality play: the obese Persian Prince is gluttonous (and played by a woman, Mathilde Comont), and the Indian Prince (African-American Noble Johnston) is haughtily angry (he glowers, says the Princess). The emaciated and avaricious Mongol Prince (Sojin Kamiyama) is the Thief's chief rival as he plots to overthrow the Caliph of Baghdad and seize the Princess — all the while wielding a fan. The Thief's stolen clothes are deliberately designed to emphasize the shape of his body and expose his bare chest — even when the Thief moves from the margins into the center of society, he emphasizes his difference as an "Arab." Viewer pleasure in Fairbanks's body is refracted through the Princess when she comes face-to-face with the Thief as "Prince Ahmed" for the first time. As she casts an admiring look at him from toe to head, a look not quite in keeping with her sheltered innocence, we follow where her eyes go. Fairbanks sees her gaze and responds to it with a look of ardent triumph mixed with adoration.

We might read Fairbanks' performance as a response to Valentino's earlier and quite scandalous performance as the Sheik. It seems as if Fairbanks deliberately sets out to recuperate a proper masculinity in his Arab role, attempting to restore to Hollywood some control over the representation of heteronormativity that Valentino undermined in *his* Arab role. For example, Valentino/The Sheik, captured by the bandit Yousaef (George Waggner), is severely whipped (an episode that is repeated in several Valentino films), and his helplessness as he recovers allows the Lady Mayo to admit her love for him. We are made voyeurs to Valentino/the Sheik's whipping, and the erotic charge inherent in the scene as well as the erotic effect on Lady Mayo is unmistakable. In imitation Fairbanks includes a whipping scene, but it is quite different in tone and effect. When the Thief is discovered to be an impostor prince, the order is given: "Flog him!" Fairbanks is stripped to the waist of his stolen finery, and he is whipped by slaves and guards. However, the scene is staged as if all were taking part in a complex, intertwined dance as the Thief sways back and forth at the center of the frame. Fairbanks' whipping

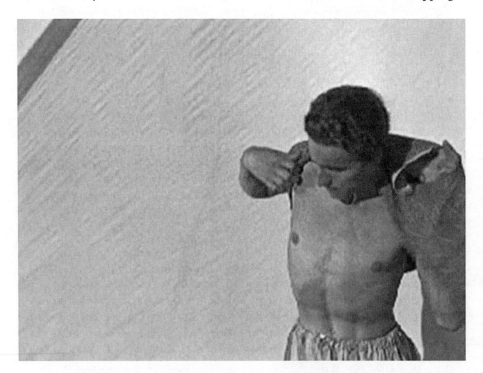

King Ahmed (John Justin) dons a simple vest in *Thief of Bagdad* (1940).

scene is thus highly stylized; the audience may thrill to the accompanying dramatic score and sympathize with the Princess as she listens outside the walls of the palace — to the same score, we presume — but Fairbanks has made Valentino's perversely erotic scene into an allegory for American endurance and stoic perseverance.[26]

While on offer to be admired for its athletic tone, Fairbanks' body stands in for subjectivity itself, for throughout *The Thief of Bagdad* Fairbanks's body, which is consistently filmed at the center of the frame, separates him from an undifferentiated mass of Arabs who are not allowed to occupy full subject positions. The other characters inhabit an Eastern past; Fairbanks/The Thief embodies the modern West. The other Arabs are extravagantly effeminate; in comparison Fairbanks is almost austerely virile, in spite of the earrings. As in all of his films, Fairbanks is clearly enjoying himself in his role as the Thief who wins the Princess through daring, pluck, and ingenuity — stereotypical American traits all. His grin belies the eye make-up, and his muscular torso contradicts the harem pants. Fairbanks does not offer an androgynous performance; his heroic masculinity is never at risk precisely because his role is such an obvious put-on. In this respect the extra-diegetic enters and informs the diegesis of the film, for the audience never loses sight of Douglas Fairbanks, movie star.

The Thief of Bagdad: An Arabian Fantasy (1940)

> Princess: *"Where did you come from?"*
> King Ahmed: *"From the other side of time — to find you."*
> —The Thief of Bagdad *(1940)*

As the second *Thief of Bagdad* (often wrongly called a remake of the Fairbanks film) was in production, Europe was at war; in 1939 Germany took Czechoslovakia and invaded Poland, and England declared war on Germany. The U.S., after much debate, declared its neutrality, despite the fact that many Americans sympathized with the British.

Producer Alexander Korda and his brothers Zoltan and Vincent (both of whom collaborated on *Thief*) had left Hungary for England in the early 30s because of increasing anti–Semitism and political and economic instability. Alexander Korda embraced Englishness with the zeal of the newly naturalized. In fact, when Chamberlain's declaration of war stopped production on *Thief* in 1940, Korda pledged his studio, London Films, to his friend Winston Churchill (about to return as prime Minister) and made a propaganda film, *The Lion Has Wings*. Korda, who then went to Hollywood to finish *Thief*, was asked by Churchill to serve as a good-will ambassador in the isolationist States.²⁷ Korda's project after *Thief* was *That Hamilton Woman* (1941), a thinly disguised pro–British, pro-war film that resulted in Korda's being subpoenaed by a Senate committee to testify in December 1941 on whether he was "inciting the American public to war."²⁸ Pearl Harbor made the question moot.

While much vilified in England for staying in Hollywood, a handful of expatriate British actors were actually asked by their government to remain in the States (David Niven had actually left and joined the British Rifle Brigade before the request came down). The British Ambassador, Philip Kerr, Lord Lothian, explained Foreign Office policy in this way:

> The maintenance of a powerful nucleus of older British actors [such as Cary Grant and Laurence Olivier] is of great importance to our own interests, partly because they are continually championing the British cause in a very volatile community which would otherwise be left to the mercies of German propaganda, and because the production of films with a strong British tone is one of the best and subtlest forms of British propaganda.²⁹

I offer these details as a prelude to explaining the appeal of John Justin in Korda's *Thief*. Justin plays the naive King Ahmed, who is deprived of his throne by a trick of the evil Grand Vizier and magician Jaffar. Ahmed starts out as an "Arab" in royal turban and robes. At the urging of Jaffar he goes among his people in disguise as a merchant. However, when he tries to return to the palace, Jaffar denies that he is the Prince, declares him mad, and has him imprisoned. The thief Abu, also imprisoned, helps him escape; together, they flee Baghdad for Basra. At one point Ahmed, in his merchant's disguise, ritually puts off his bourgeois clothes and dons a vest, leaving Justin barechested. The simple vest serves as the sign of his fallen station, as in Fairbanks' *Thief*. In an odd juxtaposition the camera lingers on Ahmed as he changes his clothes while Abu sings "I Want to Be a Sailor." But Justin is no Fairbanks, as Figure 2 demonstrates. Unlike Fairbanks Justin is rarely centered in the frame in the film. Almost too slender, Justin conveys not athletic strength, but physical weakness. What does Justin's effeteness signify?

Throughout the film Justin/Ahmed is a figure who lacks: kept isolated from his subjects, he lacks the understanding and judgment to rule wisely; restless and unhappy as king, he is dominated by Jaffar and does not possess the worldly experience necessary to see the evil in his Vizier. Justin, one might say, stands for the British Empire: stoic in the face of adversity, expecting others to behave as honorably as he does. Justin/Prince Ahmed has no strength of his own, but depends upon the muscle of colonized peoples to help him win back the Princess and destroy Jaffar. The thief Abu is played by Sabu, a young South Asian (who would go on to play Mowgli in Korda's 1942 *The Jungle Book*), and the Genie is played by African American actor Rex Ingram

King Ahmed receives evil counsel from Jaffar (Conrad Veidt) in *Thief of Bagdad* (1940).

(ubiquitous as a generic African in early *Tarzan* films) in sparkling green face paint. Ahmed can only regain his throne and win his beloved Princess by relying on the help of Abu and the Genie. Othered bodies serve as prostheses: Ahmed can do nothing by himself. Even the Princess is a prosthesis: once Ahmed falls in love with her, and she serves to motivate him to achieve the experience and wisdom necessary to rule Bagdad.

Laurence Olivier once described British actors working in Hollywood as "British by profession," a comment that captures the stereotyped Brit in tweeds that Americans were so fond of in the 30s and 40s.[30] Justin fits this stereotype whether dressed as an Arab prince or as a dethroned outcast. Justin was more of an established stage actor than a film star: his elegant good looks and lean body are appropriate to a well-tailored suit; his accent is BBC. I would argue that Korda deliberately cast Justin in his *Thief* to keep a quintessential Englishman — and English interests — before American eyes. Certainly the film served as a welcome escape from the war in both England and America, but even before *That Hamilton Woman* it may well be that Korda had in mind "the best and subtlest forms of British propaganda," in Lord Lothian's words, as he filmed the *Thief of Bagdad*—recall that Korda made a British propaganda film in the middle of *Thief*. And perhaps it is not too farfetched to read Ahmed's transformation from a weak ruler into a strong one as a parallel to the replacement of Chamberlain and his appeasement policies with the more militant Churchill.

An Englishman in Arabface might actually be inspiring in 1940, not only as stand-in for an argument to back Britain in the war, but also as a way to think through Britannia's relationship with its colonies. While I would like to read Korda's casting of Sabu and Ingram as a critique of colonialism, it is difficult to do so in the context of his best films (after *The Third Man* [1949]), which have been described as "colonial epics" and what I would call pro-colonial epics: *Sanders of the River* (1935), *The Drum* (1938), *Elephant Boy* (1937), *The Four Feathers* (1939), and *Jungle Book* (1942).[31] Moreover, Korda had hoped to film a life of T.E. Lawrence in the mid 1930s, but was blocked first by Lawrence and second by the British Foreign Office, the latter because of Korda's depiction of the Turks as villains—Turkey was a British ally. Korda apparently planned to portray Lawrence uncritically as the courageous hero who goes East and whose experiences in Arabia teach him humility.[32] For Korda the East is a convenient proving ground for Western heroes. Perhaps we might see Justin's role as fulfilling a fantasy of empire: he is a dethroned king who must regain what he has lost, and he does so triumphantly. Korda looks into the future, but cannot predict it: an Englishman in Arabface would not work at any later point, in 1947, say, when India regained its independence or in 1948 when the British Mandate over Palestine ended, or in 1956, the year of the Suez Crisis, or later, throughout the 60s and 70s as decolonization continued in Africa and the Caribbean. Korda's timing was just right.

Aladdin (1992)

> *"Like so many things it is not what is outside, but what is inside that counts."*
> —*(The Merchant in Disney's* Aladdin*)*

Disney's *Aladdin* (1992) exists in two versions; it inhabits parallel temporalities. The first version exists only as citation, that is, in references to an original film. The second version is the "authoritative" version, the one that consumers have spent over $600,000,000 in theatres, rentals, and sales of the video and DVD to see, and that includes the market for the film in the Middle East itself.[33] In the first version the opening song, "Arabian Nights," extolling the virtues of home (or "home"), contains noteworthy lyrics. (I may not quote them here because of copyright restrictions. However, the lyrics can be found on the IMDb as well as on YouTube.[34])

After public protests by the American-Arab Anti-Discrimination Committee (ADC), these lines were changed, resulting in a standard edition of the film with an opening song about "a faraway place."[35] The idea of a "faraway place" is spatially relative indeed, positioning the singer "there" and the audience "here" when the singer — an Arab merchant on a camel, voice by Bruce Adler (who also specializes in Yiddish theatre) — is actually in his own "here" since he never leaves "there." The last line in the revised version is still an offensive stet and keeps in play a temporal relativity that distinguishes civilized Western "now" from barbaric Eastern "then."[36] What was narrated in the original lyrics led to a "logical" conclusion; now, a reference to the East as "barbaric" simply asserts a stereotype that smacks of factiousness because it is unexplained. Every article and every review, as well as every discussion of the film on the Internet that I've read, recounts the history of the controversy over the lyrics and furnishes the original and revised lyrics for comparison. *Aladdin* is one of Disney's most successful animated features, yet it will always be haunted by the history of its revision.

Aladdin himself is an ambiguous figure, for behind the animation lurks Tom Cruise, himself haunted by rumors of possible homosexuality. Aladdin was initially modeled on Michael J. Fox, who was considered not sexy enough; Jeffrey Katzenberg then asked that Aladdin be redrawn to look like Tom Cruise as he appeared in *Top Gun* (1986). The resemblance is most apparent when Aladdin flashes his crooked digital smile. Cruise's body, like Fairbanks', does not belong exclusively to him; it also resides in the public domain, in the cultural imaginary. In that space Cruise's body has come under heavy scrutiny. Like the deleted lyrics to "Arabian Nights," rumors about Cruise's homosexuality persist in the media. That Katzenberg would single out *Top Gun*, which has, as Tanya Modelski points out, cult status in the gay community, is rich indeed.[37] Consider the film *Sleep with Me* (1994), in which Quentin Tarantino in the character of Sid famously launches into a monologue on *Top Gun*:

> It is a story about a man's struggle with his own homosexuality. It is! That is what *Top Gun* is about, man. You've got Maverick [Tom Cruise], all right? He's on the edge, man. He's right on the fucking line, all right? And you've got Iceman [Val Kilmer], and all his crew. They're gay, they represent the gay man, all right? And they're saying, go, go the gay way, go the gay way. He could go both ways.

Thus Tarantino dramatizes rumors about Cruise's sexual identity that had already worked their way into popular culture before *Aladdin*— rumors that circulate in part *because* of Cruise's role in *Top Gun*. Disney's Aladdin has no Iceman as a friend; rather, his best friend is a monkey named Abu. Earlier Fairbanks played a hero/thief; in Korda's *Thief*, the hero is split into two, into

Ahmed and Abu; Disney extends this split by creating a boy-hero and his trickster totem, as it were. In fact Aladdin has no homosocial allegiances whatsoever. He lives on the margins of his culture, in opposition to every other character (though women in the marketplace are affectionately indulgent toward him). Aladdin, once he meets the Princess Jasmine, sets out on a romance quest that privileges a narrative in which the effects of the feminine are transformative and civilizing, designed to help him become a responsible member of his society.

Earlier I noted how the "Arab" heroes in the two *Thief* films are distinguished from other "Arabs" through their obvious whiteness. Digitizing Arabs allows for even more exaggerated bodies in *Aladdin*. At one point Aladdin is shown in small-nosed profile versus the huge and menacing hook-nosed guard. In the words of Jack Shaheen in *Reel Bad Arabs*, the Arabs in *Aladdin* are "ruthless, uncivilized caricatures ... [with] large bulbous noses and sinister eyes" (51).[38] And Roger Ebert notes the film's "odd use of ethnic stereotypes," calling it a "distraction:"

> Most of the Arab characters have exaggerated facial characteristics — hooked noses, glowering brows, thick lips — but Aladdin and the princess look like white American teenagers. Wouldn't it be reasonable that if all the characters in this movie come from the same genetic stock, they should resemble one another?

Ebert also notes that Aladdin and Jasmine "look unformed, as if even the filmmakers didn't see them as real individuals."[39] Both Aladdin and Jasmine look unformed precisely around the nose; Jafar, on the other hand, is often shown in profile, which emphasizes the exaggerated cut of his nose. In animation when characters morph from their default bodies into other forms, the space between each change is called a "hesitation:" the morphing is made visible through these hesitations, and visibility, depending, can be a desirable or an undesirable effect. Walt Disney, for example, insisted on the integrity of the body, mandating that every change had to return the body to its original form.[40] Yet here it's as if Aladdin and Jasmine are caught in an endless hesitation, caught between competing representational paradigms of East and West. Another "unformed" body part is Aladdin's chest: he has no nipples (the Genie does). Instead, Aladdin's chest is defined by two manly slashes. Nipples, it appears, are unseemly, and may suggest effeminacy. Yousef Salem, spokesperson for the South Bay Islamic Association, says:

> Aladdin doesn't have a big nose, he has a small nose. He doesn't have a beard or turban. He doesn't have an accent. What makes him nice is that they've given him this American character. They have done everything but put him in a suit and tie.[41]

As Fairbanks represented an all–American ideal, so does Aladdin; certainly the values of *Aladdin* are based on an American master narrative of getting over — in this case, moving from a "street rat" to a Prince worthy of a Princess.

Fairbanks exhibits a robust heteromasculinity and Justin a more effete version — safe because it is not American, but British — but Aladdin offers us something altogether different because the figure of Tom Cruise shadows the animated figure of Aladdin. Aladdin and Cruise live in Bakhtin's "great time," and while Bakhtin would reserve such a temporal space for "great works," as he says, the power of the pop culture imaginary is such that there is always the potential for confusing Aladdin with his human model.

To conclude I'd like to return to the idea of masquerade from a different angle by thinking through Arabface as a manifestation of drag. To *transvest* is, more often than not, symptomized and gendered masculine in the history of Western sexuality, yet this history has certainly been under revision for some time. We appreciate the many cultural functions of cross-dressing, which has crossed over from simply a theory of the pathological to a more capacious theory of performance. We need not elide the sexual charge that may accompany cross-dressing, for dresser and viewer alike. What does it mean, then, to be Western and dress Eastern, either as a deliberate performance or disguise or as following the latest fashion trend? To wear a Palestinian *keffiyeh* or bangles from Tibet or other ethnic accessories or clothes may signify nothing more than casual consumerism, but even such consumerism (particularly because it is so unreflectively casual) suggests the degree to which the West routinely appropriates and absorbs the material goods of the East for its own purposes, severing such goods from their original cultural contexts and significances. Such consumerism has a long history: Alexander the Great made it a policy to adopt local sartorial customs as he moved East, and Crusaders sometimes wore Eastern dress during their sojourn in the Levant. Every century since has seen renascences in orientalist fashions and fads.

Earlier I cited the Ballet Russes' staging of *Schéhérazade* as an inspiration for Fairbanks's performance in *The Thief of Bagdad* and as an influence on Menzies's set design. In a wider context Léon Bakst's costumes and set designs for *Schéhérazade*, as Peter Wollen documents, had an immediate impact on fashion and the material arts.[42] As Cecil Beaton observed of 1910 Paris, "a fashion world that had been dominated by corsets, lace, feathers and pastel shades soon found itself a seraglio of vivid colours, harem skirts, beads, fringes and voluptuousness."[43] In addition to precursor films by Georges Méliès (*Le Palais des Mille et Une Nuits*, 1905) and Paul Leni (*Das Wachsfigurenkabinett*, 1924), Fairbanks was also tapping into the fashion *Zeitgeist* when he created the phantasmagoric *Thief*, which both Korda and then Disney Studios were to imitate in their own constructions of a magical, opulent Middle

East. As part of its "research" for Aladdin, Disney acknowledges medieval Persian miniatures as an inspiration, as well as the 1940 *Thief*, glossy coffee-table books on the Middle East, Victorian paintings of the Middle East — that is, works by painters that we have come to describe as Orientalists — and, as well, its own films from the classic Disney period of the 40s and 50s. And Disney cites its sources without irony: Disney depends on Western constructions of the Middle East (and its own product) to represent a Middle East that is, in its view, both magical and authentic.[44] One hardly needs the "East" when we can recycle the West's East for profitable consumption.

In *Vested Interests* Garber distinguishes between "marked" transvestism (that is, a transvestite "whose clothing seems deliberately and obviously at variance with his anatomical gender assignment") and "unmarked" (that is, a transvestite who may represent an "*unconscious* of transvestism"). One may not necessarily "signal [his] cross-gender identit[y] onstage, and this quality of crossing ... can be more powerful and seductive than explicit 'female impersonation,' which is often designed to confront, scandalize, titillate, or shock" (354). Both marked and unmarked transvestism call representation into question, but in the first instance the audience is complicit in the masquerade, while in the second the audience is left more unsettled. In the context of Western impersonations of Arabs or other Middle Eastern peoples, we thus might describe Sir Richard Burton as attempting an "unmarked" masquerade as an Arab; T. E. Lawrence, on the other hand, had no intention other than to be an Englishman in Arab dress, and he is therefore "marked." Burton took great glee and pride in his many Arab disguises, all the better to gather "authentic" experiences and savor Arab culture; T.E. Lawrence, on the other hand, while he also took pride in his Arab dress, was more invested in *being* consumed by his Arab identification than in consuming.[45]

In the two *Thief* films and in *Aladdin*, Arab-ness is very much marked in the way Garber theorizes for transvestites. Each film makes very clear that the hero is not an Arab, most clearly through contrast with other fantasized "Arab" bodies. We are invited behind the mask; it never stands between us and Fairbanks or Justin or Cruise. Garber argues:

> Psychoanalytically, transvestism is a mechanism that functions by *displacement* and *through fantasy* to enact a scenario of desire.... Transvestism on the stage, and particularly in the kind of entertainment culture that generates the phenomenon known as "stardom," is a symptom for the *culture*, rather than the individual performer.... These transvestic symptoms, appear, so to speak, to gratify a social or cultural scenario of desire. The onstage transvestite is the fetishized part-object for the social or cultural script of the fan [366].

Surely Arabface functions through displacement and fantasy in the same way — and, given the long association of Eastern customs and dress with effeminacy, when one puts on Eastern dress, one also tests the limits of gender identification as constructed in the West. Following Garber (who is following Freud and Lacan), Fairbanks and Justin and Weinger/Cruise are not acting out their own desires, but participating in a script already written by American culture, a script that privileges white heteromasculinity. In the two *Thief* films this white heteromasculinity is posited as so unshakable that play outside of its borders does not threaten, but actually reaffirms its prerogatives. In *Aladdin*, where animation makes all bodies hyperbolic (Jasmine is impossibly curvaceous, and Robin Williams's Genie is a polymorphous wonder), the exaggerated bodies of Arab villains may be read as attempting to mitigate what I'll call the Cruise-effect: less unshakable.

Recall that Disney cited coffee-table books on the Middle East as a source of inspiration for *Aladdin*. A common photographic trick of such books is to capture an image as if it could have been photographed at any time: no modern intrusions of telephone wires or automobiles are permitted to enter the frame. And of course modern Jerusalem would not have worked for Ridley Scott when he made *Kingdom of Heaven* (2005): the first long shot of CGI Jerusalem in the film is so stunning because it seduces us into belief— it is an "unmarked" representation of the past. When it comes to representations of the Middle East, our cultural script also demands a fetishization of the past, a past that belongs not to the East, but to the West. "Yesteryear's Arabland," says Jack Shaheen, "is today's Arabland."[46] We have taken their time. This Western appropriation of the past denies the Middle East its place in history and in modernity. The Middle East that is offered in the three films is, for its intended audience, safely lodged in an imagined past. These films that claim *The Arabian Nights* for themselves thus reside in no time and no place at all.

Notes

1. Quoted in M. Brodie, *The Devil Drives: A Life of Sir Richard Burton* (89).
2. The dedications and forewords to Burton's *The Thousand Nights and a Night: A Plain and Literal Translation of the Arabian Nights Entertainments* can be conveniently found at www.wollamschram.ca. This Foreword is to Vol. 4 (1888) of the *Supplemental Nights*: http://www.wollamshram.ca/1001/Sn_4/14foreword.htm, viii.
3. Burton, Foreword to The Thousand Nights and a Night, Vol. 1 (1885): http://www.wollamshram.ca/1001/Vol_1/vol1.htm, xii.
4. In addition to the three films under discussion (and in addition to the two Disney Aladdin sequels and the TV cartoon spin-off), the Internet Movie Database (IMDb) lists the following selected films made in the United States or England based on *The Arabian Nights: A Caliph of the New Bagdad* (Van Dyke Brooke, 1916); *Ali Baba and the Forty Thieves* (Arthur Lubin, 1944); *A Thousand and One Nights* (Alfred Green, 1945), with Cornell Wilde; *The Prince Who Was A Thief* (Rudolph Maté, 1951), with Tony Curtis as an Arab prince; *The Veils of Bagdad* (George Sherman, 1953) with Victor Mature; *The Wizard of Baghdad* (George Sherman 1960); (Arthur Lubin 1961) a Steve Reeves remake of the 1940 *Thief*; *The Thief from Baghdad* (Hal Seeger, 1967), part of the TV cartoon Batfink; *Thief of Baghdad* (Ravikant Nagaich, 1977);

Thief of Baghdad (Clive Donner, 1978) TV; *The Pink of Bagdad* (1978) Pink Panther cartoon; *Thief of Baghdad* short (2003) with Charlton Heston and footage from the 1940 *Thief*; *Thief of Baghdad* (2008), a TV mini-series remake of the 1940 *Thief*. Nick Haydock directed me to the oldest extant animated feature film, Lotte Reiniger's *The Adventures Of Prince Achmed* (1926), which now only exists in reconstructed form. Reiniger used a "silhouette" technique involving black cutouts. The film is remarkably mesmerizing and very different from any other treatment of *The Arabian Nights* that I know of.

 5. Both *Thief* films use the spelling "Bagdad," and both films are often cited with the spelling "Baghdad."

 6. The 1940 *Thief* is a product of more than one hand: Ludwig Berger, Michael Powell, and Tim Whelan are credited as directors, but producer Alexander Korda, who wanted a full-scale spectacle, often intervened and re-shot many scenes.

 7. See Wise 105–14 and Staninger 65–78. For other analyses of gender, see Kahf 19–25 and Addison 5–25. For reading *Aladdin* against the Gulf War, see Macleod 179–92, as well as Nadel 184–203.

 8. M. M. Bakhtin: "If it is impossible to study literature apart from an epoch's entire culture, it is even more fatal to encapsulate a literary phenomenon in the single act of its creation, in its own contemporaneity, so to speak" (3–4).

 9. See Richard Burt (217–42) for a detailed analysis of the paratext.

 10. Space does not permit me to discuss the other actors in these three films, especially when the actors themselves bring something unexpected to their respective roles, and given the complications of spectatorial identifications. I can only gesture at some possibilities: consider Conrad Veidt, for example, who plays Jaffar in Korda's *Thief*. Veidt receives top billing; Sabu follows, then Duprez, Justin, and Ingram. Veidt fled Germany in the early 1930s-like the Korda brothers, a refugee, but not Jewish. His career was made playing villains: in *Escape* (Mervyn LeRoy, 1940), Veidt plays a Nazi general; in *Contraband* (Michael Powell, 1940), he plays a Danish sea captain who tangles with a German spy ring; in *The Spy in Black* (Michael Powell, 1939) he plays the captain of a German U-boat; in *Nazi Agent* (Jules Dassin, 1942), Veidt plays *both* sides: one twin an American, anther a Nazi. But his most famous role was the Gestapo official Major Strasser in *Casablanca* (Michael Curtiz, 1942).

 11. A classic case: it is necessary that Rudolph Valentino's Sheik be not a real Arab, but an English/Spanish orphan in Arab dress: after all, he has abducted a white woman and enslaved and degraded her — and then she falls in love with him. Sarah Projansky suggests that "the colonialist setting and the threat of rape in that setting are metaphors for danger outside heterosexual whiteness" (48); for an overview of the trope of rape in the desert romance, see 47–49. Also see Ella Shohat and Robert Stam, *Unthinking Eurocentrism: Multiculturalism and the Media*, Chapter 4, "Tropes of Empire," on "symbolic fantasies of rape and rescue" (141).

 12. Eric Lott, page 6.

 13. Kaja Silverman, page 312.

 14. See the 2000 U.S. Census Bureau Short Form: http://www.census.gov/dmd/www/pdf/d61a.pdf, and "Revisions to the Standards for the Classification of Federal Data on Race and Ethnicity," in which it is recommended that "Arab" or "Middle Eastern" not be added to the Census, http://www.census.gov/population/www/socdemo/race/Ombdir15.html. The Arab American Institute, arguing that the Census does not reflect accurate numbers with respect to Arab Americans, is lobbying for a question for all Americans on ancestry on the 2010 Census: http://www.aaiusa.org/foundation/34/census-information-center. See also Werner Sollors' classic *Beyond Ethnicity: Consent and Descent in American Culture*.

 15. My narrative of this story depends upon Husain Haddawy's introduction to his two-volume translation of *The Arabian Nights*, page ix. Also see Robert Irwin's introduction and first chapter of *The Arabian Nights: A Companion*, Rana Kabbani's *Europe's Myths of Orient*, and Michael Cooperson's "The Monstrous Births of 'Aladdin'" (265–82).

 16. Haddawy, page xii.

 17. Haddawy, page xiv.

 18. Haddawy, page xiii. For Burton's account of the history of the Aladdin tale that he accepts as a genuine part of *The Arabian Nights*, see the Foreword to the *Supplemental Nights*, Vol 6 (1888): http://www.wollamshram.ca/1001/Sn_6/vol16.htm, pages vii–ix.

 19. See Emily W. Leider *Dark Lover*, pages 372–73.

20. It is common to compare Fairbanks and Valentino in the ways that I have; see an account of such comparisons in Jon Lewis (49–51) and Leider, pages 4, 87, 256.
21. Qtd. in Richard Corliss, "King of Hollywood," at http://www.time.com/time/magazine/article/0,9171,984717,00.html.
22. Corliss, "King of Hollywood."
23. Excerpts from the Souvenir Book are included on the Kino Video DVD.
24. Studlar, page 115.
25. The marketplace is a key site in all three films: not only so-called exotic goods are featured, but rope-climbers, fire-swallowers, and mystics on beds of nails. The thieves in all three films steal goods from stalls and merchants and confront potential violence and punishment there. It would be worth devoting an essay to representations of the marketplace and what Western desires such representations fulfill. Christopher Wise says provocatively: "the film vilifies Islamic law, or *sharia* ... promoting instead a largely Western notion of "freedom"—which means essentially the freedom to exchange goods" (106).
26. I must add, however, that there is something to be found in the whipping scene for a perverse spectator: in no other instance is Fairbanks's/the Thief's package so obviously outlined.
27. Churchill claimed that *That Hamilton Woman* was his favorite film. In addition to Winston Churchill, Korda also came to know Robert Vandsitart of the British Foreign Office, who apparently recruited Korda to work in his intelligence service as a courier throughout the 30s and 40s—an activity that, as much as his stature in the film world, may well have led to Churchill's nominating him for a knighthood. Bruce Eder, "Alexander Korda," Allmovie.com, http://www.allmovie.com/cg/avg.dll?p=avg&sql=B97893.
28. As recounted in and quoted in Kati Marton, *The Great Escape: Nine Jews Who Fled Hitler and Changed the World* (142).
29. As qtd. in Holden, page 161.
30. According to Michael Korda, *Charmed Lives* (149).
31. See Screenonline.com: http://www.screenonline.org.uk/people/id/446996/).
32. See Laurence Raw, http://findarticles.com/p/articles/mi_qa3768/is_200510/ai_n15957560/pg_1?tag=artBody;col1.
33. In theatres worldwide: over $479,000,000; rentals: over $111,000,000; DVD sales: over $10,000,000. Statistics at http://www.imdb.com/title/tt0103639/business, http://www.imdb.com/title/tt0103639/news. For the popularity of *Aladdin* in the Middle East, see Christopher Wise (110–111).
34. For the IMDb: http://www.imdb.com/title/tt0103639/trivia for YouTube: http://www.youtube.com/watch?v=9wRIkix_RDI.
35. The original version contained the line, "Good tiger, take off and go," which was spoken by Aladdin when Raja is growling at him. However, after the film was released on home video, many began to speculate that the line was actually, "Good teenagers, take off their clothes," meant as a subliminal message. For the DVD release, this line was omitted, presumably to prevent any further speculation. http://www.imdb.com/title/tt0103639/alternateversions.
36. Jack Shaheen comments: "Now, how could a producer with a modicum of intelligence, just a modicum of sensitivity, let a song such as that open the film?" Interview with Jack Shaheen, 19 October 2007, on the radio program *Democracy Now!* Transcript at http://www.democracynow.org/2007/10/19/reel_bad_arabs_how_hollywood_vilifies. Disney executives were slow to react to protests to the song; indeed, Ashman had alternate lines in reserve before there was a public protest. See Mark Pinsky, *The Gospel According to Disney: Faith, Trust, and Pixie Dust* (148–49); Henry Giroux, *The Mouse that Roared: Disney and the End of Innocence* (104–105). However, the song is not the only sign of a corporate recalcitrance with respect to representations of Arabs and Arab culture. The character who sings "Arabian Nights" crosses a desert to arrive in night-time "Agrabah." There is no such city as Agrabah; it is a made-up place name that the filmmakers substituted for Baghdad, the original setting (following the two *Thief* films). However, the 1990–91 Gulf War made "Baghdad" fraught indeed. "Agrabah" is semi-anagrammatic for "Baghdad"; it also has an ersatz Arabic feel, and, worse, functions as an onomatopoetic sound of disgust.
37. Tanya Modleski 101–05.
38. Jack Shaheen in *Reel Bad Arabs* (51).

39. Roger Ebert, Review, http://rogerebert.suntimes.com/apps/pbcs.dll/article?AID=/199 21125/REVIEWS/211250301/1023.
40. See Norman M. Klein (32–33).
41. Quoted in Giroux, page 104.
42. Peter Wollen, "Fashion/Orientalism/The Body," *New Formations* 1 (1987), 5–33.
43. Quoted in Wollen, page 21.
44. John Culhane, *Disney's Aladdin: The Making of an Animated Film* (89).
45. See Silverman, "White Skin," for a nuanced account of Lawrence's complex sexuality.
46. Interview with Jack Shaheen, *Democracy Now!*

Bibliography

Addison, Erin. "Saving Other Women from Other Men: Disney's Aladdin." *Camera Obscura* 31 (1993): 5–25.

Bakhtin, M. M. "Response to a Question from the Novy Mir Editorial Staff" (1970). Speech Genres and Other Late Essays. Translated by Vern W. McGee and edited by Caryl Emerson and Michael Holquist. Austin: University of Texas Press, 1986. 1–9.

Brodie, M. *The Devil Drives: A Life of Sir Richard Burton*. New York: W. W. Norton, 1967.

Burt, Richard. "Introduction: Getting Schmedieval: Of Manuscript and Film Prologues, Paratexts, and Parodies." *Exemplaria* 19.2 (2007): 217–42.

Burton, Sir Francis. "Foreword" to *The Thousand Nights and a Night*, Vol. 1. 1885.

———. *The Thousand Nights and a Night: A Plain and Literal Translation of the Arabian Nights Entertainments*. Translated and Annotated by Richard F. Burton, Vol. 4, Supplemental Nights. 1888.

"Census Information Center." Arab American Institute. http://www.aaiusa.org/foundation/34/census-information-center.

Cooperson, Michael. "The Monstrous Births of 'Aladdin.'" *The Arabian Nights Reader*. Edited and introduced by Ulrich Marzolph. Detroit, MI: Wayne State University Press, 2006. 265–82.

Corliss, Richard. "King of Hollywood." *Time*. 17 June 1996. http://www.time.com/time/magazine/article/0,9171,984717,00.html.

Culhane, John. *Disney's Aladdin: The Making of an Animated Film*. New York: Hyperion, 1992.

Ebert, Roger. Review, http://rogerebert.suntimes.com/apps/pbcs.dll/article?AID=/199 21125/REVIEWS/211250301/1023.

Eder, Bruce. "Alexander Korda." Allmovie.com. http://www.allmovie.com/cg/avg.dll?p=avg&sql=B97893.

Giroux, Henry. *The Mouse that Roared: Disney and the End of Innocence*. Lanham MD: Rowman and Littlefield, 1999.

Haddawy, Husain. *The Arabian Nights*. New York and London: W. W. Norton, 1990.

Holden, Anthony. *Laurence Olivier*. New York: Atheneum, 1988.

Irwin, Robert. *The Arabian Nights: A Companion*. London: Allen Lane/Penguin, 1994.

Kabbani, Rana. *Europe's Myths of Orient*. Bloomington: Indiana University Press, 1986.

Kahf, Mohja. "The Image of the Muslim Woman in American Cinema: Two Orientalist Fantasy Films." *Cinefocus* 3 (1995): 19–25.

Klein, Norman M. "Animation as Baroque: Fleischer Morphs Harlem; Tangos to Crocodiles." *The Sharpest Point: Animation at the End of the Cinema*. Edited by Chris Gehman and Steve Reinke. Toronto: YYZ Books, 2005. 27–48.

"Korda, Alexander." Screenonline.com. http://www.screenonline.org.uk/people/id/446 996/.

Korda, Michael. *Charmed Lives: A Family Romance*. New York: Random House, 1979.

Leider, Emily W. *Dark Lover*. Farrar, Straus & Giroux, 2003.
Lewis, Jon. *The History of American Film*. New York and London: W.W. Norton, 2008.
Lott, Eric. *Love and Theft*. New York: Oxford University Press, 1995.
Macleod, Dianne Sachko. "The Politics of Vision: Disney, Aladdin, and the Gulf War." *The Emperor's Old Groove: Decolonizing Disney's Magic Kingdom*. Edited and introduced by Brenda Ayres; introduced by Susan Hines. New York, NY: Peter Lang, 2003. 179–92.
Marton, Kati. *The Great Escape: Nine Jews Who Fled Hitler and Changed the World*. New York: Simon & Schuster, 2006.
Modleski, Tanya. "Misogynist Films: Teaching Top Gun." *Cinema Journal* 47.1 (2007): 101–05.
Nadel, Alan. "A Whole New (Disney) World Order: Aladdin, Atomic Power, and the Muslim Middle East." *Visions of the East: Orientalism in Film*. Edited by Matthew Bernstein and Gaylyn Studlar. New Brunswick, NJ: Rutgers University Press, 1997. 184–203.
Pinsky, Mark. *The Gospel According to Disney: Faith, Trust, and Pixie Dust*. Louisville and London: Westminster/John Knox Press, 2004. 148–49.
Projansky, Sarah. *Watching Rape: Film and Television in Postfeminist Culture*. New York, NY: New York University Press, 2001.
Raw, Laurence. "T.E. Lawrence, the Turks, and the Arab Revolt in the Cinema: Anglo-American and Turkish Representations." *Literature Film Quarterly* (2005). http://findarticles.com/p/articles/mi_qa3768/is_200510/ai_n15957560.
"Revisions to the Standards for the Classification of Federal Data on Race and Ethnicity." http://www.census.gov/population/www/socdemo/race/Ombdir15.html.
Shaheen, Jack. "Interview with Jack Shaheen." 19 October 2007. Democracy Now! (Radio Program.) Transcript at http://www.democracynow.org/2007/10/19/reel_bad_arabs_how_hollywood_vilifies.
_____. Reel Bad Arabs: How Hollywood Vilifies a People. New York and Northampton: Olive Branch Press, 2001.
Shohat, Ella and Robert Stam. *Unthinking Eurocentrism: Multiculturalism and the Media*. London & New York: Routledge, 1995.
"Short Form." 2000 U.S. Census Bureau. http://www.census.gov/dmd/www/pdf/d61a.pdf.
Silverman, Kaja. "White Skin, Brown Masks: The Double Mimesis, or With Lawrence in Arabia." *Male Subjectivity at the Margins*. New York and London: Routledge, 1992. 299–338.
Sollors, Werner. Beyond Ethnicity: *Consent and Descent in American Culture*. Oxford and New York: Oxford University Press, 1986.
Staninger, Christiane. "Disney's Magic Carpet Ride: Aladdin and Women in Islam." *The Emperor's Old Groove: Decolonizing Disney's Magic Kingdom*. Edited and introduced by Brenda Ayres; introduced by Susan Hines. New York, NY: Peter Lang, 2003. 65–78.
Studlar, Gaylyn. "Douglas Fairbanks: Thief of the Ballets Russes." *Bodies of the Text: Dance as Theory, Literature as Dance*. Edited by Ellen W. Goellner, Jacqueline Shea Murphy. New Brunswick, New Jersey: Rutgers University Press, 1994.
Wise, Christopher. "Notes from the Aladdin Industry: Or, Middle Eastern Folklore in the Era of Multinational Capitalism." *The Emperor's Old Groove: Decolonizing Disney's Magic Kingdom*. Edited and introduced by Brenda Ayres; introduced by Susan Hines. New York, NY: Peter Lang, 2003. 105–14.
Wollen, Peter. "Fashion/Orientalism/The Body." *New Formations* 1 (1987), 5–33.

Filmography

Aladdin, dir. Ron Clements and John Musker, 1992.
Das Wachsfigurenkabinett, dir. Paul Leni, 2002.
Elephant Boy, dir. Zoltan Korda, 1937.
Harum Scarum, dir. Gene Nelson, 2004.
The Jungle Book, dir. Zoltan Korda, 1942.
Le Palais des Mille et Universityne Nuits, dir. Georges Méliès, 1905.
Robin Hood, dir. Allan Dawn, 1922.
Sanders of the River, dir. Zoltan Korda, 1935.
Sleep with Me, dir. Rory Kelly, 1994.
That Hamilton Woman, dir. Alexander Korda, 1941.
The Drum, dir. Zoltan Korda, 1938.
The Four Feathers, dir. Zoltan Korda, 1939.
The Lion Has Wings, dir. Michael Powell, 1940.
The Mark of Zorro, dir. Fed Niblo, 1920.
The Third Man, dir. Carol Reed, 1949.
The Three Musketeers, dir. Fred Niblo, 1921.
Thief of Bagdad: An Arabian Fantasy, dir. Ludwig Berger, Michael Powell, 1940.
Thief of Bagdad: An Arabian Nights Fantasy, dir. Raoul Walsh, 1924.
Top Gun, dir. Tony Scott, 1986.

10. Chivalric Conspiracies

Templar Romance and the Redemption of History in National Treasure *and* The Da Vinci Code

SUSAN ARONSTEIN
and
ROBERT TORRY

> *"Templar history is a great store of enchanting hypothesis and also of unreclaimed speculation repeated from writer to writer. I know no greater sea on which ships of imagination and fantasy have been launched more boldly; if they have reached no final harbor, they have paused to take in further stores at innumerable "summer isles" of an imaginary Eden."*[1]

Arthur Edward Waite's 1909 vision of "unreclaimed speculation repeated from writer to writer" as the ships of "imagination and fantasy" sally forth on the sea of Templar history has proved eerily premonitory; what he could not have envisioned was the translation of this legendary history from print to film. The film industry loves the Templars, both as historical characters in cinematic epics, such as *The Crusades* and *The Kingdom of Heaven,* and as the transmitters of an occult history, a living link between the medieval and the modern world. The Templars' hidden history on film chronicles a *translatio imperii* in which the knights transfer "truth" and power—the Holy Grail, the *sang real,* the sarcophagus of Mary Magdalene, the "tomb" of Christ, the key to Satan's prison, the collected treasures of empires—from the East to the West, where they remain, guarded by an unbroken chain of initiates, a chain that assures the continuity of history in the face of apparent rupture. These Templar romances claim to extract the meaning of "History" from the "noise" of historical facts, presenting a vision of the world in which seemingly random sequences of events are actually part of an unseen whole, both motivated and teleological.

While the occult history of the Templars has long been a recurring plot device in a variety of cinematic genres, ranging from B-horror films (*Revelation* and *The Minion*) through dark fantasies of psychosis and tainted bloodlines (*Murderous Intent* and *The Blood of the Templars*) to action-adventure treasure hunts (*Indiana Jones and the Last Crusade* and *The Da Vinci Treasure*), in this essay we will focus on the Templar romance's post–9/11 manifestation in two Hollywood secret history/conspiracy films: Ron Howard's much-anticipated and mostly disappointing 2006 adaptation of Dan Brown's monumental best-seller *The Da Vinci Code* and 2004's *National Treasure*, Disney/Touchstone's successful ride on the Dan Brown/Indiana Jones bandwagon. Released in a period when, as Stephen Gaghan, director of the conspiracy thriller *Syriana*, opined, many people felt like "(they) were in the back of this car called America, and the car was accelerating rapidly and taking a sharp turn, and (they're) holding on, going 'Whoa, holy shit!,'" these films premiered with a raft of conspiracy thrillers "raising big questions about America today" (Kaufman). These Templar romances, however, sought to answer rather than raise questions; if a post–9/11 world of global terrorism, political, corporate, and religious scandals and the worsening quagmire in Iraq had "chastened the United States for its naïve optimism, and, indeed, its naïve self-absorption, leaving Americans confronting a series of unmanageable realities," with "a diminished faith in national and personal agency," both the *Da Vinci Code* and *National Treasure* employ Templar legend to revive optimism, rediscover "original truth," and restore faith — whether in a miraculous divine (*The Da Vinci Code*) or in America's privileged destiny (*National Treasure*) (Varsave 161). Secret history becomes cinematic true history, conspiracy becomes benevolent patriarchy, and an apparently random, ruptured historical past proves to be both coherent and continuous.

Templar romance may seem an odd genre in which to cast therapeutic narratives aimed at healing an American public mired in a post–9/11 paranoia exacerbated by a growing series of scandals: tainted intelligence, corporate malfeasance, Plamegate, allegations of sexual abuse and cover-up in the Catholic Church. These romances would seem to feed such paranoia, chronicling the centuries-long "secret war" between the Templars and established authority, a conspiracy plot that seems ill-suited to a revalorization of faith in either a national or religious mythos. However, as Leon Surette, in his under-appreciated study of the influence of occult ideas in the formation of literary modernism, demonstrates, in the eighteenth and nineteenth centuries secret history presupposed a benign and redemptive hidden truth. Furthermore, since, Templar history was almost immediately identified with American history, this legend of the Templars' hidden truth merged with the myth of America's privileged destiny. While later Templar romances, particularly in 1980s and 1990s films, reread the Templars as remnants of a suspect medieval past opposed to an enlightened modernity, both *The Da Vinci Code* and *National Treasure* return to these benign and redemptive early versions of Templar romance. In the following essay we will analyze the ways in which these two latest iterations of Hollywood's Templar history seek to ameliorate historical trauma in post–9/11 America. We will begin by discussing the tradition of occult history and its connection to both America and American mythos, move to an examination of Ron Howard and Akiva Goldsman's recasting of *The Da Vinci Code* as a faith-affirming Grail romance, and then conclude with an analysis of *National Treasure's* restoration of a typological reading of American history and destiny.

Ships of Imagination and Fantasy: The Templars Come to America

Templar romance stems from the occultist insistence that a hidden, conspiratorial history underlies mere surface appearance. Most often this secret history takes the form of a benign conspiracy undertaken and preserved through the generations by a group of initiates in possession of profound knowledge — a *gnosis* illuminative of the true nature of sacred, ultimate reality. In the typical form of this belief, such knowledge remains hidden and is preserved because it poses a threat to existing religious and political authority. Thus, history takes the form of a struggle between the forces of an unenlightened and repressive orthodoxy and the defensively hidden possessors of a carefully maintained and transmitted truth; "[Occultists'] understanding of historical process," Surette observes, "tends to derive from the paradigmatic case of an archaic wisdom or practice suppressed — and often opposed — by authorities committed to a degenerate or corrupt version of the true, archaic faith"(50).

In the Templar version of this secret history (now familiar to most of us through *The Da Vinci Code*), the Knights' *gnosis*— often associated with various forms of the Grail, which, according to legend, they unearthed while on Crusade in Jerusalem — comes from the Middle East, the land of religious origin; forced underground after the infamous slaughter on Friday October 13, 1307, the Order continues to guard religious truth from the corrupt Catholic orthodoxy that seeks to destroy both it and them.[2] Ironically the man whom Surette identifies as having "invented (this) secret history of Europe," Abbe Barruel — whose *Memoirs Illustrating the History of Jacobinism*, published in 1795 during Barruel's exile in England and translated within two years into English, stands "at the head of occult scholarship"— saw the Templars as anything but benign. For him they posed a threat to civilization itself (41).

Barruel "trace(d) the history of an alleged long-term conspiracy against church and king culminating in the French Revolution of 1789 ... to discredit Jacobinism by exposing it as the survival of a dark and anarchic paganism.... He apparently could not imagine," Surette observes, "that the continuity of Jacobinism with a dark and remote past would be perceived by the romantic imagination as a legitimization of that very Jacobinism he sought to discredit. But so it was" (41).

Berruel's "exposure" of the roots of a centuries long heretical and subversive conspiracy in a period increasingly animated by a romantic *zeitgeist* sympathetic with what he most detested, was received, Surrette points out, in ways that its author certainly never intended; others read his text as the revelation of a hidden history of Europe congenial to progressive and revolutionary aspirations, and his secret history, filtered through this romantic lens, has had a continual influence since the late nineteenth century among occult enthusiasts and conspiracy devotees, many of whom may never have read the original text. Barruel in many ways is responsible for the development of a peculiarly American version of the Templar romance. In his exposé Barruel identifies the secret society responsible for the historical preservation and transmission of what he regarded as a blasphemous and politically pernicious set of beliefs: the Freemasons, whom he and subsequent writers alleged to be the heirs of the medieval Templar order: "The basic principles common to all varieties of [the secret doctrine] were — according to Barruel — those of the Revolution: liberty, equality, and fraternity. His great 'find' was that atheism, republicanism, and democracy were the 'secret of masonry'" (96). Barruel would doubtless find such a "Masonic secret" equally reflected in the values of the American Revolution. Indeed, there exists a number of fascinating if relatively unscholarly books arguing that the last Templars fled to the new world, bringing their "treasure" or secret with them.[3] The Templars' ultimate hiding place in the New World, away from European interests, serves as a symbol of the westward tendency of a secret history toward an American finality; the relocation of the treasure and its guardians chronicles the westward passage of an idea formulated in Jerusalem and transported to the New World.

In its depiction of the passage of "treasure," *gnosis*, and artifacts from East to West, this version of Templar history merges with the myth of American exceptionalism. This myth, as Sacvan Bercovitch has famously argued, found a powerful impetus in the typological understanding of history practiced by the Puritans, an understanding that plays right into the premises of occult history, particularly those that invoke the Grail. Typology as a hermeneutical strategy began with the desire to discern a prophetic unity between the Old and New Testaments. Thus Old Testament events and figures were to be understood proleptically as forecasting their more perfect embodiment in a divinely ordered historical sequence governed by the movement from the initial instance, the *type*, to the fulfillment, the *antitype*. Thus, for example, the exodus from Egypt serves as a type of the later exodus from Babylon, and Moses is to be understood as a type of Nehemiah. The movement of typological history is usually but not exclusively from the lesser to the greater instance, from adumbration to achieved perfection as type succeeds type in the passage toward the realization of the antitype. Thus Moses and Nehemiah are to be understood as types of Jesus as antitype, and the exoduses from Egypt and Babylon as types of Jesus's delivery of the elect from the bondage of sin, which in turn points toward millennial finality — the end of history in the final gathering of the saved.

The New England Puritans were devotees of an expansion of the range of this hermeneutical practice. As Bercovitch notes, "With the development of hermeneutics, the Church Fathers extended typology to postscriptural persons and events. Sacred history did not end, after all, with the Bible" (36). The Puritan practice of typological historical understanding saw in the New World the site of an antitypical fulfillment of previous history. Thus the Atlantic crossing was an antitype of the Exodus crossing of the Red Sea, the puritans the antitype of the nation of Israel fleeing the European "Egypt/Babylon" for a New Israel in America:

> They were not only spiritual Israelites.... They were also, uniquely, American Israelites, the sole reliable exegetes of a new, last book of scripture. Since they had migrated to another "Holy Land" ... they conferred upon the continent they left and the ocean they crossed the literal-spiritual contours of Egypt and Babylon.... [T]hey were a "second, far more glorious Israel." ... Since they inhabited the earth's millennial fourth corner, "to which that blessed promise truly's given," and of "which the Old and New Testaments do ring," they regarded all other locales — Asia, Africa, Europe ... as backward spiritual dependencies awaiting the fulfillment of their venture" [Bercovitch 113].

In this typological history America inherits the privileged position lost by the Israelites. In the New World God's plan is both made manifest and fulfilled; similarly, the versions of Templar romance that relocate both Templars and treasure to the New World identify America as the end of history, the repository of truth and revelation. New Israelites and New Templars unite in the Freemasons. Furthermore, in its addition of Templar history to the myth of American exceptionalism, American Templar romance identifies the new nation as typological heir to Arthur as well as Abraham. The grail — and the *gnosis* and destiny it represents — moves from Jerusalem to Logres to the New World.

In its insistence on typology — a historical timeline that moves in an orderly fashion from origin to revelation — and its assertion that the "truth" of history is inscribed in the world around us (the dollar bill, the Mona Lisa, the Lincoln Memorial) Templar secret history offers a reassuring vision of past, present, and future to a postmodern audience. While traditional conspiracy narratives feed paranoia by showing that apparently random events are part of a planned and malevolent deception and generally end on a despairing note in which the hero's knowledge is suppressed and nothing has or can be changed, Templar conspiracy tales lead us back to a truth that will set us free. They are well-suited to offer reassurance to a post–9/11 America, an antidote to bleaker conspiracy films like *Syriana*; their hidden histories reestablish the continuity of both personal and national narratives.

What Matters Is What You Believe: Redeeming *The Da Vinci Code*

The Catholic Church would certainly not agree with our assertion that *The Da Vinci Code* recovers a faith-affirming truth; far from it, the Church's reaction — both official and unofficial — to Dan Brown's novel and Hollywood's decision to film that novel — was negative, emphatic and well-documented. The popularity of Brown's book — how could someone not film such a potential box office goldmine? — combined with the Catholic Church's anti–*Da Vinci Code* campaign presented Columbia Pictures with a seemingly impossible mine-field to maneuver: how to domesticate Dan Brown's explosive tale without alienating its many devoted fans. The studio's choice of director and star (Ron Howard and Tom Hanks, both known for feel-good, life-affirming films) signaled its desire to soften the novel's radical implications (George Clooney was many fans' first choice for Langdon, but Clooney's personal politics were much too edgy for this project). Howard's and Akiva Goldman's (the screenwriter he brought to the project) revisions, including Tom Hanks' translation of Robert Langdon from skeptical "symbologist" to gentle prophet, transform Brown's tale of conspiracy and cover-up from an indictment of Christianity into an affirmation of faith and belief.

The first teaser-trailer for *The Da Vinci Code* foreshadows this transformation; it begins with a long, slow tracking shot over unrecognizable fragments — puzzle pieces that refuse to resolve into a whole; the camera then dives into the crevices between pieces while the narrative voice-over announces: "It is so powerful that men have died to protect it and there are those who would kill to expose it; it is a message that has been hidden for centuries right before our eyes." "What," the voice continues, as the camera pulls back from the fragments that resolve into the familiar face of Mona Lisa, "if the world's greatest works of art held the secret that could change the course of mankind?" "No matter what you have read," we are told, as flying fragments of paper coalesce into letters and text, "no matter what you believe, the journey has just begun." This trailer promises that illegible fragments will — with the proper perspective — resolve into a legible whole and that the "truth" lies right before our eyes, ready to redirect the course of humankind, restoring us to the right path. The trailer, like the film, performs a balancing act between the promise of "truth" and the threatening possibilities of a "truth so powerful it will devastate," as the voice of Ian McKellan asserts in the second trailer, "the very foundations of mankind." As such, the film's interests are very different from the novel's; in the end it seeks not to so much to expose the secret of the Grail as it does to restore faith, reveal the coherence of the fragmentary, and reanimate the material with the spiritual. Its truth does not devastate; like all good grails, it heals.

The film begins with the same interplay between the fragmentary and unknowable and the promise of revelation. It juxtaposes two scenes that actually take place before the novel begins with the late-night call that summons Robert Langdon from his bed at the Ritz to the darkened Louvre: the murder of Jacques Saunier and Langdon's lecture. The opening frames launch the audience into the narrative *in medias res*, as Saunier flees from his pursuer; both the lighting, which plays with shadows and bars, and the constant switching of perspective — from close-ups of Saunier and fragments of artwork to long shots of the corridor to crane-shots through the skylight — impede our understanding of events, as does the utterly obscure conversation between Saunier and his stalker. We do not know who these people are, what the brotherhood is, or the identity of the disputed object. A shot rings out, and the film cross-cuts to applause and the beginning of Langdon's lecture; it continues to cut back and forth between the two scenes, Langdon's preparations and Saunier's bloody inscription of his final message, before finally settling on Langdon's opening remarks. Although some of the assertions Langdon makes here are transported from the novel, the lecture itself is unique to the film where Howard and writer Akiva Goldsman spell out ultimately conservative interests: "Symbols," Langdon explains, "are a language that can help us understand our past. As the saying goes, a picture says a thousand words, but which words? Interpret for me, please, this symbol." A picture of a head concealed by a white hood appears on the screen behind him. "Hatred," the audience responds, "Racism." "Ku Klux Klan." "Yes, interesting," Langdon agrees, "but," as the camera pulls back to reveal the "whole," which includes croziers and crosses, "they would disagree with you in Spain. There they are robes worn by priests." He repeats this part/whole party trick two more times, revealing that the devil's pitchfork is actually Poseidon's trident and the

Madonna and child is really Isis and Horus. So far, of course, this could be a standard lecture on semiotics, meant to convince the audience about the arbitrary nature of the signifier and to prove that signs have no meaning independent of context. But this is not a postmodern film. Instead, like Templar history, it insists on a necessary and recoverable continuity between the past and the present. Langdon continues,

> Understanding our past determines actively our ability to understand the present. So how do we sift truth from belief? ... Tonight this will be our quest.

Langdon promises us the Grail in a fragmentary postmodern world: original truth, free from historical distortion, that will enable us accurately to write personal and cultural history, a therapeutic narrative that will tell us who we are and who we must become. Langdon's quest to "sift truth from belief" merges, as the cross-cutting in the opening sequences suggest, with the multiple quests for the film's other Grail: the secret guarded by the Priory of Sion. As it does so, *The Da Vinci Code* moves from standard, if bizarre, *film noir* fare to Templar conspiracy romance. The clues left by Saunier lead not to his murderer, but to the occult history that occasioned it, and only in this context do these clues reveal "truth." Fache, understandably enough, interprets "P.S. Find Robert Langdon" as Saunier's identification of the murderer; lacking the context of Sophie's history, he cannot see that it actually exhorts "Princess Sophie" to seek out the American symbologist, the one person in Paris who, through his knowledge of codes, symbols, and secret history, can intepret Saunier's riddling anagrams and ancient signs. Subjected to Langdon's scrutiny, the letters of Saunier's nonsense phrases — "O draconian devil. O lame saint" — rearrange to lead them to "Leonardo Da Vinci. Mona Lisa" (conveniently, as Sophie exclaims, "over there"), which in turn poses its own puzzle: "So dark the con of man." Apparently merely another anagram, pointing to yet another conveniently accessible Da Vinci masterpiece, these words have a second meaning, one that, combined with the *fleur de lis* crest on the key Saunier left with the painting, places the signs within their proper context, introducing the film's Templar themes. "This can't be. The *fleur de lis*," Langdon mutters; "why," the audience wonders, "should it be so astonishing to find a *fleur de lis* in France?" It is the leap Langdon then makes as he fires a series of questions at Sophie that seems astonishing: "Have you ever heard those words before ... when you were a child were you aware of any secret gatherings? ... Was there ever any talk of something called the Priory of Sion?"

Langdon's series of questions recontextualizes the *fleur de lis* in the same way that his lecture recontextualized white hoods and pitchforks; in this new context the *fleur de lis* transforms from national symbol to the crest of "the

Priory of Sion ... one of the world's oldest and most secret societies ... guardians of a secret they supposedly refer to as 'the dark con of man.'... [They] protect the source of god's power on earth." Furthermore, Langdon's later chronicle of the "myth" of the Priory recontextualizes history, suggesting that accepted history distorts true history. "It all started," Langdon asserts, "over a thousand years ago when a French king conquered the holy city of Jerusalem. This Crusade one of the most massive and sweeping in history, was actually orchestrated by a secret brotherhood. The Priory of Sion, and their military arm, the Knights Templar." When Sophie tries to interject the facts of "known" history, "But the Templars were created to protect the Holy Land," Langdon replies, "That was a cover to hide their true goal, according to this myth. Supposedly the invasion was to find an artifact, lost since the time of Christ. An artifact it is said the Church would kill to possess." Langdon (and the flashback) proceeds to relate pretty standard Templar romance fare — the finding of the artifact, the return to Rome, the Order's rise to unprecedented power and wealth, the Friday the 13th massacre, the Order's flight, and the renewed search for the artifact in their keeping." When Sophie again protests, "What artifact? I've never heard about any of this," Langdon assures her that this history, far from being secret, is right before all of our eyes, "Yes you have. Almost everyone on earth has. You just know it as the Holy Grail."

This narration of an occult history in which the Templars serve as the guardians of a powerful artifact (the elusive and unspecified Grail) which they brought from the East to the West, locates, as all good Templar romances do, the origin of "Truth" in the East and its proper resting place in the West, a reassuring tale of Western manifest destiny. In the novel the "truth" of this history is never questioned; in fact, the whole tale moves towards its revelation and confirmation. The film, however, is much less comfortable with the novel's "explosive" revelation and its connotations, so it subtly sabotages this first articulation of Templar history. As Nickolas Haydock (204–206) points out, Langdon's own skepticism and equivocation and the fact that the flashback, through its use of color filters, aggressively calls attention to itself as film undermine Langdon's talking-head authority and the film's promise/pretense of unmediated access to the historical past. The cinematic version of *The Da Vinci Code* manages both to present the novel's version of events — the hidden truth — and at the same time to call that version of the truth into question.

The film continues its interrogation of Templar history as it distances Robert Langdon from the conspiracy theorists, presenting Leah Teabing as their sole advocate. Both film and novel reveal the history of the Priory and its secret through Sophie's education at Chateau Villette. In the novel this revelation unfolds as a tag-team effort as Teabing and Langdon expand upon and support each other's assertions. While Teabing is the acknowledged expert, Langdon, through his own research into the imagery of the sacred feminine, has also clearly drunk the Kool-Aid: "the historical evidence supporting this," he assures Sophie, "is substantial" (Brown 254). Furthermore, the novel's version of this exposition presents the origin of the "dark con of man" as an unambiguous political ploy. In announcing Christ's divinity, according to Teabing and Langdon, the Council of Nicaea did not resolve a theological debate, but created a theological truth in the service of political expediency, thereby hijacking Christ's message for worldly ends.

The film substantially rewrites this sequence, casting Langdon as the barely-tolerant skeptic, the voice of reason, reining in Teabing's flights of fancy. The film's Langdon is decidedly not a fan of the Priory; he tells Sophie earlier that he "hopes" their adventure has nothing to do with it, "because any Priory story ends in bloodshed." He scoffs at Teabing's assertions of a "secret war" fought by a globe-spanning Priory — that was "exposed as a hoax in 1967." "And *that*," Teabing fires back, "is what they want you to believe." This initial exchange sets the tone for what follows — Langdon's skeptical insistence of facts and evidence, Teabing's fanatical, if charming, proclamations. Their disagreement begins with the nature of the Priory's secret: Langdon asserts that it is (mythically) the source of God's power on earth; for Teabing it is "the source of the Church's power on earth." Teabing's relentless hatred of the Church also inflects his version of the Constantine history, a version that Langdon constantly corrects. Teabing blames it all on Christian aggression, and Langdon counters by noting the atrocities on both sides. When Teabing brings Sophie to "The Last Supper," Langdon groans and only grudgingly complies with Teabing's request that he show Sophie the symbols for man and woman: the wedge and the chalice.

Langdon's exasperation frames Teabing's reading of the painting, a reading that reveals the presence of Mary Magdalene, spouse of Jesus and mother of his children; each time Teabing and Sophie reach a conclusion — "it's a woman," they're "dressed as mirror images," they're "separated by the shape of the chalice," "the sign of the feminine" — the camera cuts to Langdon's incredulous and impatient expression. When Teabing, uttering one of Langdon's lines from the novel, explains why people do not usually see the woman at the table, "It's called scotoma; the mind sees what it chooses to see," Langdon has finally had enough. "This is an old wife's tale, he says, with "no empirical proof." And in the film there is none, merely Teabing's narration, his reading of Da Vinci, and some unspecified "theories," all of which Langdon dismisses, as he does Teabing's analysis of the painting ("the mind sees what it chooses to see"). The film's Teabing stands alone, without his novelistic counterpart's library of "several dozen books" (251) or Langdon's survey

Sophie (Audrey Tatou) discovers the sacred feminine (and her distant relative) hidden within Da Vinci's familiar painting in Ron Howard's *The Da Vinci Code*.

of literature and art (including the films of Walt Disney, whom Brown improbably presents as a Priory member) to support his tale of "the greatest cover-up in human history."

While the film does still reveal the "shocking" truth of Brown's novel, it works oddly against its own revelation; Teabing is an unreliable narrator at best. In spite of Ian McKellan's irresistibly charming performance, the English eccentric is obsessed, quite mad, and undeniably murderous. Teabing sees himself as a Grail knight on the quest to "explode" the truth of the Grail upon the world. He is, however, the film insists, not a knight, but the tale's one real villain, manipulating and exploiting the members of Opus Dei and willing to sacrifice Langdon and Sophie to achieve his deluded desires. In the cinematic version of *The Da Vinci Code*, as the film's true Grail knight Robert Langdon recognizes, the Priory functions to conceal, not reveal.

Goldsman and Howard's version of the novel defuses its foundation-shaking secret history and domesticates its conspiracy through Langdon's Grail quest, a quest the "symbologist" identifies in his opening lecture: truth freed from the distortions of history. Langdon's ability to read symbols makes him the perfect Grail knight. He, like Bors and Perceval — and Indiana Jones — before him, can recognize the spirit behind the letter, the hidden meaning in the familiar. While Brown's Langdon's ability to decode symbols is based in academic historical knowledge, the film-makers use cinematographic technique to recode Langdon's reading sequences. Howard films these sequences to depict not deduction, but revelation. Langdon begins by literally reading in the dark, and he finds the knowledge he seeks through cinematic illumination: letters rise from gibberish, the camera circles to the significant object, lit-up from within. The film's soundtrack — swelling and triumphant music —

reinforces this spiritual coding of Langdon's intellectual prowess, as does Howard's choice to darken the sanctuaries in which many of these scenes take place. He uses only the light glowing through the stained glass windows and the illuminated objects to light the scenes. Langdon's readings of the clues are figured as beatific visions; when the final clue, like Newton's apple, falls into his hands, he reminds Teabing in the Englishman's own words why he has failed: "Only the worthy find the Grail, Leigh. You taught me that."

Langdon finds the Grail, quite simply, because he is a man of personal faith. He, as we discussed earlier, eschews the postmodern philosophies that one might think would inform the discipline of "symbology" and argues (like Umberto Eco's Adso) that faithful signs, properly read, lead to truth: "now we see through a glass darkly, but then we will see face to face. Now I know in part but then I shall know" (I Corinthians 13:11). As a man of faith, a believer in teleology and revelation, Langdon stands apart from politics, unlike Leigh, whose Grail-obsession stems from his distrust of those in power and his misconceived notion of himself as the chivalric champion of the poor and the dispossessed. In the end, for the film's Langdon, the secret history — "the greatest cover-up in human history" — is utterly irrelevant, an irrelevance that makes the final achievement of the quest seem decidedly anti-climactic. In the novel Sophie's grandmother explains to Langdon that the Priory need not "explode" the truth upon the world, because such drastic measures are unnecessary; truth, as it were, will out, and Mary's story is already being told in songs, in art, and in Langdon's own book on the sacred feminine. The film offers no such wisdom; in fact, Sophie's grandmother, apart from assuring Sophie that the guardians are there for her, barely speaks. Langdon does not ask for advice about telling the secret history; he gives it. "Saunier took the location of Mary's sarcophagus with him," Sophie observes, "so there's no way to empirically prove that I am related to her. What would you do Robert?" Langdon responds by dismissing the need for evidence as so much "noise:" His own survival of the fall into a well as a child suggests that miracles are possible, and his researches have taught him that Christ could well have been both human and divine, as perhaps Sophie herself may be. "What matters," Langdon concludes, "is what you believe." Langdon's exhortation lies at the heart of Goldman's and Howard's domestication of Brown's Templar conspiracy tale. It slides improbably from secret history to official history, from evidence to faith. Langdon assures Sophie (and the audience) of the value of belief, but the object of belief becomes not Mary Magdalene and the Priory's secret, but Jesus himself, as Langdon admits that "evidence" can prove nothing beyond the fact that Jesus was an ordinary man. Evidence, or the distortions of history, can never lead to "original truth." Truth lies in personal experience: the praying boy who wasn't alone in that well, the water turned into wine, Sophie's healing hands. If Sophie is indeed "a living descendent of Jesus Christ," Langdon suggests, her heritage is not to destroy faith, but to renew it. And although this conversation ends with Sophie's self-deprecating attempt to walk on water, the film itself also functions to affirm faith. The conspiracy is revealed, but in the end it is inconsequential: "what matters is what you believe."

Instead of functioning as a traditional conspiracy film and chronicling the tale of its protagonists' descent into a world of corrupt authorities in charge of an inescapable system that is rotten to its very core, Ron Howard's film — oddly, given its originary text — offers us a conversion narrative. While Langdon, as we have discussed, begins on a Grail quest, Sophie herself — and by extension the audience — must become a Grail knight, but before she can do so, she must deal with the traumas of her own past. At the beginning of her and Langdon's adventures, she informs him, "I hate history." Langdon later responds," You say you hate history. Nobody hates history. They hate their own histories." And, indeed, much of the narrative depends upon Sophie's learning to interpret her own history (Saunier's insistence that she not look for her family and the half-glimpsed Priory ritual) correctly, to see the whole or truth that frames the misperceived fragments. Once she does so, the "traumas" of the past are redeemed, and Sophie can proceed on her quest. Langdon's final wish for the woman who believed not in God, but "in people," is "Godspeed."

Langdon's defense of faith redirects the film's final sequence (based on the novel's Epilogue). Both texts end with the "symbologist" kneeling at the entrance to the Louvre, where "the Holy Grail 'neath ancient Roslin waits." In the novel Langdon's pious act acknowledges the lost power of the sacred feminine; in the film it functions — in spite of the camera's reverent pan down to reveal a medieval effigy of a woman — as a beatific vision, a moment of transcendent faith, the final revelation of "truth." Music swells, the camera swirls, depth of time and space collapses as Langdon kneels beneath starry skies in a moment straight out of the end of *Il Paradiso*, where the truth of the feminine — of the rose — leads to the knowledge of God; Mary Magdalene merges with Mother Mary.

Coming to America: *National Treasure's* Templar Romance

In Ron Howard's film the Templars' secret history becomes, however unexpectedly, the means to a renewed faith; Sophie represents the continuity of history, an unfolding of the divine lineage from Christ to the present. A woman with healing hands, heir to the *sang real*, she reanimates the divine in a world that has lost touch with religious truth. Similarly 2004's *National Treasure* also uses Templar history to restore faith in the continuity of history and mission; however, its secret history relates a political rather than religious past, and so it restores faith not in the divine, but in America's national mythos and global mission. In the opening sequence of the film, young Ben Gates is initiated by his grandfather as a "knight" pledged to the values and purposes of the Templar/Masonic lineage whose narrative the grandfather has just related. The secret history rehearsed by the grandfather concerns a treasure amassed over centuries of struggle and conquest. We see images of bloody combat beneath the pyramids in ancient Egypt, Roman troops with bloodied swords, and the discovery — hidden in a vault of the Temple in Jerusalem — of this gradually acquired, immense collection of objects with, as Ben will later say, "both historical and intrinsic value." Its discoverers, Crusaders who will subsequently name their order after the site of this occulted repository, become, therefore, the Templars. In the grandfather's tale the Templars, enlightened by democratic, anti-royalist sentiments, believing that the fortune they have discovered must never fall into the hands of kings, eventually transport it to the New World, where their initiate descendents (by now having become the Freemasons), fearful that it will be discovered by the British during the American Revolution, eventually deposit the treasure in a profoundly secret hiding place, the clues to the location of which have been distributed in a series of objects and texts.

In *National Treasure* the passage of untold riches from Jerusalem, and more importantly the Templar insight of democratized wealth and power the treasure represents to the New World, serves as an essentially secular adumbration of the crucial theme of Puritan hermeneutics. The treasure moves, that is, from Jerusalem to an America understood, metaphorically at least, as the New Jerusalem, a nation whose democratic ideals may still serve a venture of profound, politically instructive significance. The film strengthens the identification of America as the realization of the democratic vision associated, in Barruel and the subsequent secret history tradition, with first Templars and then Freemasons, by beginning the story of the Gates family's involvement in the secret tradition with an unintended and unforeseen rupture in the chain of orderly transmission maintained for centuries by Templars and Freemasons. As grandfather Gates tells Ben, Charles Carroll, the sole remaining Mason with access to what we will discover to be the initial clue in the solving the mystery of the hidden location of the trove, dies on his way to inform President Andrew Jackson of the secret, but first he confers the clue he bears to the only person available: Ben's ancestor, Thomas Gates, Carroll's stable boy. This clue, a scrap of paper with the words "The Secret lies with Charlotte," will motivate the subsequent six generations of the Gates family in their search for the secret location. What had thus been an unbroken line of transmission from initiate to initiate becomes the extramasonic family initiation that opens the film. The task of interpretation having become completely democratized, it comprises the legacy of a common stable boy to his descendents.

If the chain of transmission from mason to mason was severed with the delivery of the inaugural clue by Carroll to the stable boy, an equally significant rupture is also integral to both the plot of the film and its therapeutic use of Templar romance. Ben's own father, Patrick Gates, has, we learn in the initial sequence, become utterly disenchanted with the family quest, one that he describes as "six generations of fools chasing after fool's gold." It is significant that the year in which the Gates family story is retold and in which Patrick Gates dismisses as delusion his ancestors' search is 1974: the year of Richard Nixon's resignation in disgrace of the Presidency following the Watergate revelations, the year between the American withdrawal from Vietnam and the 1975 fall of the South Vietnamese government to North Vietnamese and Viet Cong forces. The date thus evokes the political upheaval of the 1960's and early 1970's, the dispiriting prologue to a 1976 American Bicentennial celebration dogged by the tragedy and widespread suspicion of governmental wisdom and virtue, a suspicion maintained, if not magnified, the film implies, in the Bush-era setting of the main action. Patrick's cynicism reflects the cynicism of a generation that has lost its faith in America's millennial potential, in its "national treasure." Between the grandfather, John Adams Gates, and Ben lies the gap in effective transmission of both the family quest and America's manifest destiny.

Patrick's cynicism, his disavowal of the family faith and its associated quest of immense national performance, breaks the link of transmission for a generation, reinflects the "secret history" formula. In *National Treasure* "true history" has been suppressed not by a powerful organization intent on maintaining its power and position, but by a failure of belief, a degenerated capacity for faith in a protected, glorious eventuality, replaced by the mere accumulation of clues, each of which leads merely to another clue. Patrick chides Ben with having wasted his life. He states, "I have a job, a house, health insurance. What do you have?" In his catalogue of possessions and dismissal of Ben's dedication to the quest, Patrick enunciates the articles of a degenerate American faith that locates American identity in the accumulation of the indices and guarantors of middle-class security. This attitude, combined with a cynicism born of exhausted hope, functions in the film as the repressive authority of a cultural consensus that prevents Americans from seeing the truth of both their past and their future.

This truth, the film assures us, is liable to rediscovery by anyone who

Ben Gates' grandfather (Christopher Plummer) and the Masonic dollar bill in Jon Turteltaub's *National Treasure*.

has "eyes to see." Grandfather Gates shows Ben the Masonic symbol of an unfinished pyramid surmounted by the radiant all-seeing eye on the back of a dollar bill (the very commonality of which suggests the availability of enlightenment in the most ordinary of American artifacts). The bill, grandfather asserts, stands as ever available proof that the founder Masons "speak to us" in clues to be decoded. The image on the bill, a signifier upon a signifier, emblematizes the nature and solution to the Gates family's hermeneutic, intergenerational quest. The unfinished structure achieving its "completion" in the shining, comprehending eye stands as a symbol of both the method and the result of hermeneutic activity: the clue as signifier achieves its completion in the signified to be discerned precisely by the eye capable of accurate hermeneutic perception. Thus Ben's purpose, like that of his ancestors, will be to proceed from clue to clue, signifier to signifier, in search of an illuminated and illuminating signified — that "face" in the dark glass. Ben's quest, like Langdon's, is a quest for original truth animated by a vindicated belief in the power of the signifier to lead to the signified. The film visualizes this narrative of interpretation and anamneusis by deploying a literal movement from darkness to light beginning with the lighting of flares aboard the *Charlotte* and continuing through the such examples of illuminative success as the falling light at the proper hour upon the hiding place of the spectacles through which the final clue on the back of the Declaration of Independence may be seen. The spectacles themselves, the number of torches rekindled in the vault beneath Trinity Church, and the setting alight of the vastly illuminating channels of oil that reveal to Gates, his father, and their companions the extent and antiquity of the ultimately recovered treasure culminate the sequence.

The film's emphasis on illumination (the conjunction of faith with informed and accurate sight) is central to its therapeutic use of Templar romance. Ben, unlike his father, who sees in the family narrative and the concatenation of clues pursued for six generations of Gates family members mere fraud and foolishness, has faith in the family quest, and faith allows him, as the opening action sequence demonstrates, to be a practitioner of accurate and cumulative discernment. The adult Ben, with his partner Riley and Ian Howe, his villainous backer, travel across a white, featureless arctic landscape; when they stop, Ian sees nothing; "Why are we stopping?" he asks, "I thought we were looking for a ship." But Ben's research has convinced him that the spot signaled by the GPS equipment they carry is the site of the ice-sunken *Charlotte*. Inspecting the clue provided by the meerschaum pipe they discover aboard ship, Ben knows that the stem will reveal another clue, and he quickly decodes the cryptic message it reveals. He explains that a further clue is to be found on the Declaration of Independence. Ben's ability to "see" significance where others see nothing in this sequence proceeds from his immersion in American history and his faithful dedication, despite the mockery of both his father and establishment historians, to the family quest. The blank, white, arctic landscape suggests the apparently blank verso of the Declaration, and each suggests a meaning *underneath*. What is without significant feature to the uninitiated eye can become available to an informed, prepared hermeneutical vision, the significance of which, as we have seen, is emphatically registered in the film's abundant images of illumination.

Ben's faith in the family enterprise, combined with the vast knowledge of American history required by the quest, makes him an ideal interpreter of the clues he discovers and thereby resoundingly a hermeneut of the sort the Puritans viewed as exclusively able to perceive the revelatory meaning of America. Just as biblical interpretive practice depended on the intact faith of the interpreter correctly to discern the significance of sacred scripture, the Puritan sense of America as a "new, last book of scripture" demanded of the perceiver just such a faith in American millennial promise:

> Unregenerate readers kill the letter.... Hermeneutics presupposes a reader transformed in the image of the spirit he sets out to discover.... The perceiver [puritan clergy] insisted, had to identify with the divine meaning of the New World if he was to understand his environment correctly. He had to "cast his account" as an American, and his "conclusion" had to balance private and corporate redemption in the context of American destiny [Bercovitch 111, 119].

Just as the Puritan interpreters of the New World read even quotidian events from such a faith-inspired interpretive perspective, so Ben Gates reads circumambient commonalities with an informed and faithful eye.

We have noted for example the significance of the one and one hundred dollar bills, whose careful inspection yields symbolic representation of hermeneutic process in its figure of enlightened perception as completion but also specific information necessary to the ultimate discovery of the hidden treasure. Ben's attention to the exact time depicted on the clock face engraved on the hundred-dollar bill allows him to discern the proper hour at which the sun's rays will indicate the brick beneath which Franklin's multi-lensed spectacles are to be found. It is worth noting that this epiphany occurs in the shop in which Ben and Abigail exchange their formal clothing for less conspicuous outfits. Ben has to ask for the return of a bill to inspect once he has realized its hermeneutic value. Thus currency circulating unconsidered in its mundane ubiquity signs more than mere exchange value; what had been used merely to purchase goods assumes, under informed reconsideration, a far more significant meaning. Thus a mere brick in the wall of Independence Hall, viewed at the right time in the right light, is revelatory of a hidden means of further revelation.

The antique pipe discovered aboard the *Charlotte* and speculated upon by Riley concerning its potential monetary value is understood immediately by Ben as the repository of further information concerning the quest. Its stem, moistened by blood and rolled on paper, prints out the riddle Ben rapidly solves. This action inserts into the film an image of antiquity, recalling as it does the episode in Book 11 of *The Odyssey* in which Odysseus enables the shade of the prophet Tiresias to speak by supplying him with the blood of sacrificed sheep. Just as Tiresias predicts for Odysseus the stages of his *nostos*, his homecoming, so the message on the pipe stem aids Ben on the path "home" toward the recovery of the "fathers'" treasure safeguarded since the origins of the nation. This use of Ben's blood as "ink" is doubtless expedient under the circumstances, but the pipe thus "blooded" and subsequently able to "speak" its riddle suggests Ben's position in the chain of faith as generational incarnation. He holds in his blood, as it were, the faith of his fathers. Ben's immediacy of apprehension testifies to his faith in the validity and value of the quest, to his "casting of his account as an American. He "sees" in American commonalities and in singular artifacts of historical importance, in the Declaration of Independence, an antique pipe and a common brick, Ben Franklin's letters and a dollar bill, the signs and support of a valid and persistent faith.

National Treasure, by merging the vast if wildly speculative resource of pop historical speculation about the Templars with the still culturally resonant tradition of American millennialism first articulated by Puritan divines, endows its search for material treasure with allegorical significance. Templar treasure, after all, is usually associated with a *gnosis* embodied by the Grail, and Puritan typology insists upon the spirit beneath the letter. Thus the film's successfully discovered riches are both literal and figurative. The titular national treasure is literally a treasure: a massive collection of historical artifacts with immense monetary value. The cavernous vault Ben and associates discover beneath Trinity Church is filled with Egyptian, Greek, and Roman statuary; it contains scrolls from the library of Alexandria and, of course, an unimagined abundance of other sorts of treasure. However, Ben's grandfather, in the face of his son's dismissal of the quest, asserts "It has never been about the money." If it is not about money, than what is it about? Remember the grandfather's rehearsal of the treasure's history and both the Templar's proto-democratic motive for its remaining hidden and the fact that America was deemed a safe resting place for the collected treasures of history. Given the typological resonances of both Templar and Puritan history, the film implies a *historical telos* deeply embedded in the tradition of American exceptionalism. If the governing image of the unfinished pyramid surmounted by the seeing eye serves as an emblem of the method and goal of hermeneutic procedure, it also stands for the as yet incomplete project of *novus ordo seclorum*. It thus combines hermeneutic proficiency and teleologically ordered historical process. To participate as viewer in the syntagmatic relation of clue to clue toward completed meaning is to join a sensitivity to figural possibility. The treasure deposited in the New World implies an achieved plenitude, a summation of history in synecdoche by which a figural consummation in keeping with American millennial promise is imaged.

Ben's ultimate decision to redistribute the treasure to the museums of the world and his decision (to Riley's dismay) to accept as reward only 1% of the value of the hoard provide a counter discourse to the post–Iraq invasion suspicion of American motives globally and in the Middle East in particular. If many observers, both at home and abroad, of the American invasion of Iraq saw in regime change a cynical interest in the control of crucial Middle Eastern oil reserves, *National Treasure* offers its viewers a narrative therapeutically aligned with the eventual justification for invasion and occupation offered by the Bush administration following the failure to locate weapons of mass destruction anywhere in Iraq and, not coincidentally, a concomitant rehearsal of the corporatist insistence that American democracy is best disseminated and supported through global American corporate presence. If the "mission" to be completed became in White House rhetoric a divinely mandated democratization of a nation freed from despotic rule, Ben's decision to distribute the treasure to a variety of institutions (he mentions the Smithsonian, the Cairo Museum, and the Louvre as examples) suggests, at the simplest level, an America devoted not to material appropriation, but rather to global distribution, to the spreading of wealth through global corporate expansion. More subtly the gesture proceeds from the film's association of the treasure with the proto-democratic impulse of the Templars, which came to fruition in the America to which that treasure had been removed. Ben explains his decision to distribute the hoard to "everyone in the world" through reference to both the Templar/Mason legend and American political history. Noting that Templar/Masons believed the treasure was too great for any one man to hold, Ben declares, "The founding fathers believed the same thing about government. I figure their solution should work for the treasure too." Thus, the film imagines and deftly conjoins what it represents as an American dedication to distributive justice, the sharing of material wealth, with the distributive role of an America imagined by the Puritans as an exemplary light to the nations, a new Jerusalem with the divinely sanctioned duty to lead the world toward a millennial, democratic future. A treasure protected from despotism becomes the treasure of democratic dispensation.

National Treasure ends on a high note; Ben's faith in the family legend — and thus in America's privileged destiny — has been justified, and he is — as the American dream promises — rewarded with both acclamation and material benefits. What makes this conclusion possible is the recovery of an artifact that, like Indiana Jones' Ark of the Covenant and the Holy Grail (in films to which, as many have noted, *National Treasure* owes a profound debt), originates in the sacred locale of the Middle East and is transmitted to the West via the Templar-Masons. Thus the film participates in the *translatio imperii* we discussed at the beginning of this essay, one in which America stands as the destined *telos* of a divinely-inspired history that began in Holy Land. In 2004, in the wake of a tenuous patriotic enthusiasm generated by the premature declaration "Mission Accomplished," this optimistic American narrative still had some vestige of rhetorical power. However, by the time Ben Gates and his companions returned to the big screen in December 2007, the dramatically unaccomplished mission in Iraq had engendered a significant wave of American cynicism and distrust concerning the actual motives of American intervention in the Middle East. More and more citizens called for the withdrawal of American troops, a call that received at best a qualified response in a deadlock between the newly Democratic-controlled Congress and an obdurate Executive Branch. Given the national mood, it is not surprising that Ben Gates' second outing, *National Treasure: The Book of Secrets* dispenses with a myth of *translatio imperii* arguably constructed as a justification for suspect political-military designs. Instead, *The Book of Secrets* develops an essentially isolationist mythology, locating the sacred not in a relic from the old world, but rather in a recoverable, indigenous resource — a move that is interestingly echoed in Indiana Jones' latest adventure. America is no longer the heir to the Holy Land; "it is and always has been" the Holy Land.

Notes

1. Arthur Edward Waite, *The Hidden Church of the Holy Grail, Its Legends and Symbolism Considered in Their Affinity with Certain Mysteries of Initiation and other Traces of a Secret History in Christian Times.* (London: Rebman Limited, 1909), page 556.
2. Versions of the Templar History can be found in dozens of sources, some more respectable than others. For a scholarly discussion of "the secret tradition" see Richard Barber, *The Holy Grail: Imagination and Belief* (Cambridge: Harvard University Press, 2004) and Malcom Barber, *The New Knighthood: A History of the Order of the Temple* (Cambridge: Cambridge University Press, 1995).
3. The connection between the Templars, the Freemasons, and America is the subject of long-standing speculation. See John Reynolds, *Secret Societies: Inside the World's Most Notorious Organizations* (New York: Arcade Publishing, 2006); William Mann, *The Knights Templar in the New World: How Henry Sinclair Brought the Grail to America* (Rochester, VT: Destiny Books, 2004); Steven Sora, *The Lost Colony of the Templars: Verrazano's Secret Mission to America* (Rochester, VT: Destiny Books, 2004); Tim Wallace-Murphy and Marilyn Hopkins, *Templars in America: From the Crusades to the New World* (San Francisco: Weiser Books, 2004). For more academic discussions of the Freemasons in America, see Mark A. Tabbert, *American Freemasons: Three Centuries of Building Communities* (New York: New York University Press, 2005) and Vincent Bernard, "Masons as Builders of the Republic: The Role of Freemasonry in the American Revolution," *European Contributions to American Studies* 14 (1988): 132–50.

Bibliography

Bercovitch, Sacvan. *The Puritan Origins of the American Self.* New Haven: Yale University Press, 1977.
Brown, Dan. *The Da Vinci Code.* New York: Doubleday, 2003.
Haydock, Nickolas. *Movie Medievalism: The Imaginary Middle Ages.* Jefferson, NC: McFarland, 2008.
Kaufman, Anthony. "Eye on the Oscars: The Director: Passion Players." *Daily Variety* December 6, 2005: A1.
Surette, Leon. *The Birth of Modernism: Ezra Pound, T.S. Eliot, W.B. Yeats and The Occult.* Toronto: University of Toronto Press. 1993.
Varsava, Jerry. "Unmanageable Realities in Postmodern America," *American Studies in Review* 33.2 (2002): 161–169.
Waite, Arthur Edward. *The Hidden Church of the Holy Grail, its legends and symbolism considered in their affinity with certain mysteries of initiation and other traces of a secret history in Christian Times.* London: Rebman Limited, 1909.

Filmography

The Da Vinci Code, dir. Ron Howard, 2006.
The Da Vinci Treasure, dir. Peter Mervis, 2006.
Blood (Code) of the Templars, dir. Florian Baxmeyer, 2004.
Indiana Jones and the Last Crusade, dir. Steven Spielberg, 1989
The Minion, dir Jean-Marc Piche, 1998.
Murderous Intent, dir. Gregory J, Reid, 2006.
National Treasure, dir. Jon Turteltaub, 2004.
National Treasure: Book of Secrets, dir. Jon Turteltaub, 2007.
Revelation, dir. Stuart Urban, 2002.

11. On the Border

Merging East and West in Cadfael's Twelfth-Century Shropshire

WILLIAM F. HODAPP

In a medieval murder mystery series of twenty novels and one small short-story collection, all published between 1977 and 1994, Ellis Peters (*nom de plume* of Edith Pargeter) created a borderline character living in borderline country in her retired Crusader-turned-Benedictine monk, Brother Cadfael. Welsh by birth, warrior and sailor by trade, Cadfael ap Meilyr ap Dafydd of Trefriw, Gwynedd, had answered Pope Urban II's call to arms in the First Crusade at age eighteen and experienced the taking of Antioch in 1098 and of Jerusalem in 1099. At age forty and following more than twenty years in arms in the Holy Land and on Mediterranean Sea and elsewhere, Cadfael returned to England in November of 1120, having taken service with Sir Roger Mauduit on the same expedition from Normandy in which the fated White Ship sank, drowning the crown prince of England, William Adelin, King Henry I's best hope for a peaceful succession. Upon completing his service with Sir Roger, Cadfael relinquished his weapons and joined the Anglo-Norman Benedictine Abbey of Saint Peter and Saint Paul, Shrewsbury (Peters, "A Light"). As the novels unfold, covering the years 1137 to 1145, characters find themselves touched more-or-less by the Anarchy, the civil war between the Empress Maude and King Stephen that waged in England for nearly nineteen years from 1135 to 1153, that was in part a result of the White Ship disaster of 1120. At the time of the novels, Cadfael — approaching twenty years and more as a brother of the Abbey — has integrated into monastic life as the community's herbalist, yet he lives ever on the margins of that community as he tends his gardens, ministers to lepers, treats the ill and maimed, counsels troubled friends inside and outside the Benedictine house, and helps the local Anglo-Norman sheriff solve crimes. In these stories Peters' Cadfael integrates knowledge gleaned from his years in the East with an understanding of life lived in the West of England to bring physical, spiritual, and social healing on a local level to a society fractured by civil violence.

Between 1994 and 1998, Stephen Smallwood produced for Independent Television (ITV) of the United Kingdom (UK) a four-season series of 75-minute films adapting thirteen of Peters' Cadfael novels. Filmed in Hungary and starring Sir Derek Jacobi in the title role, these films popularized Cadfael in both the UK on its first showing and in the United States when shown as part of Public Broadcasting's Mystery series. In this chapter I examine these film adaptations of Peters' novels with emphasis on two: *The Leper of St. Giles* (Book 5; Season I, episode 3) and *The Virgin in the Ice* (Book 6; Season II, episode 1). In these films Cadfael's Crusader past particularly intrudes on his monastic present in the forms of a former fellow Crusader in the one and of a troop of rogue Crusaders in the other. As Cadfael works to integrate his own past and present, his Crusader life with his monastic life, he seeks to bridge his experiences of two cultures, merging East and West near the Welsh border in England. In the film adaptations ITV filmmakers strive to visualize the alterity of a twelfth-century monastic community as they dramatize the experiences of this borderline monk, thereby translating Peters' late twentieth-century medievalism and orientalism from narrative to dramatic form.

Twelfth-Century Borderlands, Frontiers, Margins

The twelfth-century world Peters creates in the novels and filmmakers translate to the screen is one rooted in borderlands, frontiers, or margins, that is, boundary lines or zones, as Nora Berend notes (148–51), between individuals or groups of peoples. Having grown up and lived most of her adult life in or near Shrewsbury, Shropshire, Peters herself was steeped in a borderland culture. In her non-fiction book *Strongholds and Sanctuaries*, on which she collaborated with photographer Roy Morgan, she writes: "Every frontier, every critical line where two separate cultures, two systems of law, two social organizations, both meet and separate presents a heightened tension, intensified colours, a sense of drama the settled hinterlands do not know" (9). In her Cadfael stories and in the films based on them, we find this borderland "sense of drama" on several levels and in various manifestations, from geographic and social frontiers to emotional and mental frontiers (i.e., a given character's "sense of identity and perceptions of difference" [Berend 151]).

Perhaps most obviously we first discern this sense of borderland culture in the stories' geographic settings. Shropshire is one of four ancient counties in the west of England bordering Wales. Most likely created in the tenth century for administrative purposes by Edward the Elder (ca. 920), Shropshire is bordered by Cheshire to the north and Herefordshire to the south. Together with Gloucestershire further south, these counties encompass the English side of the March of Wales, a fluid geographical zone separating Wales and England and variously claimed by both. The medieval history of the March of Wales — as is typical of such frontier zones (Berend 150) — is one of both conflict and trade. After Rome left Britannia in the fifth century, Wales became one of the redoubts for the Romano-Celts in the face of Germanic incursions, and the March of Wales served as the buffer zone between the Welsh and the Mercians who settled the West of England. In the late 780s, presumably to prevent Welsh raiders and to regulate cross-border trade, the Mercian King and *bretwalda* of England Offa constructed a ditch and dyke "between Wales and Mercia, stretching from sea to sea," as Bishop Asser wrote in the 890s (qtd. in Wood 94–6). Peters herself interprets Offa's dyke as follows:

> Clearly the dyke was meant as a partial defence against the Welsh, for throughout its course the ditch is kept to the westward side.... But it was as much a legal as a defensive boundary, and its very creation signified that Mercia had no intention of striking beyond in search of conquest, just as surely as it stated Mercia's intention of resisting any encroachment from the western side. The man who crossed it in either direction knew under which law he stood, and had better behave accordingly [*Strongholds* 18].

With the late eighth-century dyke in place and the formation of the counties in the tenth century, Mercians and Welsh alike apparently remained fairly content with the status quo of the borderlands. However, this stasis, such as it was, changed following the Norman invasion of 1066 when William the Conqueror appointed three Normans as Marcher Lords: Hugh d'Avranches, Earl of Chester; Roger de Montgomery, Earl of Shrewsbury; William FitzOsbern, Earl of Hereford (Peters, *Strongholds* 19–20). Loyal to William and appointed to manage the borders and expand Norman control into Wales, these Earls worked industriously to establish Norman rule in the Marches and western counties.

Roger de Montgomery is particularly important to the history of Shropshire and the development of Shrewsbury as depicted in the Cadfael novels and films. A market town about ten miles from Wales, Shrewsbury lies on the northeast side of a loop in the Severn River, a loop that essentially forms a peninsula in the landscape (Lewis, *Pargeter* frontispiece map). Upon his arrival in Shropshire, Roger established Shrewsbury as one of two centers from which to manage his affairs, the other being Montgomery, a castle and town even closer to Wales. Among other projects, Roger built Shrewsbury castle on the northeast end of the peninsula and fortified the town lying southwest of its walls, thereby creating a defensible stronghold controlling a key crossing of the Severn. Outside the town walls to the southeast and across the Severn River, on the site of an old wooden church, he also founded in about

1080 a Benedictine abbey in which he established a group of Norman monks. Roger later entered the Abbey as a monk himself shortly before he died in 1094 (Peters, *Shropshire* 55–6). To this monastic foundation, the Abbey of Saint Peter and Saint Paul, the fictional Cadfael had gone as a youth "to get my letters," as he once tells a companion (Peters, "Light" 22). There he made his monastic profession in 1120, forty years after its founding.

As with Shropshire and the March of Wales, the Benedictine monasticism shaping life at the Abbey of Saint Peter and Saint Paul was in its own right a borderland or frontier culture both spiritually and physically. When he made profession as a monk of this abbey, Brother Cadfael entered into a cloistered way of life that had been first developed in the sixth century. Fusing ideas from the early hermetic life of the Desert Fathers with ideas of communal life from the Greeks, Benedict of Nursia founded a monastery halfway between Rome and Naples at Monte Casino in about 529. There he not only built a complex of buildings to house his community of monks, but also developed a Rule or set of guidelines for organizing a life lived apart from the bustle of secular affairs yet open to serving the moral, spiritual, physical, and intellectual needs of those seeking help (Duckett 122–73). Benedict's Rule — with its fusion of ideas from the East and the West — spread in the early to high Middle Ages throughout Western Europe where numerous Benedictine foundations dotted the landscape. Following Benedict's lead at the Abbey of Saint John the Baptist at Monte Casino, most Benedictines tended to locate monastic foundations in remote places or on the borders of societies, outside the boundaries of towns and walls of cities. Yet they also established in their foundations a parochial function to serve the spiritual needs of their neighbors, a hospice to help travelers and the infirm, and a school to educate both monks and laity. Though close to Shrewsbury, the Abbey of Saint Peter and Saint Paul in the twelfth century was located outside the city gates on the east bank of the Severn opposite the fortified eastern bridge (Lewis, *Pargeter* frontispiece map). Its placement is typical of Benedictine foundations and, when Cadfael joins, he enters into a borderline cloistered community, located on the edge of a society to which he is regularly called to serve. In a sense the Abbey of Saint Peter and Saint Paul near Shrewsbury is a marginal community within the larger physical, political, and social borderland and frontier structure of the March of Wales.

While the borderland, frontier culture of western Shropshire and of Benedictine monasticism seems fairly evident, a third such culture equally important to understanding Cadfael's twelfth-century world arises in the interaction between East and West brought about by the First Crusade and the establishment of the Kingdom of Jerusalem and other Crusader states in the East. As Berend notes, medieval frontier zones such as those formed by interactions between Christian, Muslim, and Jewish cultures were marked by both military and peaceful activity: "thus negotiations, arbitration, and even trade characterized this interaction along with war" (150). For Cadfael, having spent the better portion of his first forty years in the East, the borderland, frontier experiences of the First Crusade and its aftermath shaped his sense of self and understanding of his place in the monastic community. For instance, when Cadfael first enters the stage, so to speak, in the opening scene of Peters' *A Morbid Taste for Bones*, we see an aging monk on a fine May morning in 1137 contentedly working an herb garden with "many exotic plants of his own careful raising, collected in a roving youth that had taken him as far afield as Venice, and Cyprus and the Holy Land" (2). The narrator notes:

> Brother Cadfael himself found nothing strange in his wide-ranging career, and had forgotten nothing and regretted nothing. He saw no contradiction in the delight he had taken in battle and adventure and the keen pleasure he now found in quietude. Spiced, to be truthful, with more than a little mischief when he could get it, and he liked his victuals well-flavoured, but quietude all the same, a ship becalmed and enjoying it [2].

Though Cadfael is evidently contented with his life in the monastery, like many warriors returning home, integrating the borderland, frontier experiences of his youth in the East is a life-long endeavor for him. Later the same morning while dozing during chapter Cadfael dreams he is crouching in the heat and dust of battle before the walls Jerusalem, "waiting for the trumpet to sound the final assault, and keeping well in cover while he waited" (8). The immediacy of this dream, conjuring an experience nearly thirty-eight years prior, indicates from the first introduction of this character that, though as a monk he may be "a ship becalmed and enjoying it," Cadfael's thoughts, memories, habits, virtues, even dispositions formed during his Crusader life are never far from the surface as he lives out his monastic vocation.

Cadfael's experiences in the East also clearly shape his distinctive role within the monastic community, a role that allows him to work quite literally on the margins of the monastery. Master of the herbarium, the herb garden and workshop on the edge of the abbey enclosure that plays such an important function in many of the novels and films, Cadfael serves as the community's pharmacist. In the twelfth century a European monastic herbalist like Cadfael would likely have gained knowledge of herbs and their medicinal properties from three key sources: the classical medical tradition surviving from Greek and Roman cultures, direct transmission from other herbalists, and the Arabic and Islamic medical tradition that spread to Europe in the eleventh and twelfth centuries through southern Spain and the Crusades (Baker 122–4). While in the East Cadfael particularly gained knowledge of the medicinal use of opium as well as seeds he eventually plants and carefully tends in the herbarium. Distilling a syrup from the poppies he grows, Cadfael frequently prescribes but carefully controls the use of opium in a number of instances throughout the novels and films. Though not the community infirmarer (i.e., equivalent to a modern-day general practice doctor), a role filled by Brother Edmund, Cadfael, like a modern-day combat medic or triage nurse, frequently uses knowledge and skill gained in his early life to treat a range of medical issues from traumatic injuries suffered in the field to common colds and illnesses. Knowledge of herbs and plants, as well as of trauma and death gained on the battlefields of his youth, help him perform forensic functions a modern-day coroner might when investigating an untimely death. As a former Crusader turned monastic herbalist and healer, a Welshman living in an Anglo-Norman religious house, Cadfael straddles the cultures, legal systems, and social structures at play in the stories, thereby embodying diversity in his person and exhibiting tolerance and understanding of others. Throughout the stories, as he strives to integrate his years in the East with his monastic vocation in the West, Cadfael brings to his borderland, frontier world in the West of England a skill set and knowledge base that prove indispensable both to his own monastic community and to the community at large.

Ellis Peters and the Chronicles of Brother Cadfael in Print and on Film

Over the course of the novels, short stories, and films, Cadfael appears as a multi-faceted and engaging character. Peters, however, had not initially set out to produce a series centered on this twelfth-century Benedictine; rather, she wrote a novel "to fill a gap in a tightly-packed schedule," as Margaret Lewis observes (*Pargeter* 83). Writing in 1988 about the origin of her borderline monk, Peters stated:

> Brother Cadfael sprang to life suddenly and unexpectedly when he was already approaching sixty, mature, experienced, fully armed and seventeen years tonsured. He emerged as the necessary protagonist when I had the idea of deriving a plot for a murder mystery from the true history of Shrewsbury Abbey in the twelfth century, and needed the high mediaeval equivalent of a detective, an observer and agent of justice in the centre of the action [Introduction 3].

Peters developed this one-time novel, *A Morbid Taste for Bones* (1977), around the documented incident of Shrewsbury Abbey's translation of St. Winifred's relics from Wales in 1137. Two years later, unable by her own admission to "resist the temptation to shape another book round the siege of Shrewsbury and the massacre of the garrison by King Stephen" in 1138, Peters published

One Corpse Too Many (1979). The series was born, and for the next fifteen years she averaged more than one novel a year as well as the small collection of short stories entitled *A Rare Benedictine: The Advent of Brother Cadfael* (1988). Reviewing her bibliography (Lewis, *Pargeter* 141–4), one finds Cadfael not only "sprang to life" in the late 1970s, but also took over Peters' creative world for the rest of her life, for after 1979 her only non–Cadfael books were the two non-fiction collaborations with Roy Morgan on Shropshire and the March of Wales.

Though today Peters is most well known for this series, she was a prolific author throughout her adult life, having written a total of ninety-three books in the fifty-eight years between 1936 when she published her first novel and 1994 when she published her last. Prior to Cadfael, she wrote several stand-alone historical novels, a World War II trilogy detailing the experiences of a common soldier, three series of modern-day detective-novels, a trilogy and a quartet of historical novels set in thirteenth-century England and Wales, and several translations of poems, stories, and novels from Czechoslovakian. With Cadfael she fused her creative interests in historical fiction and detective fiction, contributing to the "history and mystery" sub-genre that has burgeoned on both sides of the Atlantic in the past thirty years.

Peters also picked up on an interest first explored in 1951 with *Fallen into the Pit*, the inaugural Felse series mystery, in which she explores the theme of the return of soldiers from war. As with many writers of her generation, World War II profoundly affected Peters' sensibilities and interests. During the war, while working as a teleprinter operator in the Women's Royal Naval Service (Wrens) and ultimately rising to the rank of petty officer, she continued to write in spare time, producing a novel based on her experiences in the Wrens and the first two novels of the war-time trilogy mentioned above (Lewis, *Pargeter* 24–8). After completing the trilogy she explored the war's aftermath in *Fallen into the Pit*, which centers on the murder of a former German prisoner of war in a rural English town. On the first page of the novel, her narrator introduces the theme of the challenges facing soldiers returning home from war: "The war ended, and the young men came home, and tried indignantly to fit themselves into old clothes and old habits which proved, on examination, to be both a little threadbare, and on trial to be both cripplingly small for bodies and minds mysteriously grown in absence" (qtd. in Lewis, *Pargeter* 51). The return of the soldier after war, a theme common in Western literature since Homer and the ancient Greek *nostoi* tradition of return tales, underpins Cadfael's experience of his return to England as well. Finding himself and the world he had left behind at Shrewsbury too changed to pick up his pre–Crusader life, he embarked on a new experience in the borderland culture of Benedictine monasticism. From a certain point of view, Cadfael represents a successfully re-integrated soldier; he finds a way to use a mind and body "mysteriously grown in absence" to contribute to the society he rejoins.

Once underway the Chronicles of Brother Cadfael unfold through the years and seasons, each providing different situations in which the central figure exercises his spiritual, intellectual, and at times physical acumen to aid those in need and to see justice served. The second column in the table below details the season and year in which each novel takes place. Though the novels are distinct in detail, season, and often setting, two key narrative elements appear in nearly every one: a serious crime calling forth Cadfael's particular gifts for detection and a thwarted romance between at least one pair of lovers, whom Cadfael aids in some fashion. When adapting the novels for television movies, ITV filmmakers chose to film Chronicles 1–8, 10, 12–13, 17, and 19; however, they paid no attention to Peters' chronology when organizing the four seasons, as a brief comparison of the second and third columns in the following table illustrates.

Table: The Chronicles of Brother Cadfael in Print and Film

Title (Date of Publication)	Novels — Month, Year of Setting	Films — Season, Episode, Year
A Morbid Taste for Bones (1977)	May-June, 1137	II, Episode 3, 1995–6
One Corpse Too Many (1979)	August, 1138	I, Episode 1, 1994
Monk's Hood (1980)	December, 1138	I, Episode 4, 1994
Saint Peter's Fair (1981)	August, 1139	III, Episode 2, 1997
The Leper of Saint Giles (1981)	October, 1139	I, Episode 3, 1994
The Virgin in the Ice (1982)	November-December, 1139	II, Episode 1, 1995–6
The Sanctuary Sparrow (1983)	Spring, 1140	I, Episode 2, 1994
The Devil's Novice (1983)	September, 1140	II, Episode 2, 1995–6
Dead Man's Ransom (1984)	February, 1141	
The Pilgrim of Hate (1984)	May-June, 1141	IV, Episode 3, 1998
An Excellent Mystery (1985)	August, 1141	
The Raven in the Foregate (1986)	December, 1141	III, Episode 3, 1997
The Rose Rent (1986)	June, 1142	III, Episode 1, 1997
The Hermit of Eyton Forest (1988)	October, 1142	
The Confession of Brother Huluin (1988)	December, 1142	
The Heretic's Apprentice (1990)	June, 1143	
The Potter's Field (1990)	August, 1143	IV, Episode 2, 1998
The Summer of the Danes (1991)	Spring-early summer, 1144	
The Holy Thief (1992)	August, 1144	IV, Episode 1, 1998
Brother Cadfael's Penance (1994)	November, 1145	

Although the sequence of the films through the four seasons bears no resemblance to the stories' sequence in the Chronicles, most of the films follow the central storyline of the novels on which they are based, focusing primarily on the two main narrative elements of a crime to be solved and a match to be made. As with most film adaptations of narratives, however, screenwriters modify details of the storyline in an effort to streamline speaking parts, control each film's 75-minute running time, and minimize the need for multiple sets. In *The Pilgrim of Hate*, though, first aired in the UK on December 28, 1998, as the final film of the fourth and last season, Richard Stoneman's script has little to do with the story in the novel; rather, we have a film bearing the title of the Tenth Chronicle and featuring Brother Cadfael and Saint Winifred's shrine, but little else. It is an odd episode in an otherwise engaging series.

While Cadfael's Crusader past permeates the novels in various ways, this important biographical detail receives less attention overall in the films. In fact a number of the films, for instance *The Raven in the Foregate* (1997), *The Rose Rent* (1997), and *The Pilgrim of Hate*, have not even a whisper of reference to his early life as a soldier. Because the thirteen films were presumably conceived as a series, filmmakers seem to have decided early emphasis on Cadfael's Crusader experiences might well inform later films that concentrate on other details; thus, in the first five episodes of the series we find the most clear engagement with Cadfael's Crusader past and less in later episodes. Turning to these five films, then, I shall briefly review three from the first season before examining *The Leper of Saint Giles* and *The Virgin in the Ice* in detail.

Rather than opening the film series with *A Morbid Taste for Bones*, which does not appear until the end of the second season, ITV filmmakers chose to begin with the second chronicle, a choice that emphasizes the social upheaval of civil war and introduces Hugh Beringer, who becomes undersheriff at film's end and Cadfael's companion in solving crime throughout the remainder of the series. In *One Corpse Too Many*, written by Russell Lewis, directed by Graham Theakston, and originally airing in England on May 29, 1994, the series opens with a view of a walled town and a banner across the bottom of the screen stating "Shewsbury, 1138." Very quickly the film establishes that the characters are the midst of civil war and that Shrewsbury Castle is under siege. It also establishes the Abbey of Saint Peter and Saint Paul as a place set apart, for in spite of the battle waging within sight of the enclosure walls, the brothers strive to maintain the regular life they have vowed. By the midpoint of the film, several monastic characters are introduced, including Abbot Heribert, Prior Robert Pennant, Prior Robert's assistant, Brother Jerome, and of course Brother Cadfael. Though Benedictine brothers abound in monastic scenes throughout the films, these handful of brothers — with the occasional addition of a few more — serve as the core of the community as depicted in this and subsequent films. Shortly after Cadfael is first introduced, Lewis and Theakston add a brief scene not found in the novel in which Cadfael meets by chance an old friend with whom he had served at the fall of Jerusalem nearly forty years before and who now serves in King Stephen's army besieging the castle. As the two exchange greetings and brief reminiscences, viewers learn for the first time of Cadfael's Crusader past and mid-life monastic profession.

Unable to rely on narrative interjection to give background information, Lewis and Theakston exploit subsequent brief opportunities to reveal Cadfael's past to the viewer. For example, when talking to Godith Adeney, who is hiding in the monastery enclosure disguised as a novice monk because she is a daughter of a rebel to the King, Cadfael explains how he is able to detect she is not who she appears to be, saying "I was forty years about the world before I took the cowl." Similarly, when Abbot Heribert discusses with Cadfael the gathering and burial of ninety-four rebel soldiers executed by order of the King, he reminds his herbalist, "you have yourself been a soldier" before asking him to supervise the gruesome task. Later, after preparing the dead for claiming and burial, Cadfael himself remarks to another character, "I once put all such horrors behind me." Gathering the dead leads to the central crux of the story, for Cadfael discovers an extra corpse — a man killed by garrote rather than by hanging. The dead man turns out to be Nicholas Faintree, squire to Godith's father, and Cadfael works to solve the murder, to heal Faintree's companion Torold, wounded by an arrow, and to help Godith escape the King's agents in company with Torold. Before parting from them Cadfael gives Torold a poniard he has kept from soldiering days, saying simply "It has been of some use," a moment that passes without comment in the novel because the narrator reflects on Cadfael's thoughts instead (102). Near film's end Cadfael befriends Hugh Berenger, a Norman lord, and together they discover that Adam Courcelle, a lieutenant in the King's army, murdered Faintree. The film climaxes in a trial by combat between Courcelle and Berenger, at which Cadfael stands as Berenger's second, an unusual act for a typical monk, but not out of the realm of possibility for him. After Berenger wins the trial, King Stephen names him undersheriff and keeper of the peace, and the film draws to a close, having introduced viewers to this former Crusader turned monk.

With the second and fourth films in Season I, Lewis and Theakston again join forces to adapt Chronicles 7 and 3, respectively, for the screen. In each case they work in brief references to Cadfael's Crusader past. Episode 2, *The Sanctuary Sparrow*, originally airing in the UK on June 5, 1994, centers on a gold-merchant family of Shrewsbury and their misdealing with each other and with the jongleur Liliwin, the "Sparrow" of the title. Accused of robbery and murder following a wedding party, Liliwin claims sanctuary at the abbey during the film's opening sequence. Abbot Heribert, acting to protect Liliwin from a chasing mob, grants the youth sanctuary, and for most of the film the jongleur remains on the abbey grounds. As a result of his confinement, this film offers viewers shots of life within the abbey walls and introduces a new monk central to several subsequent films, Cadfael's assistant Brother Oswin. As it turns out, the "murdered" man — Walter Aurifaber — was only knocked senseless, but the next day a nosy townsman turns up drowned in the Severn, murdered indeed. Now with two crimes to address, Cadfael works to exonerate Liliwin of robbery and help Hugh solve the murder. All comes full circle back to the family when Cadfael and Hugh discover Susanna, Aurifaber's daughter, is both thief and killer. Caught trying to escape to Wales with her lover and the stolen gold — this is border country after all — the pregnant Susanna and her unborn child die, shot with an arrow by one of Hugh's men. At this point in the film, trying to describe his emotions over Susanna's twisted life and tragic death, Cadfael declares "I have stood on the field of battle, my armor smoking from the blood of those I've slain, and felt nothing ... but not here, not now." This brief reference reminds viewers of Cadfael's past and works intertextually with Episode 1, without which the reference makes little sense. Focusing as it does on a family corrupted by greed, *The Sanctuary Sparrow* also mirrors the larger social background of *One Corpse Too Many*, offering a domestic microcosm of England's social macrocosm, the family quarrel at the heart of the civil war.

Similarly *Monk's Hood*, Episode 4 of Season I, presents a microcosmic view of a larger social structure through a close exploration of a family dynamic. Rather than emphasizing the civil war in this case, though, viewers see the multi-cultural mix of the March of Wales at work. Originally airing in the UK on June 19, 1994, the film opens with Norman landowner Gervase Bonel moving into an abbey holding with his Mercian wife Richildis and her nearly-grown son Edwin. Bonel's natural son by a Welsh serving woman Meurig plus his two Mercian servants named Aelfric and Aldith complete the household. Bonel, who had promised Richildis when they first married to give his border manor to Edwin, has now granted it to the abbey in exchange for housing, food, and care for the rest of his life. Having been called away by the Papal Legate, Abbot Heribert has left the abbey in the hands of Prior Robert Pennant, who is overseeing this transaction. Before documents can be signed to complete the contract, however, Bonel dies violently, poisoned by a dose of monk's hood oil Cadfael had made for use in the abbey infirmary. Like many herbal medicines monk's hood oil has positive properties as a soothing ointment and negative properties as a poison if ingested: Bonel ingests it with food and makes a mess of the dinner table. Berenger immediately suspects Edwin, who had frequently quarreled with his step father, but soon other suspects come to the fore, including Meurig and Aelfric.

In an effort to clear Edwin, Cadfael meets with the young man's mother, Richildis, and discovers she is none other than the woman he had left behind in Shrewsbury when answering Pope Urban II's call for the First Crusade. During an evening visit at the herbarium workshop, Cadfael and Richildis talk through their earlier decisions in life, thereby healing any unresolved issues from forty years prior. Observing this meeting from a distance, Brother Jerome accuses Cadfael of impropriety, and Prior Robert forbids him further involvement with the investigation, a prohibition he manages to circumvent with Brother Oswin's help. In the end Cadfael discerns that Meurig murdered his father when, among other things, he observes the Welshman use monk's hood oil in the infirmary to soothe his kinsman's aches while the two sing snatches of a Crusader song Cadfael recognizes. In addition to Bonel's Norman-Mercian-Welsh household, the film depicts a Welsh court at which Cadfael thwarts Meurig's efforts to secure the manor for himself before the young man escapes further into Wales, away from Norman law. The film closes with two scenes: a final parting from Richildis at the herbarium workshop as Cadfael again chooses another life apart from her; the return of now Brother Heribert accompanying Radulfus, newly appointed Abbot. As with *The Sanctuary Sparrow*, reference to Cadfael's Crusader days is limited, but the film reveals more of Cadfael's early biography through his conversations with Richildis. While these films introduce Cadfael's past in part to explain his actions or knowledge in the present, Cadfael's Crusader life comes especially to the fore in the remaining two of the first five films in the ITV series.

Brother Cadfael and the Crusaders

Considered from a certain perspective, the world outside the abbey intrudes into Cadfael's monastic life in every novel, short story, and film. Most of these intrusions — though dramatic and at times violent — are like ones we have already encountered: largely reflecting the day-to-day world of twelfth-century Shrewsbury and environs. Cadfael then responds to the issues he faces out of his wealth of experience and wisdom gleaned from a life lived outside, inside, and on the margins of the abbey enclosure. In the final two films I shall examine, *The Leper of Saint Giles* and *The Virgin in the Ice*, however, the East in the form of returning Crusaders particularly comes into the West of England, much as Cadfael himself had returned nineteen years earlier. As these borderline figures enter into the borderland, frontier culture of Shropshire and the March of Wales, they call forth from Cadfael an even sharper engagement with his Crusader past as he again seeks to aid those in need whom he encounters.

In Peters' scheme the two novels are closely connected in time: the events in *The Leper* occur during October, 1139, and those in *The Virgin* occur one month later, during late November to mid December. The films, on the other hand, are not noticeably sequenced in time. Episode 3 of Season I, *The Leper*, originally airing in England on June 12, 1994, falls between *The Sanctuary Sparrow* and *Monk's Hood* while *The Virgin*, first airing over eighteen months later on December 26, 1995, leads off Season II. *The Devil's Novice* and *A Morbid Taste for Bones* complete Season II's three-film run, originally airing in England respectively on August 18 and 25, 1996. As individual films each demonstrates the tendencies of the ITV screenwriters and directors to streamline the narrative as they dramatize the events. Together *The Leper* and *The Virgin* offer viewers a multi-faceted view of Crusader experience as characters reflect on the past and act in the present of twelfth-century Shropshire.

Written by Paul Pender and directed by Graham Theakston, *The Leper of Saint Giles* reveals to viewers vastly different elements of the larger community the Benedictines serve by juxtaposing images of the abject and marginalized with the wealthy and powerful. Like the novel the film opens with Brother Cadfael visiting the abbey's leper hospice located at Saint Giles Church, southwest of the abbey enclosure near the London road (Peters, *The Leper* map). When Cadfael approaches, all is astir near the hospice in anticipation of the arrival of two noble parties coming to the abbey to celebrate a wedding. Lepers and townspeople alike line the roads when the first group passes by, led by the groom-to-be Baron Huon de Domville. Well past his prime but in full possession of wealth and title, the Baron proves not just indifferent to the suffering before him, but cruel when he deliberately approaches the lepers and whips them out of the way: all but one, whom he causes to fall with his whip before Cadfael, his Crusader spirit up, intervenes to prevent further abuse. Not long after the first group passes, the second arrives with the youthful Iveta de Massard accompanied closely by her guardians, her maternal uncle and aunt Sir Godfrid and Lady Agnes Picard. In short order, primarily through dialogue passing between the Baron's three squires, viewers realize the impending marriage is not only an arranged affair with wealth and greed at its center, but also a January and May union not of the young woman's choosing. She loves one of the Baron's squires, in fact, a landed though lesser noble named Jocelyn Lucy, but her guardians thwart their union, seeking only an alliance that will ensure for them expanded power, lands, and wealth.

For Iveta de Massard is the sole surviving heir to Guimar de Massard, hero of the First Crusade, and the de Massard holdings are vast. This arranged marriage would thus profit both the Baron and Picard, as they divide the de Massard lands between them. Worried that Jocelyn might intervene, Picard convinces the Baron to release his squire from service the day before the marriage is to take place and to frame him for the theft of a bracelet so that he might be imprisoned and out of the way at the time of the wedding. Jocelyn, however, escapes from the arresting officers and, with help from his fellow squire Simon Aquilon, evades capture. It is not a surprise then, when after the Baron is found murdered on a forest trail on the morning of his wedding, Picard immediately accuses Jocelyn Lucy of the murder and spurs Sergeant Warden, Hugh Berenger's chief deputy, to mount a manhunt as Hugh himself is attending to another legal matter elsewhere in the shire.

Unconvinced Jocelyn is the killer, Cadfael steps in while Berenger is away and begins to examine clues more closely, discovering that the Baron had visited his mistress, Avice of Thornbury, on the night before his wedding and was returning from the tryst when he was knocked from his horse and strangled to death by a strong person with a gemmed ring on the middle finger of his right hand. Meanwhile, Sergeant Warden and his men flush their quarry but fail to capture Jocelyn when a leper, the same man whipped by the Baron, hides the squire in a pile of hay until the searchers pass by. This man, whom Jocelyn comes to know as Lazarus, subsequently disguises the fugitive as a leper, and Jocelyn, now a temporary member of a marginalized community, soon discovers how easy it is to hide in plain sight when one is invisible to the rest of society. This disguise provides the time he needs to sort out how he might escape with Iveta while Cadfael continues to investigate the Baron's murder and the deputies continue to hunt for him. All begins to draw to a conclusion when Cadfael discovers Picard strangled to death in the woods on his return from meeting Avice, and Sergeant Warden manages to corner the fugitive squire in the abbey enclosure where, with help from his friend Simon Aquilon, Jocelyn had met Iveta, intending to escape with her. At about the same time Cadfael and Hugh arrive at the abbey courtyard, where Cadfael delivers the news of Picard's death and reveals who stole the bracelet and who murdered the Baron. As it turns out, the Baron had indeed framed Jocelyn, and Simon Aquilon — squire, nephew, and heir of the Baron — killed his uncle for fear of losing his inheritance. Cleared of all charges, Jocelyn is free to court Iveta, who is in turn free from her overbearing guardian. But who killed that guardian and why? Cadfael of course knows, but the story reaches back forty years and across the Mediterranean Sea to the battle of Ascalon and its aftermath.

In that battle Iveta de Massard's grandfather, Guimar de Massard, led a group of Crusaders, one of whom was Cadfael, against the Fatimids of Egypt, who were seeking to dislodge the Crusaders from Jerusalem. Wounded and captured at the battle, Guimar reportedly died of his wounds, and the Fatimids returned his helmet and sword to Jerusalem, from which they were eventually sent to Guimar's wife and son in England. Iveta, daughter of Guimar's son, grew up learning to cherish the helmet and sword as a link to a heroic grandfather she never met. With this information in mind the next morning, Cadfael vists Saint Giles to discuss the previous days' events with the leper named Lazarus. In the course of their conversation, he declares Picard was not murdered as many assume, but defeated in single combat, and then he names Picard's killer based on the strangulation marks: Guimar de Massard. Unmoved, Lazarus simply replies: "Should I know that name?" Cadfael replies:

> My lord, I, too, was at the storming of Jerusalem. Twenty years old I was when the city fell. I saw you breach the gate.... But there was never brutality or unknightly act charged against Guimar de Massard. Why, why did you vanish after that fight? Why let us who revered you, and your wife and son here in England, grieve for you dead?

Guimar then tells his story. After the Fatimids captured him, their physicians tended his wounds, diagnosed his leprosy, and helped him through the years until word arrived of his son's death and his granddaughter's orphaning. Healed of his leprosy, though not of its crippling and deforming effects, he traveled eight years to reach England, hoping to ensure her affairs were sorted properly: aiding Jocelyn was one step in that process; challenging and defeating Picard in honorable single combat was another. As these two old soldiers discuss the past and present, they comment on their former adversaries' nobility, an attitude Cadfael sums up when he says "I have always known that the best of the Saracens could out–Christian many of us Christians." Though at first blush modern viewers might think such a comment anachronistic, evidence suggests an attitude existed among many Crusaders "that the Muslim opponent was a noble warrior and worthy adversary, who shared many important qualities with western warriors, despite the difference in religious belief" (Nicholson 4). In *The Leper of Saint Giles*, and in the borderland culture Cadfael inhabits, such an attitude acts as a foil to the grasping, manipulative values of the Picards and de Domvilles of the world. Once again recognizing this same nobility in his fellow former Crusader, as he had when they fought together in the Holy Land, Cadfael encourages Guimar to meet and stay with his granddaughter, saying "If she cherishes your sword, how much more would she revere and delight in you?" But Guimar has been too changed by his experience in the East for him to see re-integration with his former life in the person of his granddaughter a viable option. He says, "Brother, you speak of what you do not understand; I am a dead man; let my grave and my bones and my legend alone." Preferring his own marginal existence, living in society's borderlands, Guimar chooses to leave, and the film closes with his walking away from Shrewsbury alone.

While *The Leper of Saint Giles* explores the motif of the returned Crusader and introduces the motif of the noble opponent, fallout from and resolution of Iveta de Massard's domestic situation remains the primary storyline in the film. In *The Virgin in the Ice*, just the opposite is true as these two motifs shape the film's center. Written by Russell Lewis and directed by Malcolm Mawbray, *The Virgin* adopts the novel's main storyline, but with some significant changes. To understand those changes, we do well to have the novel before us first. In early November, 1139, elements of the Empress Maud's army sack Worcester. The able bodied flee to the north, and by mid-month Shrewsbury and the abbey are filled with refugees. Three such refugees — two orphaned noble children, Yves and Ermina Hugonin, aged thirteen and eighteen, respectively, and Ermina's tutor, a young Benedictine Sister named Hilaria — have gone missing, never having arrived at the town as expected. With deep cold and winter storms blasting the border country, the children's uncle, Laurence d'Angers, a Crusader having just returned to England from the Holy Land, fears for their safety and seeks permission from Gilbert Prestcote, Sheriff of Shropshire, to enter the county and search for them. d'Angers, however, is a knight of the Angevin line and owes fealty to Maud; Prestcote denies him entrance, but promises to send out word to search for the party. Meanwhile, news arrives from Bromfield Priory that a man, Brother Elyas, has been brought in severely wounded and near death. Knowing of Cadfael's medicines and particular skills in treating traumatic injury, the Prior requests he come to attend the broken man. Cadfael sets off in a snowstorm, and his role in this story begins.

The remainder of the novel is set almost entirely in and around Bromfield Priory, twenty miles south of Shrewsbury near Ludlow castle and the Clee hills, a rugged landscape in the southeastern part of Shropshire (Peters, *Shropshire* 30, 37). As the story unfolds, the novel interweaves three main narrative threads: searching for and rescuing the Hugonin children, pursuing and defeating a group of marauding bandits brazenly operating from a stronghold on Teeterstone Clee, and solving the dual crime of the rape and murder of Sister Hilaria, the virgin of the title found frozen into a stream. Central to this three-strand plot is the presence of Olivier de Bretagne, d'Angers' squire who helps the Hugonin children to safety, defeats the bandit chief in open combat using a style of fighting Cadfael recognizes as "a manner of swordplay bred from the clash of east and west, and borrowing from both" (183), and returns Yves and Ermina to their uncle at novel's end. Reflecting on the complexity of plot, the evocation of time and place, and the depiction of civil war politics tempered by familial bonds, Lewis states "*The Virgin in the Ice* must surely rank with *The Heaven Tree* trilogy as being among Peters's finest historical fiction" (*Pargeter* 114).

Adapting the novel for the screen, Russell Lewis and Malcolm Mawbray introduce several significant changes while retaining the basics of the three-strand plot. Perhaps the most obvious change is setting. While the novel's action centers around Bromfield Priory, the film's action takes place in and near the abbey at Shrewsbury. The movie opens, for instance, with a sequence of shots alternating between Brother Oswin and the abbey in which viewers first see Oswin and Sister Hilaria, caught at night in blinding snow, finding a hut in which to shelter and holding each other close to stay warm followed by shot of a worried looking Cadfael in the abbey courtyard holding a lantern and looking for his young assistant. Then, in a tightly orchestrated set of alternating shots, Oswin — having fled from Sister Hilaria in a fit of scrupulosity — is assaulted and stabbed by a group of thugs while abbey monks sing vespers in the church choir. The next day news of the missing Hugonin children reaches the abbey. Berenger — rather than Prestcote, who does not appear in any of the films — denies Laurence d'Angers access to Shropshire, and Brother Oswin is brought in nearly dead, having been found by a shepherd. Cadfael treats the delirious, wounded brother, who shouts out "to kiss her lips, she was so warm, I meant no evil, so lovely, so beautiful," which the prying Brother Jerome overhears, and he immediately concludes the worst about Oswin. Later that evening Hugh joins Cadfael in his workshop and together they plan a search and rescue expedition of the Hugonin children for early the next day. The remainder of the film moves from the abbey close to the surrounding countryside over the course of the next several days as Hugh, Cadfael, and Olivier work independently and together to find and secure d'Angers' niece and nephew, solve the crimes of Sister Hilaria's rape and murder, and confront and defeat the marauders ravaging the countryside.

Because of the change of setting for the film, Shrewsbury monks familiar to viewers from previous episodes also take the place of the Bromfield monks of the novel. Thus, rather than Brother Elyas of Pershore, Oswin takes on the role of the critically wounded monk who blames himself for Hilaria's death and tries to rescue Yves from the bandits near the end of the film. Prior Robert and Brother Jerome, too, who make only the briefest appearance at the beginning of the novel, play a central role in the film by developing and putting forth an alternative solution to the murder of Sister Hilaria based on Oswin's ravings, the place of his wound near his heart, blood stains on Sister Hilaria's shift, and their own propensity to attribute to others the basest motives and desires. This alternative interpretation of the evidence is not in the novel, but serves as a foil to Cadfael's more reasonable reading of the details, which of course wins the day. In his own right, apart from Prior Robert, Brother Jerome is particularly cruel when, replacing Yves' well-intentioned but equally effective delivery of information in the novel, he confronts Oswin with Hilaria's death, offering information that causes the feeble man to flee raving into a stormy night with Yves at his side. Finally Abbot Radulfus himself makes occasional appearances, replacing Prior Leonard of Bromfield as father-protector of the fugitive children. In a scene not at all part of the novel, Radulfus briefly challenges Cadfael before giving him his blessing to seek Yves and Brother Oswin.

These changes are interesting and suggest much about decisions screenwriters and directors make when adapting a 220-page novel to a 75-minute film. The advantages of maintaining a small cast, using just a few sets, developing continuity of character from episode to episode, and using the interactions between these characters as a means to present the dynamics of life in a twelfth-century abbey are fairly obvious. I find, though, the most important changes Lewis and Mawbray make center on the group of marauders and Olivier de Bretagne's relationship to them.

On the first morning of the search for the Hugonin children, Cadfael, Hugh, and company come upon three dead, snow-covered bodies lying frozen in a field while on their way to John Druel's farmstead. They discover with some surprise these men are wearing white Crusader tabards emblazoned with a red cross. This discovery occasions a brief conversation between Cadfael and Hugh in which the latter wonders whether Cadfael would have known Laurence d'Angers in the Holy Land. Cadfael replies: "It has been twenty-six years since I sailed from Saint Symeon; I doubt there are any left there I would know." Hugh then teases him about "a certain Syrian widow named Mariam who had a stall among the sail makers in Antioch" as they near Druel's farmstead. Discovering it burned out they begin investigating the ruins when Druel himself approaches and tells them of the attack that destroyed his farm and of the bandits who were, as Druel declares, "dressed as soldiers of the cross." When asked if he had encountered the Hugonin party, Druel says no but reports of a stranger, "dark skinned and claiming to be a woodsman," who was also asking after such a party. As they part, Druel remembers one more thing about the stranger, saying "woodsman or no, he wore a sword." In the film's next shot viewers see a young man hiding in the woods and dressing a wound in his upper right shoulder. Hearing Cadfael and Hugh approach, the young man draws a dagger and observes them planning to split and rejoin later in order to cover more ground in their search. This young man, of course, turns out to be Olivier de Bretagne, whom we next see two nights later wearing a Crusader tabard as he rescues and hides Ermina from horsemen who are chasing her in Clee forest.

The Crusader tabard is a visually important marker in this film not only for the characters, but also for viewers. On the morning after the storm in which Yves and Oswin walk to the hut, Yves stumbles upon the group of bandits who all wear the cross. Viewers know this group, having already seen the leader beat and stab Brother Oswin in the film's opening sequence. And the leader of the troop knows Yves, for they have been searching for the Hugonins as well as sacking farms and manors. Taking Yves prisoner he declares openly his intention to ransom the boy to d'Angers. In the very next shot Ermina, too, is found yet again wandering in the woods, but by a different kind of Crusader, Cadfael. In a sequence of alternating shots between the two siblings, we first see her brought to the abbey, where she first tells her story to Abbot Radulfus before viewing Sister Hilaria's body; then we see Yves with the Crusaders on the march moving deep into the Clee hills. Next, in Cadfael's workshop, Ermina reveals to him how Olivier de Bretagne helped her in the woods; then we see the Crusaders and Yves arrive at camp high in the hills. Finally, we see Cadfael take a dagger out of a chest in his workshop: he arms himself before leaving in search of Yves and Oswin. Then the Crusaders' leader interrogates Yves about Ermina's whereabouts before ordering another Crusader to torture the boy until he talks. This sequence of scenes leads to a key point in the film, Cadfael's first meeting with Olivier and their subsequent efforts together to rescue Yves.

Having found a hut in which shepherds store fodder, Cadfael enters looking for evidence of Yves and Oswin. Already inside, Olivier jumps him, but Cadfael, having his own dagger at hand, surprises the young man with a poniard poking his ribs and declares, "you must always beware of the unexpected stroke." After Cadfael reveals he knows Olivier by name, the two join forces and determine the hut is the place where both Yves and Oswin and Hilaria and Oswin had stayed. It is also the site of Hilaria's rape and murder. In this union of effort, however, the film differs significantly from the book, where Cadfael and Hugh work together while Olivier always works alone. Moving out, Cadfael and Olivier track Yves and the Crusaders to the hideout, at which Olivier recognizes the troop and its leader. As he explains to Cadfael, d'Angers sent all of them to Shropshire to find the Hugonins. Le Gaucher — disloyal to their lord and seeking personal gain — led the majority in mutiny, killing their captain and two others. Olivier, the sole loyal survivor, escaped with a wound, which he has been treating with an unguent of his own devising: something his mother who practiced the healing arts had taught him. When night falls, the two rescue Yves, and Olivier fights a group of his former fellow soldiers to allow Cadfael and the boy time to escape. Suddenly Hugh's men attack, and in the melee Le Gaucher snatches the boy from Cadfael and threatens to kill him unless all stand down. Oswin, however, appears just as suddenly on the scene and distracts Le Gaucher enough for Yves to slip away and Cadfael with drawn dagger to face the rogue Crusader. As Le Gaucher makes his move to strike the monk, Olivier knocks down his sword and challenges him to single combat. Recognizing his challenger, Le Gaucher says through his teeth, "I'll feast on your heart, half breed," thereby hinting at Olivier's parentage. Noble Crusader versus ignoble Crusader, Olivier and Le Gaucher battle until the latter, seeming to have the upper hand, pauses and laughs, giving Olivier just enough time to mortally wound Le Gaucher with his dagger while echoing Cadfael's advice: "always beware the unexpected stroke." During the confusion of the fight's aftermath, Olivier slips away after saluting Cadfael.

In choosing to stage the bandits as rogue Crusaders and not simply as a group of lawless men taking advantage of the country's civil unrest, as in the novel, Lewis and Mawbray place the theme of the noble versus the ignoble at the center of the film, a theme suggested in *The Leper of Saint Giles*. They refine the theme by probing the difference between the noble and ignoble Crusader. A thorough-going opportunist, Le Gaucher represents a darker, ignoble side of human nature—Crusader or not—and, like Picard in *The Leper*, finds final defeat at the hands of a just and fair opponent. Emphasizing nobility of the person over that of social standing or occupation, such as Crusader, Lewis and Mawbray capture Peters' own position on the issue as suggested by the characters and stories she creates: like Geoffrey Chaucer in his short poem "Gentilesse," Peters finds nobility in a shared humanity rather than power, position, or wealth. Lewis and Mawbray also develop the return of the soldier theme we see in *The Leper* and elsewhere. In this case, however, the rogue Crusaders coming into Shropshire seek to exploit for personal gain the borderland, frontier culture they find rather than using their knowledge and skill to build something positive for themselves and others as Cadfael, Guimar de Massard, and even Olivier strive to do. Rejecting their given task to find and return the children safely to their lord, these rogue Crusaders choose a self-serving path that leads ultimately to their own destruction or capture. These rogue Crusaders also act as a foil for our heroes: their selfishness and ignomy contrasts poignantly with the main characters' generosity, humanity, and nobility.

The film draws to a close back in the abbey. Two nights after the fight Olivier comes to secret away the Hugonins. While waiting for the children, he and Cadfael meet in the herbarium workshop where Olivier reveals more of his biography. His mother was a Syrian from Antioch and his father a man-at-arms from England. As he says to Cadfael, "I am their bastard got between faiths and peoples, but for all that I think myself well mothered and well fathered." Having chosen to follow his father's faith, he entered d'Angers's service in Jerusalem, which is how he has come to be in England. Telling his story gradually reveals to Cadfael that Olivier must be his son: the coincidences and the timing all fit. When the young man tells him his mother's name, Mariam, Cadfael is convinced, which gives his parting statement to Olivier, the Benedictine blessing "My son, go in peace," a dramatically ironic double meaning. Later, at private prayer in the abbey church, Cadfael says yet again "this was an unexpected stroke." Hugh meets him at the church and asks about the mysterious woodsman with the sword; Cadfael replies with the film's final line: "He was ... a son any father would be proud of." Olivier, "got between faiths and peoples," encapsulates the best of each in Peters' twelfth-century world and suggests what might be possible from such a union of two cultures. Peters seems to have no doubts, however, that in the twelfth-century Shropshire of the novels and films the best includes embracing Christianity, but a Christianity tempered by Islam. Like his father, Olivier — "well mothered and well fathered" — joins East and West in his personal character and actions as he fulfills his duty to his lord.

Conclusion

Ellis Peters' medievalism, her imaginative view of twelfth-century Shropshire — colored as it is by her own twentieth-century experience of living

Father Cadfael (Derek Jacobi) and his son, Oliver (Robert Cavanah) in *The Virgin in the Ice.*

there — is one of fluid borders and frontiers: a place of "heightened tension, intensified colours, a sense of drama the settled hinterlands do not know" (1993b, 9). Her orientalism, her imaginative view of the East in the twelfth century, is similar: a borderland, frontier culture, as Olivier suggests, "between faiths and peoples." Her Brother Cadfael embodies both. Living on the borders of society throughout his adult life, first as a Crusader and sailor in the East and then as a Benedictine monk in the West of England in the March of Wales, Brother Cadfael strives to integrate his past with his present as he responds to the needs of those he encounters inside and outside the abbey walls. The ITV filmmakers, seeking to translate Peters' medievalism and orientalism, dramatize the experiences of this borderline monk for a late twentieth-century film audience. In two films in particular, *The Leper of Saint Giles* and *The Virgin in the Ice*, they examine the Crusade experience in the form of former Crusaders who have returned from the East. While Guimar de Massard and Olivier de Bretagne have, like Cadfael himself, gained from their experience in the East and work to help others, Le Gaucher and company in the film version of *The Virgin in the Ice* do not. Serving as a foil, in fact, Le Gaucher and his men set off Cadfael and Olivier (and, intertextually, Guimar de Massard) in sharp relief, emphasizing by their ignoble actions the nobility of those returning Crusaders who strive to merge East and West in the borderland, frontier culture of twelfth-century Shropshire.

Bibliography

Baker, Margaret. "Brother Cadfael and His Herbs." *Cordially Yours, Brother Cadfael.* Ed. Anne K. Kaler. Bowling Green, OH: Bowling Green State University Press, 1998: 121–32.
Berend, Nora. "Frontiers." *Palgrave Advances in the Crusades.* 2005. New York: Palgrave, 2005: 148–71.
Duckett, Eleanor Shipley. *The Gateway to the Middle Ages: Monasticism.* 1936. Ann Arbor, MI: University of Michigan Press, 1966.
Lewis, Margaret. "Cadfael and the Borders." *Cordially Yours, Brother Cadfael.* Ed. Anne K. Kaler. Bowling Green, OH: Bowling Green State University Press, 1998: 109–19.
_____. *Edith Pargeter: Ellis Peters.* Mid Glamorgan, Wales: Seren, 1994.
Nicholson, Helen J. Introduction. *Palgrave Advances in the Crusades.* New York: Palgrave, 2005: 1–12.
Peters, Ellis. Introduction. *A Rare Benedictine: The Advent of Brother Cadfael.* New York: Mysterious Press, 1988: 3–7.
_____. *The Leper of St. Giles.* New York: Mysterious Press, 1981.
_____. "A Light on the Road to Woodstock." *A Rare Benedictine: The Advent of Brother Cadfael.* New York: Mysterious Press,1988: 9–53.
_____. *A Morbid Taste for Bones.* New York: Mysterious Press, 1977.
_____. *The Pilgrim of Hate.* New York: Random House, 1986.
_____. *The Virgin in the Ice.* New York: Morrow, 1982.
_____. *A Rare Benedictine: The Advent of Brother Cadfael.* New York: Mysterious Press, 1988.

Peters, Ellis and Roy Morgan. *Shropshire: A Memoir of the English Countryside*. New York: Mysterious Press, 1993a.

_____. *Strongholds and Sanctuaries: The Borderland of England and Wales*. Dover, NH: Alan Sutton, 1993b.

Wood, Michael. *In Search of the Dark Ages*. New York: Facts on File, 1987.

Filmography

The Devil's Novice, dir. Herbert Wise, 1996.
The Holy Thief, dir. Ken Grieve, 1998.
The Leper of Saint Giles, dir. Graham Theakston, 1994.
Monk's Hood, dir. Graham Theakston, 1994
A Morbid Taste for Bones, dir. Richard Stroud, 1996.
One Corpse Too Many, dir. Graham Theakston, 1994.
The Pilgrim of Hate, dir. Ken Grieve, 1998.
The Potter's Field, dir. Mary McMurray, 1998.
The Raven in the Foregate, dir. Ken Grieve, 1997.
The Rose Rent, dir. Richard Stroud, 1997.
Saint Peter's Fair, dir. Herbert Wise, 1997.
The Sanctuary Sparrow, dir. Graham Theakston, 1994.
The Virgin in the Ice, dir. Malcolm Mawbray, 1995.

12. Movie Millenarianism
Left Behind, *Script/ure* and the Sleeping Dragon

CHRISTOPHER POWERS

While studies of movie medievalism have shown how films like *The Da Vinci Code* and *Kingdom of Heaven* have brought the Grail and the Crusades back into focus on the silver screen, the present inquiry will look at another projection of medievalism onto mass culture in America. "Movie millenarianism" would be the more appropriate term for the religiously motivated "Christian fiction" *Left Behind* series, which began as a series of bestselling novels and has found its Hollywood expressions in the films *Left Behind: The Movie* (2000) and its two sequels *Left Behind II: Tribulation Force* (2002) and *Left Behind: World at War* (2005). My interrogation of these novels and their corresponding cinematic adaptations will compare and contrast them both with Dan Brown's novel and its adaptation by Ron Howard as well as to several popular, novelistic examples of what I call the secular Grail story.

My essay will mobilize Theodor Adorno's theories of mass culture and fascist propaganda to undertake a socio-psychological and aesthetic ideology critique of the themes and techniques of the movies and their source novels with reference to Adorno's analysis of the rhetoric of a right-wing Christian evangelist titled *The Psychological Techniques of Martin Luther Thomas's Radio Addresses*. A reading of *Left Behind* as a mass-cultural and cinematic artifact provides the challenge and opportunity to analyze both its ideological orientation and its mass-cultural appeal, which are aligned with their explicit "dispensational fundamentalist" theology on the one hand and with the same medievalist vogue that has popularized other examples of movie medievalism on the other. By using Adorno's socio-psychological analysis as prism to read *Left Behind*, I hope to open critical categories that can in turn be related to the movie medievalism of *The Da Vinci Code*, shedding light from an oblique angle on the possibilities of its analysis. My reading of the films and novels critically approaches a broader nexus of religious hysteria and popular paranoia subsisting in American popular culture that reveals modern anxieties and desires even as it invokes medieval themes.

The *Left Behind* series by the evangelist minister Timothy LaHaye and the professional writer Jerry B. Jenkins includes sixteen novels in the main series, (comprising four tetralogies), two spin-off parallel series, corresponding audiobooks, a graphic novel series, a video game, a book series for children, an extensive website marketing the series, plus other nonfiction and religious writing by the authors and the three cinematic adaptations. Seven books have been bestsellers in the *New York Times* and *USA Today* lists; the main series has sold over 40,000,000 copies (according to dustjacket marketing), and it has established Christian fiction as a major category in popular publishing. *Next Time* is a fictional account of the future events supposedly foretold in the Bible according to dispensational eschatology. It represents the experiences of the main characters during the so-called Rapture, the Tribulation, and the Millennium. It relates the stories of the reporter Buck Williams, the pilot Rayford Steele, and Steele's daughter Chloe after the cataclysmic, sudden disappearance of millions of humans, the true Christians living or dead who have been carried to heaven by Christ in preparation for the Second Coming. As the characters cope with the abrupt loss of their loved ones and with the slow rise of the Antichrist (in the form of a Romanian politician, Nicolae Carpathia, who quickly becomes head of the one-world government established by the UN in the wake of the Rapture), they convert into true believers and prepare themselves to defend the Christian Church on Earth through the necessary period of the Tribulation. Central to the story is the Holy Land itself and the supposed biblical prophecies that require the nation of Israel to return to the Holy Land so that the Second Coming might occur.

The novels' plots schematically repeat the action-story model ubiquitous in popular literature and combine heart-pounding action with the gradual revelation of ancient secrets in the manner of *The Da Vinci Code*, while reflective passages explore the characters' "struggles" with faith and promote conservative family values. The blockbuster format exploits pop culture instinct and cheap thrills to market a sexier conservative Christianity to a younger audience even as it promotes a values-based message of faith, sacrifice, fidelity and above all, unwavering commitment to scripture and to the dispensational, premillennarial eschatology to which much of the fundamentalist theology that predominates in the United States subscribes.

Left Behind, Dispensational Fundamentalism, and Christian Zionism

Left Behind: The Movie has received repeated mention in the mass news media during the 2008 US presidential campaigns because of the cameo appearance of James Hagee, the controversial right-wing pastor of the Cornerstone Church in San Antonio, Texas, with close ties to the 2008 Republican presidential nominee John McCain. Hagee is the founder and most vocal proponent of Christians United for Israel (CUFI), a lobbying organization that has exercised increasing influence in Washington during the George W. Bush administration. Hagee is known for his demagogic end-times preaching, vehement defense of the state of Israel, anti–Catholicism, and extreme right-wing positions.[1] His bestselling *Countdown to Jerusalem*, aside from being an extended exercise in fanatical Islamophobia, is interesting for the specificity with which it translates current events into realizations of supposed Biblical prophecy, which happen to accord perfectly with the neoconservativism that has attempted to reshape the Middle East according to the geopolitical interests of the United States in the post–9/11 years. The book was reissued in 2007 at a moment when the Bush White House was beating the war drums for an attack on Iran, and it provided the occasion for the author to advocate aggressive action against the Islamic foes of Israel to prevent a purported total destruction imagined as imminent.[2] Hagee is one of the most outspoken proponents of Christian Zionism, a consequence of the mode of prophetic biblical interpretation known as dispensational fundamentalism that is associated with the influential Dallas Theological Seminary and the Moody Bible Institute and that has "increasingly shaped the presuppositions of American fundamentalist, evangelical, Pentecostal, and charismatic thinking concerning Israel and Palestine over the past 150 years" (Masalha 124).[3] While the origins of Christian Zionism can be traced to John Nelson Darby (1800–1882), who founded the prophetic movement known as the Plymouth Brethren, it has established itself as the central element of dispensational fundamentalist theology only in the twentieth century and especially since the founding of the state of Israel. Dispensationalism reads scripture as arranging worldly history in a series of phases that correspond to important biblical figures:

> Dispensationalist fundamentalists hold that there are several ages of God's history. Each age is a dispensation from God. The ages are named after Old Testament figures such as Adam, Noah, Abraham, Moses and others. These ages are followed by the Christian or "church age," which culminates in the messianic and "New Heaven and New Earth" ages [Masalha 124].

The final historical ages correspond to passages taken especially from apocalyptic scripture, the Old Testament Book of Daniel, and the New Testament

The opening shot of *Left Behind*, showing the Dome of the Rock, where dispensational fundamentalists expect the construction of the Third Temple.

Book of Revelation. They are imagined to be imminent in accordance with the millenarianist spirit familiar to students of medieval apocalyptic religious movements.[4]

Contemporary Christian Zionism advocates the absolute defense of the right of the Jews to occupy the Holy Land, which, according to dispensationalism, is a prophetic necessity for the Second Coming of Christ and the establishment of the Millennial Kingdom of God on Earth before the Final Judgment. Christian premillennialism hails the foundation of the State of Israel by the original chosen people of God as necessary for the descent of Jesus from the heavenly Jerusalem described in the Book of Revelation. The Church of God is to be a physical, earthly church led by Jesus from the time of the Second Coming to the Final Judgment, a period of one thousand years. This occurrence requires the construction of the Third Temple, something actively sought by premillennialists since the 1967 war:

> One of the important outcomes of the Six-Day War for Christians expecting the Second Coming of Jesus was the Israeli takeover of the territory on which the Temple could be rebuilt and the priestly sacrificial rituals reinstated. The

Temple, or rather the prospect of its building, excited premillennialist Christians as the one event standing between this era and the next [Ariel 91].

Some fundamentalists, such as Hal Lindsey, author of the bestseller *The Late Great Planet Earth*, call for the destruction of the Dome of the Rock to allow for the construction there of the Third Temple (Masalha 127). But the first European Crusaders, on the other hand, aside from geopolitical interests, were religiously motivated mostly by secure access to the Holy City for the sake of pilgrimage and care of the Holy Sepulchre. Millenarian eschatology was not important to the theological architects of the Crusades, who adhered to the Augustinian "amillennialism" that had been Church doctrine since its beginnings and that insisted on the separation of the earthy and the heavenly until the Final Judgment.

Bernard of Clairvaux, the main figure behind the Second Crusade, himself was most interested in the Cistercian monastery as a holy site, the "heavenly Jerusalem" being a symbol of the mystical union with God in prayer. But, as Karen Armstrong notes, "for the rank and file the holiness of Jerusalem and Palestine was vital, because it was the closest they would ever manage to get to God" (205–6). Armstrong's richly comparative study *Holy War: The Crusades and Their Impact on Today's World* traces the development of the concept of Holy War out of the original motives of the Crusades and the pertinence of this idea for contemporary politics in the Middle East. It is a rigorously judicious work that highlights a "Triple Vision" that celebrates the contributions of all the three religions. But Armstrong harshly characterizes Christian Zionism in this manner:

> Non Jewish Zionism is a form of Protestant Crusading.... [T]his fervor has increased with a new wave of American Christian fundamentalism which is aggressively Zionist.... [L]ike the Puritans, they believe that the last days are at hand and that the Jews will either have to be converted or suffer in hell. But they also passionately believe that the Jews must live in Israel to fulfill Biblical prophecy. They have returned to a classical and extreme religious crusading [Armstrong 527].

That Hagee and CUFI have positioned themselves in the Middle East politics of Washington to propagate a "Greater Israel" expansionist, radically anti–Arab politics based on fundamentalist Christian eschatology is medievalism in the sense that it reprises the Crusading Holy War motif and millenarian thinking in its motivation. It has lead to an unusual coalition of Christian right-wingers and the pro–Israel lobby during the Bush Administration years, cynically exploited by CUFI to influence Washington politics.[5] In the dispensationalist scheme the Holy Land will become the site of Armageddon, a terribly destructive war[6] after which Jews must convert or be condemned. Christian Zionism is thus ultimately anti–Semitism masquerading as philosemitism. Alarmingly, prominent fundamentalists like Lindsay, Hagee, and LaHaye have translated the religious tenets of dispensationalism not only into a fully developed Christian millenarian interpretation of the historical events in the Middle East in the last decades, but also into a highly effective political movement with a powerful lobbying machine and a large base of fanatical supporters.[7]

The *Left Behind* series is remarkable as a thoroughly developed, fictional expression of the politics and theology of dispensational fundamentalism and by its extraordinary reach, a particularly effective method for its popularization. Its plot reprises all of the central elements of dispensational premillenialism with specific details taken from the books of James Hagee. Thus it is less a critique of ideology than an example of straightforward religious propaganda. Hagee is an extreme case of the hypercommercialized, right-wing evangelist pastor, employing charismatic preaching to exploit religious sentiment toward specific political ends and foment popular opinion along doctrinal lines, with a modern mobilization of Christian end-times prophetic teaching tied to the very political and earthly concerns of modern Middle East politics. His eschatological fervor combines the excitation of religious hysteria with political fear-mongering. While Hagee's end-times apocalypticism parallels the Holy War fervor of the Crusades, it also exploits postmodern popular paranoia as does *The Da Vinci Code*. In the next section I will turn to Adorno's critique of right-wing fascist and Christian propaganda in the context of his general theory of culture and the culture industry to harvest conceptual tools useful for the reading of *Left Behind* and *The Da Vinci Code* in the last two sections.

"The American Crusade": Adorno's Critique of Christian Fascism

Theodor Adorno's *The Psychological Technique of Martin Luther Thomas's Radio Addresses* engages critical concepts of the psychoanalytical- and Marxist-oriented sociology of the Institute for Social Research, with which he had a lifelong association, in a deconstruction of the pseudofascist politics of the Christian right. It is an analysis of the rhetoric of the right-wing Christian demagogue Martin Luther Thomas, who, although today largely forgotten, delivered radio addresses in the nineteen thirties and forties to a wide audience. This text, which Adorno wrote in English during his exile in the United States, combines his critique of mass culture with his insistent philosophical/historical elaboration of a "dialectic of Enlightenment." These modern, twentieth-century manifestations of Enlightenment culture insistently reproduce the archaic, the mythic, the supposedly overcome historical past that the

Enlightenment intended to replace with the forward-looking, modern claims to progress and development. I take this text to be especially relevant to the decoding of contemporary dispensational fundamentalist discourse with special reference to *Left Behind*. Adorno's study, which remained unpublished in his lifetime, was finished in 1943, and it is the first of a series of sociological studies of popular culture, fascist propaganda, and the authoritarian personality that he carried out in the years of his American exile in the nineteen forties and early fifties.[8] In the following I will rehearse central Adornian concepts pertinent to these studies in order to situate this work within his larger critique.

Adorno's psychoanalytically tinged sociology was consistent with his analysis of modernity and the possibilities for true progress and a truly autonomous intellectual culture. *The Authoritarian Personality* (1950), a group research project led by Adorno, combined dialectical theory and empirical research methods to undertake a socio-psychological investigation of the ideological formation of the person through socialization (in an American context). The perpetuation of conformity to social hierarchies and to prejudicial and racist attitudes exists, according to the study, in a dynamic interaction between affect-laden drives and impulses on the one hand and the socialization process on the other. The project employed psychoanalytical categories to decode the influence of forces of socialization in its cultural, religious, and political dimensions on the individual. If psychoanalysts originally wanted to participate in the spirit of Enlightenment by engendering the autonomy of the person through the recognition of the dynamics of the subconscious, by "making the id an ego" (according to Freud's formulation of the liberatory potential of psychoanalysis), products of the culture industry do the opposite, making the unconscious opaque to consciousness, manipulating desire to maintain hierarchical power structures, prejudicial attitudes, and what Adorno called ticket-thinking, the unreflective urge to box, categorize, separate, and divide according to preprogrammed schemata. The authoritarian personality is not merely susceptible to manipulation by authority, but rather this personality is a structure that itself produces ever-new methods of conformity and resistance to change. Products of the culture industry reverse the liberatory impetus of psychoanalysis: they use its insights into the primordial motivations of consciousness for the sake of marketing, selling products to consumers on a libidinal level, turning the hopes and fears of persons into an opportunity for the manipulation of their consumption. Adorno's hyperbolic expressions of this process, formulated in the nineteen forties when radio, cinema, and television were gaining influence, presciently address the hegemony of the advertising industry in mass media and its concomitant effects on the consciousness of individual consumers.[9]

The Psychological Technique of Martin Luther Thomas's Radio Addresses investigates a similar process in which the rhetoric of the sermons of a demagogic bigot is subjected to a minute analysis. Like other products of the culture industry, Thomas's sermons (and by extension those of other demagogues) exploit psychological potentials in the listeners through a series of button-pushing tricks that make the id opaque to consciousness. The results of the related studies of fascist propaganda that Adorno undertook with other colleagues from the Institute are summarized in the essay "Freudian Theory and the Pattern of Fascist Propaganda," an investigation of Freud's theory of mass psychology and its application to the critical interpretation of fascist agitation. It isolates moments of psychoanalysis that are useful for the decoding of the interaction between agitator and participant in the political event, interrogating the psychological dynamics at play in the bond between the agitator, who "has to win the support of millions of people for aims largely incompatible with their own rational self-interest," and the listener who identifies with him (Adorno 1991, 135). This identification Freud explains with recourse to the concept of suggestion, in which a "love relationship is expressed ... in a sublimated and indirect way, through the mediation of some religious image," which awakens "a portion of the subject's archaic inheritance" (138).

According to Adorno's reading of Freud's mass psychology of fascism, the agitator "reanimate[s] the idea of the all-powerful and threatening father" (1991, 139). This specter is at the root of the personalization characteristic of fascist propaganda, its ability to speak directly to individuals rather than appealing to their objective, rationally deduced interests. The crux of this relationship lies in the identification of the listener with the agitator, which reaches back to the former's most basic experiences and which is narcissistic in that the agitator and his message function as an ersatz object for an ego goal frustrated and abandoned by the listener, a process which Freud labels "idealization." But the Marxist Adorno modifies Freud's argument to give it a social twist:

> The people he [the fascist leader] has to reckon with generally undergo the characteristic modern conflict between a strongly developed, rational, self-preserving ego agency and the continuous failure to satisfy their own ego demands. This conflict results in strong narcissistic impulses which can be absorbed and satisfied only through idealization as the partial transfer of the narcissistic libido to the object [Adorno 1991, 140].

Thus fascist propaganda, like the Hollywood movie, practices reverse psychoanalysis by effecting an identification of the "narcissistic libido" with the agitator, but collectively, such that the group as a whole has identified with the same object (the message of the agitator). As phenomena of modern mass culture, the Hollywood movie and fascist propaganda share a central methodological exploitation of the conflicted modern ego toward ends commercial or political.

In his analysis of Martin Luther Thomas's rhetoric, Adorno extends this interaction to the religious, to the relation between churchgoer or radio listener and sermon, in line with the overwhelmingly religious tone of much of American political life. Adorno's study is dedicated to the exposure of the psycho-aesthetic tricks employed by Thomas in his addresses, which he organizes in four categories: self characterization, methodology, the religious medium, and ideological baiting. The agitator indulges in expansive self-characterization in which he positions himself as a normal person, but one charged with great tasks, "just as Hitler posed as a composite of King Kong and the suburban barber" (Adorno 2000, 141). The self-characterization of the preacher is summed up in a series of tricks or devices: the "Lone Wolf" device, in which he paints himself as the individualist struggling in adverse conditions; the "persecuted innocence" device, in which he evokes vague forces that oppress him; the "messenger" device, in which he claims to be tasked by God with the delivery of news of great importance, like John the Baptist. Thomas's method, like his self-characterization, is similarly composed of a series of techniques that underline the predominance of "how" something is said over any particular goal. These techniques include: the "Movement" technique, in which he substitutes the inchoate idea of a great movement for any specified aims of the movement; the "Flight of Ideas" technique, in which his sermon abandons any structure of logical reasoning, the better to hypnotize listeners with rhetoric; the "*fait accompli*" technique, in which each political goal is presented as a foregone conclusion, to make it easier for the listener to subscribe to; the "Listen to Your Leader" technique, which is an unmediated appeal to preprogrammed obedience to authority. Other methodological tricks, such as the "If you only know" and "Dirty Linen" methods, belong to what Adorno calls Thomas's "strategy of terror," which appeals to popular paranoia by suggesting the improprieties or evil dealings of the immoral enemies, whether they be the government or specific groups (53). One trick of Thomas's strategy of terror is directly related to premillenial tensions and anxieties, the "Last Hour" trick, which evokes imminent disaster: "Thinking men and women across this nation are fast going to their feet, for they know that things cannot go on much longer as they are," as Adorno cites from a 1935 speech of Thomas, connecting it to a generic motto of advertising: "this offer holds good only for a few days" (64).

Since the tricks and techniques of Thomas's rhetoric are associated with religious motifs, like the parallel between the "*fait accompli*" device and the Protestant doctrine of predestination or that between the "Last Hour" trick and the "apocalyptic mood of certain sects" (2000, 74), Adorno also dissects a series of religious devices, such as the "Speaking with Tongues" device. He characterizes this method as the "maudlin sentimentality and phony dignity" (78) mixed with "senseless chatter" (80) of Thomas's sermons, which correspond to a need in popular culture for the exaggerated, for "overdoing things," and the easy credulity toward the performance and "false tones" (78–79). This credulity can be connected with the "larger-than-life" aspect of the plot development obligatory in every popular novel and movie, including in *Left Behind* and *The Da Vinci Code*. Other techniques in Thomas's religious medium include: the "Sheep and Bucks" device, the violent condemnation of the sinner and the stress on the negative element of punishment; the "Anti-institutional" trick, an American Jeremiad against the failed state of things; the "Anti-Pharisees" trick, which positions the Revivalist emphasis on the Spirit against the institutional, bureaucratic focus on the Letter of the law; the "Faith of the Fathers" device, which appeals to tradition rather than individually discovered faith, which resonates particularly with my reading of *Left Behind* below. *The Psychological Techniques of Martin Luther Thomas's Radio Addresses* concludes with a discussion of the typical ideological baiting that Thomas shares with fascist orators: attacks on communists, bankers, the "administration," and finally, of course, the Jews.

Christian millenarianism in the modern American context nominally bases its eschatology on ancient Scripture, but its appeal and value emphatically mirror the decidedly modern demands of the market and the seduction of advertising. Thus, in the spirit of Adorno's analysis of the "Last Hour" technique, one may justifiably relate the end-times, doom and gloom prophesying of a Martin Luther Thomas, a James Hagee, or the *Left Behind* series to the advertising motto "buy now before it's too late," which represents a conjuncture of mediatic and religious manipulation. While the omnipresent threat of imminent scarcity is evoked in the advertising motto (buy now before there's nothing left to buy), it also subtly teases up apocalyptic and Crusader motives deeply buried in the Western/Christian subconscious: the "before it's too late" ominously portends the coming millennium. Martin Luther Thomas himself expresses the idea willfully enough in his own evocation of the "Christian American Crusade" (Adorno 2000, 35) with reference, in good dispensational fashion, to the Mayflower and the apocalyptic eschatology of the Puritans who came to the New World to found the New Jerusalem. This Crusade is also imagined by Thomas as falling within the framework of dispensationalist eschatology and Christian Zionism (despite his overtly anti–Semitic fear mongering, a historical difference between his demagoguery and that of the contemporary Christian Zionists): "The Jews are now in the land of Palestine in answer to the prophecy of God" (125), but "one of these days they will

The Antichrist, Nicolae Carpathia (Gordon Currie), emerges intact from the flames to close *Left Behind: World at War*, fulfilling prophecy and promising a sequel.

cry to Jesus Christ to release them and he shall come and claim his ancient people" (124). The devices that, in Adorno's analysis, lend seductiveness to the psychological techniques of Martin Luther Thomas's radio addresses are mirrored in the merger of religious fanaticism with the manipulation of popular paranoia in the *Left Behind* series.

Left Behind: The Movies and Script/ure

The movie trailer for *Left Behind: The Movie* unintentionally reveals a theological contradiction in the very premise of the series and, indeed, points to a dilemma within the prophetic theology that undergirds it. In the trailer's voice-over the ubiquitous raspy, stentorian male voice (meant to evoke a sense of profound gravity and portentousness) pronounces (in a melodramatically delayed stagger) the words: "*Seeing is believing.*" The phrase refers to the movie's depiction of end-times events as if they were actually occurring, the observable presence of God intervening in the world, which should convert the last unbeliever. But faith, for any believer since Abraham, consists of not needing to see: "Now faith is the substance of things hoped for, the evidence of things unseen" (Hebrews 11:1), a favorite verse the common American churchgoer knows by heart. But if the events *fore-seen* by supposed prophecy are in fact realized, *seen*, as in the *Left Behind* series (which begins with the Rapture foretold, according to dispensationalists, in 1 Thessalonians 4:16–17) then the term *faith* does not apply. Rather God's existence becomes perfectly consistent with the methodological rules of modern scientific reasoning. In *Left Behind* the absurdity Kierkegaard philosophized in the Abrahamic act of faith's trespassing of Cartesian reason ("an absolute relation with the absolute")[10] has been replaced by the positivist assertion of observable evidence. In this section I will turn my attention to this contradiction as it plays out within specific scenes from the films from the *Left Behind* series. I will develop the concept of script/ure to tease out the parallels between the relation of prophecy and plot within the novels and script and screening within the movies to interrogate the issues of free will, faith, and reason as they play out in the narrative.

The *Left Behind* series represents a fantasy of the the end-times events supposedly prophesied in Scripture through the experiences of a group of central actors, marrying the interpretation of the Book of Revelation and other prophetic texts with the suspenseful action plot ubiquitous in the Hollywood blockbuster format. As the occurrence of the Rapture, the Tribulation, and the Wrath of the Lamb are translated into a contemporary context, the protagonists are drawn into the unfolding of a prophetic drama even as they deal with their personal dramas. The plot expresses the politics of the fundamentalist Christian right in its overt anti-feminism, its anti-choice message, its bolstering of patriarchal privilege, its anti–Catholicism, and its demonization of even the most tepid liberal or progressive politics. It furthermore invokes the anti–Semitism masked as philosemitism of CUFI and Christian Zionism generally, in that it portrays the conversion of the "144,000" Jews to Christianity that supposedly will precede Armageddon. The end-times events are portrayed with full exploitation of the larger-than-life violence and heart-pounding action of the popular movie/novel format. But in both the movies and the novels there are moments of attempted character development schematically interspersed at intervals preprogrammed by the exigencies of the blockbuster plot, in which a character's "struggle with faith" provides some character motivation. This turn generally results not only in bathos, but also in the artificial, stilted, and decontextualized performance of having to struggle to believe, an attempt to evoke the drama of coming-to-faith within a narrative in constant danger of dramatic deflation. This performance corresponds to the plot-driven necessity for a moment of relaxation, the injection of a dose of melodrama to stall the forward-driving action and violence of the Hollywood blockbuster format. It fills the gap carefully inserted within what Sir Walter Scott, arguably the inventor of the modern popular novel, called the "big bow-wow strain" (Southam 106) to provide dramatic relaxation through scenes of tenderness, intimacy, or reflection peppered throughout with swashbuckling, car bombs, and high political intrigue. The performance of the struggle for faith corresponds more to the schematic emplotment of the blockbuster format and thus to the form of the products of the culture industry, which carefully push psycho-aesthetic buttons, titillating preprogrammed emotional responses in tune to the same old melody, than it does to any plausible inner religious crisis within the character, for whom a conflict with faith should be moot anyway since the observable revelation of divine intervention in historical events has already solved the question. In the dialogue in *Left Behind: World at War* between the two converted believers Chloe and Buck, for example, the former tells the latter, with maudlin earnestness and in the pitch of high action, "We have to keep our faith in times like these: sometimes it's all that we have." The word *faith* is reduced to the confidence that things will work out all right, an American trust in good luck, along the lines of advice given in astrology columns.[11]

Left Behind: World at War, the third and latest installment of the movie series, is particularly useful for an analysis of the movie millenarianism at play in the series because its mode of adaptation differs from that of the previous two movies. *Left Behind: The Movie* and *Left Behind: Tribulation Force* are both relatively low-budget films whose viewership was largely limited to the sub-market of Christian consumers. *Left Behind: World at War* is a major production complete with special effects, extensive studio sets, high-level stunts, and the casting of the celebrity actor Louis Gossett, Jr., in the lead (the President). The Christian film company Cloud Ten, which produced the first two films, made them in conjunction with Sony Pictures Home Entertainment.

While the first two films retain a literal fidelity to the novels, *Left Behind: World at War* is a condensation of the ending of the second novel of the series, *Tribulation Force,* and the first several chapters of the third, *Nicolae,* with the addition of significant material not included in the novels at all. The ironies of *Left Behind*'s problem with faith are apparent in a transfigurative scene from *Left Behind: World at War,* when Buck has a dream-like vision (as he lifts a Bible) in which the preacher Bruce Barnes discusses faith:

> Without faith it's impossible to please Him. For those who come to God you must believe that He is, and that He is the rewarder of those who diligently seek him.... Behold the father of faithfulness. The lord asked Abraham to sacrifice his own son, and because Abraham put it all in God's hand, it was accounted unto him for righteousness. The great heroes of faith, what did they all have in common? Did they all get rewards? No. Thousands were killed, burned at the stake, crucified as our Lord. Did they all suffer? No. Countless received the greatest miracles as they crossed the Red Sea, stopped the mouths of lions, walked through the fiery furnace. So what did they all have in common? They gave it all over, they put their own ways behind them. They that wait upon the lord will renew their strengths and mount up

with wings as eagles. They shall run and not be weary. They shall walk and not faint. Stand still and wait upon the lord.

The scene, accompanied by ethereal music, is set in a basement with light from upper windows suggesting divine illumination. The shots cut back and forth between images of Buck clutching the Bible in a wide-eyed trance and Bruce Barnes far away in feverous delirium on his deathbed, suggesting a miraculous telepathic connection or shared vision. The scene follows Adorno's analysis of the "Faith of the Fathers" trick exactly. But while Bruce's sermon repeats the original Old Testament lesson of faith from the story of Abraham's interrupted sacrifice of Isaac, the scene serves no narrative purpose. Meant to bolster the action-oriented Buck in his resolve to sit in his apartment and wait rather than leave on a mission to save his wife, the scene is a transparent ploy to justify his inaction in the rest of the movie, which elevates the President to the role of main protagonist. Buck's only remaining act is to convince the President to accept the Lord, absurdly, after the latter has already been saved by miracles. The scene, in other words, rather than fulfilling any message of an already superfluous faithfulness, actually serves only to work out technical problems of narration in the script.

Another scene relevant to the issue of faith in *Left Behind: World at War* occurs in the confrontation between the President and the Antichrist, Nicolae Carpathia, who has disseminated a virus through Bibles to kill Christians. Nicolae, as leader of the new Global Community (a central aspect of the dispensational eschatology is that the Antichrist will lead a one-world government), defends himself to the President against his critics, the "militia," and the Christians:

> There's no way of knowing, is there? It's that little grain of mustard seed. That's what dissenters do Gerald, they sow seeds of doubt. The militia does it out of a sense of fear, out of an inability to trust, The Christians, well they tell you what kind of faith they want, blind. It only takes a little bit of doubt to cloud our entire dream.

The Antichrist's statements in these lines refer to Jesus's Parable of the Unprofitable Servants in Luke 17:6: "If ye had faith as a grain of mustard seed, ye might say unto this sycamine tree, Be thou plucked up by the root, and be thou planted in the sea and it shall obey you." The Antichrist's lines in this scene underline the problem of faith and evidence that I diagnose in the *Left Behind* series. Nicolae, as some assert of the Satan of *Paradise Lost*, is by far the most well-characterized and rounded of all the characters in the novels or in the movies. His sardonic, sinister and hypocritical character, as an archetype of uncontainable evil on the one hand and a charismatic and successful politician who quickly rises to prominence[12] on the other, expresses itself in clever, sarcastic witticisms, such as his mocking reference to the mustard seed metaphor in this scene. Yet faith on film is reduced to the mere absence of doubt or an ability to trust and does not compare with the "heroism" of biblical figures such as Abraham, Enoch, Moses, Joseph, and others that Kierkegaard admired. Given *Left Behind*'s "anti–Abrahamism," the movie undermines its own claims to greater faith not only in its implicit message of reliance on observable evidence, but also in the "secular" form of its presentation, its blockbuster format, which it should condemn as trading with the greatest Whore of Babylon, Hollywood. The way that *Left Behind* appeals to its audience is similar to the psycho-aesthetic tricks of Martin Luther Thomas. The appeal of the Hollywood horror movie drives the aesthetics of *Left Behind* more than its contradictory and failed message of faith, and the cinematic aesthetics of *World at War* actually wind up promoting the Antichrist in the end, against the novel's Christian message. The finale's cinematics are Hollywood-style, horror movie-satanic, as the Antichrist (played by a German who was a German or Slavic accent in English, thus invoking the bad guys of both World War II and Cold War films) walks out of the flames and into the camera with a rock-star swagger to Christian heavy-metal music. The score implies his resurrection after the President has attempted to assassinate him. The final shot is like the hand that bursts from the gravesite at the end of the monster movie to promise the inevitable sequel.

The story presents a theological problem: when action becomes divorced from free will, and what God wills is what will be — predestination. Prophetic dispensationalism, as it plays out fictionally in real time, is thus faced with the absence of free will and the absence of the necessity for faith: indeed, now all is fatalism. This circumstance creates a narrative quandary of which the movie makers seem blissfully unaware, but which cuts to the core of its message and reveals something about its being as an artifact of mass-cultural production and consumption. If faith is superfluous, since the existence of God and grace is phenomenologically observable and thus subject to verification according to scientific (Cartesian) methodology, and free will has been replaced by the predestination detailed by Scripture and its dispensationalist interpretation, there is really nothing at all that is left to motivate the characters in the film or around which to create suspenseful plot conflicts. The plot is fatalistic, and the Christian drama of redemption through faith (formulated beautifully, for example, by Renaissance thinkers such as Pico della Mirandola and Dante Alighieri) is replaced with modern, secularist, Enlightenment-style determinism. The protagonists have nothing to choose, no fateful decision to make. All is made certain by the increasingly interventionist hand of God in worldly affairs.[13] There is no struggle with faith. The characters' actions are reduced to cogs in the divine plan. But this determinism in turn is just a mirror of the formulaic Hollywood script. Because we all know how it's going to end, the fateful choice is equally reduced to a cog in the plot mechanics.

The predictability of the plot is underlined by this section of the third novel, *Nicolae*, as Rayford survives the "Wrath of the Lamb": a great global earthquake and meteor shower unleashed by the Sixth Seal of Revelation (6:12). Rayford is in a helicopter together with the Antichrist:

> Rayford had lost hope. Part of him was praying that the helicopter would drop from the sky and crash. The irony was, he knew Nicolae Carpathia was not to die for yet another twenty-one months. And then he would be resurrected and live for another three-and-a-half years. No meteor would smash that helicopter. And wherever they landed, they would somehow be safe.[14]

The moral drama of the exercise of free will disappears. The scriptures are the script: script/ure. The failure of cinematic narration in the Hollywood blockbuster mode is a result of its frozen, reified, ossified state: the script, which has become so encrusted with formulaic repetition, cannot live up to its own criteria. The dumb necessitarianism of the schematic plot mirrors the fundamentalist adaptation of biblical prophecy into "real world" events in *Left Behind*. Its narrative necessity is prophetic necessity, which undermines the foundation of faith, since faith needs free will to be faith, since the believer needs to choose "blindly," absurdly, to take the "leap," in Kierkegaard's wording. "Belief" without choice is not belief. When Nicolae mocks the "blind faith" of the Christians, it is a cipher of the film's own blind faith in the reproduction of the schematic plot script/ure. Script/ure is the confluence of script and scripture in the schematic emplotment of *Left Behind*. But script wins over scripture in the end: the formulaic Hollywood plot is the more determinant force in the life of the artifact than the religious message, and what gets communicated in the end is the violence of the medium and the failure of faith confronted with the monstrous dialectic of enlightenment and entertainment.

The Sleeping Dragon and the Millennial Sublime

While *Left Behind* combines the reductive novelistic and cinematic aesthetics of popular culture with religious extremism, *The Da Vinci Code* mobilizes the latter (in the form of Opus Dei, the Vatican, the rituals of the Priory) to exploit popular paranoia, turning the mystique of the millennium into fodder for a widespread sense of inchoate dread that the fundaments of the social order are cracking, allowing long-buried monsters to escape: just beneath the thin crust of civilization the white-hot agony of ancient chaos is bubbling and ready to burst. The sleeping dragon has been awakened, and everyone wants to see what it will do. Medievalism in popular culture finds countless formulae to tease this curiosity. The success of the Grail story as an enduring theme of popular literature since the Middle Ages lies in its fungibility: it is a floating signifier, a voided sign, a sign of signs, and thus it can be filled with nearly any content and still do the trick. In modernity it becomes a commodity fetish: the thing that drives the plot forward, the unknown object, the MacGuffin, the evocation of hidden, long-lost secrets, ancient truths carefully guarded until a moment of crisis erupts (the pseudomillennium). In the contemporary secular Grail story, however, the crisis unleashed by the discovery of secret, ancient knowledge is diverted, and order is maintained. Thus at the end of *The Da Vinci Code* the protagonist Sophie Neveu is reunited with her "family," the descendents of Jesus, but their cover is not blown: the Priory, Opus Dei, and the Vatican may continue unchanged. *The Da Vinci Code* has inspired a series of copycat novels, which I call the "secular Grail novel." In all of them the protagonists find the Grail (whatever it is) in the end, but they decide either to destroy it for the sake of harmony and religion or to leave it hidden and undisturbed. In Steve Berry's *The Templar Legacy* (2006) the Grail (the ossuary of Jesus with his documents) is relegated to the safekeeping of the (good) modern Templars. In Kate Mosse's *Labyrinth* (2006) the Grail (an ancient Egyptian ritual that contains the secret of immortality) is destroyed in an earthquake. In David Gibbins's *Crusader Gold* (2007) the Grail (the menorah from the Second Temple) is found to have been long melted down. In Raymond Khoury's *The Last Templar* (2006) the Grail (Jesus's personal diary, detailing his humanity) is destroyed in the end for the sake of the believers. As soon as the dragon is awoken, it is allowed to go back to sleep.

The secular Grail story thus rehearses the postmodern urge toward ambiguity even as it recycles the plot and stylistics of the blockbuster paperback. The secular Grail story is millenarianism lite: it avoids the final conflict with the reassuring conviction that "we've got that covered" and things won't get out of hand. The ancient religious secrets hidden by the Templars or the Priory are neither revealed nor allowed to destabilize a socio-religious order taken for granted. They stop short of representing the collapse of Christianity that they threaten to effectuate. They appeal to a lazy intellectual curiosity to understand the historical grounds of an institution (the Catholic Church) perceived as moribund but whose continued existence demands justification (they must have secrets!) without approaching the possibility of its unraveling. The secular grail story, however, in its formulaic abstention from revealing the secrets of the grail in the end reproduces the renunciation that Adorno diagnosed at the center of the products of the culture industry and in the authoritarian personality. What it offers with one hand it takes back with the other, thus enacting the model of consumption of culture-industry products that Adorno saw as both salacious and prudish, pornographic and Puritan, indulgent and stingy. The abstention from revealing the secret of the grail is the fig leaf that it hides behind in a final gesture of shamefulness, a cipher for the self-renunciation at the center of the civilized modern subject.

The Da Vinci Code and other secular Grail stories tease rationality with the possibility of its collapse, but they draw back at the last moment, thus invoking the sublime without actually getting there: they are simulacra of epic sublimity coded to appease the everyday tastes of an ordinary consumer. Characterization in the novels always features normal citizens drawn into large events. While workaday folks deal with the quotidian, divine and historical forces are seemingly preparing the explosion of the grand onto the scene, beyond all applicable measure and beyond the imagination, but this representation of nonrepresentability is revoked. As in Adorno's analysis of Martin Luther Thomas's radio addresses, the hero is always a little-big man who is just like us, but charged with a task of historical importance. This ideal has also become an obligatory staple of American politics. In *Left Behind* the airline pilot, a reporter on the beat, and a college student struggle to make sense of the sudden disappearance of millions. In *The Da Vinci Code* a professor and a code-cracker both are involved in a mystery that leads straight back to the Grail. In *The Templar Legacy* the hero is a retired agent, in *Labyrinth* a graduate student, in *Crusader Gold* a likeable adventurer, in *The Last Templar* an archaeologist. All are "called," or chosen, by unknown figures or happenings and forced to play a role in events that straddle the divine and the historical, and in all the stories those events refer centrally to the Holy Land, thus providing a common axis to both the Christian fiction version and the secular Grail story version exploiting the millennial mystique.

The secular Grail story abstains from the leap into the millennial sublime, thus satisfying the postmodern distrust of the grand narrative even as it mechanically reiterates the latter's plot structure in a hollow, abstract way. On the other hand *Left Behind*, really does aim at the millennial sublime in its attempt to concretize a theologically elaborated millenarianism. The film intends to represent the events at the end of days (what could be more sublime?), but it only serves to deprive the apocalypse of all grandeur. The result is bathos that unsurprisingly has generated a series of parodies on the internet.[15] In using the pop novel/movie as a vehicle to evoke religious sublimity, *Left Behind* leaves behind both the sublime and the religious. The representation of the calamities imagined in the film follows the scientific model of a natural disaster or a terrorist attack, and thus it is more concerned with technology than faith, narrative moments of supposed struggle with belief not withstanding. *Left Behind* has only the tricks of the Hollywood movie to revert to, in the same way that Martin Luther Thomas's hateful fear mongering has only his arsenal of rhetorical tricks to revert to. The content of *Left Behind* is erased by its medium: the manipulation of audiences in the pews and the manipulation of audiences in the cinema seats become the message itself. Yet their astounding reach and appeal to broad audiences reveals how much popular paranoia and religious hysteria can converge and how susceptible to suggestion the consumer of mass culture has become, whether the paranoia is directed toward the religious conspiracy against the social order or toward the events that the divine is supposedly preparing for us.

NOTES

1. See for example the *Bill Moyers Journal* special for a broad characterization of the political positions and importance of Hagee and CUFI: http://www.pbs.org/moyers/journal/03072008/transcript4.html (14 May 2008).
2. James Hagee, *Jerusalem Countdown*.
3. See Masalha (85–134) for a comprehensive review of the history of Christian Zionism, its origins in the Protestant Reformism, its involvement in the creation of the state of Israel, and its culmination in British policies toward Zionism.
4. See Norman Cohn, *In Pursuit of the Millenium*.
5. "[Pastor Hagee] was one of a number that certainly had some influence and was able to quickly get someone on the phone at the White House." "NPR's *Fresh Air* Interview with former White House Press Spokesman Scott McClellan," June 2, 2008, http://www.npr.org/templates/story/story.php?storyId=91061991 (14 May 2008).
6. As Hagee warns hysterically in *Jerusalem Countdown*, "It will be a sea of human blood!" (156).
7. See *Bill Moyers Journal*.
8. For the history of the composition and publication of these texts see Rolf Tiedemann, page 411.
9. As Adorno's colleague in the Institute, Leo Löwenthal said: "Hollywood is psychoanalysis in reverse." Cited in Martin Jay *The Dialectical Imagination*, page 173.
10. "Problema 1: Is there a Teleological Suspension of the Ethical?" in *Fear and Tremblling* 54–67.
11. See Adorno's analysis of the astrology column from the *LA Times* in *The Stars Down to Earth and Other Essays on the Irrational in Culture*, pages 46–171.
12. In the 2008 Presidential Election campaign the Illinois Senator Barack Obama rose from unknown outsider to become president. His cool demeanor and charisma have created a lively internet discussion about whether he is the Antichrist (see, e.g., "Barack Obama the Antichrist?" http://www.barackobamaantichrist.blogspot.com (14 May 2008), a question which Hagee was asked in an interview and denied: see "Media Matters" http://mediamatters.org/items/200803050008 (14 May 2008).
13. "God seems to be working in much more direct and dramatic ways all the time." Lahaye and Jenkins, *Nicolae*, page 253.
14. LaHaye and Jenkins, *Nicolae*, page 409.
15. As well as in print, see, for instance, Earl Lee, *Kiss My Left Behind*. Aventine Press, 2003, Nathan D. Wilson, *Right Behind: A Parody of Last Days Goofiness*. Moscow, ID: Canon Press, June 2001, and John Cosper. *Left Overs: A Left Behind Parody*. Overland Park, KS: CreateSpace, 2008.

BIBLIOGRAPHY

Adorno, Theodor. *The Authoritarian Personality*. With Else Frenkel-Brunswik, Daniel J. Levinson, and R.Nevitt Sanford. New York: Norton Library, 1969.

_____. *Dialectic of Enlightenment: Philosophical Fragments.* Stanford: Stanford University Press, 2002.
_____. *The Culture Industry.* New York: Routledge, 1991.
_____. *The Psychological Technique of Martin Luther Thomas' Radio Addresses.* Stanford: Stanford University Press, 2000.
_____. *The Stars Down to Earth and Other Essays on the Irrational in Culture.* London: Routledge, 1994.
Apostolidis, Paul. "Culture Industry or Social Physiognomy? Adorno's Critique of Christian Right Radio." *Philosophy & Social Criticism.* 24.5 (1998): 53–84.
Ariel, Yaakov S. "An Unexpected Alliance: Christian Zionism and its Historical Significance." *Modern Judaism.* 26.1 (February 2006): 74–100.
Armstrong, Karen. *Holy War: The Crusades and Their Impact on Today's World.* New York: Anchor, 2001.
"Barack Obama the Antichrist?" <http://www.barackobamaantichrist.blogspot.com> (14 May, 2008).
Berry, Steve. *The Templar Legacy.* New York: Ballantine, 2007.
"Bill Moyers Journal." <http://www.pbs.org/moyers/journal/03072008/transcript4.html> (14 May 2008).
Brown, Dan. *The DaVinci Code.* New York: Doubleday, 2003.
"Christians United for Israel." <http://www.cufi.org/site/PageServer> (14 May 2008).
Cohn, Norman. *In Pursuit of the Millenium: Revolutionary Millenarians and Mystical Anarchists of the Middle Ages.* New York: Oxford University Press, 1970.
Cosper, John. *Left Overs: A Left Behind Parody.* CreateSpace, 2008.
Gibbins, Dave. *Crusader Gold.* New York: Bantam, 2007.
Hagee, James. *Jerusalem Countdown: A Prelude to War.* Saint Mary, Florida: Frontline, 2007.
Jay, Martin. *The Dialectical Imagination: A History of the Frankfurt School of Social Research, 1923–1950.* Boston: Little Brown and Company, 1973.
Kierkegaard, Soren. *Fear and Tremblling/ Repetition: Kierkegaard's Writings, Vol. 6.* Princeton: Princeton University Press, 1983.
Khoury, Raymond. *The Last Templar.* New York: Signet, 2007.
LaHaye, Timothy and Jenkins, Jerry B. *Left Behind: A Novel of the Earth's Last Days.* Wheaton, Illinois: Tyndale House, 1995.
_____. *Tribulation Force: The Continuing Drama of Those Left Behind.* Wheaton, Illinois: Tyndale House, 1996.
_____. *Nicolae: The Rise of Antichrist.* Wheaton, Illinois: Tyndale House, 1997.
Lee, Earl. *Kiss My Left Behind.* San Diego, CA: Aventine Press, 2003.
"Left Behind." <http://www.leftbehind.com/> (14 May 2008).
Masalha, Nur. *The Bible and Zionism: Invented Traditions, Archaeology and Post-Colonialism in Israel-Palestine.* London: Zed Books, 2007.
"Media Matters" <http://mediamatters.org/items/200803050008> (14 May 2008).
Mosse, Kate. *Labyrinth.* New York: Putnam, 2006.
Southam, B.C, ed. *Jane Austen: The Critical Heritage.* London: Routledge, Kegan and Paul, 1968.
Tiedemann, Rolf. *Gesammelte Schriften 9.1.* Ed. Theodor Adorno. Frankfurt am Main: Suhrkamp Verlag, 1975.
Waggoner, Matt. "Reflections from a Damaged Discipline: Adorno, Religious Radio, and the Critique of Historical Reason." *Culture and Religion.* 5.1 (March 2004): 23–40.
Wilson, Nathan D. *Right Behind: A Parody of Last Days Goofiness.* Moscow, ID: Canon Press, 2001.

Filmography

Left Behind: The Movie, dir. Vic Sarin, 2000.
Left Behind II: Tribulation Force, dir. Bill Corcoran, 2002.
Left Behind: World at War, dir. Craig R. Baxley, 2005.
The Da Vinci Code, dir. Ron Howard, 2006.

Epilogue

Resisting Manichean Delirium

E. L. RISDEN

This volume serves partly as a follow-up to Professor Haydock's *Movie Medievalism*—this ever-growing subfield of medievalism deserves a good deal more study from diverse interpretive points of view. We sought also to address a subject matter overdue for detailed critical treatment: how movies have treated the Crusades. Cinema—not only an endeavor of enormous profits (and losses) and perhaps, with the possible exception of television, the medium of our most active if truncated exchange of aesthetic, cultural, and interpersonal values—documents our affective response to our own times and, more and more, to times past. In some instances, of course, it even attempts to dictate that response. Films have replaced books as our primary source of verbal imaginative experience. Formerly students came to me having read Tolkien's *The Lord of the Rings* nearly desperate to share their deep love of Middle-earth and perhaps to learn about a poem they'd heard Tolkien liked and taught, *Beowulf.* Now more often they come having seen the movies and having heard that those movies come from books. They wonder, even if they don't phrase the question just this way, if the books are good enough to tear them away from their favorite video games. They don't necessarily want to struggle with the "great ideas"—though they may end up doing just that—but they do want briefly to live amidst an entertaining fictional world that values heroism and great deeds from big people and small people alike, a step beyond childhood experiences with Harry Potter. I try to help them transport their imaginations from the screen to the page and thereby to enlarge their understanding of how we have responded imaginatively to the past.

Occasionally someone will approach me simply wanting some kind of trustworthy information about the effects of the Crusades on the Middle Ages or on our time; typically they want what I can't give in other than broad, doubtful strokes, a way to understand how events ages past continue to influence the politics of our time. The literature of the time, and subsequent histories upon which we base our notions of the time, has until recently hardly encouraged readers' trust in their verity. Now (maybe since World War II?) scholars have begun (in theory) to replace polemic with something like scientific study based on evidence rather than persuasion, and so an effort has begun to reduce rhetoric and aim instead at understanding. More intrepid (or simply disgusted) types have tired of the flash-and-dash, soundbite newslessness of CNN or the mean-spirited, downright propaganda of the Fox (so-called) News Channel; they have seen documentaries (sometimes good) and Hollywood films (often bad) depicting possible events of long ago and far away that for the most part never should have happened, but that subsequent ages have recapitulated for their own purposes rather than to gain any sort of true or mutual evaluation of their impact on cultures that have continued to grow apart even as technology and education should have brought them together. For such readers and filmgoers I can merely suggest a few options and encourage them to share their analyses with me and similarly motivated friends or colleagues (and of course to let me know if they encounter any good movies I should see).

As subject matter Crusades stories, of course, constitute an entirely different learning (and cultural) experience than much other twentieth-century (and beyond) medievalism: less (if at all) aesthetically pleasing and with few admirable characters, they have what some audiences consider the advantage of claiming to be in some way true or at least *historical*, though of course we should know better. *Kingdom of Heaven*, for instance, has drawn a good deal of commentary about its authenticity or historicity, following fears from both Muslim and Christian audiences that it would offend their beliefs. Writers and filmmakers (fortunately) have a harder and harder time using the Crusades as a backdrop to depict simple notions of the virtues of the West; they may more readily than ever use their medium, though, to address the global need for the West to interact with the Middle East on equal footing, without assumption of moral superiority, without commercial/political goals of exploiting oil reserves, with the desire to promote understanding, mutual appreciation, and healing. Like Balian and Saladin in *Kingdom of Heaven*, peoples of the Middle East have not forgotten the horrors of the First Crusade (and those subsequent), and the rest of should not, either: what we forget (or distort) we too readily repeat.

Each contributor to this volume has included relevant scholarship, so here I need not rehearse background material "essential" to this collection, if one would call any essential: we intend this book also as a useful beginning point for further study. One can find many interesting and well-assembled scholarly volumes on all the individual topics that the essays address; for those readers looking for a different place to begin a study of this kind of print medievalism I would recommend: for history see Christopher Tyerman, *God's War: A New History of the Crusades* (Belknap, 2008), Carole Hildebrand, *The Crusades: Islamic Perspectives* (Routledge, 2000), and Francesco Gabrieli's *Arab Historians of the Crusades* (University of California Press, 1984); for movie medievalism see John Aberth's *A Knight at the Movies: Medieval History on Film* (Routledge, 2003), Susan Aronstein's *Hollywood Knights: Arthurian Cinema and the Politics of Nostalgia* (Palgrave 2005), Kevin Harty's *The Reel Middle Ages* (McFarland 1999), George MacDonald Fraser's *The Hollywood History of the World* (Fawcett Columbine, 1988), *Exemplaria* 19.2 (2007) edited by Richard Burt and Nickolas Haydock, and *Studies in Medievalism 12, Film and Fiction: Reviewing the Middle Ages* (2002), edited by Tom Shippey and Martin Arnold, as well as Haydock's book, which I mentioned above; for art and culture background see John Ganim's *Medievalism and Orientalism: Three Essays on Literature, Architecture and Cultural Identity* (Palgrave Macmillan, 2005). Those sources will lead to many others. We have taken literally the etymological significance of *essay*: Middle English and Old French "to try," late Latin "to weigh out."

Any volume like this one must have its limitations. You, the reader, may already lament, as we the editors do, the lack of Arabic perspectives here. Most Arab scholars, if we could even reach them, have far too many pressures from their own constituencies, institutions, and personal research agendas to have time to have contributed to our volume. Even for Western Arabists the number of films available in the U.S. from which one may consider Arab perspectives is fairly limited, and one may have difficulty even gaining access to them. Having extremely limited exposure to them myself, I would particularly welcome a volume, monograph or collection, that would explore that subject, since I feel that lack acutely as I look retrospectively at our collection. No book can do everything its authors, editors, publishers, or readers wish it could.

But I believe I can say that this book still includes much work that has importance, that adds significantly to the current scholarship on the Crusades in film, that includes searching and sensitive scholarship, and that treats the available films in illuminating ways. Nick Haydock's introduction does more than introduce the studies to come; it establishes a wider context for our volume, ranging from historical oddities to novels old and new to video games and current and upcoming animated series. It warns of the dangers of the "power of imagined continuities" and of "Manichean delirium," false notions of what we "know" derived from "artificial memory" and motivations less than laudable. Many writers, speakers, and artists have imagined and promulgated a "history" of the Crusades that never happened with goals to sell books, points of view, and international hostilities.

John Ganim (Chapter 1) aptly begins our study by comparing Hollywood films about the Middle East to Westerns. He places them in the broader context of cinematic history and technique, drawing attention to visualizations of the Middle East, not only landscapes, but also and especially interiors, which often fall quickly into stereotypes of "oriental fantasy" and magic. Nearly half of the scenes of *Kingdom of Heaven*, Ganim notes, depict interiors or enclosed streets. External images, too, depended often unfortunately on a "pre-existing iconography of the landscape ... [that] operated beneath and in conflict with the imperial gaze": no film, even had the filmmakers wished it, escapes political subtext, even while "Crusades films are often surprisingly sympathetic ... to the Islamic defenders." Cinematic visualizations, particularly of the sort we see in David Lean's *Lawrence of Arabia*, have had such a strong influence that even Youssef Chahine's *Saladin* constitutes a specific response to the images that Western films inculcate.

In the most theoretically intricate and technically detailed essay in our collection, Nick Haydock (Chapter 2) casts his eyes toward eastern Europe for films by Sergei Eisenstein (especially), Aleksander Ford, and Frantisek Vlacil (with a closing section on more recent film medievalism) to observe the "film frame as a stage for border transgressions and containments." He also addresses a number of other essential critical issues, including one often raised in reviews written by medievalists — lack of historical veracity — asserting that "mainstream movie medievalism's failures typically stem not from its infidelity to history, literature, or legend, but rather from the lack of any thoughtful commitment to provocative anachronism and compelling idiosyncrasy." To what degree should filmmakers accept an obligation to follow sources or aim for verisimilitude rather than to create an artwork that stands on its own? Must it comment on the past, the present, or both? How must it express the filmmaker's politics, and how much must it allow alternatives in a market where "historical analogy is colonized to the new world order of an empire among whose chief exports are Hollywood spectacle and [politically charged notions of Western] 'freedom'"? Don't "recent turns on Eisenstein's old Manichean strategies" and a "renewed fascination with [his] medieval Nazis ... suggest a certain growing unease with the other in ourselves?" Haydock asks in concluding. The idea of "Other" sits as powerful subtext or pretext for many of our essays just as it does in contemporary politics.

Lorraine Stock (Chapter 3) uses the characters Robin Hood, Richard I, and Saladin, both in television and cinematic representations, along with Barbara Tuchman's idea of the "distant mirror" to show how "western imperialism was [often] constructed" as a [quoting Adam Knobler] "'direct linear descendent of medieval crusading against Islam,'" and how that practice continues into the present. Filmmakers, she argues, "reinterpreted the ... Crusades as 'distant mirrors' of not only medieval history/myth, but also political events and especially wars waged" in their own time. She asserts the "richness of the cinematic Crusades corpus" and shows how the heroes of the stories became "rallying points around which assembled political and cultural constructions of the Crusades," even eventually re-inventing the Muslim antagonists of the Christian Crusaders into more 'politically correct' figures...." Artistic support of contemporary political agendas, for the most part unfortunately, sells — and sells and sells.

Chapter 4, Paul Sturtevant's essay on Gamal Abdel Nasser's "political Crusade" in Youssef Chahine's *El Naser Salah Ad-Din,* serves an essential function in our collection for its close examination of notions of the Saladin character over time and particularly the Saladin of Chahine's famous film. Depictions in Western literature and popular culture tends toward a static, even "hagiographic" nobility, almost a "predictable part of the background scenery," an "infidel ... more chivalric than the flower of Western chivalry that he opposes." However, after World War II in the Middle East "Saladin began to be specifically appropriated as an anti–Western figurehead," one of opposition to the incursions of the West. Sturtevant calls the 1963 *El Naser Salah Ad-Din* "the only successful attempt by the filmmaking industries of the Middle East to portray the events of the Crusades," and he argues even more significantly that it "appropriates Western ideological structures to create a propagandistic portrait equating Saladin with the Egyptian President Gamal Abdel Nasser." The film "still regarded by critics as a rare achievement in Middle-Eastern cinema," represents another part of the (passionate, but often flawed) artistic dialogue of which both West and Middle East need to know more.

Lynn Ramey (Chapter 5) addresses another difficult-to-acquire piece of the puzzle: Frank Cassenti's 1978 film version of the essential French epic *Chanson de Roland.* The medieval epic, ca. 1100, had nothing to do with a faithful record of history, and the film version similarly takes its own narrative course. The poem, bound up in "nascent nationalism" and notions of kingly and chivalric virtue (as well as what happens when they fail), stakes its own course for the rhetorical purpose of inspiring its audience through heroic adventure. The movie places Roland's story almost Chaucer-like amidst a frame of pilgrims on their way to Santiago de Compostella; Ramey outlines the plot: a minstrel relates Roland's story when the pilgrims stop for the evening. Those pilgrims later encounter a group of fleeing peasants: a local peasants' revolt has been brewing. The leader of the pilgrims asks the peasants to join their pilgrimage, but they refuse and are soon killed by heavily armed, noble-class horsemen. The pilgrims, without knowledge of that event, continue on, but the actor among them who plays Roland departs north to join another peasant revolt in Flanders. The narrative interweaves plotlines of different classes and different folk, upsetting simple notions of authorship, character, and storytelling and suggesting thematically that "all stories are worth telling and that there is nobility even in everyday life," an "egalitarianism ... not reflected in the textual record," but often part of the message of modern film. Cassenti, Ramey concludes, turns "the conflict to one of Christian on Christian, class on class, erasing what he perceived to be the racism of the medieval epic"; that turn exhibits the growing discontent in the West with the idea of the Crusades as heroic enterprise.

Kevin Harty (Chapter 6), well known for his considerable contributions to scholarship in movie medievalism, approaches *El Cid*, observing how the "myopic geopolitical view we may hold today can easily lead to a misreading" of the film as foreshadowing our post–9/11 world. He finds it very much a work of its time, its politics clearly those of the 1950s and 60s, a response to the Cold War: *El Cid* served both as a star vehicle and also as an expression of continuing worry over the "red menace." He concludes, "Such political agendas seem appropriate to a film about a historical figure who through the centuries has been used to advance a continuing series of conflicting agendas"; the movie life fills "yet another stage in the ever-shifting legend of the Cid from historical outlaw to mythic figure." Our films do what epics and Romances have often done, and similarly we can misunderstand them (willfully?) if we take them out of historical context.

Tom Shippey (Chapter 7) also treats the epic 1961 *El Cid*, starring Charlton Heston and Sophia Loren, as cinematic incarnation of its literary forebears. Like King Arthur El Cid has since the Middle Ages "retained a presence in the popular imagination," and "modern revisionist attempts to play down [his] role ... in nation formation have been met ... with dogged or angry rebuttal even from scholars...." Twentieth-century historians felt pressure to "prove that modern nations are natural units that always have or always should have existed," and filmmakers have often taken that view for granted. While taking the usual liberties, the movie manages, Shippey argues, "to raise its stylistic level at some moments without forfeiting credibility, a considerable achievement," as well as to interlace its themes and plot strands successfully. It does, though, give in to the imposition of "modern credos onto its medieval material: tolerance is good, unity is good, a nation is the most important focus of unity ... in short, *E Pluribus Unum*." Once again we observe the overlay of contemporary political purpose on medieval story.

My contribution (Chapter 8) looks at three movies, *The 13th Warrior*, *Kingdom of Heaven*, and *Robin Hood, Prince of Thieves*, as examples of the popular "buddy film" genre through the equally popular critical lens of "Othering." Not all "Crusades films," the first shows the kind of friendship possible in the contemporary cinematic imagination between Arabs and Europeans before the Crusades; the second shows a "best case" for a relationship during the time of the Crusades; the third shows a friendship between "Others" after a Crusade. The tensions among the characters in the films parallel those in the culture that produced them. More recently Western filmmakers, whether intentionally or not, express a need to place the "Arab other" on more equal ground, but only to the extent that he doesn't prove dangerous to the Western hero — even better if he is willing to assume the capacity as servant. In *The 13th Warrior* the Arab proves an equal (and in many ways a superior) to the Norseman with whom he forms a friendship, but then he follows monotheism, and they are after all "vikings," and no Crusade has yet marred their possible relationship. In *Kingdom of Heaven* the potential friendship between Balian and Nasir is stunted by the battles that take place around them: the Crusade makes true friendship impossible, even while their gifts and expressions of mutual respect distinguish them from their conflict — even a more culturally sensitive contemporary film can allow them no more than that. *Robin Hood* places the titular hero's Moorish friend in a position of obligation to him: he fulfills it, even insisting on walking a few paces behind his English friend as a public "acknowledgment," however sadly ironic, of deference to his temporary "master." Pre-text complicates any hope of equal friendship.

In Chapter 9 we turn to Kathleen Kelly's readings of Disney's 1992 animated *Aladdin* and two early film versions of *The Thief of Bagdad* (1924 and 1940). Kelly uses Richard Burton's prefatory remarks to *The Book of a Thousand Nights and a Night* and Edward Said's *Orientalism* as theoretical backdrop to our understanding of the "debates over ownership of the discourses and narratives that construct the Middle East" from the Western vantage point. She attends to those films not for the purpose of general cultural critique (common enough in previous criticism), but to "read the representation of ... the heroic male body," which creates interesting temporal and cultural dislocations. Along with Kelly the reader may find both pleasure and confusion in "contemplating a set of impossibilities in each film," what as viewers we recognize as *body, heteromasculinity* (either hyper- or hypo-), *whiteness, Arab*, all fantasy constructs in which the audience shares complicity. Our cinematic representations of the Middle East, our "cultural script," suffers from a "fetishization of the past" that may preclude our acquiring a realistic view of the present and its thoroughly real problems.

Susan Aronstein and Robert Torry's chapter (10) on *National Treasure* and *The Da Vinci Code* argues that "Templar romances" readily become "conspiracy thrillers" that aim to relocate the idea of "Holy Land" from the Middle East to the United States, perhaps as "justification for suspect politico-military designs." They aim also, the authors suggest, to heal "an American public mired in a post–9/11 paranoia exacerbated by a growing series of [political and corporate] scandals": film serves a purpose not prophetic in the old sense (seeing what a society needs to set itself right in the present), but prophylactic, yet dangerous. They continue to reinforce through adventure narrative the idea that Americans have in our midst the "truth" and the artifacts necessary to use that truth to broker an international socio-economic order that will instill peace and harmony bulwarked by "American values" (a fulfillment, in a sense, of Puritan typology, but also of corporate expansionism). Such films have, despite entertainment value as "thrillers," helped us grow little from the early days of cinema that reinforced racial and cultural stereotypes.

Bill Hodapp's essay (Chapter 11) details a series of films produced not for cinemas, but for television: the neatly done Brother Cadfael detective mysteries, adapted from Ellis Peters' (Edith Pargeter) novels and released for British Independent television in the 1990s, no less significant than work for release in theaters. The monk brings with him to his duties as herbalist and healer for Shrewsbury Abbey the history the experience of a soldier in the First Crusade. While the thirteen episodes make less use of Cadfael's Crusading past than do the novels, still in the films his military experience provided knowledge of healing, the impetus to retire from secular to religious life, and the experience and wisdom pertinent to the solving of crimes and mysteries. Thematically they deal more with "borderland phenomena" and "frontier culture" of twelfth-century Shropshire than with the Holy Land itself. But as we see more typically in recent productions, Cadfael's Crusading background also taught him a degree of tolerance and, as Hodapp observes, *gentilesse*, both in a desire to serve peacefully rather than to gain victory and in his finding a "Christianity tempered by Islam."

In the final essay in our collection (Chapter 12), Christopher Powers considers "movie millenarianism" through a discussion of the *Left Behind* series and *The Da Vinci Code*, looking to examine both their "ideological orientation" and their appeal to pop culture. While one derives from dispensational fundamentalist theology and the other from the fictionalizing of an extant theory of the meaning of "holy grail" (*Holy Blood, Holy Grail*, by Michael Baigent, Richard Leigh, and Henry Lincoln, Dell 1983), the author applies Theodor Adorno's method of socio-psychological analysis to address both the content and peculiar medievalism of both films. They arise in part, Powers argues, from "religious hysteria" and "popular paranoia" of current American culture and their creators' desire to exploit the now-past (one may hope) "millennial mystique." In such secular grail stories the "manipulation of the audience becomes the message," as once again we see ideas of Holy

Land refocused on Americans and America under the guise of vast religious conspiracy. Whether for ideological or monetary gain (or both), writers and filmmakers count on audiences' fears trumping their rationality — not an exclusively contemporary phenomenon, but a ploy we might by now have learned to resist with a little more fortitude and simply by recognizing the differences between entertainment and indoctrination, propaganda and scholarship.

While we assembled this volume with scholarly concerns foremost in mind, I hope it will also appeal — as McFarland's books so often do — to at least a little broader audience as well, readers who enjoy films of all sorts and film study and those interested in cultural matters outside the confines of academe. The difficulties of Middle Eastern/Western relationships won't dissolve away any time soon — they have settled too deeply and for too long — but I can't help but hope that any attempt to understand how we shape and deal with them has value, eventually, however small, for all the cultures involved, particularly if we engage it with open minds and hearts, as authors have here — that idea in fact constituted our major criterion as we sought and assembled the essays. Books such as this one seldom have political impact, but I also dare to hope that readers will think about what they found here, share their responses and ideas of their own with others, and urge their political representatives to approach the issues that study of the films raises with less posturing and pugnacity and more generosity and tolerance. Art doesn't itself bring peace, but persons who think about it and appreciate it, and therefore one another, can.

About the Contributors

Susan Aronstein is professor and English MA director at the University of Wyoming. She is the author of *Hollywood Knights: Arthurian Cinema and the Politics of Nostalgia* (Palgrave, 2005) and has published articles on medieval Welsh and French Arthurian romances, medievalism and popular culture, Steven Spielberg and Disney. Her current project (with Robert Torry) is *Mourning in America: Loss and Redemption in the Films of Steven Spielberg*.

John M. Ganim is professor of English at the University of California, Riverside. He is the author of *Style and Consciousness in Middle English Narrative*, *Chaucerian Theatricality* and *Medievalism and Orientalism*. He has served as president of the New Chaucer Society (2006–2008) and has been a Guggenheim Fellow. He is a collaborator on an Australian Research Council multi-year project on Australian medievalisms, and has recently published three other articles on film and the Middle Ages, including essays on teaching medieval cinema, on Chahine's *Saladin* and on the connections between medieval-themed cinema and film noir.

Kevin J. Harty is professor and chair of English at La Salle University in Philadelphia. He is the author or editor of twelve books including three published by McFarland: *King Arthur on Film*, *The Reel Middle Ages*, and *Cinema Arthuriana: Twenty Essays*.

Nickolas Haydock, co-editor of this volume, is professor of English at the University of Puerto Rico, Mayagüez, where he has taught for the past fourteen years. He is the author of *Movie Medievalism: The Imaginary Middle Ages*, co–guest editor (with Richard Burt) of a special edition of *Exemplaria* 19.2 on "Movie Medievalism" (2007), and has written a number of articles on movie medievalism and on late medieval literature. Current projects include a book on *The Place of Robert Henryson's Testament of Cresseid*, an edition of Gavin Douglas' *Eneados*, and a novel entitled *Quod Dunbar*.

William F. Hodapp is professor and chair of English and coordinator of medieval and Renaissance studies at the College of St. Scholastica, Duluth, Minnesota. He holds a Ph.D. in English from the University of Iowa and has published on Avianus, Geoffrey Chaucer, the *Gawain*-Poet, John Lydgate,

John Peckam, and Richard Rolle among others. In addition to his research interests in medieval languages and literatures, he is also interested in 19th and 20th-century medievalism, particularly representations of medieval culture in novels and films.

Kathleen Coyne Kelly has published in *Allegorica, Arthuriana, Assays, Exemplaria, Parergon, PRE/TEXT*, and *Studies in Philology*. She is co-editor (with Marina Leslie) of *Menacing Virgins: Representing Virginity in the Middle Ages and Renaissance*, co-editor (with Tison Pugh) of *Queer Movie Medievalisms*, and author of *A.S. Byatt*, and *Performing Virginity and Testing Chastity in the Middle Ages*. She has a cyberpunk trilogy in progress, the first of which is titled "Upon a Peak in Darien."

Lorraine Kochanske Stock teaches medieval texts and cinematic medievalism (including the Third Crusade) at the University of Houston. Publishing widely on such medieval authors as Chaucer, Langland, Dante, Froissart, Chretien de Troyes, the *Gawain*-Poet, and others, her topics of interest include the medieval Wild People, werewolves, giants, female warriors, female Others, Sheela-na-Gigs, gender issues, Robin Hood texts and films, Arthurian texts and films, and the pedagogical use of technology. After winning the 2008 Award for Innovative use of Technology in Teaching, she is completing a monograph about primitivism and the medieval Wild Man.

Christopher Powers is associate professor of comparative literature in the Humanities Department at the University of Puerto Rico–Mayagüez. He has published articles on Ralph Ellison, Toni Morrison, and nineteenth century European philosophy. His current book project is a study of the influence of the jazz aesthetics of Ralph Ellison's writings in late twentieth-century African-American literature.

Lynn Ramey is associate professor of French and an affiliate of the film studies program at Vanderbilt University. She is author of *Christian, Saracen and Genre in Medieval French Literature* (2001) and co-editor with Tison Pugh of *Race, Class, and Gender in "Medieval" Cinema* (2007). She has published numerous articles on medieval and Renaissance perceptions of self and other and is currently working on the legacy of medieval notions of difference in modern-day perceptions of race.

E. L. Risden, co-editor of this volume, teaches medieval and Renaissance literature at St. Norbert College in Wisconsin. He has published criticism, fiction, poetry, and a dozen books including *Heroes, Gods, and the Role of Epiphany in English Epic Poetry* (2008) and *Sir Gawain and the Classical Tradition* (2006, edited) from McFarland.

Notes on the Contributors

Tom Shippey is professor emeritus at Saint Louis University. He has published extensively on medieval studies, Tolkien, and medievalism, including medieval movies. His edited collection *The Shadow-Walkers: Jacob Grimm's Mythology of the Monstrous* has just won the Mythopoeic Society's Award for myth and fantasy studies, 2008, while his interest in philology and the growth of romantic nationalism has been signaled by a theme-oriented festschrift, edited by Andrew Wawn and titled *Constructing Nations, Reconstructing Myth* (2007).

Paul B. Sturtevant is a Ph.D. candidate at the Institute for Medieval Studies at the University of Leeds. He completed a BS in theatre and English textual studies at Syracuse University and an MA in medieval studies at the University of York, where he submitted a dissertation entitled "The Sword, the Cross, and the Camera: Modern Myths of the Crusades in Film." He has published on a wide range of topics including medieval film, apocalypse cinema, and the Polynesian expansion. His current research focuses on popular culture's impact upon the public understanding of the past, with a specific focus on the big-budget medieval epics of the past decade.

Robert Torry is associate professor of English and adjunct professor of religious studies at the University of Wyoming. He has published a number of articles on American film and is co-author, with Paul Flesher, of *Film and Religion*. He is currently at work with Susan Aronstein on a book-length study of the films of Steven Spielberg.

Index

Abdulhamid II 16
Aberth, John 72
Abject 10, 23, 258
Abu Ghraib 10
Acre 4–5, 9–10, 16, 23–26, 37, 40, 42, 60–61, 89, 92, 106–107, 116, 127, 137, 139, 140, 152, 155, 157, 198, 208, 227, 229, 233–237, 241, 244
Adorno, Theodore 269, 274–279, 282, 285–288, 297
The Adventures of Robin Hood 107–108, 110, 115
Afghan Knights 12, 28
Afghanistan 1, 12–13, 28
Agamben, Giorgio 15, 73
Aguirre: The Wrath of God 83
Aladdin (film) 200, 202–206, 214–219, 296
"Aladdin and His Magic Lamp" (story) 205–206
Alexander Nevsky 7, 8, 25, 41, 42, 43, 46, 47, 48–73, 84, 85, 90, 92, 94, 95
Alfonso VI, King 161, 164, 171, 174, 176–182
Alfred, King 169, 170
Algeria 157–158
Ali, Tariq 2
Ali Barbajou et Ali Bouf à l'Huile 35
Alien 12, 42, 43
Allegory 14, 48, 73, 82–83, 113, 126–127, 132, 211, 242
Almoravides 172, 173, 176, 179
Althusser, Louis 83
The Ambassadors see Holbein, Hans
American Exceptionalism 229, 243
American Revolution 228, 238, 245
Anamorphic Distortion 52–53, 57
Andalusian Spain (al-Andalus, Andalusia) 3, 38, 161, 179, 184
Andrei Rublev 47, 91
Angel of Light 162, 173, 181
Anglo-Norman *see* Normans
Antichrist 270, 279, 282–284, 287, 288
Anti-imperialism 130

Apocalypse Now 116
The Arab 38, 46
Arab Nationalism 110, 129, 130
Arabface 204, 214, 217, 218
The Arabian Nights (film) 201
The Arabian Nights (book) see *A Thousand and One Nights*
Ariosto 17
Armstrong, Karen 273, 288
Arthur, King 8, 28, 121, 162, 166, 169, 170, 206, 229, 295
Arzachel (al-Zarqali) 176
Assassins 5–6
Assassin's Creed (video game) 5–7
Asser, Bishop 248
Auerbach, Erich 1
Auteur 43, 47–48, 54, 72, 74, 110, 143, 149, 153, 155
Auteur Medievalism 47
Authoritarianism 56, 71, 91, 275, 285, 287
Averroës (ibn-Rushd) 176, 184
Axial Cut 52, 55, 56, 58–59, 65, 68
Azeem 117–119, 188, 193–195

Babylon 229, 283
Baha al-Din 4, 30, 128
Bakhtin, M.M. 15, 51, 203, 217, 220, 222
Bakshi, Ralph 84–85, 93, 95–96
Baldwin IV 41, 191
Balian of Ibelin 7, 26, 40–42, 110, 113, 120, 183, 188, 190–193, 291, 296
Ballet Russes 208, 217
Barbarossa, Frederick 88–89
Barruel, Abbe 227–228, 238
Barthes, Roland 65, 84
Basque 147, 155, 158–159, 170
Battle of Grunwald *see* Battle of Tannenberg
Battle of Hattin (Hittin) 110, 123, 136, 198
Battle of Tannenberg 74, 78, 93, 95
Battle of the Bulge 85
Battle on the Ice 7, 64–69, 79, 86, 87
Battleship Potemkin 49, 57, 70, 71, 89n1, 90
Bédier, Joseph 154

Ben-Hur 153
Ben Jussuf (Jussef, Jusuf) 26, 161, 165–166
Benedict XVI, Pope 2, 20, 249
Benedictine Rule 246, 249, 251, 252, 254, 258, 261, 265, 267
Beowulf 162, 166, 169, 189, 190, 290
Bercovitch, Sacvan 228, 229, 241, 245
Berend, Nora 247–249
Berengaria 25, 104–108, 118
Bergman, Ingmar 47
Bernard of Clairvaux 273
Berry, Steve 285
Bezhin Meadow 50
Bhabha, Homi 13
Biddick, Kathleen 28–29
Birth of a Nation 70
Black Adder 8
Blackface 144, 146, 204
Blade Runner 42, 43
Blockbuster 104, 110, 117, 120, 270, 280–281, 283–284, 285
The Blood of the Templars 226
Book of Revelation 272, 280
Boormn, John 170, 185
Border(s) 37, 47, 50, 52, 55, 57, 69, 75–76, 80–84, 109, 219, 246–268, 293, 297
Bordwell, David 61, 68, 71, 72, 73
Borges, Jorge Luis 4
Braveheart 28n13, 90
Braudy, Leo 54
Brecht, Bertolt 65
Bresson, Robert 67
Bricolage 67
Bronson, Samuel 162–163, 167
Brooks, Mel 119
Brown, Dan 9, 60, 226
Buddy Films 186, 197
Bulgakowa, Oksana 70–72
Burton, Sir Richard Francis 200–201, 204–206, 218–222, 296
Bush, George W. 1, 2, 7, 9, 13, 18, 27, 29, 63, 97, 111, 175, 202–203, 243, 271, 273, 297
Butch Cassidy and the Sundance Kid 14, 28, 186
Butler, David 108–109, 110, 146

Cadfael 246–267, 297
Cahiers du Cinéma 155, 159–160
Cassenti, Frank 147–159
Castration 62–65, 86
Catholic Church, Roman Catholic Church, Catholicism 19, 50, 53, 58, 74, 91, 144, 226, 227, 230, 271, 280, 285

Chahine, Youssef 26, 40–41, 43–44, 47, 109–112, 113, 125, 127, 135, 140, 143
Chanson de Roland (poem and film) see *Song of Roland*
Charlemagne 18–19, 147–152, 155, 157–159
Chaucer, Geoffrey 14, 74, 265, 294, 299
Chimene 161, 165–167, 174–179, 182–184
Christian American Crusade 278
Christian and Moor 34, 40
Christian Right Wing 274, 280
Churchill, Winston 108, 211, 221
El Cid *see* Rodrigo Diaz de Vivar
El Cid (film) 3, 25, 37, 38, 42, 85, 161–166, 168–185, 295
Le Cid see Corneille, Pierre
Clash of Civilizations 9, 27, 29, 88
Closed films (frames, style) 54–55, 57, 71–72, 75, 80–83
CNN 291
Colbert, Claudette 204
Cold War 75–76, 84, 86, 87, 161, 163, 283, 295
Colonialism 28, 81, 110, 113, 126, 130, 133–134, 142, 214
Communism 49, 72, 164, 183
Compostella 148, 156, 294
Connery, Sean 114, 116, 119, 197
The Conqueror 12, 30, 38–40, 46
Conrad de Montferrat 5, 129, 137
Conspiracy 6, 7, 9–10, 11, 90, 226–230, 232–233, 235, 237, 287, 296, 297
Containment 47, 59–60
Convivencia 3, 175, 176, 183
Coppola, Francis Ford 116
Corneille, Pierre 162, 167, 174, 175, 182–183
Costner, Kevin 117
Council of Nicaea 234
Crescentade 169, 180
Crichton, Michael 189–190
Cross 1, 3, 7, 10, 19, 22–28, 25, 31, 42–43, 45, 48 59, 60–67, 75–76, 78, 84–85, 88, 91, 100, 106, 108, 113, 119, 123, 132, 133, 134, 138, 152, 165, 178–179, 181, 183, 187, 191, 200, 217, 218, 221, 229, 231, 241, 248, 254, 259, 263, 277, 281
Crouching Tiger, Hidden Dragon 39
Cruise, Tom 12–14, 202, 204, 215–219
Crusade in Europe 25
Crusader Gold 285–286, 288
Crusades *see* First Crusade; Northern Crusades; Third Crusade
The Crusades (1935) 3, 24, 38, 40, 42, 44–45, 100–107, 108, 110, 123, 128, 225

Cultural Imaginary 3, 203, 215
Culture Industry 274–275, 281, 285
Curtis, Tony 204
Cycloramas 33

Damascus Arabs Exhibition 34
Dances with Wolves 117
Daniel, Norman 19–20
Danse Macabre 51
Dante 21, 124, 145, 283, 300
Darwish, Mahmoud 15–16, 18, 28–29, 47
Da Vinci Code (film) 225–235, 245, 269, 274, 285, 286, 289, 296, 297
Da Vinci Code (novel) 7, 9, 60, 64
Day for Night 155
Death Instinct 1, 21–23
Declaration of Independence 240–242
Defamiliarization 67
Deleuze, Giles 54, 56
DeMille, Cecil B. 3, 11, 24, 26, 30, 38, 40, 42–45, 100, 104–110, 112, 121–122, 128, 146
DeMille, Katherine 25, 105
Derrida, Jacques 203
Description de l'Egypte 32
De Sica, Vittorio 110
Destiny 47
Dialectic of Enlightenment 274, 288
al-Din, Baha 4, 30
al-Din Sinan, Rashid 5
Dispensationalist 270–275, 278–279, 283
Disney (company) 202, 214, 215–219, 221–223, 235, 296
Disney, Walt 107, 216
Distanciation 55, 65
Distant Mirror 97–98, 114
DNA 87
Drang nach Osten 48, 51, 53
Dreyer, Carl Theodore 47
Dwan, Allan 99–104, 106–107, 108, 110, 115

Eastern Church 58, 70
Easterns (film genre) 31–45
Ebert, Roger 216, 222
Eco, Umberto 9
Edison, Thomas A. 35
Egypt 14, 33, 44, 46, 98, 109–110, 125, 128, 129, 133–134, 138, 140, 142–145, 229
Eisenhower, Dwight D. 25, 108
Eisenstein, Sergei 7, 25, 41, 47–73, 75, 77, 79, 80, 83–84, 85, 86, 87, 89, 110
England, Lynndie 10

Engle, Herbert 72
Enlightenment 11, 13, 16, 17, 19, 240, 274, 275, 284
Epic film 8, 45, 125, 153, 156, 164
Erasmus 17
Eschatology 8, 34, 270, 273, 278, 282
Excalibur 170, 185

el Fadl, Abou 2
ibn Fadlan 15, 188–191, 194
Fairbanks, Douglas 99–100, 104, 120, 202, 204–205, 207–212, 215, 217–219, 221, 223
Fanon, Frantz 158–159
Fascism 51, 72, 92, 94, 157–158, 183, 269, 274–278
Fate neurosis 21–22
Fatimids 259–260
Fellowship of the Ring 86
Ferdinand, King 164, 174, 175, 177, 183
Fetish 61–62, 65, 77, 79, 84, 91
Figuralism 18, 243
Film noir 35, 76, 82, 105, 184, 232, 299
First Crusade 2, 21, 100, 127, 140, 145, 172, 183, 246, 249, 250, 257–258, 291
First Knight 7, 170
The Flowers of St. Francis 47
Ford, Aleksander 47, 48, 73–80
Foucault's Pendulum 9
Fox, Michael J. 215
Fox News 291
Frame (film frame) 37
Franco, Francisco 45, 163–167, 183
Franklin, Benjamin 242
Freeman, Morgan 117, 118
Freemasons, Freemasonry 70, 228, 229, 238, 239–240, 244, 245
French New Wave 149, 155, 157
French Revolution 227–228
Freud, Sigmund 21–23, 28, 61, 71–72, 203, 219, 276
Friday the 13th 227, 233
Frodo 181, 187, 190
Frontier(s) 76, 177, 179, 247, 248–249, 250–251, 267, 297
Frost, Robert 32
Fundamentalism 2, 9, 27, 29, 183–184, 271, 273–274
Fuqua, Antoine 48, 64, 86–87

Gabrieli, Francesco 292
Gaghan, Stephen 226
Gallipoli 18
Ganelon 151–153

Index

Gender 48, 61, 62, 64, 92, 98, 104, 107, 122, 137–138, 187, 217–220, 244, 275
The General Line 49
Genghis Kahn 11–12, 28, 30, 38–39, 92
Genocide 60–61, 87
Gentilesse 265, 297
Geoffrey of Monmouth 169
Gerusalemme Liberata *see* Tasso, Torquato
A Gest of Robin Hood (medieval ballad) 114
Geste 147–157
Ghering, Wilhelm 71
Gibbens, David 285, 288
Gladiator 40
Gnosis 227–229, 242
Godard, Jean-Luc 67
Godfrey of Bouillon 172
Goebbels, Josef 71
Golden Horde 12, 56–57
Goldsman, Akiva 227, 231, 235
Gormaz, Don 174, 180–181
Gower Gulch Gang 11
Grand Tours 33–34
Graner, Charles Dean 10
Griffith, D.W. 70, 95, 207
Grunwald Monument 75
Guantánamo Bay 10
Guinevere 64
Gulf War: first 8, 12, 117, 119, 203, 220–221, 223; second 101, 243; syndrome 12
Guy de Lusignan 110

Haddawy, Husain 205, 206, 220, 222
Hagee, James 271, 273–274, 278, 287–288
Hanks, Tom 230
Harris, Richard 115–116
Harry Potter 290
Harum Scarum 200
Harvey, Lawrence 109
The Heaven Tree 261
Hepburn, Audrey 116
Heraldry (heraldic devices) 61–62, 67, 91
Herbalist 116, 246, 250–251, 297
Herzog, Werner 83–84
Heston, Charlton 25, 42, 164–168, 181–184, 220, 295
Heteromasculinity 203, 217, 219, 296
Hildebrand, Carole 292
Himmler, Heinrich 51, 53, 54
Hindenberg, Paul 74
Historia Roderici 169, 174, 183
Historical Uncanny *see* Uncanny
Hitchcock, Alfred 78
Hitler, Adolf 51, 64, 85, 90n7, 94, 221, 223, 227

Hofman, Otto 53–54
Höhne, Heinz 53
Holbein, Hans (the Younger) 52
Holsinger, Bruce 2, 72
Holy Blood/Holy Grail 60, 297
Holy Grail 8, 9, 54, 60, 61, 90, 93, 225, 227–229, 231–233, 235, 237, 244, 245, 269, 285, 286, 297
Holy Land 3, 7, 22, 25, 32–34, 37–38, 40, 44, 45, 82, 89, 100, 102–103, 105, 114–117, 123, 135–136, 159, 193, 229, 233, 244, 246, 250, 260–261, 263, 270, 272–273
Homosexuality 48, 71, 80–83, 103, 121, 215
Homosocial 23, 82–83, 103, 122, 216
Hospitallers 5
Howard, Ron 95, 226–227, 230, 235, 237, 245, 269, 289
Hrolf Kraki 169
Hughes, Howard 12, 38–39
Huntington, Samuel P. 18
Hussein, Saddam 8, 12, 14, 144

Iliad 4
Imad Al-Din 136
Imperialism 8, 9, 11–12, 16, 18, 28, 97, 132, 142, 182
Indiana Jones 90, 117, 244–245
Indiana Jones and the Last Crusade 226, 245
Interiors (shots) 33, 40–45, 111
Iraq 1, 101, 117, 119, 142, 226, 243–244
Iraq War *see* Gulf War, second
Isolationism 26, 59, 107, 244
Israel 113, 126, 130, 229, 270–273
Issa 8, 130, 137
Ius Prima Noctis 50, 89
Ivan the Terrible, Parts I, II 49, 86
Ivanhoe (novel) 38, 99, 120

Jackson, Andrew 165, 238
Jackson, Peter 64, 86
Jacobi, Sir Derek 247, 266
Jacobinism 227–228
Japanese landscape painting 69
Jaws 66
Jerusalem, Kingdom of Jerusalem 3, 22, 24–26, 33, 36–38, 40–45, 94, 99, 107, 111, 120, 126, 127, 129, 130, 132, 140, 142, 145, 192, 196, 198, 219, 228, 229, 238, 244, 246, 249, 255, 272, 273, 287, 288
Jesus 181, 229, 234, 236, 272, 279, 282, 285

Jews 19, 28, 38, 71, 91, 94, 106, 126, 131, 135–136, 144–146, 157–158, 165, 167, 178, 196, 201, 220, 250, 272, 273, 278, 280
Jihad 27, 29, 134, 144
Jimena see Chimene
Joan of Arc 8, 137, 167
Joan the Woman 25
John of Segovia 19
John Paul II, Pope 24
Jones, Owen 33
Jones, Terry 2
The Jungle Book 212
Justin, John 202, 210, 212–214, 217–220

Kabuki 70
Kagemusha 47
ibn Kathir 15
Kennedy, John F. 31
KGB 75, 77
Khoury, Raymond 9, 29, 285, 288
Kierkegaard, Søren 280, 283–284, 288
King Arthur (film) 8, 28, 48, 86–87, 170
King Richard and the Crusaders 108–109, 110, 118, 119
Kingdom of Heaven 2, 3, 7, 16, 26, 27, 30, 37, 40–43, 86–88, 95, 101, 111, 112–113, 120, 122, 123, 136, 1144, 146, 185, 187, 188, 190, 191–193, 196, 199, 219, 225, 269, 291, 295, 296
Kingdom of Jerusalem 126, 132, 249
A Knight's Tale (film) 8
Knobler, Adam 97–98, 117–118
Koran see Qur'an
Korda, Alexander 202, 211–217, 220–224
Korean War 107, 109
Kracauer, Siegfried 54–56, 59, 90, 91
Kristeva, Julia 23, 29, 67, 196, 198
Krushchev, Nikita 166
Krzyzacy 43, 47, 48, 73–80
Kurd(s) 133–134, 136, 144
Kurosawa, Akira 47, 84

Labyrinth 285, 286, 288
Lacan, Jacques 52, 68, 95, 203, 219
Lane, Edward 33
Lang, Fritz 54, 63, 65, 70, 91, 95
Last Supper (Da Vinci) 78, 234
The Last Templar (novel) 9, 29, 228, 285–286, 288
Lawrence, T.E. 36, 37, 204, 214, 218, 222–223
Lawrence of Arabia 31, 36, 37, 38, 44
Lean, David 25, 26, 31, 36, 46
Left Behind: The Movie 271, 279, 281

Left Behind: World at War 269, 279, 281–283, 289
Left Behind II: Tribulation Force 269, 281, 288–289
The Legend of Robin Hood 114
Leonardo Da Vinci 71, 78, 232, 234
Leper 154, 166, 178–181, 246–247, 253–254, 258–260, 265–268
The Leper of St, Giles 247, 267
Lester, Richard 114, 116
Lev, Yaacov 123–124, 133
Lindsey, Hal 273
Lions for Lambs 12–13
The Lion Has Wings 211, 224
Lord of the Rings 41, 46, 48, 63, 86, 87–88, 93, 95, 181, 185, 186, 187, 290
Loren, Sophia 166, 167, 173, 181, 184, 295
Lott, Eric 204, 220, 223
Louvre 231, 237, 243
Lucas, George 84, 85, 86, 88, 96
Luther, Martin 17
Luttrell Psalter 120

Madden, Thomas F. 2, 16
The Magnificent Seven 8
Maher, Bill 196
Manchurian Candidate 6
Manesse Codex 62
Manichaeism (Manichean Delirium, Manichean Nationalism, Cold War Manichaeism) 9–10, 13, 47, 48, 54, 70, 71, 73, 75, 83, 84, 86–89, 292, 293
Mann, Anthony 3, 90, 161–166, 170–180, 182, 184
Manuel II Paleologus 20
March of Wales 248–249, 252, 257
Marian (Maid Marian) 108, 113, 119
The Mark of Zorro 202
Marx, Karl (Marxism) 12, 48–51, 78, 91, 274, 276
Mary Magdalene 225, 234, 236
Masculinity 61, 64, 184, 197, 202, 203–204, 207, 210, 217, 219, 296
Masefield, John 18–19
Masons see Freemasons
Masquerade 49, 205, 217, 218
Mass culture 269, 274, 287
Mastnak, Tomaz 17
Maude, Empress 246, 261
Mayer, Luigi 32
Mayo, Virginia 108–109, 205, 210
McAlister, Melanie 28
McCain, John 271
McKellan, Ian 231, 235

meconaissance 27
Medievalism 1–3, 12–13, 16, 18, 22, 100, 101, 108, 187, 247, 266, 267, 269, 285, 290–292, 297, 299, 300; Futurist 5; Orientalist 12–13, 14; Romantic 101
Mein Kampf see Hitler, Adolf
Meliès, Georges 35, 201
Memento Mori 51, 56
A Memory for Forgetfulness see Darwish, Mahmoud
Menéndez Pidal, Ramón 162, 167, 170, 171, 176–177, 180, 183, 185
Mexico 49–51, 53, 90
Michaud, Joseph François 16
Mid-Evil 11–13
Millennialism, Premillennialism, Amillennialism 6, 23, 229, 241–244, 272–273, 284, 286, 297
The Minion 226
Misogyny 64–65, 76, 80–83
Mizoguchi, Kenji 47
Las Mocdeades del Cid 162, 174
Mohammed 19–20, 159
Mona Lisa 230, 232
Mongols 11, 12, 22, 38, 39, 51, 56–57, 73, 92, 209
Monkey Dust: The Crusades 8
Monk's Hood 256
Montage 51–52, 55, 58, 61, 65, 71–72, 80, 90–92, 110, 139, 140, 144
Monty Python 8
Moor(s) 34, 40, 46, 161, 164–166, 169, 171, 174–175, 180, 183–184, 194–195, 296
A Morbid Taste for Bones 250, 251, 253–254, 258, 267–268
More, Sir Thomas 17
Moses 229, 271, 283
Moses Maimonides 135
Moss, Kate 285, 288
Moutamin 164, 180, 184
Mouvance 156, 203
Murderous Intent 226
Murnau, F.W. 54
My Lai Massacre 116

El Naser Salah Ad-Din see *Saladin*
Nasir 113, 188, 191–193, 198, 296
Nasser, Gamel Abdel 15, 43–44, 109–110, 113, 123, 125–135, 137, 139–145, 184, 294
National Cinema Council (of Egypt) 126
National Treasure 225–227, 237–245, 296
National Treasure: The Book of Secrets 244
Nationalism 47, 70, 74, 84, 90–91, 110, 113, 134, 147, 294

Nazi Medievalism 22, 53, 60, 89, 90
Naziism 22, 53, 60, 62–64, 83, 87, 89–91, 93, 95, 220
Neanderthal 190
Nesbet, Anne 68
Neurosis 21–22
New Testament 18, 228, 229, 271
Die Nibelungen (film) 63, 65, 70, 71, 95
Nicholas of Cusa 19
9/11, post-9/11 8, 9, 16, 87–89, 97, 188, 195, 202, 226–227
Nispel, Marcus 48, 87–88
Nixon, Richard 239
NKVD see KGB
Non-Aggression Pact, German-Soviet 73, 75
Nonindifferent Nature (book and concept) 68–69, 84, 86–87, 92
Normans 119, 131, 246, 248, 249, 251, 255–257
Northern Crusades 47, 53, 87, 92, 94
Nostos 242, 252
Nur al-Din 125, 128, 133

Obama, Barack 287–288
Objet Petit a 52
Occidentalism 40, 130, 139, 201
Occult 6, 51, 54–55, 60, 70, 72, 225–228, 232–233, 238, 245
October 48, 49
Odyssey 242
Old Testament 14, 228, 271, 282
Olivier, Laurence 212, 213, 222
One Corpse Too Many 252, 253–254, 256, 268
Open films (frames, style) 54–55, 57, 63, 68, 71–72
Operation Barbarossa 89
Opium 250, 251
Opus Dei 235, 284, 285
Ordene de Chevalerie 124
Ordensritter see Teutonic Knights
Ordoñfiez, Garcia 165, 172, 174, 175, 177, 180–182
Orientalism 1–3, 12–13, 17, 23, 31, 36, 37, 39, 45, 88, 98, 102, 106–107, 108–109, 117, 118, 122, 123, 131, 138, 139, 143, 145, 197, 200, 201, 204, 209, 215, 217, 218, 222, 223, 247, 267, 292, 293, 296, 299
Osama bin Laden 2, 6, 8, 16, 27, 184
Other Buddy 27, 186, 187, 189, 190, 197
Outremer 15, 141, 144, 172
Owen, Wilfred 19

Palestine 36, 46, 100–103, 145, 198, 214, 271, 273, 288
Pantomime 35
Paradise 6, 20, 92, 237, 282
Paradise Lost 92, 282
Paranoia 49, 83, 165, 226, 230, 274, 277, 279, 284, 296–297
Paratext 204, 220, 222
"The Pardoner's Tale" 14
Parsifal (Wagner opera) 90n7
Partisan camera 55, 58, 68–69
The Passion of Beatrice 47
The Passion of Joan of Arc 47
Pathetic fallacy 69
Pathfinder 48, 86–88
Pathos 68–69, 87
Peters, Ellis (Edith Pargeter) 246–253, 257, 258, 261, 265–268, 297
Phallus 60–64
Pickford, Mary 207
Pilgrimage (Pilgrims) 24, 26, 34, 40, 43–44, 51, 100, 109–111, 130, 140–143, 148–156, 253–254, 267–268, 273, 294
Pleasure Principle 21
El Poema de Mio Cid 161–162, 169, 174, 182–183, 185
Political correctness 117–118
Priory of Sion 232–237, 261–262, 284–285
Prokofiev, Sergei 51, 58, 80, 85
Propaganda 8, 13, 16, 20, 51, 60, 74, 84, 90, 95, 125–128, 145, 183, 211–214, 269, 274–277, 291, 298
Prosthesis 24, 72, 86, 213
Prosthetic memory 72, 86
Psychoanalysis 23, 275, 276
Pudovkin, Vladimir 11–12, 70
Puritans 228, 229, 238, 241, 242, 244–245, 273, 278, 286, 297

al-Qaida (El Qaeda) 6–8, 16, 161
Que Viva, Mexico! 49–51, 53
Queer, Queering 64, 205
Quest 9, 43, 90, 133, 187, 188, 189, 193, 195, 197, 216, 232, 235, 236, 243
Quint, David 64
Quixote, Don 162
Qur'an (Koran) 19–20

Rambo 14
Ran 42
Rapture 270, 279, 280
Raymond II of Tripoli 5
Reagan, Ronald 86

Reality effects 141–142
Reconquista 170
Redford, Robert 13–14
Reformation 17
The Return of the King 28n19
Revelation (film) 226
Reynaud de Châtilson 43, 44, 110–111, 130, 137, 140–144
Richard I 5, 7, 11, 25–27, 30, 42–44, 90, 93, 95, 97, 98–110, 112, 114–124, 128–130, 132–133, 135, 137, 139, 142, 146, 159, 167–168, 172, 184, 188, 193, 198, 200, 207, 218–222, 239, 245, 254, 268, 292, 293, 296, 297, 299, 300
Riefenstahl, Leni 85, 91, 96
Riley-Smith, Jonathan 1, 2, 16–17, 24, 30
Robin and Marian 114–117
Robin Hood 99–103, 104, 106, 108, 114, 166, 188, 293, 296
Robin Hood (1922) 99–104, 106, 119, 202
Robin Hood (2006–7) 119
Robin Hood: Men in Tights 119
Robin Hood: Prince of Thieves 117–119, 187, 193–195
Rodrigo Diaz de Vivar, Don (El Cid) 161, 162, 169, 171, 174–184
Roosevelt, Eleanor 108
Rope 78
Rosicrucians 70
Rossellini, Roberto 47, 55, 95, 110
Rotoscope 84–86
Runciman, Steven 16, 22

Sabu 202, 212, 215, 220
Sacred Feminine 234–236
Said, Edward 31, 32, 138, 197, 200, 201, 202, 296
Saladin 5, 7–9, 15, 16, 24–27, 30, 38, 40–46, 89, 97–99, 103–113, 117–125, 127–135, 137–145, 184, 185, 187, 191–193, 198, 291, 293, 294, 299
Saladin (*El Naser Salah Ad-Din*, film) 26, 40–41, 43, 109–113, 118, 123–143
Saladin: The Animated Series 7
Sam (*Lord of the Rings* character) 181, 187
Sancho, King 164–165, 171–172, 174, 176–177, 182
The Sanctuary Sparrow 253, 255–256, 268
Sansho the Bailiff 47
Saracen(s) 3, 13, 17, 18–20, 25–27, 38, 70, 74, 86, 88, 92–93, 104, 106, 124, 260; doxology 19–20
Sassoon, Siegfried 19
Satan 14, 92, 173, 225, 282–283

Index

Saxons 86–87, 119
Scarry, Elaine 77
Schéhérazade (ballet) 209, 217, 223
Scott, Ridley 2, 3, 16, 26, 40–43, 112–113, 125, 219
Scott, Sir Walter 3, 11, 16, 38, 99, 100, 124–125, 129–130, 140, 280
Secret history 39, 226–230, 232, 235–239, 245
Secular grail story, novel 269, 285, 286, 297
September 11, 2001 *see* 9/11
Seven Samurai 84
The Seventh Seal 38, 47, 76
Sex/gender complication 104
Shah of Iran 12
Shaheen, Jack 28, 30, 184–185, 216, 219, 221–223
The Sheik 38, 46, 139, 146, 205, 210
Shi'ite (Shi'a) 133, 142
Shrewsbury 246–249, 251–252, 254–255, 257, 260–262, 297
Shropshire 246–249, 252, 257, 261–262, 264–268, 297
Siegfried 63, 75, 162
Sienkiewicz, Henryk 74, 77
Silverman, Kaja 204, 220, 222–223
Six Day War 272
Sleep with Me 215
Socialist realism 55
Soldier of God 26–27
Song of Roland (poem and film) 18–19, 44, 144, 147–159
Spanish Civil War 163, 170, 183
Spain 3, 17, 25, 36, 120, 147–148, 161–167, 170–171, 175–176, 178–179, 180, 183–185, 231, 250
Spencer, Robert 2
SS (Nazi Secret Service) 51, 53, 60
Stalin, Joseph 48, 56, 73, 90
Star Wars 42, 48, 84, 87
State of emergency 12
States of Exception *see* Agamben, Giorgio
Stephen, King 246, 251, 255
Stereographic projection 34
Storm Over Asia 11–12, 70
The Story of Robin Hood and His Merry Men 107–108
Streets of Cairo exhibitions 33, 35
Strike 49, 73, 89, 90
Suez Canal 127
Sunni 5, 133, 42, 45, 142, 201
Syria 98, 125, 128, 133–134, 136, 145, 206, 226, 230, 263, 265
Syriana 28, 226

Taking the Cross *see* Cross
Taliban 13, 161
The Talisman 3, 11, 16, 38, 107, 108, 119, 124–125, 129–130, 135
Talisman energy 11
Tannenberg Monument 74–75
Taqiyya 5–6
Tarantino, Quentin 215
Tarkovsky, Andrei 47, 91
Tartars 39, 191
Tasso, Torquato 17, 21
Tavernier, Bertrand 47
Tears of the Sun 14
The Templar Legacy 285, 288
Templars (Order of the Knights Templar) 5, 7, 9, 26, 42, 54, 82, 144, 225–244, 245, 285
Templar Romance 225–229, 233, 237, 239, 296
Ten Commandments 110, 153
Terrorism 5–7, 13
Teutonic Knights, Order of 5, 26, 47–48, 50–51, 53, 57, 65–69, 71, 73–83, 86, 89
Thanatos *see* Death Instinct
That Hamilton Woman 212
Thelma and Louise 42
Thief of Bagdad (1924) 36, 200, 202, 203, 207–211, 214, 217, 224, 296
Thief of Bagdad (1940) 36, 211–214
Third Crusade 5, 8, 88, 94, 97–99, 101–105, 107, 109–111, 113–121, 124, 127, 128, 130, 136–137, 139, 144–145, 183, 300
Third Temple 272–273
The Thirteenth Warrior 3, 7, 27, 28, 30, 187–191
Thomas, Lowell 36
Thomas, Martin Luther 269, 274, 276–279, 283, 288
Thousand and One Nights, Book of (*Arabian Nights*, by Burton) 37, 104, 201, 203, 205–207, 214, 215, 219–222, 224
300 153
Three Kings 8, 11, 14
The Three Musketeers 202
Tolkien, J.R.R. 47, 60, 85, 86, 87, 190, 290, 301
Top Gun 202, 215, 223–224
Torture 10–11, 20, 58, 77–78, 93, 264
Totenkopf(bande), Death's Head Ring 53, 90
Tracking shot 8, 78–80, 230
Transgression 47
Translatio Imperii et Studii 97, 225, 244–245

Transvestism 64, 71, 217, 218
The Treasure of the Sierra Madre 14
Tribulation 270
Triumph of the Will 85, 91n20
Troy (film) 40
Truffaut, François 155
Turks 17, 19, 40, 45, 106, 117, 133, 136, 214, 223
Turolde 148–150, 154–155, 158–160
Turpin 151
Twin Towers 8, 196
Tyerman, Christopher 90, 92, 93, 95, 125, 140, 141, 143, 144, 146, 197, 199, 292
Typology 1, 40, 228–230, 242, 297

Ulysses 70
Uncanny 4, 8, 14, 15, 18, 19, 23, 65, 75, 83
Unheimlich(e) see Uncanny
United Arab Republic 127, 133, 140, 144
Urban II, Pope 2, 17, 101, 147, 183, 246, 257
Urraca 165, 174–175, 177, 179, 180, 184
Usamah 15

Valentino, Rudolph 205, 207, 209–211, 220, 221
Valley of the Bees 26, 47, 48, 80–83
Vatican 9, 28, 90–91, 165, 167, 284–285
Vaudeville 35
Vertical montage 55–56, 65, 72, 80, 90
Victoria and Albert Museum 37
Vietnam War 13, 14, 84, 114, 116–117, 120, 239
Vikings 3, 87, 169, 188, 191, 296
Virgil 21
The Virgin in the Ice 247, 253, 254, 257, 261, 267

Virgin Mary 26, 76, 80, 144, 237
Virgin Spring 80
Vlacil, Frantisek 26, 47, 48, 80–83
Voltaire 19

Wales 109, 247–252, 256–257, 267–268
Die Walküre (Wagner opera) 71
Wallace, William 8
The War Lord 89–90, 96
War on Terror 2, 13
Wayne, John 12, 38, 181
Wedge (German Wedge, symbol for man) 64, 79, 82, 234
Weinger, Scott 202, 219
Wilcoxon, Henry 25, 104–107, 108, 115
Wilhelm II, Kaiser 124
William of Tyre 93, 141
Williams, Robin 202, 219
With Allenby in Palestine and Lawrence in Arabia 36
Wizards 84–86, 87
World War I 25, 59, 63, 70, 71, 100, 101, 102, 107
World War II 25, 37, 70, 89, 107, 108, 109, 125, 163, 252, 283, 290, 294

Ximena *see* Chimene

Young, Loretta 104–107, 108

Zionism, Christian Zionism 15, 135, 271–273, 278, 280, 287–288
Zizek, Slajov 13, 23, 30, 52, 88, 95, 183
Zucker, Jerry 170
Zulu 85
Zumthor, Paul 153